Policy, Planning, and People

THE CITY IN THE TWENTY-FIRST CENTURY

Eugenie L. Birch and Susan M. Wachter, Series Editors

A complete list of books in the series
is available from the publisher.

POLICY, PLANNING, AND PEOPLE

Promoting Justice in Urban Development

Edited by

Naomi Carmon and Susan S. Fainstein

PENN

UNIVERSITY OF PENNSYLVANIA PRESS

PHILADELPHIA

Published by
University of Pennsylvania Press
Philadelphia, Pennsylvania 19104-4112
www.upenn.edu/pennpress

Printed in the United States of America
on acid-free paper

10 9 8 7 6 5 4 3 2 1

Library of Congress Cataloging-in-Publication Data
Policy, planning, and people : promoting justice in urban development / edited by
Naomi Carmon and Susan Fainstein. — 1st ed.
    p.   cm. — The city in the twenty-first century
  ISBN 978-0-8122-2239-5 (hardcover : alk. paper)
  Includes bibliographical references and index.
    1. Urban policy—United States. 2. City planning—United States. 3. Urban policy.
4. City planning. I. Carmon, Naomi. II. Fainstein, Susan S. Series: The city in the
twenty-first century
HT167.P643   2013
307.760973   2012038308

*Urban planning is people-oriented
and future-oriented*

*This book on planning is dedicated
to our people of the future
our grandchildren*

What is the city but the people?
—William Shakespeare, Coriolanus

Contents

III. PLANNING AND EXCLUDED GROUPS

IV. HOUSING AND COMMUNITY

Introduction: Policy, Planning, and People

Goals in a Changing Context

This collection of invited essays, especially written for this book, provides the readers with the state of the art of urban studies and planning oriented to the theme of planning for people. They all cope with the challenge of enhancing quality of life *for all* in the built environment.

Our first goal in initiating this book was to provide a stage for well-known authors who do not accept that there must be a "tradeoff between equality and efficiency" (Okun 1975), saying instead that economic efficiency without consideration of social equity is unacceptable for both moral and practical reasons. The second goal was to emphasize the importance of both process and outcomes in making urban policy and planning in general, and especially in producing more equitable results. The third goal was to show how research that examines planning in action can inform future policy and plans.

We initially talked with our colleagues about this book in 2007 at the height of the neoliberal era. At that time much urban policy and planning focused on increasing the competitiveness of cities. Embedded in the ideology of neoliberalism—a belief that markets offer the best approach to improving the human condition—the focus on competitiveness by urban governments essentially made an analogy between the efforts by businesses to gain a lion's share of their market and by cities to capture productive enterprises. This approach presents at least two serious problems to those concerned with the well-being of urban residents. First, we cannot simply write off the places that do not prevail in the contest, as we would for businesses that are obsolete; second, if success in the battle for investment depends on winning the race to the bottom—competing on the basis of low wages, deregulation, weak environmental protection, displacement of residents from valuable land, etc.—then increase in aggregate wealth will benefit only a few and contribute to widening inequality.

The effect of globalization in conjunction with neoliberal ideology and strategies has been to heighten inequality in many countries (OECD 2008, 2012). Until recently this outcome has largely been ignored in public discourse, as the dominating belief was that a rising tide lifts all boats. Still, not everybody shared this belief. There have been colleagues who thought differently; they advocated public intervention rather than assuming the market would cause benefits to "filter down." They worked to improve the situation of less advantaged groups and individuals directly, and thus, to promote equality of opportunity and increased equality of results.

Between 2007 and the time this book is published in 2013, the socioeconomic context has changed. The belief in the "rightness" of neoliberalism has been shaken following the global economic and financial crisis that has been with us since 2008. Most salient have been the protest movements, which spread in 2011 to 951 cities in 82 countries around the world. People, many of them middle-class and highly educated young adults, went on the march, first in Arab Middle-Eastern capitals, then in Madrid, New York, London, Frankfurt, Rome, Tel-Aviv, Sydney and Hong Kong. Around the globe, the protesters raised their voice in opposition to tyranny of governments and markets and against austerity measures (Rogers 2011). As a result, both the public and the professional discourses are changing, and terms like inequality and social responsibility are once again being heard.

The Occupy Wall Street movement, which coined the phrase "We are the 99 percent," highlighted the huge increase in income enjoyed by the top 1 percent of the population as opposed to the stagnation in income of the rest. Its spread led Peter Dreier (2011) to conclude that it had changed the national conversation in the United States: "At kitchen tables, in coffee shops, in offices and factories, and in newsrooms, Americans are now talking about economic inequality, corporate greed, and how America's super-rich have damaged our economy and our democracy." An analysis of the Lexis/Nexis database shows that whereas in October 2010 U.S. newspapers published 409 stories with the word "inequality," in October 2011, after the start of Occupy Wall Street in September, the frequency soared to 1,269 stories. During the same period the parallel change in Israeli media was times 6 and in the UK times 2.5 (Google News). *Time* Magazine in December 2011 selected *The Protester* as Person of the Year. In January 2012, the annual meeting of the World Economic Forum in Davos, Switzerland, featured Occupy Wall Street protesters, and a newspaper report commented that the Forum participants, who included the world's richest and most influential financial leaders, "will discuss not only the Europe's debt woes but also the future of capitalism, [noting that] even some billionaires in Davos are worried about income inequality" (Vafeiadis 2012). This changed context sheds a new light on the theme of this book and its various chapters.

Toward Quality of Life for ALL in the Built Environment

Guided by the above-mentioned goals and the focus on social equity, we initiated a unique process for writing this book:

- We selected senior scholars in North America, the European Community, and Israel whose work has expressed deep involvement with social aspects of urban policy and planning; the group included planning theorists as well as researchers who investigate practical fields, united in their longstanding interest in *planning for and with people*.
- We requested essays regarding the state of the art in each author's subject of expertise; authors were asked to include in their writing both a theoretical approach/analysis and evidence-based conclusions and recommendations. The guiding principle was *looking back for the future*, that is, describing and analyzing evidence from the past and using it to draw significant conclusions, possibly suggest paradigm shifts, and propose policy recommendations and/or "best practices" for future planning.
- We provided an arena for mutual exchange of ideas. In June 2009, the authors were invited to an international workshop at the Technion-Israel Institute of Technology, where they spent four days and evenings listening to one another's presentations, taking planning-related tours, and spending hours discussing issues raised by the participants. It was a very special opportunity to

benefit from the perspective and insights of a unique assembly of colleagues.
- We subjected the essays to rigorous peer review process after which they were substantially revised.

The seventeen chapters of this book, each based on decades of personal involvement and research into the presented subjects, were written to serve policy and planning in the early twenty-first century. The chapters summarize the accumulated experience and its lessons regarding planning processes and development outcomes. Both intended and unintended consequences are considered, with a focus on impacts on people in general and disadvantaged groups in particular. Much of the evidence comes from the United States, but some of the European experience—in western, eastern, and southern Europe—as well as Israeli research and practice, is also analyzed and lessons are suggested to the readers.

In the opening part of the book the authors discuss issues of goal setting and ethics in urban planning as well as questions of achieving just outcomes in Western urban areas and post-communist European cities. The second part focuses on equity-oriented planning with a chapter on its general practice and more specific chapters on regional development, transportation planning, and the implications of the Network Society. Chapters in the third part are devoted to disadvantaged/excluded groups, especially elderly people, migrant workers, the poor, and welfare dependents. Essays in the last part deal with community development, with community safety, and with issues of neighborhood policy and planning.

Readers who search for empirical research-based conclusions and guidelines may find this book especially useful. The authors were asked by the editors to offer practical advice to future policy makers and practitioners. Below are a few examples of policy considerations and planning "best practices," with an emphasis on uncommon or nonconventional ones.

In the field of housing, neighborhood and urban redevelopment
- Planners hear *housing* as a verb; architects hear it as a noun; but residents hear it as "my home." Achieving progress on the relationship among housing, planning, and people means remembering that housing is always simultaneously a process, a piece of the built environment, and an emotional attachment to a place (Vale).

- Urban renewal programs have too often caused massive demolition of residential buildings and displacement of their residents. Decision makers are advised to take into consideration that eliminating a housing project differs from solving its problems. Because a large body of empirical research has shown that typically the negative consequences of implementing demolition and redevelopment are more significant—socially, economically and environmentally—than their positive outcomes, planners need to avoid forced displacement and to consider alternative approaches to housing and neighborhood regeneration wherever housing demolition involves displacement of residents (Vale, Fainstein and Fainstein, and Carmon).
- Even if concentration of poverty perpetuate disadvantage, it does not necessarily follow that simply moving the poor into proximity with the better-off will change their lot. Neighborhood social mix can be beneficial if done right. The main factors that should be considered in shaping the social mix for a certain housing project are: composition, concentration and scale parameters, and in addition, the facets of maintenance, design, community building, location, and function are to be taken into account (Galster).
- Ending the isolation of the least advantaged poor is to be achieved by increasing their proximity to and intermixing with upwardly mobile working poor rather than by interspersing them with the rich. What seems needed is a broader application of a narrower mix (Vale).
- Preventive planning is a powerful concept. An example of preventive planning: identify a neighborhood on the verge of deterioration and encourage "incumbent upgrading" (Carmon's Table 1.1).

In the field of urban design
- Public spaces are increasingly under assault by modernist planning practices, privatization, and since 9/11 especially by measures of surveillance. In order to prevent a situation in which the voluntary city becomes an exclusionary city, plans and designs that promote rather than preclude human interaction among city users are suggested; the ways that buildings relate to the public realm, the articulation of ground floor uses, the relationship between open and enclosed space, and the land use mix could all encourage the

kind of "manned surveillance" advocated by Jane Jacobs and the authors (Banerjee and Loukaitou-Sideris).

In the field of poverty alleviation

- Planners must be especially sensitive to policies promoted to cope with the challenges of globalization and climate change; the poor disproportionally bear the costs of such policies (Teitz and Chapple).
- The importance of the local level for alleviating poverty and shaping effective welfare policies is increasing in the U.S. (Teitz and Chapple) as well as in Europe (Andreotti and Mingione).
- Although equity planners are generally advised to work locally and consider specific local characteristics and circumstances, they are also counseled to work toward regional collaboration; to use regional programs in transportation to connect inner-city poor to suburban opportunities, to link regional economic development programs to anti-poverty goals, and to require "fair-share" of affordable housing in the suburbs (Krumholz).

In the field of the network society

- As societies increasingly function in a networked manner, planners will require greater awareness of both the evolving nature of network structures and the spatial-rootedness of community interests (Gurstein).

In the field of transportation

- The focus of transportation planners on mobility improvements blinds them to the ways in which transportation systems promote social exclusion. Reform requires changing paradigms, choosing accessibility over mobility, and examining transportation within the much wider context of equitable land use and social need (Levine).

In the field of resident participation

- Strategies for resident participation in community development should be adjusted by three contextual variables: level of economic resources, level of support for community development/participatory planning, and concentration of power within the local community; each of these variables is shown as a continuum: the more hostile the context, the more residents will need to start their efforts through activism and protest (Bratt and Reardon).

In the field of planning for the aged
- The number of older people in the world will triple in the next forty years, while the number of very old will quadruple. It is at the local level that we live our daily lives and thus land use and development standards frame the environment that will hinder or support one's ability to meet needs that change with age; by following specific guidelines, planners can create environments that are supportive of people of all ages, including the elderly, and thus make more possible the option of aging in place (Howe).

Concluding Comments

More than two thousand years ago, Aristotle posed the most basic question: *How should we live*? One of the famous answers was given by the Danish philosopher Søren Kierkegaard in *Either/Or* (1843/1992), in which he portrayed two alternative approaches: the esthetic/hedonistic approach that focuses on the individual, his/her utilities and pleasures; and the ethical approach that focuses on the civic realm of existence and calls for involvement and responsibility.

This book demonstrates the role of scholarship and research in the field of urban policy and planning. It says that this role cannot be fulfilled with an "either/or" exclusive method such as the one described above; it is rather based on inclusive "both/and" approach, on taking into account individual and specific groups' benefits simultaneously with the public interest. Among other inclusive elements that our book embraces is the recognition that urban planning is both a discipline and a profession; thus, contributions to this book deal with understanding urban phenomena and reflecting on professional planning projects. Policy and planning are built on both theoretical analysis and empirical research; this empirical research should be excellent, and excellence can and should be achieved by both "rigorous" quantitative works and "softer" qualitative studies; accordingly, one of the scholars who wrote for this book on housing and neighborhood based his analysis on numerous quantitative studies, while another colleague who dealt with issues of housing and neighborhood drew his conclusions from case studies and more qualitative analysis. Furthermore, unlike some disciplines and professions that claim to be value-free, urban policy and planning should not and cannot exclude discussion of values. This book stands clearly on a certain side of the value debate; its authors believe that quality of life *For All* should direct urban scholars and professionals. Needless to say, economic development is a critical means; both efficiency and economy should be included as very important considerations, but not as *the* goals of city development.

Finally, another aspect of "both/and" is the following suggestion to urban policy makers and planners to adopt "a commandment to do" and "a commandment not to do." Based on the essays in this book as well as our own analysis and experience, we suggest these two commandments. (1) *Primum Non Nocere*, that is, *Above all, Do No Harm* (the first rule of medical ethics). Due to the mistakes of the past, one should always be aware that acts of good intention may have unwanted consequences, especially from the point of view of society's worst-offs; hence, avoiding disruptive side effects (including second-order consequences) on people and their communities as well as on the natural environment and on historic sites should be a guiding criterion. (2) Consideration of *who pays and who benefits*. The outcomes from the various points of view of all those who are influenced by a policy or plan should always be part of urban and regional policy making and planning and their implementation processes.

It is our hope that this volume will increase the commitment to social justice among students, scholars and practitioners who work in the field of urban development and will provide them with some useful tools to realize the potential imbedded in their profession to promote better quality of life for all. Especially we hope that we contribute to changing the conversation around urban issues so that quality of life for all rather than competitiveness becomes the metric employed when policies and plans are being discussed, selected for implementation, and evaluated.

References

Dreier, Peter. 2011. Occupy Wall Street: Changing the topic. *Huffington Post*, November 1. http://www.huffingtonpost.com/peter-dreier/occupy-wall-street-media_b_1069250.html, accessed January 2012.

Kierkegaard, Søren. 1843/1992. *Either/or: A fragment of life*. Ed. Victor Eremita; abr. and trans. Alastair Hannay. London: Penguin.

Okun, Arthur M. 1975. *Equality and efficiency: The big tradeoff.* Washington, D.C.: Brookings Institution.

Organization for Economic Cooperation and Development. 2008. *Growing unequal? Income distribution and poverty in OECD countries.* http://www.oecd.org/document /4/0,3343,en_2649_33933_41460917_1_1_1_1,00.html, accessed January 2011.

———. 2012. *Divided we stand: Why inequality keeps rising.* Paris: OECD.

Rogers, Simon. 2011. Occupy protests around the world: full list visualised. *Guardian Data Blog.* http://www.guardian.co.uk/news/datablog/2011/oct/17/occupy-protests-world-list-map, accessed March 2012.

Vafeiadis, Michail. 2012. Davos meeting: Gloomy about economy, worried about capitalism. *Christian Science Monitor*, January 26.

PART I

Planning in an Era of Turbulence

Chapter 1

The Profession of Urban Planning
and Its Societal Mandate

Naomi Carmon

Modern urban planning is over a hundred years old, yet there is still no internal agreement about its mission and little external recognition of its societal role. This opening essay is intended to promote agreement among planners regarding their societal responsibility, a step that in turn may enhance external recognition of the planning profession and its societal mandate.

The chapter may be viewed as a personal statement. It is based on observations, findings, and interpretations regarding the knowledge field and the profession of urban planning, which have been evolving from the time I first attended classes at the Department of Urban Studies and Planning at MIT—some forty years ago. Since then I have been a planning scholar, a planning educator, and a planning consultant, mainly in Israel but also in the United States, and I have had the opportunity to travel and talk to, and with, colleagues and practitioners on four continents.

Is Urban Planning a Profession?

In order to answer this question, we must first analyze the meaning of the term profession. A "profession"[1] is a special kind of community of persons who share the same special kind of occupation. Occupations whose practitioners assume responsibility for the affairs of others and provide a service that is indispensable for the public good are granted the standing of a profession (Kultgen 1988). Being recognized by the broader society as the sole or primary provider of this indispensable service, or, in other words, having a mandate from the society to provide services in a specific field (medicine, law, engineering), is a basic attribute of a profession. Another trait of professions is their organization through professional communities (Goode 1957). A professional community is characterized by three communal-organizational attributes: (a) It develops and maintains an elaborate training program; newcomers to the community have to study for several years, acquire comprehensive knowledge of the theory and practice of the occupation, and absorb its special professional values; they have to pass formal examinations before being allowed to practice what they have learned. (b) It creates a code of conduct, or professional ethics, which includes at least three distinct elements: responsibility toward colleagues within the profession, responsibility toward those who use the services of the profession, and responsibility toward society at large. (c) It establishes professional institutions to oversee proper training and proper conduct of its members and to censure or punish those who transgress.

Defining an occupation as a profession is not a binary matter of either "yes" or "no." The various professions are part of a continuum, with medicine, which conforms to practically all the above noted characteristics of a profession, at one end, and barbers, who maintain very few of the attributes of a profession, at the other. Between these, one finds distributed along the continuum all the other occupations. Because professionals carry out work that is considered interesting, and for which they are usually well remunerated, occupations seek to progress toward professionalization. They develop a distinct body of knowledge and obligatory training programs with requirements for entry and graduation, create codes of professional ethics, establish institutions for internal inspection, and lobby legislators to approve laws that will grant them exclusivity in their work. In this manner, through the years, many occupations (social work, for example) have succeeded in advancing themselves along the professional continuum.

Let's now turn back to the question of whether urban planning is a profession, or at least a vocation in a process of professionalization. The answer appears to be positive. For more than a hundred years there have been university programs to train urban planners, many of which are subject to an accreditation process. Gradually, a theoretical and practical body of knowledge has formed, which is distinct and has its particular objectives, although based on knowledge from other disciplines. Associations of professional planners have been established and processes of professional certification are now institutionalized. Planners' associations usually have an elaborate ethical code (e.g., the APA code, AICP 2009) and issues of planning ethics play an important part in theoretical and professional debates. Hence, the communal-organizational conditions required of a profession are already in place among the community of planners. Planners, however, still lack a crucial element of a profession: a societal mandate to work in a specific field in which they are regarded as the primary (although not necessarily exclusive) experts.

Nathan Glazer identified a main difference between the "major professions" of medicine and law and the "minor professions," including town planning: while the major ones "are disciplined by an unambiguous end," the goals of the minor ones remain unclear and under debate (Glazer 1974: 363). It seems that some forty years later, planners have not yet reached internal agreement regarding their goals and societal mission, an agreement that seems to be a precondition for achieving a societal mandate. I believe it is both possible and desirable to define the unique expertise and mission of planners and would like to submit an offer.

The Mission of Urban Planning, Its Societal Mandate, and Its Values

The mission of each profession is tied to its societal mandate. Society gives physicians a mandate to care for health, and teachers are responsible for schooling education; what is the mandate we ask for as urban planners?

For decades, the noble but vague concern of the public interest has served as the flag of urban planning. There have been numerous attempts to translate it into more concrete terms, one of which may be found (in 2011) in the website of the American Planning Association. The section explains "What is planning?" as follows:

> Planning, also called urban planning or city and regional planning, is a dynamic profession that works to improve the welfare of people and their communities by creating more convenient, equitable, healthful, efficient, and attractive places for present and future generations.
> Planning enables civic leaders, businesses, and citizens to play a meaningful role in creating communities that enrich people's lives.

Good planning helps create communities that offer better choices
for where and how people live. Planning helps communities to
envision their future. It helps them find the right balance of new
development and essential services, environmental protection,
and innovative change.

In line with these concerns and with an emphasis of people-sensitive
planning ("people" are mentioned in each of the above three paragraphs), I
suggest adopting the following statement as both the mission and the domain
of expertise of urban planning: ***Planning with and for People to Enhance
Quality of Life for All in the Built Environment.*** This phrase expresses both
the practical-instrumental role and the value orientation of the profession.
The meaning of "planning," "with and for people," "quality of life," and "for
all" should continuously be discussed, both within the profession and with
those who are expected to use the work and products of planning. Yet, as is,
this phrase seems to broadcast the essence of the profession. Let us look more
deeply into the meaning of the components:

(a) *Planning as a process of communication* with the people who are af-
    fected by the plans and those who have an impact on them *and in-
    tegration* of this communication with the vocational knowledge and
    techniques that are required for *producing plans for the future.*
(b) *Quality of life in the built environment* indicating the aggregation of
    the outcomes of planning, the various components of quality of life
    in the built environment like housing, transportation, community
    development, environmental protection, and many more. The built
    environment includes cities, towns, and their regional surroundings,
    emphasizing place-based comprehensive development.
(c) *For all*—as the composite of several meanings. First, planning is about
    making the various components that comprise a good quality of life
    accessible to all and affordable by all individuals as well as specific,
    relevant groups of people. Second, planning must consider not only
    the interests of the current generation but *also the well-being of future
    generations*, that is, environmental responsibility is an integral part
    of planning. Third, even though the emphasis here is on individuals
    and groups, the *all* is inherently related *also to some kind of "common
    good"* (in Friedmann's sense of the term; 2000: 465).

This suggested formulation of the planners' mission is grounded in what planners actually study and do, and it emphasizes the *uniqueness of urban planning* vis-à-vis others who are involved in the development of the built environment, from architects and engineers to elected officials and developers. That uniqueness is inherent in its *comprehensiveness*, encompassing as it does the various components of the quality of life in urban areas, with their social, economic, spatial, and environmental aspects; in its *integrative approach*, integrating all the above into the complexity of urban development, working with citizens, businesses, and public agencies; and beyond all these, in *the inseparable connection between what planners do and their value commitment*. The suggested formulation clarifies that planning is committed to a specific value orientation.

In practice, however, planning has its dark side (Yiftachel 1998); evils have been perpetrated under the auspices of professional planning, especially toward disadvantaged groups, including indigenous populations, and certainly toward the natural environment. This does not imply that planning is inherently bad or that society would be better off without planning. It does imply that *a more formal adoption of a mission statement with a clear value orientation is of utmost importance* and that continuous procedures of evaluation should be implemented to ensure that values are part of the day-to-day work of planners. The process of planning and its outcomes should be evaluated using the criterion of "who pays and who benefits?" with special attention to unintended consequences. This criterion must be applied when selecting between alternatives as well as for ex post evaluation. Needless to say, this is not a sole evaluation criterion; planners should always take into consideration the trio of economic efficiency, environmental protection and social equity (Campbell 1996). Yet in most planning teams there are other professional advocates for economic growth and for environmental aspects, while concern for social equity is the unique contribution of urban planners to the discussion of public policies, one that should come to be expected when planners are involved.

In other fields there may be a separation between scholars who deal with theory and research as a means to understanding the world and social actors whose work is value-related and context-related (Castells 1998: 359), but urban planners, including planning scholars, are always social actors. John Friedmann (2000: 461) talks about the problem of young people in higher education who are being trained in a narrow body of knowledge and skills, in isolation from larger, vital, value-related questions of our world. This cannot or at least should not happen in a school of urban planning. Planning is always directed toward some kind of "the good city" (461), and is constantly involved in search of "the good city" (Linch, 1981) and "the just city" (Fainstein 2010).

Social Equity as a Leading Value in Urban Planning

As a proposed leading value, social equity—the planning version of social justice—deserves further discussion. The discussion below is divided into three parts: the first focuses on the point of view of planners, while the other two cope with claims that are often raised by those who see the world mostly from an economic point of view. In a world in which economic considerations and the struggle for economic growth take center stage, it seems especially important to discuss common economic assumptions.

The central position of social equity in urban planning. The rise of modern urban planning was motivated by a desire to correct the evils of the slum city of the nineteenth century (Hall 1988). In the 1960s, Herbert Gans led "the goal-oriented approach to planning" (Gans 1968a), placing social equity at the head of the ladder of goals for desirable public policy, claiming that human potential can be better realized by "more equality" (Gans 1973). The roles Melvin Webber (1963) suggested that planners adopt, including extending access to opportunities and expanding freedom of choice in a culturally diverse society, express the value of social equity. Since the 1960s, social equity has been probably the most commonly mentioned value in the discourse of urban planning. It has been the point of departure of specific planning branches such as Advocacy Planning and Progressive Planning. In their essay for this book, Norman Fainstein and Susan Fainstein reach a conclusion that coincides with my own. If planners wish to promote a better world, social equity ought to be the number one value in urban planning; when it clashes with the values of diversity and democracy, planners are called upon to prefer equity (Fainstein and Fainstein in this book).

The special position of social justice in determining human behavior. According to mainstream economic thought, human behavior is motivated by the desire to maximize one's utility, to extract the maximum amount of benefits. I suggest that a better starting point is the assumption that most human beings, most of the time, consider the moral implications of their desires before they set out to accomplish them, an assumption that contradicts the conventional concept of "rational" behavior. This conventional concept is negated not only by sociologists but also by behavioral economists, including Amos Tversky and Nobel laureate Daniel Kahneman. Arieli (2008, esp. chap. 4), another renowned behavioral economist, supports the claim that moral commitments and social norms, which stem from socialization within certain social groups, explain much of human behavior. Thus, for example, people persist in speaking truthfully or giving charity not because it necessarily pays off, but because that is what a "good person" (or a "good Christian") does. Hence, behaving justly, that is, in accordance with one's own definition of justice, is one of the fundamental building blocks of human behavior.

The dilemma of social equity versus economic efficiency. There is a common claim that social equity and economic efficiency are always in competition, so that if one increases the other must decrease. Moreover, it is also often argued that a moderate increase in social equity inevitably causes a substantial loss of economic efficiency. Given this premise, and since economic growth is important to societies, the argument goes, policy makers should forsake equity to promote growth. In contrast to this premise, the claim here is that deliberate policy and planning can result in relatively small reductions in efficiency when social justice is promoted; *moreover, planning can even bring about simultaneous increases in both social equity and economic efficiency.* This approach is not so foreign, even to economists. Okun (1975) explored it years ago. Michael Bruno, chief economist of the World Bank, said that "there is no intrinsic tradeoff between long-run aggregate economic growth and overall equity; policies aimed at helping the poor accumulate productive assets—especially policies to improve schooling, health, and nutrition—are important instruments for achieving higher growth" (Bruno et al. 1999). EU economists have said it loudly and clearly as well: "the European Union's economic evolution for the last sixty years . . . has been characterized by a higher efficiency level (growth in productivity, in the labor occupation degree), which favored the reduction of inequalities related to incomes through the redistribution process" (Socol et al. 2008; see also Barca Report 2009 and OECD 2011). This line of thought has found its way even to the *American Economic Review.* Based on a theoretical model and empirical data from 56 countries, researchers found a significant negative correlation between economic growth and social inequality, in other words, around the world, when inequality increases, growth declines (Persson and Tabellini 1994; see also Alesina and Rodrik 1994). Banerjee and Duflo (2003) analyzed

the methodological difficulties in measuring the aggregate relationships between inequality and growth and recommended a more microeconomic approach. Their recommendation was implemented by Banerjee et al. (2001)
and Panizza (2002), who used detailed regional data and found a highly
significant negative correlation between inequality and growth in India as
well as in the United States. The conclusion derived from these findings is
that *at least in democratic regimes*, increasing social equity, that is, *decreasing inequality between the "haves" and "have-nots" does not prevent economic
growth but rather is essential for securing it.*

Hence, the emphasis on social equity is justified on the basis of its intrinsic value, on being a cornerstone of human behavior (each group with its
own definition of justice-based behavior), and on the paradigm that is accu-
mulating support since the recent global financial crisis in 2008, according to
which more social equality is a necessary condition for sustainable economic
growth.[2]

Having a clear societal mission and a value commitment serves the public good and is an indispensable characteristic of a profession. Next we turn
to discussing another prominent characteristic, the knowledge base of the
profession.

Knowledge in Urban Planning:
Linking Research and Practice

The point of departure for this discussion is two assumptions: first, a considerable part of the knowledge in urban planning is based on, and will continue
to be based on, empirical research (empirical research is a way of gaining
knowledge by means of direct observation or experience); second, a stronger
link between theory, empirical research, and professional practice in urban
planning is highly desirable, in order to improve planning processes and outcomes and also to enhance the field's status as a profession.

When Glaser and Strauss (1967) presented "grounded theory," they had
a similar goal: a stronger link between systematic field work and theoretical
conclusions. Donald Schon called for developing a feedback loop of experience, systematic learning, and practice, notably in his seminal book *The
Reflective Practitioner* (Schon 1983). In recent decades, the volume of research
in urban studies and urban planning has grown significantly; professors and
professionals have access to an immense amount of new information along

with research findings and conclusions. "Intellectual capital" in urban planning is being built (Sanyal 2000). Does this imply that the required link
between research and practice has been established? Are many research projects designed to solve practical urban problems and are planning practitioners using research-based findings and conclusions? It would seem that the
answer to these questions is negative and that there is little progress in connecting research and practice in urban planning (Friedmann 1987; Palermo
and Ponzini 2010).

The difficulty of linking research and practice is inherent in all professions; this issue is widely recognized and discussed. As a result, several
professions have devoted considerable attention to strengthening this link
by raising requirements for evidence-based practice (EBP). Most notably,
medicine (Sackett et al. 1996; Montori and Guyatt 2008) and the health sciences (Murray and Lopez 1996), including pharmacology (Mayo-Smith 1997)
and nursing (DiCenso et al. 1998), have introduced EBP requirements, but
the same is true for other professions, including management (Pfeffer and
Sutton 2006) and public administration (Sanderson 2002), psychology (APA
Presidential Task Force 2006), education (Slavin 2002), and social work
(Matthew et al. 2003). Some initial attention is now being given to EBP in
urban planning, as will be detailed below.

EBP does not mean relying necessarily on quantitative testing of hypotheses. It is true that more and more rigorously managed experiments and
quasi-experiments are being conducted and there are researchers who call
for using them alone as reliable evidence, while defining "expert opinion" as
the least valuable basis for professional decision-making. Still, a large share
of those who write about EBP, even in medicine, advocate "integrating individual clinical expertise with the best available external clinical evidence
from systematic research" when it comes to guiding practitioners (Sacket
et al. 1996, cited by more than 5,000 authors). Moreover, in parallel with
the evidence-based movement, a narrative-based medicine is being developed, based on the assumption that there are "limits of objectivity in clinical
method" and "there is an art to medicine as well as an objective empirical
science" (Greenhalgh 1999: 323).

The reservations mentioned in the last paragraph are certainly relevant
when considering the merits of evidence-based practice in urban planning.
In addition, much can be learned from the introduction of EBP into the field
of program evaluation; Vedung's (2010) description of the historical development of EBP in program evaluation seems particularly relevant:

Four waves have deposited sediments, which form present-day evaluative activities. The scientific wave entailed that academics should
test, through two-group experimentation, appropriate means to reach
externally set, admittedly subjective, goals. Public decision-makers
were then supposed to roll out the most effective means. Faith in scientific evaluation eroded in the early 1970s. It has since been argued
that evaluation should be participatory and nonexperimental, with
information being elicited from users, operators, managers and other
stakeholders through discussions. In this way, the dialogue-oriented
wave entered the scene. Then the neoliberal wave from around 1980
pushed for market orientation. Deregulation, privatization, contracting-out, efficiency and customer influence became key phrases.
Evaluation as accountability, value for money and customer satisfaction was recommended. Under the slogan "What matters is what
works" the evidence-based wave implies a renaissance for scientific
experimentation. (Vedung 2010: 263)

In the urban field, the objection to so-called "objective research" is probably wider and has deeper roots, and therefore, in contrast to developments
in other professions, the combination of the term "evidence-based" with
"urban planning" is still rare. Yet, some beginnings can be found. Faludi and
Waterhout (2006) took the initiative of "introducing evidence-based planning." In an article that opens a series of papers on the subject, they present
three revealing observations. (a) The essence of evidence-based planning is
not new; actually, it has been with us since antiquity, when the Romans conducted a general census (according to the Bible, a census was conducted 1,500
years earlier, when Moses commanded counting the Sons of Israel N.C.), and
reached its culmination in the modernist period, when professionals tended
to believe in scientific and technical progress and instrumental rationality.
(b) The reentry of an evidence-based approach into planning came not from
the field itself but from external sources: British policy makers and European
Union spatial planning organizations. (c) Faludi and Waterhout conclude
that evidence-based planning is "one of the important trends of this century."
U.S.-based researchers have joined the discussion more recently, trying
to answer the question: "Is there a role for evidence-based practice in urban
planning and policy?" (Krizek, Forysth, and Slotterback 2009). The bottom
line of their paper is that in view of frequent failures in achieving the stated
goals of plans, and without ignoring the limitations and special challenges

related to EBP, they recommend adding it to the list of common sources of knowledge used by planning practitioners.

Their line of thought goes the same direction as my own conclusion. I believe that planning practice, its process and its outcomes, can be significantly improved by more extensive use of systematic empirical research and by meta-analysis of studies. I also believe that evidence-based research in urban planning may encompass a variety of systematic research methods, including the narrative tradition in planning. Moreover, where a variety of research methods reach similar, practice-oriented conclusions, the reliability of those conclusions is enhanced

The path to integrating evidence-based research into planning practice requires researchers and practitioners to reach out to each other. Given the current state of the art in urban planning, the main burden should fall on the shoulders of researchers. They can contribute to the required integration by

(a) Selecting research questions that focus on practical problems (in addition to studying theoretical issues).

(b) Studying outcomes, in addition to processes.

(c) Emphasizing the search for "what works."

(d) Providing the necessary service of meta-analysis, that is, developing methods to combine and evaluate the results of many studies that address a set of related questions/problems, in spite of the different research methods the researchers use.

(e) Using all the above to create lists of "best policies" and "best practices"; these are lists of practical recommendations, which represent *the best currently available research-based findings and conclusions,* which can then be used by practitioners; they should be periodically updated in accordance with the advancement of systematic research.

All this may sound like a proposal to turn planning research publications into cookbooks, but that is not at all my intention. There are and there should always be theory and history studies that gradually build the foundations of planning; in fact, many may have implications for planning practice, but by their very nature they are not the most appropriate means for developing "best practices." Moreover, empirical studies in planning, be they semi-experimental evaluations, case studies, or action research, are based (unlike cookbooks) on analysis and explanation, and the request for practical recommendations is meant not to replace analysis but to complement it.

It seems that often planning researchers either try to avoid practical issues that may disturb their "clean" analysis or hesitate to take on the responsibility of advising practitioners. Of course, every case has its specific characteristics and is different from all others, but this does not mean that there are no common denominators or no good, evidence-based practices that can and should be derived from systematic research and then taken into consideration by those working in the field. (I wish we could replace "best" by "good" or "appropriate," but the term "best practices" has become rooted in the commonly accepted terminology of many professions.)

Table 1.1 draws on my own research to illustrate several of the above suggestions regarding ways of tying research to practice. It focuses on practical questions in a defined area, housing and urban regeneration, highlighting "what works"; it uses studies with a variety of systematic research methods; and it presents evidence-based and practice-oriented recommendations in the form of "best policies" and "best practices." Elaborating on one "best practice" in the table (the third one) may clarify the idea. In my studies I found, as did empirical studies conducted in different cultures using various research methods, that housing demolition, which frequently goes hand-in-hand with forced displacement of residents, is usually bad for the people, for the environment, and for the urban architectural fabric; moreover, often it takes far longer than planned to complete such projects, so that they cause financial and other losses to the involved actors. On the basis of these findings, the recommendation to a planning practitioner is to check your case, consider alternatives, and as far as possible try to avoid demolition, especially demolition with enforced displacement of residents, because of its unintended consequences.

A general recommendation for planning researchers, in particular those conducting empirical studies, is to try to end their reports by answering the question "*so what?*" from the point of view of planning practice. If they do so, their conclusions can be considered and possibly adopted by practitioners who encounter similar cases. Moreover, at some point in time a scholar is able to collect their answers and make a meta-analysis of studies that can be used to draw "the best currently available" policies and practices. In parallel, a general recommendation to planning practitioners is to search for research on the type of plan they are developing and make educated use of its findings and inferences.

Table 1.1. "What Works" in Housing and Urban Renewal

Evidence-based best policies	Evidence based best practices related to policies on the left and grounded in the same studies
Differential intervention in different deteriorated residential areas[a][d][g]	Remedies should differ by level of social capital within the neighborhood, location in Hot Demand Area or elsewhere, and also type and physical situation of buildings[a][d][g]
Preventive Planning[b][h]	Identify neighborhoods on the verge of deterioration and encourage "incumbent upgrading"[b][h]
A gradual and "soft" approach to housing and neighborhood improvements[a][d]	Wherever possible, avoid demolition of the old housing stock and plan for gradual physical and social regeneration of old neighborhoods[a][d]
Prevent segregation of the lower classes in re-planned residential areas[c][e][f][g]	Desirable outcomes of social mix in residential areas are achieved where: differences among neighbors are moderate and not extreme; homogeneous clusters reside within a heterogeneous area with joint public and social services[c][e][f][g]
Work simultaneously for social equity and economic growth and efficiency[b][d]	Encourage user-controlled upgrading of housing in distressed neighborhoods, and thus promote simultaneously: better housing conditions and housing maintenance, place attachment and the motivation to work that increases the income of the households [b][d]
Regeneration through partnerships[a][b][g]	Public-Private-Partnerships (PPPs), Public-Civic Partnerships (PCPs) and Public-Private-Civic-Partnerships (PPCPs)[a][b][g]

The statements in the table are based on studies conducted over 35 years, using a variety of research methods. The table draws on my studies only (studies published in accessible English publications), but partly similar conclusions and recommendations were proposed by others, including contributors to this book; see essays by Galster, Fainstein and Fainstein, and Vale.
(a) Literature survey and historical analysis of "waves" of urban renewal policies in Western countries (Carmon 1999).
(b) A series of empirical studies of user-controlled housing upgrading, based mainly on interviews with households (Carmon and Oxman 1986; Carmon and Gavrieli 1987; Carmon 2002b).
(c) A critical review of research literature (in sociology and in urban planning) regarding neighborliness and ethnically mixed housing (Carmon 1976).
(d) An empirical social-architectural-economic-organizational evaluation study of 10 case studies, 10 distressed neighborhoods selected for Project Renewal (Carmon 1997).
(e) A quasi-experimental study with rigorous statistical analysis of 52 Project Renewal neighborhoods, compared with carefully selected control group of 67 neighborhoods (Carmon and Baron 1994).
(f) A household survey on inter-enthnic relations in a peripheral rural region (Yiftachel and Carmon 1997).
(g) A longitudinal study using a variety of research methods to invetigate the process and outcomes of adding a middle-income neighborhood to a small low-income town (Carmon 2006; Ziflinger 2005).
(h) The same research methods mention in (b) above (Carmon 1998, 2002a).

In Conclusion

A majority of the rapid changes in technology, demography, economic structure, and sociocultural settings that are occurring in the twenty-first century are taking place in urban environments—environments that are expected to absorb and support these changes. Under these circumstances, society needs a body of knowledge on urban development, a body that is being produced by researchers of many disciplines, especially geography and the social sciences, including planning. In addition, society needs a group of carriers of this knowledge, who have a holistic view of the many components involved in the development of the built environment and who can assist public decision makers, community leaders, and citizens to create appropriate policies and plans that lead to improved urban environments. Urban planners may be granted the societal mandate to cultivate this holistic view and lead the creation of urban policies and plans. For that to happen, planners have to take additional steps in their progress toward becoming a publicly recognized profession.

"Whether planning is a profession is a matter of some dispute: a recent outside opinion suggests it isn't yet but may make it very soon" (Marcuse 1976). More than three dozen years after these words were published, it is still a matter of dispute and it is unclear whether planning is about to make it. This essay supports advancement toward professionalization as something beneficial to planners and to the societies in which they live. The way forward involves three processes that were detailed above:

- Working toward an accepted definition of the planning expertise, which requires first internal agreement and then public recognition; here the proposal is to adopt *Planning with and for People to Enhance Quality of Life for All in the Built Environment* as both the mission statement and the domain of expertise of urban planning.
- Renewing the commitment to values by planners, those "professional values" that according to Rein (1969) are one of the basic sources of legitimacy of planning; *Social Equity* with relation to present and future generations is offered here as a leading value, along with several justifications for selecting it.
- Strengthening research and the connection between research and practice as a way to improve the process and products of planning

and strengthening its recognized credibility; a way to do that is by critically analyzing findings from various studies that focus on one issue or problem and use the analysis to suggest evidence-based "best policies," "best procedures," and "best practices"; thus, the best currently available research-based evidence is made accessible to practitioners, under the assumption that the analysis is updated when additional research findings are published.

Pursuing these proposals does not mean that the ultimate goal is an institutionalized profession which is exclusively responsible for urban development. In my judgment, such a goal is both unattainable and undesirable. Planning is, by its very nature, a field and a profession that works with other fields/disciplines and professions. Moreover, in countries and periods that reached advanced institutionalization of the planning profession (for example, the British Town and Country Planning Act 1947), planning seemed to be reduced to procedural-technical activities, and in the process it lost its spirit and its connections with the public for which it works (Upton 2010). Hence, what may be both attainable and desirable, if planners move along the above-mentioned lines, is a stronger sense of purpose and a more identifiable and coherent collection of procedures and practices; a collection which is constantly developed by researchers and practitioners, which is used by members of the profession and which is respected by the society they are part of and for whom they choose to work.

With an eye to the revolutionary processes that seemed to start with the protest movements of 2011—movements that rapidly spread to close to a thousand cities around the globe, from Occupy Wall Street in New York to the May 15 Movement in Madrid and the People Demand Social Justice in Tel Aviv—the above discussion and suggestions seem especially relevant.

Notes

The author wishes to thank her colleagues and students for their contributions to shaping the ideas and suggestions presented in this essay. Special thanks are due to Susan Fainstein and Emily Silverman for helpful comments on early versions.

1. Etymology: professiōn- (s. of professiō) taking the vows of a religious order. http://dictionary.reference.com/browse/profession. In modern times, the term means taking the vows of a professional order.

2. The World Economic Forum in Davos (2012) found that "Severe Income Disparity" was number 1 out of 50 global risks, in terms of perceived likelihood over the next ten years.

References

AICP, 2009. *AICP Code of Ethics and Professional Conduct*. Adopted March 2005, revised October 2009. http://www.planning.org/ethics/ethicscode.htm, accessed February 2012.

Alesina, Alberto, and Dani Rodrik. 1994. Distributive politics and economic growth. *Quarterly Journal of Economics* 109: 465–90.

APA Presidential Task Force on Evidence-Based Practice. 2006. Evidence-based practice in psychology. *American Psychologist* 63, 4: 271–85.

Arieli, Dan. 2008. *Predictably irrational: The hidden forces that shape our decisions*. New York: HarperCollins.

Banerjee, Abhijit, Dilip Mookherjee, Kaivan Munshi, and Debraj Ray. 2001. Inequality, control rights, and rent seeking: Sugar cooperatives in Maharashtra. *Journal of Political Economy* 109: 138–90.

Banerjee, Abhijit, and Ester Duflo. 2003. Inequality and growth: What can the data say? *Journal of Economic Growth* 8: 267–99.

Barca Report. 2009. An agenda for reformed cohesion policy: A place-based approach to meeting European Union challenges and expectations. http://www.eurada.org/site/files/Regional%20development/Barca_report.pdf, accessed February 2012.

Bruno, Michael, Martin Ravallion, and Lyn Squire. 1999. *Equity and growth in developing countries: Old and new perspectives on the policy issues*. World Bank Policy Research Working Paper 1563. SSRN: http://ssrn.com/abstract=604912.

Campbell, Scott. 1996. Green cities, growing cities, just cities? Urban planning and the contradictions of sustainable development. *Journal of the American Planning Association* 62(3): 296–312.

Carmon, Naomi. 1976. Social planning of housing. *Journal of Social Policy* 5(1): 49–59.

———. 1997. Urban regeneration: The state of the art. *Journal of Planning Education and Research* 17(2): 131–44.

———. 1998. Preventive planning: housing updating as a tool for preventing and combating neighborhood decline. Keynote lecture at ENHR-European Network of Housing Research Conference, Cardiff. *Book of Abstracts*, 21–23.

———. 1999. Three generations of neighborhood remedies: Research-based analysis and policy implications." *Geoform* 2: 145–58.

———. 2002a. The Phoenix strategy for updating housing stock: Preventing neighborhood deterioration and promoting sustainable development. *Journal of the American Planning Association* 68(4): 416–34.

————. 2002b. User-controlled construction and renovation: Desirability and feasibility. *European Planning Studies* 10(3): 285–303.

————. 2006. Turning a low-income small town into a sustainable mixed-income place. Paper presented at World Planning Schools Congress, Mexico City. *Book of Abstracts*, 70–71.

Carmon, Naomi, and Mira Baron. 1994. Reducing inequality by means of neighborhood rehabilitation: An Israeli experience and its lessons. *Urban Studies* 31(9): 1465–79.

Carmon, Naomi, and Tamar Gavrieli. 1987. Improving housing by conventional versus self-help methods. *Urban Studies* 24(4): 324–32.

Carmon, Naomi, and Robert Oxman. 1986. Responsive public housing: An alternative for low-income families. *Environment and Behavior* 18(2): 258–84.

Castells, Manuel. 1998. *End of millennium.* The Information age: Economy, Society and Culture 3. Oxford: Blackwell.

DiCenso, Alba, Nicky Cullum, and Donna Ciliska. 1998. Implementing evidence-based nursing: Some misconceptions. *Evidence Based Nursing* 1: 38–39.

Fainstein, Susan, S. 2010. *The just city*. Ithaca, N.Y.: Cornell University Press.

Faludi, Andreas, and Bas Waterhout. 2006. Introducing evidence-based planning. *disP—The Planning Review of ETH* 165: 4–13.

Friedmann, John. 1987. *Planning in the public domain: From knowledge to action.* Princeton, N.J.: Princeton University Press.

————. 2000. The good city: in defense of utopian thinking. *International Journal of Urban and Regional Research* 24(2): 460–72.

Gans, Herbert J. 1968. *People and plans: Essays on urban problems and solutions.* New York: Basic Books.

————. 1973. *More equality*. New York: Pantheon.

Glaser, Barney G., and Anselm L. Strauss. 1967. The discovery of grounded theory. *British Journal of Sociology* 20(2): 227.

Glazer, Nathan. 1974. The schools of the minor professions. *Minerva* 12(3): 346–64.

Goode, William J. 1957. Community within a community: The professions. *American Sociological Review* 22(2): 194–200.

Greenhalgh, Trisha. 1999. Narrative based medicine in an evidence based world. *British Medical Journal* 318(7179): 323–25.

Hall, Peter. 1988. *The cities of tomorrow: An intellectual history of urban planning and design in the twentieth century.* Oxford: Blackwell.

Hardin Garrett. 1968. The tragedy of the commons. *Science* 162(859): 1243–48.

Innes de Neufville, Judith. 1987. Knowledge and action: Making the link. *Journal of Planning Education and Research* 6(2): 86–92.

Krizek, Kevin, Ann Forsyth, and Carissa Schively Slotterback. 2009. Is there a role for evidence-based practice in urban planning and policy? *Planning Theory and Practice* 10(4): 459–78.

Kultgen, John H. 1988. *Ethics and professionalism*. Philadelphia: University of Pennsylvania Press.

Mannheim, Karl. 1950. *Freedom, power and democratic planning*. New York: Oxford University Press.

Lynch, Kevin. 1981. *A theory of good city form*. Cambridge Mass.: MIT Press.

Marcuse, Peter. 1976. Professional ethics and beyond: Values in planning. *Journal of the American Planning Association* 42(3): 264–74.

Matthew, O. Howard, Curtis J. McMillan, and David E. Pollio. 2003. Teaching evidence-based practice: Toward a new paradigm for social work education. *Research on Social Work Practice* 13(2): 234–59.

Mayo-Smith, Michael F. 1997. Pharmacological management of alcohol withdrawal: A meta-analysis and evidence-based practice guideline. *Journal of the American Medical Association* 278(2): 144–51.

Meyer, Dietmar, and Lackenbauer Jörg. 2005. EU cohesion policy and the equity-efficiency trade-off. European Regional Science Association series, ERSA conference papers ersa05p564.

Montori, Victor M., and Gordon H. Guyatt. 2008. Progress in evidence based medicine. *Journal of the American Medical Association* 300(15): 1814–16.

Murray, Christopher J. L., and Alan D. Lopaz. 1996. Evidence based health policy: Lessons from the global burden of disease study. *Science* 274(5288): 740–43.

OECD. 2011. *Social justice in the OECD: How do the member states compare?* Gütersloh: Bertelsmann Stiftung.

Okun, Arthur M. 1975. *Equality and efficiency: The big tradeoff*. Washington, D.C.: Brookings Institution.

Palermo, Pier C., and Davide Ponzini. 2010. *Spatial planning and urban development: Critical perspectives*. Springer Series on Urban and Landscape Perspectives 10. Dordrecht: Springer, 2010.

Panniza, Ugo. 2002. Income inequality and economic growth: Evidence from American data. *Journal of Economic Growth* 7: 25–41.

Persson, Torsten, and Guido Tabellini. 1994. Is inequality harmful to growth? *American Economic Review* 84(3): 600–621.

Pfeffer, Jeffrey, and Robert I. Sutton. 2006. Evidence-based management, *Harvard Business Review* 84: 62–84.

Piccione, Michele, and Ariel Rubinstein. 2007. Equilibrium in the jungle. *Economic Journal* 117(522): 883–96.

Rand, Ayn. 1957. *Atlas shrugged*. New York: Random House.

Rein, Martin. 1969. Social planning: The search for legitimacy. *Journal of the American Planning Association* 35(4): 233–44.

Royal Town Planning Institute. 2001. *A new vision for planning*. http://www.rtpi.org.uk/download/245/RTPI-New-Vision-for-Planning.pdf., accessed February 2012.

Sackett, David L., William M. C. Rosenberg, J. A. Muir Gray, R. Brian Haynes, and W.

Scott Richardson. 1996. Editorial: Evidence based medicine: What it is and what it isn't. *British Medical Journal* 312(7023): 71–72.

Sanderson, Ian. 2002. Evaluation, policy learning and evidence-based policy making. *Public Administration* 80(1): 1–22.

Sanyal, Bishwapriya. 2000. Planning's three challenges. In *The profession of city planning: Changes, images, and challenges 1950–2000*, ed. Lloyd Rodwin and Bish Sanyal, 312–33. New Brunswick, N.J.: CUPR Press, Rutgers University.

Schon, Donald A. 1983. *The reflective practitioner: How professionals think in action.* New York: Basic Books.

Slavin, Robert E. 2002. Evidence-based education policies: Transforming educational practice and research. *Educational Researcher* 31(7): 15–21.

Socol, Cristian, Aura Gabriela Socol, and Marius Corneliu Marinas. 2008. The analysis of equity-efficiency trade-off in the European Union economy. *Annals of Faculty of Economics* (University of Oradea) 2(1): 442–48.

Upton, Robert (2010). Rising to the challenge: Planners and the planning profession. *Planning—Journal of the Israel Association of Planners* 7(2): 16–28 (Hebrew with English abstract).

Vedung, Evert. 2010. Four waves of evaluation. *Evaluation* 16(3): 263–77.

Webber, Melvin M. 1963. Comprehensive planning and social responsibility: Towards an AIP consensus on the profession's roles and purposes. *Journal of the American Planning Association* 29(4): 232–41.

World Economic Forum. 2012. *Global risks 2012.* Insight report, seventh ed. Davos, Switzerland: World Economic Forum.

Yiftachel, Oren. 1998. Planning and social control: Exploring the dark side. *Journal of Planning Literature* 12(4): 395–406.

Yiftachel, Oren, and Naomi Carmon. 1997. Socio-spatial mix and inter-ethnic attitudes: Jewish newcomers and Arab-Jewish issues in the Galilee. *European Planning Studies* 5(2): 215–37.

Ziflinger Yulia. 2005. Promoting social justice through urban regeneration. Ph.D. dissertation supervised by Naomi Carmon, Technion-Israel Institute of Technology.

Chapter 2

Restoring Just Outcomes
to Planning Concerns

Norman Fainstein and Susan S. Fainstein

Creating a more just world has been a human goal ever since injustice was recognized and defined. Needless to say, the definitions of just outcomes and the methods for attaining them have differed widely across cultures and epochs. Some visions of justice have been entirely ethereal or otherworldly. Many, however, have been presented in the context of a physical utopia embodying, at least implicitly, a conception of justice. In fact, the rise of town planning as a professional and academic field in the nineteenth century was strongly propelled by the desire to shape a more just world through explicitly rational human interventions in the built environment.

In this chapter, we explore the ways urban planning and social justice have been intertwined in the West during the modern period. We show that ideas about justice were an integral part of the principal utopian models that influenced planning from the mid-nineteenth to the mid-twentieth century. But we also see that the idea of social progress gradually became dissociated from physical plans for the built environment. The plans that were implemented lost their egalitarian content, while the emergent vision of activists concerned with justice turned away from physical answers to social questions. In their place, they developed theories of democratic processes that rejected the goal of a specific "outcome," much less of an actual urban vision of the built environment and pattern of human settlement that would animate it. We find that these "talking cures" have always been flawed and inadequate. We conclude by arguing that just outcomes can and should be restored to planning concerns and can, to some extent, be specified. For us, looking back for the future is no mere academic exercise; it is in fact essential to identifying the most virtuous goals of planning so that they can provide us with guidance in shaping a built environment for a more just world.[1]

The Utopian Moment in Town Planning

The objectives of town planning have been multiple—defense, sanitation, transportation, religion, housing, economic production—and removing noxious neighborhoods and the people within them has long been claimed to benefit the poor as well as city aesthetics.[2] Yet while "ideal" cities had been envisioned by Plato, Sir Thomas More, and Jonathan Edwards, to name but a few, it was the particular confluence of rapid urbanization, industrialization, and various forms of political democracy that gave birth in the West to the modern utopian vision of the just city—the city where the "common man" would be better off.

By the latter half of the nineteenth century, the industrial city—with its crowding, filth, and miserable poor—was seen by many reformers as not merely the form of the built environment that encompassed the working class and the destitute, the dangerous factory and the tenement house, disease and "immorality." It was also regarded as the *cause* of much that was wrong with modern society: its extremes in economic inequality, its class conflict, its prostitution, and its loss of the traditional norms that bound people together (Ward 1989). The city itself had cut the masses off from their "natural" rural roots and from the benefits of the clean water and fresh air they once enjoyed. So it was no wonder that a new urban *form* was seen as necessary if there were to be genuine social *re-form*. Although the social forces that would implement this improved way of living needed to be found—variously, in an enlightened public, a government freed from corrupting politics, or the charitable inclinations of the wealthy—progress required a vision, a plan, a utopian alternative to the frightening dystopias places like New York, London, Paris, and Berlin had become.

The most influential of these utopian "urban" visions can be found in the work of the English Ebenezer Howard, the American Frank Lloyd Wright, the German Bauhaus group, and the French Le Corbusier, who have arguably bestowed on us the essential models for how life is to be lived in real space.[3] They were horrified by cities as they knew them, and conceived of their grand plans as offering a better, more equitable, more just life to the citizens of their new worlds.

Howard imagined modest-sized garden cities (30,000 people or so), with artisanal workshops within an easy walk of homes (and larger factories on the outskirts), which would prosper through communal, socialistic economies. Cities would be connected by railroads to form metropolitan areas. Still, no one would be very far from the countryside. As Howard's plans evolved and realities set in, his modernistic housing was replaced by Raymond Unwin's neo-Tudor country villages and much of the socialism got lost. Nonetheless, the utopian ideals of reasonable social equality, access for all to both town and rural spaces, and cities full of light and greenswards remained intact. Formally, at least, the garden city has very much molded today's New Urbanism.

In contrast to Howard, Wright rejected the whole idea of a city, even one on the scale of an English country village, and he loathed socialism. Wright's model was a fantasized—some would say fetishized—"little house on the prairie," from which people drove to highly decentralized workshops and stores. Bizarrely, and prefiguring Mao's cottage-communist backyard blast furnaces, he thought of each home unit as a farm-factory of capitalist enterprise. Everyone would have at least an acre of land, and equality would be defined by the number of cars a family would own (not less than one, not more than four). His Broadacre City would be spread across the entire United States without boundaries or centers. The countryside would be privatized into the large yards surrounding single-family "ranch style" houses. In fact, much of American suburbia, especially in the newer parts of the continent, embodied the utopian Broadacre vision, minus of course Wright's economic ideas, which could not have been more out of touch with the emergent forces of corporate capitalism.

Le Corbusier was also attached to technology and the automobile. But perhaps in a typically French way, he placed great faith in rational management and in the benefits of large cities. He also believed in equality—even between the sexes—and established a syndicalist government for his "Radiant City." This was to be a city of high-rise buildings that contained quotidian services within themselves, were surrounded by parks, and were connected by highways, many of them elevated. The Radiant City was strictly segregated by function into residential, commercial, industrial, governmental, and other zones, yet it was also premised on a reasonable level of economic equality and equal access to the "center" for all classes. Much urban planning in the post-World War II period was influenced by the Radiant City—by its form of strict zoning and order, its residential towers in parks for rich and poor alike, and its auto-centered street life.

While its utopian visions were never quite so detailed, the Bauhaus School also emphasized the impact that design would have on shaping the New (socialist) Man in the New City. When the school was closed by Hitler in 1933, after only fourteen years of existence, many of its leaders fled to Israel, where they helped plan Tel Aviv and filled it with Bauhaus architecture. Around the world, the Bauhaus designers' functional elements were highly influential in the postwar period. Merged with LeCorbusier's designs, they were propagated by the Congrès International d'Architecture Moderne (CIAM). But as in the case of Howard, Wright, and Le Corbusier, the social content of Bauhaus thinking was largely lost, except, perhaps, in the case of the Israeli Kibbutzim (Fiedler 1995; Girard 2003).

An optimistic, modernist model of the future city was elaborated in great detail even as war clouds broke over Europe. Visitors to the 1939 New York World's Fair were presented the strictly free-enterprise-based "Wonderworld of 1960," courtesy of the General Motors Corporation, a vision directly from the drawing boards of Wright and Le Corbusier (but cleansed of their "unrealistic" economic ideas).[4] Thousands of visitors a day sat on a conveyor that moved them through GM's sanitized America: a sprawling Broadacre-like countryside consisting of detached, single-family homes with big yards, with cities here and there of towers in parks, all knit together by highways and traversed by family cars that never collided or polluted. In an accompanying movie, the public was assured that "on all express city thoroughfares, the rights of way have been so routed as to displace outmoded business sections and undesirable slum areas whenever possible. Man continually strives to replace the old with the new."[5] In this way, urban renewal—a term not yet coined—would solve both the "urban problem" of antiquated industry and the "social problem" of class inequality. It was an automotive, corporate utopia that perfectly combined the most palatable elements of Wright and Le Corbusier.[6]

In that same fateful year of 1939, the American Institute of Planners projected its own utopian and physical solution to the problems of industrial capitalism in an hour-long film with Hollywood production values and the modest title, *The City*.[7] Written by Lewis Mumford, scored by Aaron Copland, and narrated by Morris Carnovsky, the movie depicted the golden past of the pre-industrial American farm town and the English village, when home and work, master and apprentice, men and women, built and natural environments all comprised a single, harmonious landscape. This classless and organic form of life was destroyed by the industrial revolution and the filthy, chaotic, and conflict-ridden "city" that embodied it. The formula for returning to the communal existence that preceded industrial capitalism—and simultaneously for eradicating the evils of the city that accompanied it—would in fact be Howard's garden city.

Without reference to Howard himself, we are presented with a scenic break from the horrible extant city, after which technology, planning, and the right vision literally take off in the form of a shining aluminum DC-3 that eventually lands us in a new town, this time with modern Bauhaus structures, small workshops, bicycle paths, open spaces, limited automobile usage, and all the other accouterments of the updated Garden City. Capturing the rushing water and tweeting birds of the agrarian past, the musical score and narrative tell us that the physical transformation of urban space could provide the key to a new way of life. Again, a planned physical utopia would help form the "new man" and society.

The Postwar Fate of Grand Plans

Although the "utopian mix" of Wright, Howard, Le Corbusier, and the Bauhaus, as well as the timing of critique, was different on the two sides of the Atlantic, the faith in grand physical solutions to social inequality rose everywhere in the West after the war and fell everywhere by the 1980s. At the risk of gross simplification, the two stories can be told briefly.

In the United States, slum clearance and highway construction were the rationales for the major urban redevelopment projects that began with the Housing Act of 1949, and continued under increasing fire and opposition through the 1970s. But in America the support for public (i.e., social) housing was strictly limited, while the alternative of mass, privately constructed "popular" housing of the Levittown variety was powerfully advanced by an alliance of bankers, estate agents, corporate house builders, and conservative politicians. The vast suburban subdivisions that arose were idealized as "the American dream" and taken to represent an egalitarian solution in which everyone could aspire to property ownership. The definition of equity underlying this vision can be traced to Wright's picture of a society in which people controlled their lives individually rather than as part of a collective. Class difference disappeared, as everyone became middle class.

In the diminishing urban core, large-scale slum clearance, along with accompanying highways, was strongly advanced by planners, with the same promise and premise offered by General Motors in its 1939 vision of the future: a physical, "grand" solution to urban poverty and economic obsolescence through large-scale clearance of dense urban neighborhoods and replacement with modern housing and commercial development along Corbusian lines of functional segregation, towers in parks, and easy automobile access.[8] As southern rural blacks and off-shore Puerto Ricans streamed into older American cities, enthusiasm for social housing further eroded, so that except for a very few large cities—especially New York and Chicago—the utopian vision of housing for the masses, mainly in Le Corbusier-inspired towers, quickly expired (see Baxandall and Ewen 2000; Gelfand 1975; Warner 1972).

By the time urban renewal entered its second decade in the United States, its projects became famous, or rather infamous, worldwide. They not only gave rise to opposition on the ground, but inspired an academic literature in planning, sociology, and political science that quickly became iconic. Thus, Herbert Gans documented the destruction of Boston's West End in his *Urban Villagers* (1962), Jane Jacobs ridiculed the "radiant garden city beautiful" in *The Death and Life of Great American Cities* (1961), while Floyd Hunter in *Community Power Structure* (1969) found the power structure behind the reconstruction of Atlanta. In a magnum opus that traced the erosion of social commitment in the face of American economic and political realities, Robert Caro in *The Power Broker* (1974) adumbrated not only the damage in New York City over the decades by master-builder Robert Moses, but also the plans finally thwarted in the 1960s to build great, elevated expressways across lower and midtown Manhattan, to transform that island into a simulacrum of Le Corbusier's prewar "Plan Voisin" for the right bank of the Seine.

By the time Caro laid the last nail in Robert Moses's coffin in 1974, American cities had been wracked by citizen mobilization, racial conflict, and large-scale riots. The effect on planners and intellectuals concerned with social justice was to destroy the utopian vision of urban physical transformation as the way to address social inequality and political instability. The real applications of earlier utopian ideas in "comprehensive planning" were identified mainly as programs for "Negro removal" and bourgeoisification of valuable central-city spaces.[9]

Nor was the answer an alternative plan for a "just city." With faith lost in grand visions and their proponents, planning from "above" was countered with a political program from below—a program of community control, black power, and bureaucratic enfranchisement.[10] Progressive planners and likeminded professionals became advocates for the poor, for persons of color, and for "inner-city" neighborhoods (Hoffman 1989). The "advocacy planning" Paul Davidoff (1965) championed as early as 1965 became *the* progressive paradigm for planning as social reform, while Manuel Castells (1977), David Harvey (1973), and others on the neo-Marxian left dismissed planning altogether, redefining the "urban question" as a crisis in capitalism that could be resolved only through class conflict, social restructuring, and possibly revolution.

In Britain, France, and throughout Western Europe, the faith in grand projects that would modernize cities and "benefit all" waxed and waned along a rather similar timetable. The construction of the Montparnasse tower and destruction of Les Halles market in Paris, the building of the Southbank Concert Halls in London, and similar massive urban redevelopment projects quickly drew critics, as in America. For similar reasons of a newfound appreciation for historical preservation (catalyzed in the United States by the destruction of the Pennsylvania Railroad Station in New York in 1963 and the attempt to demolish Grand Central Terminal a few years later), Covent Garden in London was preserved and restored, and the Seine autoroute in Paris was rejected.

But the differences between Europe and America in grand ideas about progressive urban reconstruction were also significant and long-lasting. For one thing, the need for massive reconstruction from war damage in England, the Low Countries, Germany, Italy, and, to a somewhat lesser extent, France, empowered national planning regimes in Britain and the Continent. For another, labor, social democratic, and even centrist governments engaged in social housing construction on a mass scale, and this housing consistently embodied equity objectives (Harloe 1995). Thus, grand, housing-centered planning proceeded across Western Europe from the epoch of postwar rubble and hunger, through the economic "renaissance" of the 1950s and 1960s, until well beyond the popular "uprisings" of 1968. With racially marginalized former colonial populations and Islamic guest workers appearing on the urban stage only in the 1970s and later, huge social housing projects were viewed in the 1950s and 1960s as accomplishments in social justice for the national working and even middle classes. Equally important, and for the same reasons, they retained widespread electoral support.

Nonetheless, one could see a slow waning of the utopian vision in European urban planning as time went on. A decade before the Thatcher neoliberal revolution in 1979, the construction of garden city new towns came to a halt in Britain. The *grands ensembles* in France and Bijlmermeer in Amsterdam were criticized both for their anti-urban aesthetics and for geographically isolating and homogenizing the working classes in a stigmatized urban periphery (Mengin 1999; Luijten 2002). The terms "cités" ("projects") and "banlieues" ("suburbs") turned negative even while the vast majority of their occupants were still native born, white, and French.

In retrospect, European faith in large-scale brick-and-mortar approaches to social justice eroded as the metaphorical 1960s petered out in the stagflation of the actual 1970s. Working-class parties weakened and lost their influence over public policy to no small degree because their industrial bases rusted. The drab and monotonous urban models offered by state socialism in Eastern Europe and the Soviet Union seemed to show the future of the planned society taken to scale. Equally important, and integrally related, was a simultaneous efflorescence and transformation of ideas on the left (Fainstein and Fainstein 1978). Neo-Marxist urbanists continued to delegitimize planning and urban development as routes to a just society under capitalism (see, inter alia, Harvey 1978; Foglesong 1986). In the following decades, a European "new left"—rather like that of the U.S. without its racial dimension—grew in strength. This left strongly opposed top-down planning, a unitary conception of social citizenship, and utopian dreams of a just city (see, inter alia, Hajer 1989; Mouffe 1992). Its radicalism centered on democratic processes that would empower multiple publics. Thus was a pictured urban utopia in whatever form washed out by a torrent of words.

Neoliberalism, Diversity, and Planning Response

In response to the global economic restructuring that began in the mid-1970s, planning became increasingly preoccupied with enhancing the competitiveness of cities and regions (Fainstein et al. 1986; Harvey 1989, 2005). The shockingly rapid decline of manufacturing industries in Western European and American cities, accompanied by the massive shedding of jobs, made a commitment to economic growth seem imperative. Even planners on the left acquiesced to the pressure of stimulating development, and earlier emphases on community involvement and benefits became combined with this aim (Mier 1993; Clavel 1986). The one significant exception was Norman Krumholz and his colleagues, who in the famous *Cleveland Policy Planning Report* abjured efforts to promote downtown development and instead called for "government institutions [to] give priority attention to the goal of promoting a wider range of choices for those Cleveland residents who have few, if any, choices" (Krumholz et al. 1975: 299).

Although attacks on the concepts of trickle-down and public-private partnerships permeated much of the critical literature from the academy (see, inter alia, Stone 1989; Squires 1989), planning professionals largely cheered for private-sector involvement, leveraging, and entrepreneurship. Often they themselves became actively involved in deal making (Frieden and Sagalyn 1989; Fainstein 2001a). There was a substantial shift in the focus of planning staff, which now began to find itself employed in offices of economic development rather than land use planning. To the extent that equity remained a concern, it was embodied in demands for commitments from developers to jobs or public amenities ("planning gain," community benefit agreements) in return for public subsidies and regulatory relief.

Communicative planning theory accompanied the rise of neoliberalism (Purcell 2008). Rooted in Habermasian critical theory, American pragmatism, and post-modernist/post-structural textual analysis, the focus of critique shifted from outcomes to discourse. Despite an underlying concern with justice, this movement avoided judging planning outcomes and focused on the process by which these outcomes were achieved. It paralleled and referred to a corresponding movement in political theory calling for deliberative democracy (Gutmann and Thompson 1996). The logic was that if decision-making were inclusive of the multiplicity of interests affected and if all elements were listened to, then the final outcome would be just. The underlying sentiment was that speaking truth to power would change circumstances. To objections that power would not be so easily budged (Flyvbjerg 1998), the response was that either speech was being distorted or planners were not listening carefully enough (Forester 2001). In repudiating Marxian political economy, communicative planning theory ignored the economic structure of global capitalism. The assumption seemed to be that since the economy was a social construction, changing discourse could change its distribution of benefits (Healey 2005).

The communicative turn represented a rebellion against the utopianism of earlier epochs, which was seen as embodying a top-down authoritarianism (Scott 1998) and a totalizing discourse (Beauregard 1989). Instead, a sort of utopianism of participation took its place, in which the "ideal speech situation" became the objective. The theory moved from the abstractions of philosophy to the everyday activities of planners:

> The state upholds justice by ensuring the rights of free and equal citizens to choose between different conceptions of the good. . . . Justice therefore becomes concerned with the process and procedures through which choices are made, leading to a focus on deliberation and public reasoning. . . . In a sense the "what" question about justice has been placed to one side and substantive issues about values and the good placed in the realm of the private. (Campbell 2006: 97)

Having premised their argument on the view that any conception of the just is achieved through discourse, proponents of discourse ethics put themselves in the position of being unable to set forth any criteria of justice beyond the character of discourse itself.

Even though the leaders of the discursive turn would probably repudiate a neoliberal, market-oriented public philosophy, their vision of the planner as an intermediary among competing interests fits well into this framework. As development planning became increasingly privatized and a product of individual deals between private firms and the public sector, the planner as mediator among politicians, business executives, and affected community groups essentially became a facilitator of market processes. Whatever compromise resulted would be legitimated by participation. Given the imbalances of power in such situations, however, and the structural prerequisite that no firm could accept an outcome in which it could not make a profit, the outcomes were necessarily skewed in favor of investors. In their most Pollyanna-ish form, the precepts of communicative planning took on the character of many of the self-help books popular at the time: "promoting win-win situations," "getting to yes" (see Friedman 2008). Doubtless there *are* win-win situations that can be produced by open processes, but they do not exist where there are deep-seated conflicts of interest.

Communicative theory also fits into the cultural left's preoccupation with diversity and recognition of the "other." Gender and race, ethnicity and immigration status, and the resulting biases and outright discrimination surrounding them pointed to the inadequacy of economic analysis in explaining disadvantage. Although inferior status based on ascriptive characteristics was intertwined with economic structure, it nevertheless had an independent base that would not be dissolved simply through increasing economic justice (Kymlicka 1995; Sandercock 1998). Analyses of hierarchy and difference correctly identified multiple sources of repression besides economic inequality, but there was a tendency for those concerned with accommodating diversity to ignore economic causes altogether (Fraser 1997: chap. 1). Moreover, a belief that "where you sit is where you stand" implied that each group had its own viewpoint and set of interests and that there could be only coalitions rather than unity among those economically disadvantaged. The stress on difference inevitably reinforced the political weakness of low-income groups:

> The proliferation of special interests fostered by multiculturalism is . . . conducive to a politics of "divide and rule" that can only benefit those who benefit most from the status quo. There is no better way of heading off the nightmare of unified political action by the economically disadvantaged that might issue in common demands than to set different groups of the disadvantaged against one another. Diverting attention away from shared disadvantages such as unemployment, poverty, low-quality housing and inadequate public services is an obvious long-term anti-egalitarian objective. Anything that emphasizes the particularity of each group's problems at the expense of a focus on the problems they share with others is thus to be welcomed [by opponents of redistribution]. If political effort is dissipated in pressing for and defending special group privileges, it will not be available for mobilization on the basis of broader shared interests. (Barry 2001: 11–12)

Although such disunity was not merely a consequence of "the politics of difference" (Young 1990), and the history of the left has been notorious for its failures to address non-economic forms of discrimination within its ranks, exhortations to listen to everyone's "unique" story offered little that would allow imposition of a unified way to evaluate outcomes. In practice, the theory and politics of difference have generally reinforced the very differences that militate against the "unities" essential to a successful planning and policy outcome for subaltern groups. The single-metric ideology of neoliberalism— the metric, of course, being money—has, in contrast, united dominant elites as never before. The leaders of local and global capitalism have thus learned from the "diversity" left to "respect" differences in race, ethnicity, gender, and religion. They have effectively learned how to provide symbolic satisfaction to potential challengers even as they exploit them economically for their own gains. While the proponents of discourse and diversity have spent their time mediating in theory and practice the differences they have legitimized, the owners of capital have continued to capture an increasing share of the income distribution in most countries, especially in the British and American cities where communicative approaches originated.

Competitiveness and Cohesion

The neoliberal paradigm became embedded in national regimes to varying extents. Its strongest impact was in the United States and the UK, where the Reagan and Thatcher administrations rejected governmental interventionism as limiting freedom and development. Continental (Western) Europe was slower to relinquish the commitment to social equity embodied in social housing programs, which continued to be the main planning mechanism for implementing concepts of the just city. A particular vocabulary associated with the European Union came to express social justice goals: poverty was regarded as the consequence of social exclusion, and the social aim of planning was indicated with the terms of inclusion and social cohesion. Under this formulation competitiveness and cohesion were deemed to be mutually reinforcing rather than in conflict, as critical theorists who pitted growth against equity would have it. With the election of the Blair government in Britain in 1997 and proposals for a "Third Way," optimists dreamed of the end of class and ethnic antagonisms; thus they revived in a new language the utopian frame of a unified public interest (Giddens 1998).

The argument that social cohesion and economic competitiveness were mutually supportive countered the perception that a purely market-driven society resulted in growing social division, and that such division was ultimately inimical to economic success (Levitas 1998: chap. 6). It did not, however, directly confront the thesis, presented in a huge volume of literature on the effects of globalization and economic restructuring, that growing social inequality is an inevitable consequence of deregulation, ratcheting down of government welfare programs including social housing, and greater competition among places.[11] Rather, the conviction that cohesion and competitiveness were synergistic drew from the literature focused on social capital, communitarianism, trust, and deliberative decision-making and was quite compatible with the communicative turn in planning theory (Gordon and Buck 2005).

One can visualize the possible relationships between competitiveness and cohesion in terms of virtuous and vicious circles (see Figure 2.1).[12] The virtuous circle is the one envisioned within the Third Way:

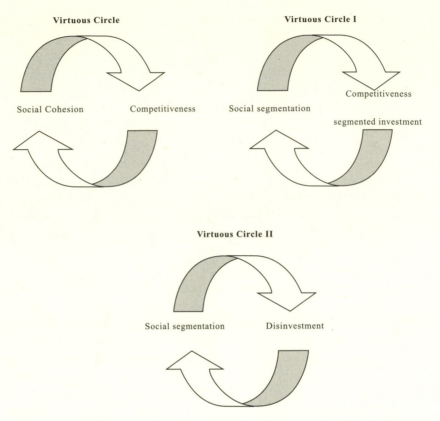

Figure 2.1. Possible relationships between competitiveness and social cohesion.

The third way suggests that it is possible to combine social solidarity[13] with a dynamic economy, and this is a goal contemporary social democracy should strive for. To pursue it, we will need "less national government, less central government, but greater governance over local process," as well as opening out in the direction of the global community. (Giddens 1998: 5)[14]

Thus, the advocacy of social cohesion did not imply a repudiation of neoliberal principles of privatization nor a move away from greater reliance on individual responsibility in place of government-provided social welfare benefits. The underlying argument was that within an inclusive society people would be motivated to gain skills, work harder and become more economically productive. At the same time increased affluence would trickle down to the bottom levels of society, muting social conflicts that manifest themselves in terms of ethnic and lifestyle differences, encouraging trust and the acquisition of social capital, and thereby further enhancing economic capacity while allowing individuals to access opportunities. In Europe, the Scandinavian welfare states provided a model of such a possibility.

The vicious circle scenario took two forms. In the first, global competition promoted more ruthless behavior by governments and firms. The "race to the bottom" meant that governments, in order to retain or attract business, reduced their social welfare expenditures, thereby increasing human misery. Private firms, in order to compete with low-cost producers elsewhere, lowered labor costs through depressing wages, substituting capital for labor, and outsourcing production. The outcome was high unemployment as well as poverty among those in low-skilled occupations and rising social tension (e.g., attacks on immigrants by native workers). At the same time, if the economic development strategy succeeded in increasing production, the upper strata of earners and owners gained an ever-increasing share of a growing income pie and increasingly segregated themselves from the rest of society.

The second, related scenario described the situation if efforts at economic development failed to stimulate growth in domestic product. Then, instead of simply a rise in relative inequality in a metropolitan area, we would see a withdrawal of both investment and population accompanied by abandonment of sections of the city. The absence of the super-rich might lessen the inequality at the municipal level, but income disparity would become expressed regionally and nationally in terms of both income and spatial inequality.

The notion of a Third Way was strengthened by the collapse of socialism in Eastern Europe and the associated discrediting of the socialist alternative. Along with the discarding of the socialist panacea went the class analysis that accompanied it. The Third Way, while a utopian formula of sorts, did not really address the question of economic justice. Rather it presented a moderately progressive approach to smoothing the bases of social conflict, primarily by fostering labor market attachments among the excluded, facilitating better relations among ethnic groups, and improving social services. Nancy Fraser (1997: 2), commenting on what she terms the "postsocialist" condition, noted correctly that "no comprehensive progressive vision of a just social order has emerged to take socialism's place." Neither communicative planning nor the Third Way offered a vision of an end state, as opposed a commitment to processes for improving social relations.

The Just City

In 1993 a conference was held at Oxford University to commemorate the twentieth anniversary of the publication of David Harvey's (1973) landmark book *Social Justice and the City*.[15] Susan Fainstein participated in this conference; its topic caused her to begin thinking more systematically than previously about the applicability of theories of justice to urban planning decisions. Her paper on social justice and urban space marked the beginning of a series of publications exploring this topic.[16] By the end of the decade, the question of social justice was gaining increasing attention more generally among planning scholars. Sayer and Storper (1997), introducing a special issue of the journal *Environment and Planning D*, raised the question of why normative concerns had been neglected in urban theory. In the next century the question became moot as more and more thinkers interrogated planning norms and, while not necessarily rejecting the concerns of the communicative theorists with participation, sought to provide a substantive content to the values governing planning (see, e.g., Friedmann 2011). Recently, this renewed interest in a wider vision has inspired a whole series of conferences, including the one that inspired this chapter.[17] At the same time, grass-roots groups calling themselves the Right to the City movement have begun to organize activities promoting social justice in American cities.[18] The goal of both the intellectual and activist wings of these movements has been to unify opposition to neoliberalism and mobilize commitment toward egalitarian aims. Both proceed with the understanding that ideas require support of social forces to gain purchase but also that movements for justice require a more specific agenda than simply a call for democratic participation.

Around what values should such an agenda be organized?[19] There can be considerable debate concerning the content of urban justice. Nevertheless, we would posit three general principles that characterize a just urban policy: equity, diversity, and democracy.[20] The criterion of *equity* follows on the work of John Rawls, which has become the dominant philosophical argument in liberal democratic societies. As Hayward and Swanstrom (2011) assert: "People with a very wide range of philosophical commitments and beliefs about justice . . . should, from principle, repudiate the inequalities of resources, opportunities, and powers that characterize the contemporary metropolis." It follows that just policies do not reinforce inequality but rather result in more equitable outcomes.

The principal criticism of Rawls by those who wish to broaden his definition of justice is that he overemphasizes material outcomes and does not sufficiently concern himself with discrepancies of power and self-esteem resulting from differences in gender, ethnicity, or other group characteristics (see especially Young 1990; Honneth 2003). Although group differences often correlate with material disadvantage, they still have an autonomous element that is not simply overcome by income equalization. Based on these arguments and their obvious relevance to issues of metropolitan segregation and inferior access to housing and services, we name *diversity* the second value dimension of urban justice. Philosophers use the term "recognition" to refer to just treatment of the "other"; however, in the context of the metropolis and in accordance with common usage, diversity or social inclusion seems the more appropriate term.

Democracy, our third value, is a principle in accordance with the traditions of liberal societies and usually considered by its advocates to contribute to just outcomes. The logic is that inclusion of subordinate groups in decision-making processes not only is a good in itself by making people feel empowered and acting as a vehicle for education, but would force elites to take non-elite interests into consideration. Proponents of deliberative or thick democracy regard participation beyond periodic elections into the policy-making process as essential to justice (Gutmann and Thompson 1996). As a practical problem, however, inclusion in situations where power is unequally distributed initially does not usually lead to redress of inequality. When, as is frequently the case, participation is dominated by propertied interests—whether homeowners or developers—the result is frequently exclusion and unequal distribution. Moreover, lower-income people often lack the personal resources to participate effectively even if they are nominally included and, due to the dominance of certain ideas promulgated by ruling regimes—for instance, that everyone benefits from policies promoting economic development—they may opt for policies not in their best interests. Thus, while democracy needs to be included in the list of guiding principles of justice, it is not sufficient, and an evaluation of its impact in relation to equity is always necessary.

At times equity, diversity, and democracy will clash; when such contradictions occur, the presumption ought to be in favor of equity. As discussed above, the pressure for diversity can lead to unproductive identity politics, while democratic rule can result in exclusionism. Thus, if the aim of planning is to increase social justice, consciousness of who are the beneficiaries of a policy should weigh heavily in decision-making, and Krumholz's dictum ought to apply: *priority attention should be directed to the goal of promoting a wider range of choices for those residents who have few, if any, choices.* At the same time, the aspirations of the majority of the population should not be ignored. This means that each situation requires judgment and, while it is possible to list general rules, their particular application depends on context. The aim is a just city, but justice requires sensitivity to the claims of many different groups, and one cannot decide a priori which is the most deserving.

Notes

1. John Friedman 2008 similarly argues that utopian thinking should be a component of good planning.

2. Parisian authorities asserted they were assisting the poor when, in the seventeenth century, they razed the medieval quarters around Notre Dame. Victor Hugo, whose hunchback had guarded its precincts three centuries previously, protested this early instance of slum clearance.

3. The following discussion of Howard, Wright, and Le Corbusier is drawn mainly from Fishman 1977; see also Mumford 1961. Most significant among the voluminous writings of these three seminal thinkers are Howard's *Garden Cities of Tomorrow* (1902), Wright's Broadacre City article (1935), and Le Corbusier's *The City of Tomorrow and Its Planning* (1987).

4. See "To New Horizons," exhibited at the GM Futurama Pavilion, New York World's Fair, 1939, http://www.archive.org/details/ToNewHor1940, accessed February 13, 2012.

5. Ibid.

6. It is interesting to compare this particularly bright American capitalist vision of the future made concrete with the darker European and socialist *Metropolis* of Fritz Lang (released in 1926). Lang's city of the future also has strong Le Corbusian design elements, but it is animated by an exploited proletariat that inhabits the subterranean world of the nightmarish capitalist industrial city. The utopian future can be realized for Lang only when this proletariat revolts.

7. http://www.archive.org/details/CityTheP1939_2, accessed December 6, 2008.

8. "And now we see a great river city of 1960." Its population has grown from one million twenty years earlier. "It is much larger, rebuilt and re-planned. Residential, commercial and industrial areas have all been separated for greater efficiency and greater convenience" (GM Futurama, Part II, 1: 40).

9. An excellent history of the entire period, but especially of events in Boston and San Francisco, may be found in Mollenkopf 1983.

10. See, inter alia, Fainstein and Fainstein 1974; Needleman and Needleman 1974; and Fainstein et al. 1986.

11. A 2008 OECD report records growing inequality among two thirds of its member nations, with the exception of France, Greece, Ireland, Spain, and Turkey (OECD 2008: 27).

12. Buck et al. 2005 refer to triangles rather than circles.

13. Giddens here uses social solidarity as a synonym for social cohesion.

14. The internal quotation was drawn from Massimo D'Alema, Italian prime minister at the time, presented at a U.S. White House conference held April 25, 1999.

15. The papers were subsequently published in Merrifield and Swyndegouw 1996.

16. See Fainstein 1996, 1999, 2000, 2001b, 2005, 2007, 2009, 2010.

17. Recent conferences include Searching for the Just City, Columbia University, New York, April 29, 2006; Urban Justice and Sustainability, University of British Columbia, August 22–25, 2007; Spatial Justice, University of Paris X, March 12–14, 2008; The Right to the City, Technical University of Berlin, November 6–8, 2008; Justice and the American Metropolis, Washington University, Saint Louis, May 8–10, 2009.

18. http://www.righttothecity.org/, accessed December 7, 2008.

19. Space precludes operationalizing these values in specific policies. For that, see Fainstein 2010, 2009; Markusen and Fainstein 1993.

20. Sustainability, interpreted as producing environmental equity between present and future generations, is a corollary to the principle of equity. For the purpose of this essay, it is collapsed into that principle, but it does produce an additional constraint to redevelopment policy.

References

Barry, Brian. 2001. *Culture and equality*. Cambridge, Mass.: Harvard University Press.

Baxandall, Rosalyn, and Elizabeth Ewen. 2000. *Picture windows: How the suburbs happened*. New York: Basic Books.

Beauregard, Robert. 1989. Between modernity and postmodernity: The ambiguous position of U.S. planning. *Environment and Planning D: Society and Space* 7: 381–95.

Bennett, Larry, Janet L. Smith, and Patricia A. Wright, eds. 2006. *Where are poor people to live?* Armonk, N.Y.: M.E. Sharpe.

Bluestone, Barry. 1972. Economic crisis and the law of uneven development. *Politics and Society* 3 (Fall): 65–82.

Buck, Nick, Ian Gordon, Alan Harding, and Ivan Turok. 2005. *Changing cities: Rethinking urban competitiveness, cohesion, and governance*. New York: Palgrave Macmillan.

Campbell, Heather. 2006. Just planning: the art of situated ethical judgment. *Journal of the American Planning Association* 26(1): 92–106.

Caro, Robert. 1974. *The power broker: Robert Moses and the fall of New York*. New York: Knopf.

Castells, Manuel. 1977. *The urban question: A Marxist approach*. Cambridge, Mass.: MIT Press.

———. 1978. *City, class, and power.* Trans. Elizabeth Lebas. London: Macmillan.

Clavel, Pierre. 1986. *The progressive city.* New Brunswick, N.J.: Rutgers University Press.

Davidoff, Paul. 1965. Advocacy and pluralism in planning. *Journal of the American Institute of Planners* 31(4): 331–38.

Fainstein, Norman, and Susan S. Fainstein. 1974. *Urban political movements.* Englewood Cliffs, N.J.: Prentice-Hall.

———. 1978. New debates in urban planning. *International Journal of Urban and Regional Research* 3(3): 381–403.

Fainstein, Susan S. 1996. Social justice and the creation of urban space. In *The urbanization of injustice,* ed. Andrew Merrifield and Erik Swyngedouw, 18–44. London: Lawrence and Wishart.

———. 1999. Can we make the cities we want? In *The urban moment,* ed. Sophie Body-Gendrot and Robert A. Beauregard, 249–72. Thousand Oaks, Calif.: Sage.

———. 2000. New directions in planning theory. *Urban Affairs Review* 35(4): 451–78.

———. 2001a. *The city builders.* Lawrence: University Press of Kansas.

———. 2001b. Competitiveness, cohesion, and governance: Their implications for social justice. *International Journal of Urban and Regional Research* 25(4): 884–88.

———. 2005. Cities and diversity: Should we want it? Can we plan for it? *Urban Affairs Review* 41(1): 3–19.

———. 2007. Planning and the just city. *Harvard Design Magazine* 27: 70–76.

———. 2009. Planning and the Just City. In *Searching for the just city,* ed. Peter Marcuse, James Connolly, Ingrid Olivo Magana, Johannes Novy, Cuz Potter, and Justin Steil, 19–39. New York: Routledge.

———. 2010. *The just city.* Ithaca, N.Y.: Cornell University Press.

———. Forthcoming. Spatial justice and planning. In *Justice spatiale et politiques territoriales,* ed. Frédéric Dufaux and Pascale Philifert. Nanterre: Presses Universitaires de Paris-Ouest.

Fainstein, Susan S., Norman Fainstein, Richard Child Hill, Dennis R. Judd, and Michael Peter Smith. 1986. *Restructuring the city,* rev. ed. White Plains, N.Y.: Longman.

Fiedler, Jeannine, ed. 1995. *Social utopias of the twenties: Bauhaus, kibbutz, and the dream of the new man.* Wuppertal: Bauhaus Dessau Foundation.

Fishman, Robert. 1982. *Urban utopias in the twentieth century: Ebenezer Howard, Frank Lloyd Wright, Le Corbusier.* Cambridge, Mass.: MIT Press.

Flyvbjerg, Bent. 1998. *Rationality and power.* Chicago: University of Chicago Press.

Foglesong, Richard E. 1986. *Planning the capitalist city.* Princeton, N.J.: Princeton University Press.

Forester, John. 2001. An instructive case-study hampered by theoretical puzzles: Critical comments on Flyvbjerg's *Rationality and Power. International Planning Studies* 6(3): 263–70.

Fraser, Nancy. 1997. *Justice interruptus: Critical reflections on the "postsocialist" condition.* New York: Routledge.

Frieden, Bernard J., and Lynne B. Sagalyn. 1989. *Downtown Inc.* Cambridge, Mass.: MIT Press.

Friedmann, John. 2008. The uses of planning theory: A bibliographic essay. *Journal of Planning Education and Research* 28: 247–57.

———. 2011. *Insurgencies: Essays in planning theory.* London: Routledge.

Gans, Herbert J. 1962. *The urban villagers.* New York: Free Press.

Gelfand, Mark I. 1975. *A nation of cities: The federal government and urban America, 1933–1965.* New York: Oxford University Press.

Giddens, Anthony. 1998. *The Third Way and its critics.* Cambridge: Polity Press.

Girard, Xavier. 2003. *Bauhaus.* New York: Assouline.

Goetz, Edward G. 2003. *Clearing the way: Deconcentrating the poor in urban America.* Washington, D.C.: Urban Institute Press.

Gordon, Ian, and Nick Buck. 2005. Cities in the new conventional wisdom. In *Changing cities*, ed. Nick Buck, Ian Gordon, Alan Harding, and Ivan Turok, 1–21. New York: Palgrave Macmillan.

Gutmann, Amy, and Dennis Thompson. 1996. *Democracy and disagreement.* Cambridge, Mass.: Harvard University Press.

Hajer, Maarten A, 1989. *City politics: Hegemonic projects and discourse.* Aldershot: Avebury.

Harloe, Michael., ed. 1977. *Captive cities.* New York: Wiley.

———. 1995. *The people's home? Social rented housing in Europe and America.* Oxford: Blackwell.

Harvey, David. 1973. *Social justice and the city.* Baltimore: Johns Hopkins University Press.

———. 1978. Planning the ideology of planning. In *Planning theory in the 1980s*, ed. Robert Burchell and George Sternlieb, 213–34. New Brunswick, N.J.: Rutgers University Center for Urban Policy Research.

———. 1989. "From managerialism to entrepreneurialism: The transformation in urban governance in late capitalism." *Geografiska Annaler, Series B, Human Geography* 71(1): 3–17.

———. 2005. *A brief history of neoliberalism.* New York: Oxford University Press.

Hayward, Clarissa R., and Tod Swanstrom. 2011. *Justice and the American metropolis.* Minneapolis: University of Minnesota Press.

Healey, Patsy. 2005. On the project of "Institutional Transformation" in the planning field: Commentary on the contributions. *Planning Theory* 4(3): 301–10.

Hoffman, Lily M. 1989. *The politics of knowledge.* Albany: State University of New York Press.

Honneth, Axel. 2003. Redistribution as recognition: A response to Nancy Fraser. In Nancy Fraser and Alex Honneth, *Redistribution or recognition? A philosophical exchange*, trans. Joel Golb, James Ingram, and Christiane Wilke, 110–97. London: Verso.

Howard, Ebenezer. 1902. *Garden cities of tomorrow.* London.

Hunter, Floyd. 1969. *Community power structure*. Chapel Hill: University of North Carolina Press.

Jacobs, Jane. 1961. *The death and life of great American cities*. New York: Modern Library.

Krumholz, Norman, Janice M. Cogger, and John H. Linner. 1975. The Cleveland policy planning report. *Journal of the American Planning Association* 4(5): 298–304.

Kymlicka, Will. 1995. *Multicultural citizenship*. Oxford: Oxford University Press.

Levitas, Ruth. 1998. *The inclusive society? Social exclusion and New Labour*. Basingstoke: Macmillan.

Le Corbusier, *The city of tomorrow and its planning*. 1987. Mineola, N.Y.: Dover.

Luijten, Anne. 2002. A modern fairy tale. In *Amsterdam Southeast: Centre Area Southeast and urban renewal in the Bijlmermeer, 1992–2012*, ed. Dick Bruijne, Dorine van Hoogstraten, Willem Kwekkeboom, and Anne Luijten, 7–25. Bussum: Thoth.

Markusen, Ann R. and Susan S. Fainstein. 1993. Urban policy: Bridging the social and economic development gap. *University of North Carolina Law Review* 71 (June): 1463–86.

Mengin, Christine. 1999. La solution des grands ensembles au vingtième siècle. *Revue d'Histoire* 64 (October): 105–11.

Merrifield, Andrew, and Erik Swyngedouw, eds. 1996. *The urbanization of injustice*. London: Lawrence and Wishart.

Mier, Robert. 1993. *Social justice and local economic development*. Newbury Park, Calif.: Sage.

Mollenkopf, John. 1983. *The contested city*. Princeton, N.J.: Princeton University Press.

Mouffe, Chantal, ed. 1992. *Dimensions of radical democracy*. London: Verso.

Mumford, Lewis. 1961. *The city in history*. New York: Harcourt, Brace and World.

Needleman, Martin, and Carolyn Needleman. 1974. *Guerrillas in the bureaucracy: The community planning experiment in the United States*. New York: Wiley.

OECD. 2008. *Growing unequal? Income distribution and poverty in OECD countries*. Paris: OECD.

Pickvance, Chris, ed. 1976. *Urban sociology*. London: Tavistock.

Purcell, Mark. 2008. *Recapturing democracy: Neoliberalization and the struggle for alternative urban futures*. London: Routledge.

Sandercock, Leonie. 1998. *Towards cosmopolis: Planning for multicultural cities*. New York: Wiley.

Sayer, Andrew, and Michael Storper. 1997. Ethics unbound: For a normative turn in social theory. *Environment and Planning D: Society and Space* 15(1): 1–18.

Scott, James C. 1998. *Seeing like a state: How certain schemes to improve the human condition have failed*. New Haven, Conn.: Yale University Press.

Squires, Gregory, ed. 1989. *Unequal partnerships: The political economy of urban redevelopment in postwar America*. New Brunswick, N.J.: Rutgers University Press.

Stone, Clarence N. 1989. *Regime politics: Governing Atlanta: 1945–1988*. Lawrence: University Press of Kansas.

Ward, David. 1989. *Poverty, ethnicity, and the American city: Changing conceptions of the slum and ghetto*. Cambridge: Cambridge University Press.

Warner, Sam Bass. 1972. *The urban wilderness: A history of the American city*. New York: Harper and Row.

Wright, Frank Lloyd. 1935. Broadacre City: A new community plan. *Architectural Record* 77 (April): 243–54.

Young, Iris Marion. 1990. *Justice and the politics of difference*. Princeton, N.J.: Princeton University Press.

Chapter 3

Environmental Equity:
Is It a Viable City Planning Goal?

Eran Feitelson

The improvement of environmental conditions, primarily of the urban poor, has been one of the main driving forces and goals of planning in the past century. Indeed, the environmental degradation induced by the industrial revolution and borne mainly by the urban poor, a condition graphically described by various nineteenth-century writers and analysts, was one of the stimulants for urban planning thereafter (Hall 2002; Hunt 2005). However, the direct coupling of environment and equity implicit in the term "environmental equity" is relatively new, having been advanced largely in the last twenty-five years, primarily in the United States.

As city planning has long been concerned with poverty alleviation, social equality, and the mitigation of environmental externalities, it could have been expected that environmental equity would be widely embraced by planners. Yet, that has not been the case. Actually, until recently the term environmental equity, or the closely related term environmental justice, could hardly be found in the planning literature. This perhaps can be attributed to the civil rights origins of the environmental justice movement that promulgated and advanced these notions. This movement essentially came out against the institutionalized inertia of land use decision-making, of which planners were part. In the United States, where the environmental justice movement emerged, the activists and advocates of this movement were often alienated from planners and planning, because they viewed planning as a mechanism through which Euro-Americans institutionalized the neglect that resulted in the perceived inequity of exposure to hazards (Diaz 2005). Thus, while planners focused on the environmental implications of urban form, the urban metabolism, and the inter-relations between the urban and the rural (sometimes termed a "green" agenda), environmental justice activists focused on intra-city or community exposure to hazards (a "brown" agenda).[1]

In recent years, with the emerging empowerment of minorities in large American cities and the shift in discourse within the planning community, and beyond the U.S., there have been increasing calls to incorporate environmental equity aspects into environmental planning practice at the city/region scale (Petts 2005; Pijawa et al. 1998; Rast 2006). These calls have been driven in part by the realization that the equity-environment dimension is central to attempts to advance sustainability notions (Agyeman and Evans 2004; Campbell 1996; Haughton 1999). Harvey (1996) takes the potential for merging planning and environmental justice a step farther, as he argues that the environmental justice movement shifts the focus of attention back to the urban scale and place-related issues, thereby countering the tendency of the environmental movement to focus on abstract supranational concerns. By doing so the environmental justice movement focuses attention on the scale at which most planners operate, thereby providing an opportunity to make a more substantive contribution to the advancement of sustainability notions (Feitelson 2004).

This chapter asks to what extent environmental equity can indeed become a viable city planning goal. To this end I begin with a brief review of environmental equity notions and the debate over their definition, generation, and implications. I go on to ask what issues, scope, and problems may need to be addressed if environmental equity is to become a viable planning goal in the urban realm. I deal with the special case of transportation, which I argue is fundamentally different from other issues relating to environmental equity. Based on these discussions, I identify some possible goals for city planning whose purpose is to reduce adverse environmental distribution effects, but note that these are limited. In the final section I discuss the role environmental equity may play in city planning, if indeed its role as a direct goal is as limited as I find.

Background: The Difficulties Associated with Defining Environmental Equity

The definition of environmental equity is fraught with difficulties (Holifield 2001). It is usually seen as contrary to environmental inequity, whereby the environmental burden is disproportionately placed on specific groups, identified by ethnicity, race, or class (Mennis and Jordan 2005). The assumption behind the possible correlation between weak groups in society and sources of pollution or risk is that some malicious siting process has directed these facilities toward areas in which the ability to oppose them is less, or that there has been discrimination in the application of environmental standards or in the decision-making processes, resulting in lesser protection of the rights of people in these areas.[2] For this reason, perceived environmental inequities have been at the base of the environmental justice movement and in some cases have been termed as environmental racism.

But the establishment of a correlation between exposure to environmental externalities and population attributes (usually class, ethnicity, and race) is not simple. Many studies attempt to find correlations between the jurisdictions or zip codes in which hazardous waste treatment storage and disposal facilities are sited and attributes of the population in these and neighboring jurisdictions or zip codes. These studies were facilitated by the increasing availability of GIS and the readily coded lists of superfund sites. The results of these studies, however, have been mixed (Cutter 1995; Mohai et al. 2009), their variance attributed to the sensitivity of results to the choice of spatial unit for analysis, geographic scope of analysis (and hence control groups analyzed), type of facility, data sources, and model specification (Anderton 1996; Baden et al. 2007; Mennis and Jordan 2005; Noonan 2008; Ringquist 2005). These studies have also been criticized for focusing on the siting of risk and pollution sources rather than on the extent of exposure or health effects (Brulle and Pellow 2006), which arguably should have been the dependent variables (Bowen and Wells 2002).

A more fundamental question is what are the implications of inequities, if found. This question has two facets. The first, raised by Been (1993), is the extent to which inequities reflect unfairness (injustices). Been identifies seven possible definitions of what fair siting may imply, and asks the implications of each one: (1) even apportionment of locally unwanted land uses (LULUs) among neighborhoods; (2) compensation to host communities by neighborhoods in which LULUs are not sited; (3) progressive siting, in which wealthier communities are obliged to receive greater number of LULUs; (4) a market-type system whereby all communities receive equal number of vetoes they can use to bid against other communities for the privilege of excluding LULUs; (5) a beneficiary-pays system, whereby those that benefit from a LULU pay its full (social) cost; (6) the absence of discriminatory intent in

Table 3.1. Environmental Justice Definitions and Their Implications

Definition/goal	Spatial implications	Difficulties
Equal apportionment	Dispersion of LULUs	Individual rights Availability of suitable sites Measurement and definitions
Compensation	LULUS in low-income areas	Moral objections Valuation Identification of recipients Power effects
Progressive siting	LULUS in high-income areas	Moral objections Individual rights "escape" options
Competitive bidding	Unclear: some LULU dispersion	Transaction costs Definitions and measurement Representation in bids Uncertainty in predictions
Beneficiary pays	LULUs largely in low-income areas	Not all beneficiaries can pay Valuation of "full" costs Transaction costs Allocations of receipts Pollution havens

Lack of discriminatory
intent
	Unclear whether
	different from existing
		Proofs—differentiating
		    among valid siting
		    considerations

Treatment as equals	Unclear	Illusion of neutrality Illusion of consideration

This table is based on Been (1993). However, the spatial ramifications and some of the terms used are my interpretation of her work.

siting; (7) a process that shows "equal concern and respect" for all neighborhoods and groups.

But the application of these approaches faces considerable (and arguably insurmountable) practical and theoretical difficulties, summarized in Table 3.1. Moreover, each of these definitions of fairness leads to a radically different spatial outcome. If equal apportionment is desired, the LULUs have to be distributed "equally" over space, negating the agglomeration economies often found in LULU siting (Schweitzer and Stephenson 2007). Therefore, equal apportionment may lead to a wider dispersion of LULUs, potentially afflicting a much wider area than would be the case under a market mechanism. If beneficiary-pays or compensation definitions are adopted, weaker communities with a lower tax base may be more willing to accommodate LULUs, as these will be seen as a source of income and jobs. Indeed it has been alleged that such considerations have induced Native Americans to accept hazardous facilities in their reserves, prompting Bullard (1993) to term such decisions "environmental blackmail." Hence, the choice of fairness criteria has substantial implications for the planning goals chosen, the outcome sought, and the likelihood that it can be achieved.

A second facet of the critique of spatial inequities as a basis for determining injustice pertains to the "who was there first" question. Several analysts have argued that a crucial question is whether the noxious facility was sited near a "weak" neighborhood (primarily through a bureaucratic or planning process) or whether the residences encroached on the facility as part of market dynamics (Been 1994; Been and Gupta 1997). This question can be subsumed under a wider question, how the inequality came about. That is, what are the causal factors behind the inequality (Pulido et al. 1996; Schweitzer and Stephenson 2007)? Feitelson (2001) identifies four spatiotemporal processes in the metropolitan economy that may lead to the disproportionate exposure of weak groups to pollutions or risks (see Figure 3.1). These may be of particular importance to planners.

The first process pertains to the legacy of the industrial revolution, during which working-class neighborhoods were built in proximity to industrial plants to be within walking distance. With deindustrialization and the decentralization of employment, such sites often became "brownfields" contaminated by industrial waste,[3] while the adjoining neighborhoods have remained either white or minority working-class neighborhoods. The second process pertains to the implications of motorization, which led to increasing decentralization and intensifying of radial traffic flows, often through or near inner-city neighborhoods. Thus, it can be expected that inner-city neighborhoods will suffer disproportionately from the negative externalities of radial transportation corridors. The third process pertains to the encroachment of residential areas on infrastructure facilities intended to address the intensifying metabolism of the metropolis (energy, water, waste, and wastewater streams), as well as industrial estates, airports, and other

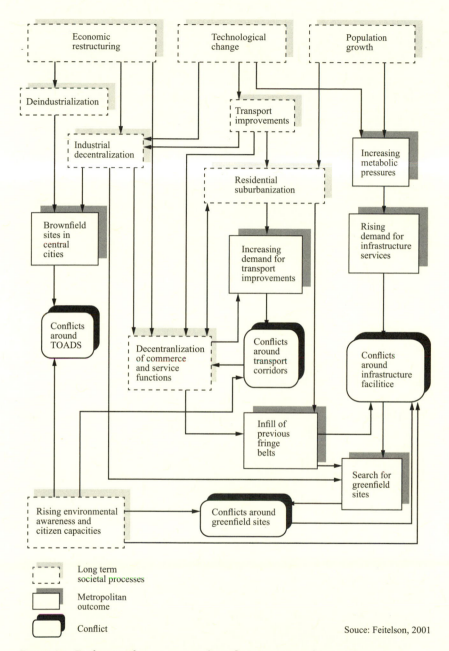

Figure 3.1. Evolution of environmental conflicts in metropolitan settings. Eran
Feitelson, "Malicious siting or unrecognised processes? A spatio-temporal analysis
of environmental conflicts in Tel Aviv." *Urban Studies* 38 (2001): 1143–59.

land-intensive facilities. These were originally sited at the outskirts of the city (in then-"greenfield" sites). But as the metropolis grew and land values rose, residential areas encroached on these facilities. The fourth process is a result of the increasing scarcity of sites in the urban setting. The combination of tightening environmental standards and empowerment of local communities led metropolitan authorities and private capital to search farther afield for sites for both production and metabolism management functions (in "greenfield" sites), turning intra-urban issues into regional ones (Rast 2006). However, widening local-national and, in some cases, international coalitions increasingly stem such efforts (Feitelson 1997). Such coalitions are empowered by environmental justice arguments, which can serve as a basis for anti-growth discourse coalitions. Consequently, an impasse may develop, whereby LULUs are increasingly locked into their existing sites (Feitelson 2001). This impasse raises the market value of the dwindling number of possible sites, thereby raising the specter of "pollution havens" where different noxious activities cluster in areas unable to muster an effective resistance to them (Blowers and Leroy 1994). However, the formation of such "pollution havens" is not only an outcome of the dynamics depicted in Figure 3.1. Rather, as Harvey (1996), Pulido et al. (1996), and many others have argued, they are an outcome also of discriminatory practices in the housing market, residential segregation, the spatial division of labor, and agglomeration economies (Schweitzer and Stephenson 2007). Hence, environmental equity issues clearly overlap with social justice concerns and wider societal processes.

Environmental Equity in Planning: The Questions

The difficulties in conceptualizing what a "just" environment is, beyond the obvious lack of discriminatory intent—or identifying what an environmentally equitable outcome is—raise the question to what extent environmental equity or justice can be a truly meaningful planning goal.

Before addressing this question, however, it is necessary to lay out the type of planning within which the goals are to be set, the environmental issues that are meaningful in a planning context, and the practical questions planners will need to address if they are to incorporate environmental equity as part of their planning goals.

The Type of Planning

Much of the preceding discussion on environmental (in)equity focuses on the outcomes—the spatial array of sources of pollution or hazards and the communities affected by them. The types of planning that focus on outcomes are the traditional rational planning, which strives to direct the various land uses to their socially "best" location, and more recently the design-oriented approach termed New Urbanism (Fainstein 2000). Thus, one possible focus of planners may be to identify the "best" locations for the various facilities, including equity considerations (however defined), and to establish the appropriate spatial inter-relations that will preclude the encroachment of residences, particularly of low-income housing, on such sites. Wherever minority or low income groups are already exposed to hazards or pollution (or suffer from a lack of environmental amenities), planners may strive to facilitate a change in land use or to introduce mitigation measures that will reduce the exposure (or provide better access to amenities). Yet, in doing so they are likely to face the problems associated with the first five goals noted in Table 3.1.

The second possible focus is on the processes that led to the disproportionate exposure of minority or low income groups to hazards or nuisances. The type of planning that focuses primarily on process, rather than outcome, is often associated with the discursive turn in planning (Healy 1993; Innes 1996). The assumption behind this type of planning is that if all concerns by all groups are raised and discussed, a just outcome is likely to emerge (Innes 1996). However, as several critics of this approach have argued, such processes do not alter power relationships and may actually serve to accentuate power imbalances, because the capability of different participants to manipulate the discourse in their favor is a function of power (Allemendiger and Tewdwr-Jones 2002; Fainstein 2000; Flyvberg and Richardson 2002; Purcell 2009). Thus, in structuring deliberative processes with environmental equity in mind, planners have to pay particular attention to the identity of those invited and provide the necessary facilitation to assure that weaker, less eloquent participants are indeed part of the process. But Petts (2005) warns even that may not assure equity.

Fainstein (2000) advances, or resurrects, a third type of planning, which she terms "the just city." This type of planning seeks to generate a "just" or "equitable" outcome directly, taking into account the various population groups (whether differentiated by class, gender, ethnicity, race, or other similar attributes). It thus combines elements from the two previous approaches. Yet, the means for achieving the "equitable" or "just" outcome remain obscure. One possibility is to evaluate outcomes according to equity criteria. These criteria can conceivably be extended to include environmental equity.

The Issues

Historically, much of the discussion of environmental equity has focused on hazardous waste treatment storage and disposal facilities or on highly polluting industrial plants. More recently the scope of issues discussed increased to include environmental amenities, particularly parks (Boone et al. 2009), transportation (Forkenbrock and Schweitzer 1999; Ogneva-Himmelberger and Cooperman 2010), and water issues (Bond and Dugard 2008). Equity issues have also been raised with regard to global issues such as climate change (Ikeme 2003), but as these are less amenable to intervention at the scale planners usually work in, they are not discussed herein.

Overall, the issues planners can analyze and affect thus include the distributional effect of the management of the urban metabolism,[4] the siting of production enterprises, transportation facilities, environmental amenities, and small-scale LULUs. The facilities needed to manage the urban metabolism include water supply works, wastewater and waste treatment storage and disposal facilities,[5] and energy facilities (particularly electricity generation). It should be noted that efforts to reduce the negative distributional effects of the urban footprint on other parts of the world are not discussed here as part of the environmental equity agenda: the desirability of reducing the urban footprint is universal, regardless of the location of effects. That is, from a sustainability perspective it is imperative that the urban footprint be minimized, regardless where the effects are felt, and thus it should be viewed as part of the environmental agenda, not the environmental equity agenda. This issue is taken up again in the concluding sections.

The second type of issues planners may try to tackle from an environmental equity perspective are those that pertain to the economic base of the city. These include primarily the location of production facilities. A closely related but distinct issue is the effect of transportation. As I argue below, this topic is inherently different from all others, and thus merits particular attention. A third issue planners might heed is the distributional facets of environmental amenities, particularly access to parks and open spaces. Finally, planners need to address the equity aspects of local public services, such as rehabilitation centers, some of which may have environmental facets.

The Questions Planners Need to Address

Due to the complexities outlined above, once planners have decided on the form of planning they focus on (that is, to what extent they focus on the outcome vis-à-vis on the process[6]) and the issues to be addressed in an environmental equity frame, they will need to address a series of questions.

First, planners should ask what the temporal dimension of equity they seek to address is. Do they seek to assure that a specific outcome is "equitable" (however defined) at a certain time or that the process is inclusive for a specific decision, or do they seek to affect the equity of decisions and processes over a longer time period. The answer is likely to be a function of whether planners view themselves as social reformers or followers of the critical social justice approach, to use Marcuse's terms (this volume).

Second, planners should consider how differences in suitability among sites should be accounted for in an environmental equity framework. For example, if some sites for waste disposal are better suited from a geo-hydrological perspective than others (though all are possible) but might affect a larger minority population, how should the tradeoff be decided? This is essentially the question that faced Israeli planners in siting waste facilities, as the more suitable sites from both an economic and a geo-hydrological perspective are in the sparsely populated northern Negev (Kedmi 2006), an area characterized by economically stressed development towns and a sizable minority Bedouin population.

Third, planners should ask how the relevant groups should be identified, as the specification of groups determines who is invited to participate and on whom the analyses will focus. In particular, planners should ask how finely specified should these groups be. For example, is it sufficient to have people from certain minority groups represented, or should there also be care that there is adequate participation from both genders in each group? In many cases, ethnic, racial, or minority groups are segmented internally and stratified socially and economically. In such cases planners should ask to what extent those participating reflect the internal diversity (Cohen-Blankshtain and Perez 2007). At the same time, as Petts (2005) notes, it is impossible to have meaningful deliberations if there are too many participants. Thus, the balance that should be struck between repetitiveness and effectiveness of deliberations (or extent of analysis) is difficult to define.

Fourth, planners should ask how individual and group differences in perceptions of risk should be accounted for and addressed. Such differences often arise in discussions pertaining to the issues noted above (Flynn et al. 2006). While environmental assessments may help to gain insights regarding the nature and extent of risks, they rarely attenuate the differences in perceptions and attitudes toward risk. Hence, in balancing the distribution of environmental costs planners cannot ignore the variance in perceptions of such costs.

Finally, planners have to consider how differences in the benefits that accrue from a certain facility should be accounted for, given the difficulties noted in Table 3.1. Specifically, planners should ask whether compensation or beneficiary pays mechanisms are sufficient to account for such differences, or whether additional measures should be introduced. Moreover, identifying beneficiaries may be crucial for understanding the power politics behind the stance of the various actors in the planning process, and hence for assessing the contributions made by such actors.

The Special Case of Transportation

As noted above, most of the studies of environmental justice and equity, as well as most of the references to environmental equity and justice in the planning and policy literature, pertain to various LULUs—mainly waste treatment storage and disposal facilities or to industrial plants. These are, essentially, point sources that can conceivably be sited in various locations in the metropolitan area. Environmental amenities, such as parks, can also be located in a wide variety of sites within the metropolis. Transportation, however, is arguably very different from the "normal" issues identified above. Because people travel on transport vehicles (and hence those benefiting are direct users), transportation is comprised of networks which have more stringent location requirements than point sources and in which there are inter-effects among different parts of the network. Moreover, it has a wide number of environmental externalities.

Feitelson (2002) argues that the differences between transportation systems and the "normal" point sources discussed above have several implications for environmental equity discussions in planning contexts. One, due to transportation being a network and the consequent greater stringency in locating transportation links, it is erroneous to take the whole metropolitan area as the control group (the unaffected population) when assessing equity effects (as is often done with regard to point sources). Because the identification of the control group—the area in which the facility could conceivably have been sited, but which was left unaffected—is crucial for determining whether there was discrimination (Anderton 1996), the restrictions on possible alignments of transportation corridors has potentially major implications for assessing their environmental equity effects. Moreover, any change in the capacity of the network at one point may have implications for traffic flows in distant parts of the network. Hence, the problem of defining the geographic scope of equity analyses is more complex in the case of transportation networks than in cases of point sources.

Two, as transportation systems are used directly by people, users are a distinct group of beneficiaries. Given the difficulty in identifying control groups due to the network facet, Feitelson (2002) suggests that, in the case of transportation environmental equity, discussions should focus on the relationship between users and those adversely affected, mainly those residing near major transportation facilities.

Three, transportation systems generate multiple externalities, differing in severity and scale between places. Thus, while in most other cases the main environmental externality is singularly defined, this is not the case with transport. Virtually any land transportation system emits multiple air pollutants, whose composition is a function of the mix of traffic, as well as green house gases and noise (Rodrigue et al. 2009). In addition highways and rail infrastructure affect water flows and constitute barriers. Thus, the identity of those potentially affected by a certain transportation facility (and hence those that should be part of the planning process or considered within it) varies by the type of externality discussed. Moreover, different policies are implemented to address the various externalities of transport. These policies may have distributional implications too (Levinson 2010, for example). Hence, in environmental equity analyses it is also necessary to take into account the equity implications of the different policies implemented to address transport's environmental externalities.

Four, transportation has significant land use effects, which in turn have substantial equity implications (Levine, this volume). Transportation systems attract various land uses, among them uses that generate negative externalities. They thus have secondary environmental effects. The issue of the evolving spatial relationships between source and recipient is therefore particularly complex in the transportation case. Moreover, both the time in which land use effects materialize and the time between inception and completion of transportation projects are particularly long, often measured in decades. The discussion of such long-term effects in environmental equity analysis is thus fraught with greater uncertainties than in other cases.

Five, transportation development and the layout of transportation systems often differ from the institutional structures and jurisdictional boundaries that deal with residential development or siting of point sources. Hence, the data needed for relating transportation externalities to population attributes may not conform to the spatial array of units according to which data are collated (zip codes, statistical areas, jurisdictions, etc.).

Due to the particular difficulties in assessing the environmental equity implications of transport, I suggest that, in the case of transport, the emphasis should be placed on the options for compensation by users to those adversely affected, and on the distributional implications of policies implemented to mitigate transport's multiple environmental externalities (Feitelson 2002). The goals planners may adopt for transportation projects to mainstream environmental equity considerations should reflect these two suggestions. It should be noted, however, that these suggestions, and resulting goals, pertain only to direct environmental equity effects. They do not reflect the potential second-order effects—environmental equity effects of land use change induced by transportation infrastructure.

The Potential and Limitations
of Environmental Equity as Planning Goals

In Table 3.1 a series of definitions for "fair" siting are enumerated. Each can be viewed as a planning goal (hence the column title: definition/goal). The first five definitions can be viewed as goals in an outcome-oriented planning framework, while the last two can be seen as goals for a process-oriented framework.

However, all these definitions face substantive difficulties from an applicative perspective, as noted in the right-hand column of Table 3.1. Thus, it seems that none of these definitions can be applied in "ideal" (first-best) form—the form presented in the table. That is, none of them can be applied in a manner that will lead to a fully "fair," "just," or "equitable" outcome in practice. Moreover, it is clearly impossible to evaluate which of these definitions is unequivocally superior to the others, and there are contradictions in the spatial implications among them. Thus, it seems that environmental equity cannot serve as a basis for determining planning goals in its idealized versions.

However, planners do not work in a "first-best" idealized world. Planners work in a second- (or third-) best world. The visions of an idealized future city (as described by Hall 1992) have long been abandoned. Thus, while some forms of utopian planning are advanced (e.g., Marcuse, this volume), most planning practice is conducted in a second-best world where pragmatism rules supreme, and hence idealized "fairness" or "justice" is simply not sought (Campbell and Marshall 1998). Rather, planners seek in practice an improvement on the existing situation, even if this improvement falls short of what they may have wanted in an idealized setting (Faludi 1987). In this second-best world, some of the definitions noted in Table 3.1 may serve as a base for defining goals.

The first and least controversial of the goals in the table is an inclusive nondiscriminatory planning process. This is actually a basic premise of "good planning" in general. The contribution to this goal from an environmental equity perspective is to incorporate a social analysis into environmental impact assessments (EIA) to assure that all potentially adversely affected groups are identified and hence included in the process. Although the desirability of determining the identity of the people affected, rather than merely their number, and discussing their vulnerability and hence the distributional aspects of EIA has long been noted, it is too often overlooked (Vanclay 2004). Thus, by introducing into the goals of a plan or planning process the need to assure that environmental equity concerns are fully reflected in the deliberation, through identifying all potentially adversely affected groups, planners may ensure that this "best practice" is indeed implemented. Moreover, this may lead to taking the proactive steps sometimes needed to bring marginalized groups into the process (Petts 2005).

A second possible goal that may improve on the existing situation is to introduce compensation schemes to those adversely affected by the siting of the various facilities noted above, particularly when they have regressive distribution implications. These may take the form of direct compensation or of compensation in kind. Direct compensation may be assessed directly, as a function of exposure, or indirectly, as a function of loss of property value. While the loss of property value is also affected by the level of exposure, it is also a function of other property attributes. Hence, the level of compensation can be expected to be higher for high-value properties, controlling for other attributes. Thus such compensation is likely to have a regressive element. From an equity perspective, therefore, direct compensation based on tort law may be preferable to compensation based on loss of property values. Alternatively, a community-level in-kind compensation can be sought in the form of planning gain ("exactions" in American terminology). These, however, may also be regressive, as better-off or politically more astute communities are able to extract more gains and the burden of the gains falls on all service users, regardless of their income. Still, while compensation will not lead to full cost pricing and will not necessarily compensate households for the full welfare loss they suffer, it may reduce the otherwise regressive outcome, and increase the likelihood that adverse effects on disadvantaged groups will not be overlooked or ignored.

A third possible goal is to assure that all population groups are provided with similar attenuation measures from negative externalities (controlling for level of exposure) and have reasonable access to environmental amenities, particularly parks and open spaces. Although even such a direct equity goal may not eliminate inequities, it may improve the quality of life of disadvantaged groups, providing them and advocacy planners a measure to demand that urban or regional governing bodies invest in the provision of attenuation measures or such amenities in disadvantaged areas; or at the very least in the improvement of accessibility from disadvantaged areas to existing amenities.

Environmental inequities arise from societal processes and power relations. As a result the spatiotemporal processes depicted in Figure 3.1 may lead to an impasse whereby existing sources are "locked" into their current locations. This, perhaps paradoxically, is an outcome of the increasing awareness and empowerment of local communities (Feitelson 1997, 2001). The result of this increasing spatial fixity may be the creation of "pollution havens" (Blowers and Leroy 1994). Thus, a fourth potential goal planners may adopt is prevention of the concentration of multiple LULUsin a single community or near it, to preclude the creation of such pollution havens. In doing so, planners will de facto follow the Rawlsian approach, whereby they focus on those most at risk, rather than on questions of disproportionality (Perhac 1999).

It can be argued that these four goals are too minimalistic. However, environmental equity goals are not the only ones pursued in any plan or planning process. They should, thus, be considered in tandem with other social and environmental goals. As Pulido et al. (1996) argue, the structural processes that drive disadvantaged population groups to highly polluted areas usually stem from failures in the housing market (such as "redlining" in the mortgage industry, lack of affordable housing, or lack of public transportation to employment opportunities) and from the spatial division of labor, as well as developments in the industrial landscape and structure. These should be addressed directly. Environmental equity is thus an additional, often minor reason to address these fundamental underlying factors. Similarly, the exposure of residential communities or neighborhoods to unacceptable levels of hazards or risks is often an outcome of failures in the environmental policy field, such as insufficient enforcement of environmental standards or inappropriate standards. These too should be addressed directly, regardless of whether those affected are disadvantaged or not.

This discussion seems to suggest that the potential of environmental equity to serve as a basis for meaningful implementable goals in planning is limited, at least if a largely technocratic approach is taken. However, planning is embedded in political processes. In the public sphere, environmental justice has proven to be a powerful discursive tool, as nobody can object to it. Planners can use this concept as a discursive tool, much as the environmental justice movement has, to advance wider environmental and social justice goals. Thus, by relating more general environmental or social equity goals (such as tightening environmental standards in siting decisions or widening affordable housing schemes) to environmental justice concerns, planners may be able to obtain greater leverage in the public sphere, and thus widen the coalitions that will be ready to support the plans they prepare. In other words, rationalization of planning goals in environmental equity or environmental justice terms has a political facet, and thus should not be seen only in terms of the implementability of these concepts.

By using environmental equity or environmental justice terms in enumerating the goals of planning, planners may re-direct some of the political attention back to the local issues that affect communities. These have been increasingly overlooked in the environmental discourse due to the widespread attention to global, and particularly climate change, issues. These terms may also help planners build brown-green coalitions at the regional scale to address the structural impediments to social mobility and to empower weak groups (Rast 2004). Thus, incorporating environmental equity language in planning goals may assist planners to become more influential players in the local and regional level.

Conclusions

Environmental equity or justice concepts may be too nebulous to serve as practical goals for positivistic planning. Essentially, it is impossible to derive clear positive goals that will implement environmental equity or justice ideals, as these ideals are largely defined by negating environmental inequity or injustice. Yet, such negation is also fraught with theoretical, methodological, and practical difficulties, as it is not readily possible to define the inequities or injustices except in the most extreme situations. Still, once the first-best world is abandoned in favor of the more practical second-best world in which most planners actually operate, four possible practical goals can be derived, the efforts to meet any of them being an improvement on the existing situation. However, I argue that the use of environmental equity or environmental justice language in setting goals can be a very useful discursive tool that planners may use to advance the plans they prepare in the public and political arenas. Thus, environmental equity may be sought as a goal less for practical purposes and more as a tool for building discourse coalitions[7] that will advance wider social goals.

This conclusion does not mean, however, that environmental equity is purely a discursive tool. One of the main roles of goals in the planning process is to serve as criteria for assessing proposed actions and the subsequent success of a plan. Environmental equity can and should be considered in the planning process. Specifically, it is necessary to introduce equity perspectives into environmental programs and plans, and environmental considerations into social programs, as at present these programs and the tools in their preparation too often do not give adequate consideration to each other. To this end, it will be useful to better merge EIA with social impact assessment (Vanclay 2004). If the introduction of environmental equity language into planning goals will indeed induce more intensive discussions of distributional impacts in environmental programs and environmental considerations in social programs, they will indeed contribute to the advancement of sustainability concepts in practice in the planning field.

Notes

1. On the roots of the split and the complexities of reconciling the environmental and environmental justice movements in the U.S., see Tarlock 1993.

2. These processes can be seen also at the global scale. But as planners operate mainly at the local or regional level, this chapter follows suit.

3. Greenberg et al. 1992 termed these Temporary Obsolete Derelict Sites, TOADs, the term used in Figure 3.1.

4. The urban metabolism is the throughput of materials through the urban system (Wolman 1965).

5. These include the full scope of waste streams, including household waste, garden waste, hazardous materials, building waste, etc.

6. This is the specific question posed. However, it reflects a much deeper split between two paradigms of moral philosophy: deontological (rights-based) and consequentialist (goal-based). See Ikeme 2003 for further discussion in an environmental equity frame.

7. On the definition and importance of discourse coalitions, see Hajer 1995.

References

Agyeman, Julian, and Bob Evans. 2004. "Just sustainability": The emerging discourse of environmental justice in Britain? *Geographical Journal* 170: 155–64.

Allmendiger, Philip, and Mark Tewdwr-Jones. 2002. The communicative turn in urban planning: Unraveling paradigmatic, imperialistic and moralistic dimensions. *Space and Policy* 6: 5–24.

Anderton, Douglas L. 1996. Methodological issues in the spatiotemporal analysis of environmental equity. *Social Science Quarterly* 77: 508–15.

Baden, Brett M., Douglas S. Noonan, and Rama Mohana Turaga. 2007. Scale of justice: Is there a geographic bias in environmental equity analysis. *Journal of Environmental Planning and Management* 50: 163–85.

Been, Vicki L. 1993. What's fairness got to do with it? Environmental justice and the siting of locally undesirable land uses. *Cornell Law Review* 78: 1001–85.

———. 1994. Locally undesirable land uses in minority neighborhoods: disproportionate siting or market dynamics? *Yale Law Review* 103: 1383–422.

Been, Vicki L., and Francis Gupta. 1997. Coming to the nuisance or going to the barrios? A longitudinal analysis of environmental justice claims. *Ecology Law Quarterly* 24: 1–56.

Blowers, Andrew, and Pieter Leroy. 1994. Power politics and environmental inequities: A theoretical and empirical analysis of the process of "peripherialisation." *Environmental Politics* 3: 197–228.

Bond, Patrick, and Jackie Dugard. 2008. Water, human rights and social conflicts: Experiences from South Africa. *Law Social Justice and Global Development Journal* 19(1) (February).

Boone, Christoper G., Geoffrey L. Buckley, J. Morgan Grove, and Chona Sister. 2009. Parks and people: An environmental justice inquiry in Baltimore, Maryland. *Annals of the Association of American Geographers* 99: 767–87.

Bowen, William M., and Michael V. Wells. 2002. The politics and reality of environmental justice: A history and considerations for public administrators and policy makers. *Public Administration Review* 62: 688–98.

Brulle, Robert J., and David Naguib Pellow. 2005. Environmental justice: Human health and environmental inequalities. *Annual Review of Public Health* 27(3): 3.1–3.22.

Bullard, Robert D. 1993. Race and environmental justice in the United States. *Yale Journal of International Law* 18: 319.

Campbell, Heather and Robert Marshall. 1998. Acting on principle: Dilemmas in planning practice. *Planning Practice and Research* 13: 117–28.

Campbell, Stuart. 1996. Green cities, growth cities, just cities? *Journal of the American Planning Association* 62: 296–312.

Cohen-Blankshtain, Galit, and A. Perez. 2007. *Drafting a new outline plan for the Isawiyah neighborhood in East Jerusalem: A public participation process with a deprived population in a divided city.* Research Report, Tami Steinmetz Center for Peace Research, Tel Aviv University.

Cutter, Susan L. 1995. Race, class and environmental justice. *Progress in Human Geography* 19: 111–22.

Diaz, David R. 2005. *Barrio urbanism: Chicanos, planning and American cities,* London: Routledge.

Fainstein, Susan S. 2000. New directions in planning theory. *Urban Affairs Review* 35: 451–78.

Faludi, Andreas. 1987. *A decision-centered view of environmental planning.* Oxford: Pergamon.

Feitelson, Eran. 1997. The second closing of the frontier: An end to open-access regimes. *Tijdschrift voor Economische en Sociale Geografie* 88: 15–28.

———. 2001. Malicious siting or unrecognised processes? A spatio-temporal analysis of environmental conflicts in Tel Aviv. *Urban Studies* 38: 1143–59.

———. 2002. Introducing environmental equity dimensions into the sustainable transport discourse: Issues and pitfalls. *Transportation Research D* 7: 99–118.

———. 2004. The potential and limitations of planning in advancing sustainability at the sub-national level: An introduction. In *Advancing sustainability at the sub-national level: The potential and limitations of planning,* ed. Eran Feitelson, 1–9. Aldershot: Ashgate.

Flynn, James, Paul Slovic, and C. K. Mertz. 2006. Gender, race and perception of environmental health risk. *Risk Analysis* 14: 1101–8.

Flyvbjerg, Bent, and Tim Richardson. 2002. Planning and Foucault: In search of the dark side of planning theory. In *Planning futures: New directions for planning theory,* ed. Philip Allmendinger and Mark Tewdwr-Jones, 44–62. London: Routledge.

Forkenbrock, David J., and Lisa A. Schweitzer. 1999. Environmental justice in transportation planning. *Journal of the American Planning Association* 65: 96–111.

Greenberg, Michael, Frank Popper, Bernadette West, and Dona Schneider. 1992. TOADS go to New Jersey: Implications for land use and public health in mid-sized and large U.S. cities. *Urban Studies* 29: 117–25.

Hajer, Maarten A. 1995. *The politics of environmental discourse: Ecological modernization and the policy process*. Oxford: Clarendon.

Hall, Peter. 2002. *Cities of tomorrow: An intellectual history of urban planning and design in the Twentieth Century*. 3rd ed. Oxford: Blackwell.

Harvey, David. 1996. *Justice, nature and the geography of difference*. Oxford: Blackwell.

Haughton, Graham. 1999. Environmental justice and the sustainable city. *Journal of Planning Education and Research* 18: 233–43.

Healy, Patsy. 1993. Planning through debate: the communicative turn in planning theory. In *The Argumentative turn in policy analysis and planning*, ed. Frank Fischer and John Forester, 233–53. Durham N.C.: Duke University Press.

Holifield, Ryan. 2001. Defining environmental justice and environmental racism. *Urban Geography* 22: 78–90.

Hunt, Tristram. 2005. *Building Jerusalem: The rise and fall of the Victorian city*. New York: Henry Holt/Metropolitan.

Ikeme, Jekwu. 2003. Equity, environmental justice and sustainability: Incomplete approaches in climate change politics. *Global Environmental Change* 13: 195–206.

Innes, Judith E. 1996. Planning through consensus building. *Journal of the American Planning Association* 62: 460–72.

Levinson, David. 2010. Equity effects of road pricing: A review. *Transport Reviews* 30: 33–57.

Mennis, Jeremy L., and Lisa Jordan. 2005. The distribution of environmental equity: Exploring spatial nonstationarity in multivariate models of air toxic releases. *Annals of the Association of American Geographers* 95: 249–68.

Mohai, Paul, David N. Pellow, and J. Timmons Roberts. 2009. Environmental justice. *Annual Review of Environment and Resources* 34: 405–30.

Noonan, Douglas S. 2008. Evidence of environmental justice: A critical perspective on the practice of EJ research and lessons for policy design. *Social Science Quarterly* 89: 1153–74.

Ogneva-Himmelberger, Yelena, and Brian Cooperman. 2010. Spatio-temporal analysis of noise pollution near Boston Logan airport: Who carries the cost? *Urban Studies* 47: 169–82.

Perhac, Ralph M. 1999. Environmental justice: The issue of disproportionality. *Environmental Ethics* 21: 81–92.

Petts, Judith. 2005. Enhancing environmental equity through decision-making: Learning from waste management. *Local Environment* 10: 397–409.

Pijawa, K. David, John Blair, Subhrajit Guhathakurta, Sarah Lebiednik, and Suleiman Ashur. 1998. Environmental equity in central cities: Socioeconomic dimensions and planning strategies. *Journal of Planning Education and Research* 18: 113–23.

Pulido, Laura, Steve Sidawi, and Robert O. Vos. 1996. An archaeology of environmental racism in Los Angeles. *Urban Geography* 7: 419–39.

Purcell, Mark. 2009. Resisting neoliberalization: Communicative planning or counter-hegemonic movements. *Planning Theory* 8: 140–65.

Rast, Joel. 2006. Environmental justice and the new regionalism. *Journal of Planning Education and Research* 25: 249–63.

Ringquist, Evan J. 2005. Assessing evidence of environmental inequities: A meta-analysis. *Journal of Policy Analysis and Management* 24: 223–47.

Rodrigue, Jean-Paul, Claude Comtois, and Brian Slack. 2009. *The geography of transport systems*. 2nd ed. New York: Routledge,

Schweitzer, Lisa, and Max Stephenson, Jr. 2007. Right answers, wrong questions: Environmental justice as urban research. *Urban Studies* 44: 319–37.

Tarlock, A. Dan. 1993. City versus countryside: environmental equity in context. *Fordham Law Review* 21: 461–94.

Vanclay, Frank. 2004. The triple bottom line and impact assessment: How do TBL, EIA, SIA, SEA and EMS relate to each other? *Journal of Environmental Assessment Policy and Management* 6: 265–88.

Wolman, Abel. 1965. The metabolism of cities. *Scientific American* 213(3): 179–90.

Chapter 4

From Socialism to Capitalism:
The Social Outcomes
of the Restructuring of Cities

Iván Tosics

The past twenty years or so brought the largest and quickest changes in the history of the Eastern-Central European cities. Within this short time, three periods can be distinguished, each with a different economic basis: the socialist system; the transitory, unregulated free market system; and the recent attempts at regulated capitalism.

This chapter explores the changes in the urban development processes of the East-Central European cities (represented mainly through a close examination of Budapest) across the three periods, with special regard to the social inequality aspects of development.

After an introduction of the conceptual framework, the discussion is structured around the three main periods. I describe the challenges, macro-level processes, and main restructuring policies; the socio-spatial outcomes, including changes in social inequalities and segregation patterns; and the local planning policies, illustrated by case studies from Budapest—the social aims of particular policies and the extent to which these aims can realistically be achieved. The chapter closes with a critical evaluation of the post-socialist transformation of East-Central European cities and some remarks about the ability of urban planners and researchers to influence urban policies.

A Conceptual Framework
of the Post-Socialist Transition of Cities

The development of the East-Central European countries in the 1990s is usually referred to as the period of "transition" from socialism to capitalism. To understand the transition, the starting point has to be the socialist socioeconomic and political system, central features of which were a state monopoly of the means of production, a system of one-party rule, and a single-rank hierarchical social order with the cadre elite at the top (Szelényi 1996: 308).

From an urban development point of view, the essence of the socialist system was state control over both the supply and demand sides of the housing market:

> the state strongly determined the income of the citizens, defining it on a low level, eliminating from it all those cost components (education, housing, health care) which were to be given free to citizens through state services. At the same time, the state acquired virtually all-important means of production and centralised all important investment decisions [Hegedüs and Tosics 1996: 6; UNECE 1997: 1]. Price control over the whole economy was an additional tool in the enforcement of political goals. (Tosics 2005a: 47)

In the socialist countries all aspects of urban development were directly controlled by the central state. The transition brought the collapse of strong direct state control, replacing it with less direct political and economic mechanisms, including multilevel administrative government systems and fiscal systems of revenue creation and distribution. In parallel, market actors and market processes were allowed, even pushed, to play an increasing role.

As noted above, the transition from socialism is a process of changes in three stages, starting from the centrally controlled socialist stage, through an intermediate, free market stage, and arriving finally at the regulated market society (see, e.g., Tosics 2006: 133).[1] Analysis of the three stages has to pay special attention to the turning points between them: first to the application of privatization and decentralization techniques to establish the market-based system, and then to the introduction of new public policies and reform of the institutional structure, as efforts are made to gain back some public control over the unregulated market processes.

These national-level factors create the macro-level framework for the development of urban areas, which are the concern of this chapter. There are a range of political, economic, environmental, and social consequences at the local level, depending on the nature and performance of national-level systems; we focus here on social outcomes. In each of the three stages, local policies and planning have very different levels of power and independence to establish their own strategies, with consequences for both outcomes and planners' own ability to take action in dealing with the most serious problems faced by their community.[2]

The chapter pays special attention to the social outcomes of the transition from socialism to capitalism. Two aspects of these outcomes will be discussed: the factors distinguishing the groups of population in better and worse situations as well as the measurable extent of social inequalities between these groups, and the changes in the sociospatial positions of different social groups, describing the patterns and extent of their segregation. Comparable information about changes in social inequalities and segregation, however, is very scarce. In the socialist period this research was considered "delicate" from a political perspective and forbidden or very much restricted by those in power. In the market society another problem emerged: decreasing funding for sociological surveys.

The Socialist Period of Urban Development

The Macro Processes—Determining the Functioning of the System

The ideology as well as the day-to-day functioning of the socialist political and economic system are widely described elsewhere (see, e.g., Andrusz et al. 1996) and so will not be discussed in detail here. It should be noted, however, that although direct state control over the demand and supply sides of the economy was the essence of the system, this control could not be either fully established or maintained. During the many decades of socialist governance of both supply and demand, alternative mechanisms ("cracks") for supply and demand developed, decreasing the efficiency of state control, as illustrated by the historical overview of the development and changes in the socialist housing model (Hegedüs and Tosics 1996).

The Social Outcomes

According to official statements in the socialist countries, urban development followed equalitarian principles with regard to allocation of advantages among people and among different parts of the city. The general and equal accessibility of social services was one of the important, stated political goals. This, however, was only partly achieved, just in some services (education and health care), and only at a low standard, beyond which large inequalities developed. In other services, such as housing, the politically determined processes of the planned economy functioned to produce outcomes that were, one might say, the opposite of an outcome under equalitarian principles. This was first demonstrated by Szelényi and Konrád (1969) in their empirical sociological analysis of the residents of four new housing estates in Hungary.

The results of this analysis showed—even to the surprise of the researchers—that the more "deserving" members of society had received systematic advantages in their access to the new state-owned units that were either free or very cheap. This access was at the expense of blue-collar workers, who were substantially underrepresented in the housing allocation despite the propaganda that had shown them as the main beneficiaries of state housing policy.

Szelényi and Konrád interpreted these results as a systemic outcome of socialist housing policy. They argued that housing was not considered a market good, so people's incomes did not contain a "housing element." For this reason the physical output of the housing sector and the allocation of the new units were largely determined by the state sector. The state, however, never considered housing construction a priority—instead industry was developed at great expense. Housing was considered part of infrastructural services, which were subordinated to the "productive" sector—as the saying said, "do not cut the chicken before the golden eggs come out."

From this it logically follows that housing was one of the scarcest goods, for which long waiting lists developed. New housing became a prime object with which the state could reward some members of society. For these "deserving" people, a cheaply allocated flat was a compensation for their low income (income distribution was very much flattened out in the socialist system). As a result, the allocation of housing was based on "merits": party and state functionaries were the main beneficiaries.

As an important part of their theory, Szelényi and Konrád proved that this allocation mechanism was neither a failure nor a corruption, but rather followed from the functioning of the system. This one-sided, inequality-generating mechanism was determining housing allocation throughout the

Figure 4.1 Urban rehabilitation of Block 15 in Budapest District VII, Erzsébetváros. The lower photograph shows the careful renewal of the old buildings, resulting in limited "socialist gentrification." Photos by author.

socialist period, resulting in systematic advantages in housing consumption and spatial segregation of the new ruling class. Taken together, the empirical works of Szelényi and Konrád show that in the socialist period, despite ideological statements, housing inequalities were growing: "from 1950 to 1968 class inequalities in housing did not diminish, they increased. . . . But the people themselves were not generally conscious of increasing housing inequalities, or depressed by them, chiefly because the housing situation of all classes had visibly improved through the years" (Szelényi 1983: 73)

The inequality-generating outcomes of the socialist allocation policies were probably true for all socialist countries, although systematic research was very scarce, and practically forbidden by the ruling powers. The general statement about the state housing allocation could be made more precise in Hungary, where the state sector did not become as dominant as in other countries (e.g., the Soviet Union) and a market sector was always present as well. In both the state and the market housing sectors there were better and worse housing classes. Housing policy systematically favored the richer classes, as these received more state subsidies and could more easily improve their situation in both the state and the market sector. As Szelényi noted, "the richer classes get better housing for less money and effort, while the poorer classes get worse housing at the cost of more money or effort, or both" (1983: 63).

From this analysis it can be seen that segregation of rich and poor was produced in socialist cities by different mechanisms from those in Western European and American cities. A comparative analysis of the spatial structure of cities (Szelényi 1983: 148) has also shown spatial differences: slums in the socialist cities were in the transitional belt, American ones in the inner city, and Western European ones at the edge/periphery.

Local Planning Policies

In the first decade of socialism, especially in the 1950s, the central state had a dominant position in shaping planning policies in all socialist countries. The role of the local, municipal level would only gradually gain in importance and only in countries with relatively relaxed (i.e., less repressive) forms of central control, so the following Hungarian example cannot be taken as representative of all socialist countries.

Policies aimed at rebuilding the stock of deteriorating, older parts of inner cities became prevalent only in the last ten to fifteen years of the socialist period. Prior to that time, planning policies concentrated exclusively on new developments, mainly in the form of large housing estates in previously unbuilt areas or total reconstruction of the existing urban fabric in places considered slums. From the 1970s, Hungarian urban researchers argued for investing in the poor areas of the cities (at the outer part of the inner city and in the transitional belt). It is important to understand that the socialist regime increasingly accepted debates about poor areas of cities; however, directly addressing the case of the poorest strata of society was still not allowed officially.

The sociologists and planners who argued for the rehabilitation of poor, inner-city areas warned that renovation of housing stock might result in pushing out the poor from those areas. It is worth exploring the socialist period interventions to understand the extent to which the changes in the social structure followed the physical changes.

According to a study in the late 1980s, the urban rehabilitation of Block 15 in Erzsébetváros (District VII in Budapest) in the 1980s resulted in limited gentrification. All the tenants of the state-owned old and run-down tenement houses were moved out and rehoused in other parts of the city. The buildings remained in the public rental sector after total renovation. Two-thirds of the flats were allocated to families in nearby rundown houses; approximately one-third of the new tenants represented higher-status groups who got the renovated flats through exceptional allocation channels, as a reward for political or economic positions. Thus, the selective mechanisms of the state allocation could be traced and empirically proved, although the magnitude of the social change was much smaller than it would have been in the case of free market processes. Hegedüs and Tosics called this case "socialist gentrification," referring to the gentrification-type changes caused by state allocation instead of market forces (1991: 131, see Figure 4.1).

The Free Market Period of Transition

The Macro Processes

The change from socialist to free market economic system in 1989–1990 came suddenly in most countries (e.g., GDR, Czechoslovakia, Romania), as a consequence of the collapse of the socialist political system. In some countries, such as Hungary (and even more Yugoslavia), the market-oriented economic transition started well before the political turnover.

The first turning point—preceded by a kind of "vacuum" before the introduction of a consistent system of basic laws (Tosics 2006: 133)—was a major change: as a consequence of the collapse of the socialist system the "historic pendulum" went to the other side (Bertaud-Renaud 1995). When it came to privatization of housing stock and decentralization of administrative structure, it was clear that the oversized public housing sector had to be reduced and the top-down political and planning system changed. The restructuring processes, however, went much farther to the other extreme, replacing overarching state control in most post-socialist countries with dominance of free market relations.

Housing Privatization

The post-socialist period started with mass-scale, large-discount, low-price housing privatization, called by American economists "give-away privatization" (Buckley et al. 1994: 18). This was probably the largest property transfer in history, and accomplished in a very short time, being in this regard much more "efficient" than the heavily criticized privatization efforts of Margaret Thatcher in the 1980s.

There were some differences among post-socialist countries in how privatization was implemented. The quickest and deepest changes were in the Southeastern European countries (e.g., Albania, Romania), while Poland and the Czech Republic were much slower. Compared to compulsory Right to Buy privatization in Hungary, the Czechs left it to local governments.

The speed of privatization was closely correlated with the size of discount from market value. In Budapest, for example, most rented dwellings were sold at an 85 percent discount from their market value. As a result, the share of public rental sector dropped from over 60 percent of the housing stock to below 10 percent within a couple of years. The main push for this give-away privatization came, on the one hand, from local governments (they wanted to get rid of the unprofitable public stock as soon as possible) and, on the other, from the main beneficiaries, the families living in the best publicly owned rental flats.[3]

Administrative Decentralization

In each of the transition countries one of the first new laws aimed to establish a democratic system of local governments. There were substantial differences among the post-socialist countries, in the extent to which this change pointed toward the local independence of municipalities. In Hungary, as part of a total reversal of the previous system, complete administrative decentralization was carried out: "There is no direct involvement of any central government officers or politicians in local decision-making and central supervision is restricted to checking the legality of procedures" (Bennett 1998: 38).

In principle, handing over real decision-making power to the local self-governments was a very important step toward the establishment of democratic societies. However, in the course of administrative decentralization in most post-socialist countries, local self-governments became very small (the number of Hungarian municipalities almost doubled around 1990. Their average size decreased to around 3,000 residents), and the administrative middle-tier (counties, regions, provinces) lost substantial power. As a result, the local public sector became too fragmented to create any meaningful public policy. Metropolitan-level policies, for example, are almost unthinkable due to the selfish behavior of even of the smallest local self-governments.

The Socio-Spatial Outcomes

As a result of the collapse of the socialist housing model in Hungary the dominant state redistribution system became insignificant while the market allocation, which was previously of secondary importance, became dominant. Obviously, this dramatic change, replacing the extreme power of the state by an even more extreme dominance of the market sector, had a large effect on inequality, mostly shaped by the dominant allocational channel.

Privatization and decentralization were carried out *en masse* in the post-socialist countries despite the fact that the negative social consequences of such processes were already widely known at the beginning of the 1990s[4]. It can be proven empirically that both discussed changes lead to the further increase of socio-spatial inequalities.

The Social Consequences of Give-Away Housing Privatization

In the process of give-away housing privatization, the unequal distribution of advantages of the socialist period became marketized. In 1992, the Metropolitan Research Institute, Budapest, and the Urban Institute, Washington, carried out an empirical analysis of a sample of Budapest public tenants. The aim of the Budapest Rental Panel Survey (BRPS) was to compare the rent subsidies (socialist period) with the value subsidies developed in the process of privatization. According to the 1992 BRPS survey data, privatization turned the unequal distribution pattern of rent subsidies into an even more unequal pattern of value subsidies. Thus "give-away" privatization was a large gift to sitting tenants in general, and to higher income tenants in particular (Hegedüs and Tosics 1994).

The marketization of the value of the housing unit enabled the ex-tenant, new owners to become mobile on the housing market: the larger the value subsidy was, the larger the mobility chances were. In this way housing privatization strengthened socio-spatial segregation. This general rule in Hungary was accompanied by a special one, the "condominium effect."

In Hungary, the law on housing privatization prescribed the condominium form as the new legal framework for privatized houses. Each privatized building was turned into a condominium, in which the new owners became shareholders according to the share of the floor space of their flat in the total building. The "normal" decisions in the condominium (e.g., about smaller repairs) were regulated by simple majority rule. Larger decisions, for example, about the renovation of the façade, however, require a qualified majority. Until 2004 the requirement was 100 percent (a unanimous decision); since then it has been 80 percent.

The old multi-family buildings of Budapest (built as private rental tenement houses) had greater "inner" than "outer" segregation: the social differences were larger within the buildings (higher-status families living in the bigger and better equipped flats with street windows, while lower-income families in the smaller flats with windows only to the inner courtyard) than between buildings in different parts of the city. After privatization, when virtually all tenants became owners, the chances for overarching improvement of the condominiums became more differentiated across the different parts of the city. In the lower-status parts of Budapest, it was more difficult to achieve a unanimous decision about overarching improvements for a building, as the share of low-income and/or elderly families was substantial. Thus, many better-off families sold their units and moved to higher-status areas where the financial situation of the residents was better and more equal, allowing for larger-scale improvements of the buildings. So, the "condominium effect" led to substantial changes in the socio-spatial structure of the city and to increased segregation. This pattern might be different in other post-socialist cities with other legal forms of multi-family housing after privatization.

Privatization also brought unexpected side effects. Empirical surveys in the early 2000s have shown a sudden decrease in socio-spatial segregation in some parts of Budapest, especially as a result of the increase in the social

Figure 4.2. Urban renewal program in Budapest District IX, Ferencváros. The lower photograph shows high quality private developments, mixed with public renewal of old buildings and public spaces, leading to moderate gentrification. Photos by author.

status of the worst housing estates. This was because many of the poorest households (often belonging to the Roma ethnic minority), after receiving market value for their apartments, sold their expensive-to-run housing estate apartments and moved to single-family houses in smaller towns or villages. The out-moving, low-status families were usually replaced by in-moving young families, resulting in an increase in the social status of the housing estate. This unexpected consequence of give-away housing privatization, however, will most probably be temporary, and after a while the socio-spatial differentiation in the housing classes will increase again, according to "normal" (land value-based) logic.

The Social Consequences of Administrative Decentralization

As already mentioned, the new, independent local governments became very small in size. In this situation, the role of the large cities, especially the capitals, increased. The fragmentation of the territorial system, coupled with the decision-making independence of each of the municipalities, led to a sharp differentiation in their development opportunities. Generally speaking a west-east slope has been developed (in almost all post-socialist countries), with higher development chances in the western part of the country. Another important differentiating factor is the distance to urban centers which offer greater chances for attracting investors.

The worst situation can be found in municipalities that are on the "losing side" as judged by both factors—the smaller municipalities in the eastern parts of the country in areas that lack large urban centers. Changes in these areas have led to irreversible processes, to deep poverty accompanied by ethnic segregation. According to Hungarian reports there are already at least one hundred totally segregated villages in the country with exclusively Roma population, and this number will likely double in the future. Everyone in these villages is unemployed, except the mayor.

Similar or even worse situations can be found in Roma settlements or urban areas in and around Romanian cities (see, e.g., Berescu and Celac 2006). These examples, although different in territorial patterns (Hungarian rural ghettos are in remote areas, while Romanian ones are close to the cities), show the total failure of all post-socialist countries in handling extreme poverty and in the development of preventive measures against the self-reinforcing processes of socio-spatial segregation under market circumstances.

Local Planning Policies

As a direct consequence of the change of the political system, central planning completely disappeared: socialist five-year planning has been discredited to such an extent that forecast planning in general has been given up and only yearly budgetary plans have been prepared. All the central institutions for planning (such as the Central Planning Office in Hungary) have been dissolved. The total elimination of the planning power of the previously very influential middle administrative level (e.g., counties) in all post-socialist countries also shows the effects of the anti-planning mood of the first half of the 1990s.

The post-socialist changes created a set of contradictory circumstances for local planning policies. On the one hand, administrative decentralization resulted in increasing power at the municipal level: locally elected politicians could decide about all aspects of local development, unthinkable in the socialist period. On the other hand, privatization of much of the real estate (land, nonresidential buildings) and privatization of housing to sitting tenants took away key elements of local social policies. It is a well-known fact in Western countries that segregation can best be fought with an active housing policy, involving not only new construction but also renewal of existing stock. After almost total privatization of the housing stock in many post-socialist countries, housing (and land) has been eliminated from the list of tools with which the public sector can influence the processes creating greater inequities and socio-spatial segregation.

Under these circumstances the first post-socialist years can be labeled the "non-planning" period, when yearly budgets were almost the only documents determining activities at the local government level. Since that time, planning has reappeared but in a very different form: opportunity-led planning, in which, wrote Tasan-Kok, "the aim was no longer to ensure oversight but to enable piecemeal development; the latter generates financial support for municipal governments. Although this change in attitude leads to new types of development, it also leads to fragmentation in cities" (2006: 91).

Opportunity-led planning also meant that, without strong central government redistributive mechanisms, capital investors became dominant, increasing the already existing spatial inequalities between the different categories of municipalities (large versus small, western versus eastern). Typical local planning in larger cities became decisions about the next shopping centers or office buildings, usually accepting submitted plans and supporting with subsidies the expectations of the investors. Municipalities wanting to pose environmental restrictions for large investments risked loss of the investments because developers could easily reach more favorable agreements in neighboring municipalities. This fragmented planning and decision-making system also led to urban sprawl as well as uneven and uncoordinated development in all post-socialist countries.

An interesting and exceptional case for local planning policies was the urban renewal program in Ferencváros (District IX in Budapest), where the local leadership aimed to introduce new, indirect methods of public control, in which revenue from private developers was used to fund city efforts. With the early approval of a renewal plan, the district was able to avoid the otherwise compulsory privatization of the multi-family housing stock. Empty plots and run-down buildings were sold to investors who were attracted to the area for new housing construction, while the district government used the revenues from the sale of the development opportunities for the renovation of the remaining part of the old housing stock (and privatization only happened after the completion of renovation); see Figure 4.2.

The Ferencváros example can be judged as a modestly gentrifying, area-based urban renewal program. This seems to be an unavoidable compromise and a reaction to the disappearance of public financial means—the deteriorated area could only be made attractive for investors and middle-class families through a substantial change in the local social structure, starting with the displacement of those that were thought to be the most problematic lower status social (ethnic) groups. Although no precise data are available, the level of gentrification could exceed that of the socialist case (previous example) while remaining much lower than pure market processes would have produced.

Toward a Regulated Market System: The Search for More Public Control over Unregulated Market Processes

The second turning point is a change from the free market system into more regulated capitalism. The date of this change is not as clearly identifiable as the collapse of socialism and there might be larger differences among the different post-socialist countries as to when and how the new period started.

In Hungary, by the very end of the 1990s, it had become increasingly clear that free market processes had led to very high external costs as inequalities grew to a level that was causing considerable problems. Although subsequent central governments recognized the need for new types of public interventions that could better regulate market processes, sharp conflicts between the political parties made it very difficult to introduce these new regulations (to change the basic laws a two-thirds majority is needed in the Parliament).

Another reason for change emerged along with these processes. A number of sectors in the economy, especially those providing basic services for the population (pension system, health care, education), were still using methods and institutions inherited from the socialist period. Their chronic inefficiencies and/or costliness meant that it became very urgent to introduce basic changes into these sectors. This led to what Szelényi called in a presentation as the "second reform crisis of transformation" (presentation at the Economics University in Budapest in 2008).

Although the two challenges came about the same time, they are different regarding their origins and the methods required for a solution. Even so, both types of problems had to be addressed to arrive to the end of the transition and the launching of a more or less stable, functional version of capitalism.

The Macro Processes

By the end of the 1990s, the need for longer-term urban development planning had been recognized once more, as the free market processes, combined with the very fragmented local government system had led to very high external costs, including

- Clear inefficiencies in economic development: competition and rivalry (instead of cooperation and joint strategy) between neighboring small municipalities, leading to incoherent decisions with too high costs and little chance of being efficient in a market sense;
- Clear inefficiencies in infrastructure development: as a consequence of massive suburbanization the quickly growing agglomerated municipalities had to build new social infrastructures, such as kindergardens and schools, while the large cities the population was leaving had to close down similar facilities;
- Growing negative environmental externalities: the consequences

of sprawling development were traffic congestion, increased travel times and more air pollution around the cities;
- Growing negative social externalities: the formation of social/ethnic ghettos in inner parts of cities as the middle class residents moved into new housing in other parts of urban areas, including gated communities of the rich.

All these problems threatened the economic competitiveness of functional urban areas. With the growing equalization of "hard" infrastructure conditions, the decisions of economic actors selecting where to invest began to depend more on the "soft" factors. Both governance conditions (willingness of public and private actors to cooperate) and environmental conditions are playing increasing roles (Tosics 2005c), as is the social protection system (social sustainability, socio-spatial position of the different strata), which is becoming more and more important.

As a result of the growing problems with the free market oriented mechanisms and the fragmented administrative system, in the early 2000s new types of public interventions were gradually introduced in post-socialist countries and cities. These are based on new approaches, in both financial and institutional terms.

Several attempts were made on the national level to strengthen supra-local control over the very independent local self-governments, with a goal of awakening interest in cooperation instead of fierce competition between neighboring municipalities. The idea of such an attempt is to introduce a strong administrative middle-tier, self-governing regions, to exert control over local municipalities. This happened in Poland, but implementation proved unsuccessful in Hungary (the law on regional self-governments did not get the needed two-thirds vote in the Parliament in the second half of the 2000s). The law on initiating noncompulsory cooperation at the level of small regions can be considered more successful: although cooperation of municipalities in the small regions could not be enforced from the top down, most cooperate in the prescribed composition as it is a precondition for additional central financing of public services.

From a social policy point of view, one sign of the new approach is the national system for targeted housing allowances. Until the early 2000s the social allowance systems were regulated and financed exclusively by the municipalities, which created huge disparities according to the financial positions of the municipalities. In the early 2000s, a national system for targeted

Figure 4.3. Social renewal program in Magdolna Quarter of Budapest District VIII, Józsefváros. The lower photograph shows significant changes in the central square: renovated residential buildings, community center, and desegregated school in the back. Photos by author.

housing allowances was introduced, allowing even poor families living in poor municipalities to get allowances, as these are financed largely by the central state according to a unified scheme.

In Budapest's two-tier administrative structure (one municipal and 23 very independent district local self-governments), only the first efforts to increase higher-level public control over the fragmented administrative system are observable. The modification would aim to regain rights to the municipality from the districts so as to create more balanced territorial policies (unified parking regulation, limitation of car traffic, etc.).

The cooperation problems are even worse around the capital city, where the 82 municipalities belonging to the Budapest Agglomeration (which is only a statistical unit) have absolute freedom to decide all planning issues on their own. It was only in 2005 that a parliamentary law was introduced to limit the freedom of the local self-governments in the Agglomeration area to rezone the non-urban parts of their territories into urban land use categories. It remains to be seen how effective this regulation will be in reality (in the course of the long discussion of this law, all agglomerational municipalities rezoned large areas to create sufficient "reserves" against the higher-level control). The establishment of a metropolitan level transport system is also on the agenda and has been for a long time. It has been proceeding very slowly, although it would be advantageous for all municipalities. Cooperation between large cities and their surroundings is problematic in all post-socialist countries.

The new approach toward the role of the public sector is also observable in the decisions about large developments. In the 1990s the usual solution was to sell public properties and let the private sector do the development. In the 2000s the number of public-private partnerships, in which the public sector plays an active role, is increasing, and local governments have the ability to sign agreements with developers requiring additional projects in return for rezoning or building permission.

The Socio-Spatial Outcomes

As the discussed changes are very recent, only hypotheses can be raised about their effects and consequences while empirical evidence is, in most cases, still lacking.

The increasing role of the public sector in urban development is in itself not enough to ensure more just social outcomes. As seen in the socialist period, there is no guarantee that public allocation will follow social considerations. Besides, the new public sector attempts are very limited, and the hard factors (housing, land, development means) remain largely private. Moreover, the chances for corruption endanger the social orientation of innovative methods, such as public-private partnerships, that are intended for the better cooperation between the public and the private sector.

Local Planning Policies

Although the belief in pure market processes has weakened and there are some emerging central policies for more public steering, examples of local government interventions toward an equalizing role of the public sector are still rare. One such case is the Budapest pilot social rehabilitation program in the Magdolna Quarter in District VIII, Józsefváros, launched in 2004.

Since the late 1990s the municipality of Budapest has contributed a limited amount of public money to the renewal of the inner-city districts. In the framework of the Budapest Urban Renewal Program (BURP) the inner-city districts have the opportunity to bid for "action-area" status within deteriorated smaller neighborhoods. The action-areas receive financial support from Budapest municipality to fulfill their urban renewal plans.

This program was a step forward compared to the market-led restructuring of the inner-city housing stock, which usually led to changing functions of buildings in the best ecological positions (residential houses turning into hotels and office buildings) or to gentrifying private residential buildings. The BURP, however, lacked a social orientation. Among the deteriorated areas of Budapest it was not the socially most problematic ones that became action areas for urban renewal, but those in which the district self-government was the most able to develop a concept for urban (re)development. This can easily be shown by the fact that at least half the municipal support for action-area urban renewal went to only one district, the most professionally planned area-based renewal in District IX (discussed in the previous section).

Under such circumstances, the pilot social renewal program in the Magdolna Quarter of District VIII, Józsefváros—one of the most deteriorated areas of the city—was an especially important innovation. This is the first case in Budapest where the aim of the urban renewal efforts was not exclusively to improve the physical fabric but instead to give social, health care, and educational aspects equal weight. The final aim of the program is to improve living conditions in the area, working together with families who live there now (although a better social mix is also something to be achieved through new construction).

The Magdolna program has four main "pillars." The first is a special program for tenants that aims to create ways public tenants might contribute to the renovation of their buildings. The second seeks to build communities on the basis of a community house (converted from an industrial building), the third is oriented toward improvement of public spaces, and the fourth addresses problems of safety and education. According to the strategy, Magdolna will never become a rich area. However, the colorfulness and diversity of Józsefváros should be brought back, the deep poverty should disappear, and segregation should decrease, ending the so-called ghetto character of the neighborhood. The pilot program was financed initially for three years jointly by the municipality and the district. Recently, EU funding became available which opens up the possibility for more costly interventions, such as refurbishment of residential buildings; see Figure 4.3.

Compared to the case of Block 15 (socialist gentrification) and Ferencváros (publicly steered and largely market-financed gentrification) Magdolna quarter is the first example in Budapest of the public sector playing a new role: to ensure the social orientation of the renewal process with concrete interventions protecting the most needy strata of society.

The Magdolna quarter case, however, is still exceptional. It is very difficult, even today, to convince local politicians to prioritize social policy considerations over aims such as investment in physical improvements or economic development. This is what has happened with the EU Structural Funds programs, where there are far fewer demands by local politicians for integrated interventions into deteriorated areas than for infrastructure developments in the central parts of cities.

Summary and Evaluation: Post-Socialist Transition and the Role of Urban Planning

Critical Summary: How Well Do Post-Socialist Cities Perform?

Almost two decades after the political changes and the move to market principles, urban development plans and procedures in post-socialist cities are still determined almost exclusively on the local, municipal level. This strong decentralization, coupled with the significant influence of free market mechanisms (as a consequence of widespread privatization) has led to extreme

Figure 4.4. Visual differences in the urban development of three central European capitals. Top to bottom: Prague, Warsaw, and Budapest. Photos by author.

weakness of all social aspects of post-socialist urban development processes. In this regard there are striking differences between Western European and post-socialist cities in their institutional systems, governance methods, urban development plans, economic development strategies, and housing concepts. In many Western cities, the public sector controls substantial amounts of urban land and a percentage of the housing sector that corresponds at least to the percentage of poor residents. These tools are necessary for active use of social criteria in urban development processes and decisions. The post-socialist cities have lost these opportunities over the last two decades.

Despite recent attempts at public efforts to decrease socio-spatial inequalities, the final balance regarding the social aspects of post-socialist urban development is quite negative. In the face of a fragmented administrative system and largely privatized and marketized property relations, the public sector has little opportunity to fight for greater equity and to protect minorities. Moreover, there is very little interest or political will from politicians to deal with these difficult issues as they bring little reward in the short run from the majority of society.

We can argue that the first attempts to strengthen the influence of the public sector over the market processes mean, in a formal sense, the end of the transition of the post-socialist countries from socialism to capitalism. The weakness of the public sector shows that these countries arrived at the end of their transition to the Southern European less regulated version of capitalism, quite far away from the Northwestern European more interventionist social welfare-oriented version.

In both their rhetoric and in political statements, many of the post-socialist countries would like to continue strengthening the public sector, building toward a Scandinavian or German model (sometimes called "social market systems"). However, the public policies needed for this development path are very costly and presuppose strong public power and the possibility of new regulations being developed at the higher (supra-local) administrative level, while also keeping strong public leadership on the local level. Such ideas are not feasible in most post-socialist cities at the moment, neither financially (both because they are relatively poorer countries and because of the public spending limits imposed on those looking to meet the Maastricht criteria in order to introduce the Euro) nor politically—the idea of a strong administrative middle tier in the form of self-governing regions has been rejected, for different reasons, by the ruling parties in most post-socialist countries.

The aim of this chapter has been to give an overview of post-socialist urban development, although most of the concrete examples came from Hungary. Given this, can the situations of the post-socialist countries be compared, or should the hypothesis of growing divergence be considered? After all, under socialism the same basic model (with some variation) was introduced in all East-Central European countries. The first change, marketization, the change toward a free market system, went on with some differences in depth and speed of changes in individual countries. The second change, development of new public policies, showed even larger differences: the public sector had to be strengthened from both financial and political points of view, for which budgetary conditions and political ideas (decentralization versus strong centralistic leadership) seem to vary substantially among post-socialist countries. The largest differences in this regard can be seen between the Visegrad countries and both the Balkan countries and post-Soviet states; see Figure 4.4.

- Prague: the restituted inner city was renovated, lost most of its residential function, and resembles an open air architectural museum;
- Warsaw: the central business area was taken over by skyscrapers, which can also be discovered in outer parts, where plots were available randomly as a consequence of restitution;
- Budapest: the inner city is a patchwork of renovated and dilapidated houses with renovation decided by the condominium owners.

It remains to be seen whether the present divergence—largely due to differences in economic positions and ideologies of ruling parties in these countries—will last. It is certainly possible that the common challenges to the East-Central European area (peripheral position in Europe, migration losses and aging of population, energy vulnerability, climate change) will bring them closer again in their development path.

Opportunities for Urban Researchers and Planners to Influence Urban Policies

In the socialist period planning was strong in a technical sense, while not allowing any discussion of either the politics of plans or their political consequences. Social researchers had very limited opportunities, as the analysis of the poor strata of society and deprived areas was not wanted or allowed. Beginning in the 1970s, sociologists became more accepted partners in the planning processes, but still concentrating mainly on technical (brick and mortar) aspects.

The first turning point, the collapse of socialism and development of the free market capitalist system, brought interesting changes in the relationship among research, planning, and policy-making. Many researchers or planners suddenly became politicians on the local or even national level. Such changes, however, did not mean that the actual influence of research and planning increased. In the early 1990s, medium- and long-term urban development planning completely disappeared, replaced by short-term budgetary planning. Real decisions were made through sectoral policies, with decisive consequences for the spatial and social processes. Urban researchers and planners could aim only at influencing these changes. Even in this respect their influence was marginal—the "hard and direct" short-term interests of politics always overcame their warnings, which usually pointed out foreseeable negative long-term effects. Alternative proposals had little chance of being implemented.[5]

With the second turning point in the transition process, from the late 1990s onward, planning has gradually returned in the post-socialist cities, without, however, a strong public sector able to implement overarching urban development plans. Strategic plans for the larger cities have been developed (for Budapest see, e.g., Tosics 2001), but these general plans have had only marginal influence over real-life processes. In the new period, social researchers have gotten more chances to develop new ideas for sectoral policies (see the pilot program of social urban renewal in Budapest), as politicians had to become more open to avoiding the deepening of social crises.

More recently, EU accession with its extensive planning requirements has created a good deal of work for planners. The European level prescribes the involvement of affected groups in planning procedures (public participation). For the time being, the European level is the strongest in pushing for a modernization of the planning process. The national and local level follows behind, mainly interested in getting the financial support from the structural funds.

All these positive changes, however, have had little effect on social outcomes (social equality is not even among the main priorities of EU programs). To a large extent, the limited chances given to social research and planning to influence policy has contributed to the weak social achievements of post-socialist urban development in the East-Central European cities.

Notes

1. Iván Szelényi conceptualizes the matter differently. In his view, the transition from socialism to capitalism leads through two crises: the first connected to the establishment of the basic institutions of the market system, and the second to the need to rework the social institutional structure inherited from the socialist period (from a presentation at the Economics University in Budapest in 2008). The two ways of conceptualization are not far from each other: the first crisis of transition is in close connection with the first turning point, following it with some delay. There are some differences, however, in the timing of the second crisis and second turning point.

2. A somewhat similar conceptual framework has been developed for the analysis of urban changes in the post-socialist cities by Tsenkova 2006: 24.

3. For more detail see Tosics 2005b: 262–63.

4. Cf. the analysis of Margaret Thatcher's housing privatization in the many publications of Alan Murie and Ray Forrest in the late 1980s, summed up, e.g., in Forrest-Murie 1991.

5. An example of this can be found in the story about a concise system for local public housing policy without privatization, in Hegedüs et al. 1993.

References

Andrusz, Gregory, Michael Harloe, and Ivan Szelényi, eds. 1996. *Cities after socialism: Urban and regional change and conflict in post-socialist societies.* Oxford: Blackwell.

Bennett, Robert J. 1998. Local government in postsocialist cities. In *Social change and urban restructuring in Central Europe*, ed. György Enyedi. Budapest: Akadémia Kiado.

Berescu, Catalin, and Mariana Celac. 2006. *Housing and extreme poverty: The case of Roma communities.* Bucureşti: Ion Mincu University Press.

Bertaud, Alain, and Bertrand Renaud, B. 1995. *Cities without land markets: Location and land use in the socialist city.* World Bank Policy Research Working Paper 1477. Washington, D.C.

Buckley, Robert M., Patric H. Hendershott, and Kevin Villani. 1994. *Rapid housing privatization in reforming economies: Pay the special dividend now.* TWURD WP 12. World Bank Urban Development Division. Washington, D.C.

Forrest, Ray, and Alan Murie. 1991. *Selling the welfare state: The privatization of public housing.* London: Routledge.

Hegedüs, József, Katie Mark, Raymond Struyk, and Iván Tosics. 1993. Local options for the transformation of the public rental sector: Empirical results from two cities in Hungary. *Cities* (August): 257–71.

Hegedüs, József, and Iván Tosics. 1991. Gentrification in Eastern Europe: The case of

Budapest. In *Urban housing for the better off: Gentrification in Europe*, ed. Jan Van Weesep and Sako Musterd. Stedelijke Netwerken: University of Utrecht.

———. 1994. Privatization and rehabilitation in the Budapest inner districts. *Housing Studies* 9(1): 41–55.

———. 1996. Disintegration of the East-European housing model. In *Housing privatization in Eastern Europe*, ed. David Clapham, József Hegedüs, Keith Kintrea, and IvánTosics (with Helen Kay). Santa Barbara, Calif.: Greenwood Press.

Szelényi, Iván. 1983. *Urban inequalities under state socialism*. New York: Oxford University Press.

———. 1996. Cities under socialism, and after. In *Cities after socialism: Urban and regional change and conflict in post-socialist societies*, ed. Gregory Andrusz, Michael Harloe, and Ivan Szelényi. Oxford: Blackwell.

Szelényi, Iván, and George Konrád. 1969. *Az új lakótelepek szociológiai problémái*. (Sociological problems of the new housing estates). Budapest: Akadémiai Kiadó.

Tasan-Kok, Tuna. 2006. *Budapest, Istanbul, and Warsaw: Institutional and spatial change*. Delft: Eburon Academic.

Tosics, Iván. 2001. The dilemma of strategic planning in Central European cities: The examples of Vienna and Budapest. In *Fighting poverty together*, ed. Katalin Talyigás and Erzsébet Vajdovich-Visy. Budapest: Budapest International Workshop, Social Science Foundation.

———. 2005a. City development in Central and Eastern Europe since 1990: The impact of internal forces. In *Transformation of cities in Central and Eastern Europe: Towards globalization*, ed. F. E. Ian Hamilton, Kaliopa Dimitrovska Andrews, and Natasa Pichler-Milanović. Tokyo: United Nations University Press.

———. 2005b. Post-socialist Budapest: The invasion of market forces and the response of public leadership. In *Transformation of cities in Central and Eastern Europe: Towards globalization*, ed. F. E. Ian Hamilton, Kaliopa Dimitrovska Andrews, and Natasa Pichler-Milanović. Tokyo: United Nations University Press.

———. 2005c. Metropolitan cooperation as a precondition for international competitiveness. Special difficulties in preparing post-socialist cities for international competition: The case of Budapest. In *Competition between cities in Central Europe: Opportunities and risks of cooperation*, ed. Rudolf Giffinger. Bratislava: Road.

———. 2006. Spatial restructuring in post-socialist Budapest. In *The urban mosaic of post-socialist Europe: Space, institutions and policy*, ed. Sasha Tsenkova and Zorica Nedović-Budić. Heidelberg: Physica-Verlag.

Tsenkova, Sasha. 2006. Beyond transitions: Understanding urban change in post-socialist cities. In *The Urban mosaic of post-socialist Europe: Space, institutions and policy*, ed. Sasha Tsenkova and Zorica Nedović-Budić. Heidelberg: Physica-Verlag.

UNECE. 1997. *Human settlement trends in Central and Eastern Europe*, New York: UN Economic Commission for Europe.

Chapter 5

The Past, Present, and Future
of Professional Ethics in Planning

Martin Wachs

Planning has historically been about shaping our shared built environment, but over time it has also come to be about forming our collective institutional and social environments. The meaning of plans is in their impacts on communities and in the actions that affect relationships among people within social and physical environments. Every collective or social decision is based in part on explicit or implied moral values, and it is inevitable that every act of planning is to some extent inspired by thought about morality. Programs addressing housing, air quality, mobility, and economic development all have complex technical content but are motivated ultimately by social concerns about achieving the right and the good.

As we look back over fifty years, we can see that analytic techniques have attained primacy in guiding academic curricula and planning practice. Gradually increasing status has been accorded to the professors and practitioners who developed sophisticated analytical tools and a commitment to utilitarian analysis. The field of economics has become increasingly quantitative and increasingly influential, and schools of public policy have emerged in many places, competing with planning programs for resources, the best students, and the most influential faculty members. In a number of universities, schools or departments of planning have been eliminated and replaced by programs in public policy. In other cases, urban planning departments have been moved from schools of architecture to schools of public policy. Even where this has not happened, curricula in planning programs have shifted. Classes in modeling, simulation techniques, and statistical methods have become more central, and design studios and courses dealing with legal structures and decision-making processes less so. This reflects current trends in planning as well; practice justifications for planning decisions are usually framed in terms of data analysis rather than contributions to just outcomes. Thus, both theory and practice reflect a commitment to a particular view of scholarship and action that is basically utilitarian—it gives increasing weight to the calculation of benefits, costs, and predicted consequences of policies rather than the morality or ethical content of the actions taken by those in positions of authority. This says something about current worldviews of ethics and morality.

On the Difficulty of Aligning Social Morality with Planning

In the current environment, the recognition that planning is inherently about social morality does little to help us prepare better plans, become better planners, or even be more ethical people. Planning is a collective or social undertaking and societies have much more difficulty reaching consensus about what is right or good than about which plans to adopt and on how to deploy resources to implement them. People and institutions often are able to reach consensus on a plan or policy precisely because plans can be made and actions affecting the environment can be taken even when those who plan or take action together retain different—even dramatically different—ethical or normative positions. To put it perhaps too simply, the acts of planners and policy-makers are widely recognized as being richly imbued with ethical and moral content whether or not they make the world better, and plans most often fail or succeed not because they promote particular moral imperatives but because they are silent, ambiguous, or accommodating to alternative ethical positions (Lindblom and Cohen 1979).

A second issue complicates the application of ethics to planning. Planning almost always is about shaping the future, and the future is always characterized by uncertainty. For most practical purposes, pervasive uncertainty reduces our ability to assess plans and policies on the basis of fundamental approaches to morality. The extent to which an action will be inherently supportive of worthy principles—or to which the consequences of plans or policies will be on balance beneficial—is almost always at least partly unknown. Plans must by definition be made in advance of the actions they are intended to guide. Moreover, even if we could predict the moral impact of an action in advance of planning it, the society in which the plan is to be adopted most likely would still not be able to agree on the inherent moral value of the projected outcome. Indeed, if society could agree on the material outcomes of a plan or policy and also agree that it places positive moral value on that outcome, planning would be merely a technical or administrative activity. Planning exists as a social function precisely because there is uncertainty about both ends and means, and the moral values associated with each. Those uncertainties are fundamental to our work, yet they also ensure that the ultimate morality of planners' actions is, to a great extent, always unknown (Thatcher 2004; Lempert et al. 2003).

Since the stated goal of this book is to "think social," we might be tempted to be guided by hedonistic philosophies that value the goodness of actions, plans, and policies in terms of their most direct impacts on the well-being of people (Frankena 1973). Yet, with accelerating concern for the long-term well-being of the earth, we could just as well make the case that anthropocentric views of what is right are ultimately shortsighted and incomplete (Beatley 1994). Again, the uncertainty that confronts us is greater than our ability to foresee. We can debate whether there is a moral imperative to protect our planet primarily because doing so eventually benefits people or whether we have a moral imperative to protect the earth even if doing so in the end reduces the well-being of people in relation to other elements of nature (Silva 2008). But, once again, the uncertainty that always confronts us far outweighs our ability to decide. We cannot comprehend all the longer-term implications for the earth of current plans and the impacts of earth-changing actions on the people who inhabit the planet, so our values must guide us even as we know our understanding of the choices is dominated by uncertainty.

Planners are not going to resolve by consensus fundamental disagreements based on differences in values. Planning is fundamentally about taking action to change the nature of the world around us in uncertain situations when value differences dominate public debates. We must, therefore, be prepared to take action and support policies cognizant of their moral dimensions while accepting that the most fundamental moral dimensions of our practice present pervasive contradictions as well as the uncertainties already noted. For example, we try to preserve the individual rights of all people and advance the well-being of the most needy and underrepresented. These values suggest different and often competing actions. Planners can and should focus always on the rightness or goodness of our activities, but we cannot let such concerns immobilize us. As professionals, we must try to arrive at positions that align our personal actions with our values. Yet, we must do so while understanding that the societies in which we work will often be unable to arrive at plans or policies clearly based on moral imperatives.

Professional Ethics, Codes, and Sanctions

Given the broad scope of these persistently unsolvable dilemmas, planners have historically—probably inevitably—separated the moral content of plans and programs from the ethical content of the daily professional practice of planning. Professional ethics are encapsulated in codes that have been adopted by planners in many countries with a degree of institutional formality. Our values, however, are imbued in us less by our profession than by our parents, by our teachers, and by the religious and cultural dimensions of the world. They are not primarily the result of planning education, not fundamentally affected by our professional roles and formal codes of ethics, not deeply affected by technical analysis of alternative courses of action (Wachs 1990).

Professional codes of ethics state ideals of the profession and seek to protect the public and planners themselves from improper actions on the part of individuals who might act improperly in the course of their work (Silva 2008; Kaufman 1990; Lawton 2003). Professional ethics do much less to help us decide whether the content of a plan, design, or program is or ever can be morally right.

In a classic paper that remains timely, even though it was published nearly forty years ago, Peter Marcuse (1976) reminded us that even the very motives for adopting professional codes of ethics themselves can be interpreted as less than morally pure. Knowing that planning was not widely regarded as a "profession," and seeking the self-aggrandizement that comes with professional recognition, planners decided that they needed codes of ethics in part because medicine, law, and accounting were widely recognized as professions and were distinguished by having such codes. In other words, adoption of professional codes was intended to show the world that planners are worthy of special recognition, status, and financial rewards because we are, after all, a "profession." Silva (2008) points out that professional planning codes of ethics have, in most countries, been introduced quite recently. While the Town Planning Institute in the United Kingdom adopted its first code in the 1930s, the organization now known as the American Institute of Certified Planners (AICP) did not adopt a code until 1971, which, perhaps surprisingly, was earlier than organizations in most other countries. Ethical codes have been published with a degree of pomp and enforced with a degree of solemnity. Yet, in many cases, their enforcement is quasi-legal in terms of rules of evidence and procedures.

In the many countries in which professional planners have adopted codes of ethics, these rules are intended to bind us together by having planners accept as a collective responsibility the prosecution of those among us who violate principles encapsulated in the codes. In exchange for professional status and its associated rewards, we agree to regulate and police ourselves to assure ethical behavior. Having made this "bargain," we hopefully benefit society by adhering to codes of professional behavior, but our goal in adopting the codes was not only for the protection of the societies we serve, but also for our own protection. Professional codes protect both planners and the public from a wide variety of inappropriate behaviors on the part of other planners such as lying, cheating, reliance on political influence, harassment and overt discrimination on the basis of personal characteristics, price gouging, and making improper claims when advertising qualifications or competing for commissions to do professional work. Fortunately, it is easier to recognize and regulate improper professional behavior than to recognize the essence of morality in the content of actual plans.

It is important that codes of ethics govern professional practice even as we advance the more philosophical position that great and lasting uncertainties in society limit our ability to know the ultimate moral value of a plan or policy. This is because adoption of a plan or policy inevitably redistributes wealth and other measures of well-being to a greater extent than it improves the world for all. Plans can bestow immediate benefits on some and costs on others, even when their long-term impacts are not fully understood and remain open to further analysis and debate. Populations are relocated, windfall profits accrue to owners of some land, and environmental "externalities" improve the lives of some and harm those of others. If planners have deliberately taken action to benefit some or harm others and their principal motives were to obtain direct financial or status rewards for themselves, their families, or their associates, such actions can do substantial harm, and we must collectively respond by sanctioning those responsible. If we do not act on the basis of relatively clear principles of professional ethics, we risk a loss of respect for planning on the part of society at large. The motivation to act collectively to sanction behavior defined as unethical could originate in a self-motivated concern for the loss of income, privilege, and status that might follow from a diminution of our professional standing. Yet most of us are honestly more concerned that a failure to prosecute ethical violations will diminish the public welfare.

Some planning codes of ethics also tip their hats to the deeper moral questions that are far more abstract and yet are intellectually more important to the definition of our field. For decades and through several revisions of its code, for example, the American Institute of Certified Planners (AICP) has included in its code hortatory language that is significant despite being ambiguous. The code asserts that "our primary obligation is to serve the public interest." The requirement that the public interest be served is addressed through a list of principles, including the following, among others:

a) We shall always be conscious of the rights of others.
b) We shall have special concern for the long-range consequences of present actions. . . .
d) We shall provide timely, adequate, clear, and accurate information on planning issues to all affected persons and to governmental decision makers.
e) We shall give people the opportunity to have a meaningful impact on the development of plans and programs that may affect them. Participation should be broad enough to include those who lack formal organization or influence.
f) We shall seek social justice by working to expand choice and opportunity for all persons, recognizing a special responsibility to plan for the needs of the disadvantaged and to promote racial and economic integration. . . .
g) We shall promote excellence of design and endeavor to conserve and preserve the integrity and heritage of the natural and built environment. (American Institute of Certified Planners 2010)

A small number of planners have been brought up on charges and dismissed at the recommendation of Ethics Committee after formal action of the elected Commission of the AICP. The AICP web site informs us that the number is well under a dozen per year over the last several years, and most of those accused of ethical violations have avoided prosecution by simply letting their memberships lapse and thus avoiding the prospect of being expelled. In some cases, the civil or criminal justice system more formally prosecuted individuals when their actions were considered illegal as well as unethical. There are comparable examples in Britain, Canada, Israel, Sweden, and elsewhere of planners punished for infractions including bribery and fraud. I could not find a single case of a planner who was dismissed from membership because he or she violated the public interest, failed to have special concern for the long-range consequences of planning actions, or failed to protect the integrity of the natural environment.

Part of each professional code of ethics is intended to be the basis for action in cases of clearly recognizable ethical failings by practicing planners. But it is also important that the codes are intended to be hortatory and perhaps inspirational. The goal of such provisions is to elevate the thought processes of practicing planners, urging them to consider the broader philosophical and moral dimensions of their work along with their immediate statutory and technical responsibilities. It is certainly possible for us to elevate our thought processes and clarify the ways personal commitments to policies reflect our values, but doing so is not equivalent to endowing particular policies, plans, or actions in the larger society with explicit ethical content.

Unquestionably, in the past fifty years, practicing planners have become increasingly aware of the existence of codes of ethics (Silva 2008), and concerns for ethical behavior by professional planners have become a more significant theme in the education and professional lives of planners (Barrett 2001). Professional societies require that ethics be addressed in the curricula of university programs, and practitioners in a number of countries are eligible to be "certified" to practice planning only after they have graduated from universities that include such courses and have taken professional entrance or certification examinations that include questions relating to ethical principles. Professional planning societies in a number of countries—most aggressively in the United States—include sessions on ethics in their annual conventions and encourage their constituent bodies or "chapters" in particular cities, states, or provinces to hold periodic "ethics awareness" sessions. They publish ethics columns in newsletters, magazines, and journals, and practicing planners have published a wide variety of books and pamphlets on themes relating to professional ethics (Barrett 2001). The AICP publishes "ethical advisory rulings" that elaborate on the precise language of the code by detailing circumstances in which planners can be accused of sexual harassment, gender discrimination, conflict of interest, and bias in forecasting.

Professional planning ethics awareness programs, training sessions, and publications demonstrate similarities to one another and taken together reveal some important characteristics of ethical considerations in the field of professional planning. Many of these are presented as scenarios or situations in which a planner or organization is confronted with a complex or difficult situation in which someone has made a proposal for a project or an offer to a planner that reveals multiple dimensions of consideration or can be interpreted in different ways. The planner or organization is portrayed as being in a situation taken to be an "ethical dilemma" in which several choices can be made, depending on alternative interpretations of available data, competing demands on loyalties of different sorts, and alternative readings of different ethical principles that comprise relevant professional codes. Readers and participants in workshops are invited to engage in dialogue or debate the alternatives, all to try to reach consensus on what adoption of a particular course of action (in some cases multiple courses of action) would imply about their understanding of the particular ethical dilemma. Many of the books, articles, and workshops feature a "discussion" of the ethical implications of these exemplary situations, while very often leaving conclusions to be drawn by the reader or the workshop participants (Barrett 2001). In other words, the ethical dilemmas to be considered are rarely clearly structured to give rise to a "right answer."

It is not surprising that discussions of practical professional ethics in planning are typified by the presentation of dilemmas that often confront practitioners and are amenable to discussions supportive of different and sometimes competing courses of action. It is easy to see how the principles in the AICP code could suggest alternative and competing actions that would be viewed as appropriate under particular circumstances. One clause requires that a planner be loyal to his or her employer, while another requires responsiveness to the public interest. Planners are expected to pursue protection of the natural environment while paying attention to the needs of diverse and underrepresented groups. One clause suggests that decisions be based upon data and analysis, while another suggests that due consideration be given to the long-run interrelatedness of policies and actions. Thus, while discussions of ethics inform and enrich thought processes of practitioners in hypothetical situations, those actually faced by planners are rarely so clear-cut that ethical implications of alternative actions are obvious or trivial.

Still, we have to hope and very much want to believe that practicing planners benefit from exposure to such dilemmas through their professional training and by reading continuing coverage of the ethical issues in planning in their professional newsletters, magazines, and journals. David Thatcher (2004) writes that this concept—use of analytical case studies and careful review of precedents—is an important way in which professions elucidate collective understandings of ethical principles. Case law is an extremely important element of legal scholarship, and in medicine individual cases are studied and compared in order to deepen professional understanding. In what he calls the "casuistical" approach to planning ethics, Thatcher argues that careful study of cases can also advance planners' understanding of more complex ethical principles. When confronted with genuine ethical dilemmas in their professional practice, we hope that planners mobilize and act somewhat more decisively based on this understanding and that the professional practice of planning is thereby enriched by continuous analysis of complex cases that have actually occurred.

Planners' Perceptions of Their Ethical Roles as Revealed in Research

Some evidence from empirical studies of planners' attitudes toward ethics may shed light on practicing planners' perceptions of ethics. In their landmark study of ethical attitudes and beliefs of a sample of roughly a hundred practicing planners, Elizabeth Howe and Jerome Kaufman found wide variation in the ways in which North American planners conceived of their roles in relation to the public interest (Howe 1994). They asked participants to respond to "scenarios" of the sort discussed above and developed a typology of planners based on their orientation to planning ethics. Practicing planners were considered "politicians" if their responses led to the conclusion that they defined their role as active intervention to promote ends related to their value-driven commitments. These planners wanted to make change and their commitments to change were ethically charged; they were activists who pursued "causes." They wanted, for example, to advance the well-being of the poor or to promote investments in environmental betterment. This group of planners sought to practice what Peter Marcuse (2011: chap. 56) refers to as the "critical social justice" model of planning. Planners were labeled "technicians" if they consistently conceived their role as carrying out analysis and developing plans in pursuit of goals that to a great extent had been identified by others. Technicians thought of themselves as relatively value neutral and of their work as consisting mostly of manipulating data, models, and methods. They developed plans in detail while following through on commitments and goals set for them by more senior policy-makers including elected officials.

A third group of planners, classified in Howe and Kaufman's typology as "hybrids," appear to me the most complex and intellectually interesting of the three groups. Hybrids were professional planners who possessed some of the traits both of the first two groups. Sometimes they perceived their roles to be the promotion of particular ends that were purposely chosen, and sometimes their judgments were more consistent with the role of the technical expert, in that they were relatively value neutral and data driven, operating within bounds set by more senior planners and elected officials. To some extent hybrids were people who found that planning placed different requirements on practitioners depending upon circumstances.

Howe and Kaufman analyzed and interpreted the patterns of belief revealed by their data. They compared the groups on the basis of personal traits and whether they considered themselves to be primarily deontologist (i.e., rule-oriented), consequentialist, or utilitarian in their orientation. While most planners would support the notion of "serving the public good," they could legitimately differ with respect to what that obligation required of them. This reflected planners' "need to balance the various, sometimes competing, procedural obligations to provide independent professional advice, to be responsive to the public, and to be accountable to decision makers" (Howe 1994: 60). Marcuse (2009) points out that the field of planning has in particular situations seen tension between "subservient" and "activist" perspectives, but in the end the hybrids dominate the field, meaning that the two perspectives for all practical purposes coexist in planning organizations and even within individual professional planners.

Morality in Planning and Policymaking

Thus far, I have dealt with ethics of individual planners as they might encounter challenges when working on particular assignments or devising particular plans or policies. When examining planning ethics in this way, it is not difficult to arrive at the conclusion that our profession remains indecisive and clumsy about the meaning of ethics within its work despite many decades of observation and analysis. We agree that ethical behavior is a critical element helping define our profession and the roles of planners, but we agree only in abstract generalities as to what this requires us to do in particular situations.

Beyond particular issues faced in daily work assignments, any serious review of ethics in planning also must turn to broader challenges that face us collectively as a profession and even as a society. To be ethical and for planning as a profession to have virtue, we must address global environmental sustainability, the alleviation of deep and sustained inequality, and the provision of fundamental human rights to those who are deprived of them. Indeed this is a basic tenet that brings us together as planners: we believe our work involves technical application of tools of analysis, but we apply our analysis and methods in the service of moral and ethical commitments to the well-being of people and their environment. We must consider the ethics *of planning* as well as the ethics of individuals engaged *in planning*. Saying this in another way, consideration of ethics in planning requires us to address the collective morality of our professional work as well as the ethical dimensions of acts carried out by individual planners in particular situations.

But, if we cannot be confident about what constitutes ethical behavior in a narrowly defined situation affecting a particular individual or team, how can we possibly arrive at a consensus as to what makes for an ethical land use policy (Beatley 1994) or a plan for controlling the emission of greenhouse gases that is based on morality? What does it mean to agree that such questions have at their roots even more fundamental questions about the right and the good, while we struggle to understand what they require of us as planners?

The Ethics of Forecasting: An Illustration of Moral Dimensions of Collective Planning Practice

Forecasts are used regularly in the process of planning and designing a variety of public facilities. Plans for housing, economic development, schools, hospitals, power plants, water supply systems, and transportation facilities all begin with forecasts of population, economic activity, and demand for a service or product. Countries and international financial organizations require that the demand for and cost of public programs be forecast in advance and that the anticipated benefits versus the expected costs be shown to justify a particular project. In addition, many private sector organizations depend on such forecasts to evaluate whether to invest private capital in public works projects, including many privately financed bridges, tunnels, ports, and toll roads that are becoming more common as "public-private partnerships" proliferate around the world.

Most planning activities are collectively performed by individuals who work as part of the numerous teams that make up complex organizations and interact with teams in other organizations. A housing plan for a developing country, a comprehensive airport plan for an industrialized country, and an air pollution reduction program for a province or metropolitan area are but three examples showing that plans produced by interactive processes are crucial among complex organizations. Application of professional ethics in such planning processes has proved difficult or impossible. Professional codes of ethics are all written as though they are intended to apply to individual or personal behavior, while such planning processes involve many people and organizations, and in collective social undertakings it is difficult to assign responsibility to any one person or group. In addition, by their nature such plans are intended to guide actions in the future, and it is difficult to identify the ethical consequences of actions that have yet to be taken. When they are eventually taken, it may be decades since the planning has taken place and thus impossible to find the people who exercised critical judgments affecting the moral consequences of the plans.

The ethical dimension of large-scale public works planning has in recent years received increased attention as the result of recurrent, widely publicized dramatic cost overruns in public works projects. The Central Artery Project in Boston, Massachusetts, known popularly as the "Big Dig," cost more than five times the original forecast, and construction took three times as long. The "Chunnel" or rail tunnel under the English Channel also cost many times its original forecast cost and proved to be far less cost-efficient than its planners had asserted (Flyvbjerg et al. 2006). When bids were opened to construct the new structure to replace the earthquake-damaged eastern span of the San Francisco-Oakland Bay Bridge, the lowest bid from a contractor was roughly for five times the budget estimated by consultants only a few years earlier. Why does this happen and what can be done about it? Can societies learn from experience to make better forecasts of costs and benefits when undertaking major public investments? While some scholars believe this is a simple technical matter involving the tools and techniques of cost estimation and patronage forecasting, there is growing evidence that the gaps between forecasts and outcomes are the results of deliberate misrepresentation and thus amount to a collective failure of professional ethics (Flyvbjerg 2005).

Planning firms in many countries specialize in preparing forecasts for policy assessment, based in theory on the understanding that regional plans, large capital investments, and long-term commitments of public resources to operating and maintaining networks of facilities will certainly be controversial. Often, however, firms making the forecasts stand to benefit if a decision is made to proceed with the project. Contracts to perform preliminary engineering and design follow early planning exercises if a decision is made to proceed with implementation of the plan, but such funding opportunities do not eventuate if projects are not approved, so optimistic forecasts can be used to "generate business" (Wachs 1990).

Interest groups including industries that would be served by the projects, community residents, environmentalists, and local chambers of commerce surely pursue different objectives from the policymaking process. Some communities desperately want growth and the expansion of facilities to serve them; others organize in fierce opposition to certain plans for projects or to particular design characteristics that are proposed. If forecasts are honestly prepared, it should be possible to find compromises and decide on options that perform better than others with respect to widely accepted criteria such as cost effectiveness. Demand and cost forecasting is not expected to prevent or resolve political differences or debates. Rather, it is intended to inform and facilitate debate, contribute to rational decision-making, and facilitate compromises, especially in complex and politically charged situations. If this goal is to be served, the professional values of the forecasting community must be based on the principle that forecasts should influence political processes rather than vice versa. Forecasts are always subject to error and uncertainty, but they should be honestly prepared, data should not be falsified, and assumptions should be chosen on defensible and technical grounds, not because they favor certain outcomes over others.

A lively debate has emerged over the past twenty years about the extent to which demand and cost forecasts are objective or influenced by politics. In a well-known and controversial report, Don H. Pickrell (1992) argued that in the United States the majority of a sample of seven rail transit projects he studied were forecast to have ridership levels higher than actually achieved when the projects were built, and the vast majority experienced higher capital and operating costs than forecast at the time funds were committed to their construction. Thus, actual costs per rider turned out to be consistently much higher than the forecasts. Pickrell was judicious in explaining these observed divergences, but his work leaves the reader with the strong impression that they were the result of deliberate misrepresentation. Other authors, including Jonathan Richmond, argue that the outcomes of such forecasts are politically inspired, and that for reasons that can be explained in terms of planning consultants' behavior, forecasts deliberately reach beyond reasonable expectations. To put it very directly, it is widely believed that consultants prepare forecasts of the costs and future use of large public works projects that are falsified in order to justify expenditure of public funds on those projects. In the minds of many analysts, this is a major reason there have been enormous cost overruns in projects like the "Chunnel" and the "Big Dig" (Richmond 2005).

The late Robert Moses, public works czar of New York City, actually boasted that lying was his best strategy for justifying large public investments. Once construction was underway, he said, public officials had no option but to spend the funds to complete the projects. So lying to get big projects started was always an effective political strategy (Caro 1975: 218).

A group of European scholars led by Professor Bent Flyvbjerg added fuel to the fire that has characterized this debate. His team has studied hundreds of projects in many countries, including roads, highways, and bridges, built over as span of more than fifty years. They found that costs are far more likely to be underestimated than overestimated prior to construction, while actual patronage or facility use is far more likely to be overestimated than underestimated. If estimates were truly unbiased and deviations from actual patronage and cost were the result of honest errors, overestimation and underestimation should be roughly equally likely. Interestingly, this research team argues that the margins by which differences between forecast and actual patronage and cost have occurred have not declined in almost a century. This trend suggests that the performance of forecasting models and cost estimation techniques is not improving despite many efforts by sponsoring agencies to improve the mathematical models and computer algorithms in such forecasts. They also found that such differences were persistent across investment sectors and from country to country (Flyvbjerg et al. 2006).

There are different interpretations of these findings, so they are often the basis for suggesting alternative courses of action. On one hand, perhaps consistent with the technocratic planning tradition, such findings suggest the need for deeper and continuing research to isolate the specific causes of divergence between forecast and actual performance. This is made more difficult by the fact that funds are rarely made available by public bodies in any country to do follow-up analyses of the performance of forecasts after facilities have been built. Others have described the apparent "optimism bias" in forecasts as innocent and unsurprising. There is a sort of "selection bias" clearly at work. Projects are less likely to be built and plans less likely to be implemented, it is said, if their forecasts of cost are high and predictions of expected use are low, so it is not surprising that errors of the opposite sort dominate among projects and investment programs that have actually been built. While this might be true, others respond that optimism bias is hardly the result of innocence, and in some cases researchers have been able to document "strategic misrepresentation" in the form of "adjusted" model coefficients and "refined" parameters from one model run to another. Modelers have told stories of political influence and threats that they would lose their jobs unless they produced forecasts that supported certain outcomes (Wachs 1990). It is, of course, quite likely that some or part of the observed divergence between forecasts and outcomes is not intentional while some is quite deliberate. This illustrates how critical professional ethics can be in cases of collective action in the policy arena, yet I am not aware of a single example of the application of professional codes of ethics to an organization that has prepared an analytical forecast.

It is both necessary and possible to chart a responsible and ethical course even as debates rage in academia and the media as to the causes of this apparent problem. The Department for Transport in Great Britain has issued a "white paper" on procedures to control "optimism bias" in forecasting (Flyvbjerg et al. 2004). Requirements that assumptions be reported and explained by consultants, that critical "outside" peer review be performed of forecasts, and that standards be published for data use and assumptions in forecasting are all helpful. The Federal Transit Administration in the United States has gradually—over more than a decade—been developing a set of guidelines and procedures designed to ensure that "best practices" are routinely employed in forecasting for rail and bus transit project "new starts." These would, at the very least, allow egregious deviations from objectivity and good practice to be recognized and criticized.

The divergence between forecasts and performance of large public works projects is a complex multidimensional problem rich in ethical or moral content. It is likely to be illustrative of issues that arise in every aspect of planning and policy making. While it is possible to state with naive optimism that ethical planning requires that forecasts *should be* as free as possible from deliberate distortion or misrepresentation, it remains difficult to prescribe mechanisms that ensure this outcome. Heightened awareness of the extent of the problems and increased familiarity with the debates and the data do, however, contribute to the inclusion of these concerns in the development of planning and evaluation processes. Inclusion of case studies of these problems in graduate planning curricula also help to alert the next generation of practitioners to ethical challenges they are likely to face in practice. Documentation and dissemination of information about the problem itself can contribute to limiting the most egregious exaggerations. But recognizing the problem does not resolve it; rather, it demonstrates that the planning profession has little to bring to concerns for ethics in one of the most fundamental aspects of planning practice.

Applying Ethical Principles
to Collective Actions by Planners

Nearly four decades ago, Brian Barry and Douglas Rae (1975) wrote that planning and policy-making should strive to meet several criteria that can help us understand our view of ethics and morality in planning and policy. They argued that effective policy should be judged in part on its *internal consistency*. By this they mean it is logical to come to a conclusion that a policy is effective or appropriate only if the criteria by which it can be judged are clearly understood and can be hierarchically ranked. In addition, they argued that standards by which policies are judged must be *interpretable*—a standard for judging a policy outcome must be understood by different parties to mean something they have in common. Furthermore, a policy or plan must lead to a *choice even in the face of risk or uncertainty.* Failure to make a decision or choice is to make one by default. This means that it is necessary to *aggregate or combine multiple criteria* to reach a judgment about any policy or plan. It also means that *short-term and long-term consequences must be weighed and balanced* against one another. In addition, while society must make decisions collectively, the decision-making process should make some logical connection between a collective social decision and a conception of *individual or personal welfare.*

Criteria such as these for judging the outcome of planning processes and utility of planned or implemented programs do appeal to our rationality as planners and help justify the growing focus on analytical methods and tools in planning thought. This is a trend I do not necessarily criticize; I have learned through application of more sophisticated methods of analysis that some conclusions I considered reasonably obvious have proved to be quite incorrect.

But it is also true that scholars including Charles W. Anderson (1979) and Alasdair MacIntyre (1977) almost immediately responded to such arguments by asserting that they were incomplete: while valid, they were mechanistic in that they did not include "principles" such as justice, freedom, and community which are critically important if planning is to serve us well in the pursuit of human ideals. To return to words I used earlier when referring to relatively formal codes of ethics in planning, they did not address "the public interest" nearly as well as they described the process of reaching a decision. While the public interest is extremely difficult to define, we must continue to explore the notion that it consists of something more than an aggregation of disparate individual interests.

In order to add moral or ethical content to plans and public policies, three more considerations are needed, not only for those in schools of planning and public policy but also for consideration of judgments about public policy when they are exercised by people whose backgrounds lie in any discipline. Planners should define their scholarship and our practice in terms of the following considerations.

First, plans and policies need to be attentive to the nature, role, and exercise of *authority*. This means that the person, group, or government reaching decisions and implementing them must be legitimate and justifiable. Conclusions and decisions must be arrived at through due process. Decisions that weigh benefits versus costs and emphasize efficiency may be appropriate, but perhaps not when undertaken by a decision-making body or individual who does not have legitimate authority to speak or decide on behalf of those for whom the decision is being made and who must live with the consequences of that decision.

Second, plans and public policies also need to be based on the concept of justice (see Fainstein and Fainstein in this volume). Justice is, of course, a difficult criterion to implement, but it deals ultimately with fairness and especially with regard for those who have less power and recourse to the control of resources than do others. Policies and plans must be attentive to distributive consequences and especially to impacts on those in disadvantaged positions.

Third, and finally, we also have an ethical obligation to attempt to use public resources with *efficiency*. Means and ends must be logically linked to achieve wise use of public resources, whether the resources under consideration are human or composed of land or capital.

The criteria outlined by Barry and Rae and the evolution of planning thought and public policy all seem to fit most easily with the search for efficiency. Modern approaches to planning, the application of tools and techniques of program and project evaluation, innovations in planning curricula described earlier, and distribution of rewards and prestige in the field all tend to reward improvements in efficiency rather than being concerned with the legitimacy of authority and obtaining justice. If, however, planning ethics is to guide the worldview of our scholarly and professional communities over the coming decades, it will be because we have the courage and commitment to assert that issues of authority and justice ought to have at least equal weight with efficiency. It is not clear that this can be achieved. Nevertheless, examination of current planning crises in particular countries as well as a whole set of international issues from sustainability to human rights suggests that this is the core issue facing planners today just as it was fifty years ago.

References

American Institute of Certified Planners. 2009. *Code of Ethics and Professional Conduct.* Adopted March 19, 2005; effective June 1, 2005; revised October 3, 2009. http://www.planning.org/ethics/ethicscode.htm, accessed May 2011.

Anderson, Charles W. 1979. The place of principles in policy analysis. *American Political Science Review* 73: 711–23.

Barrett, Carol D. 2001. *Everyday ethics for practicing planners.* Chicago: American Planning Association.

Barry, Brian, and Douglas W. Rae. 1975. Political evaluation. In *Handbook of political science,* vol. 1, ed. Fred I. Greenstein and Nelson W. Polsby, 337–401. Reading, Mass.: Addison-Wesley.

Beatley, Timothy. 1994. *Ethical land use: Principles of policy and planning.* Baltimore: Johns Hopkins University Press.

Caro, Robert. 1975. *The power broker: Robert Moses and the fall of New York.* New York: Vintage.

Flyvbjerg, Bent. 2005. Design by deception: The politics of megaproject approval. *Harvard Design Magazine* 22: 50–59.

Flyvbjerg, Bent, Nils Bruzelius, and Werner Rothengotter. 2006. *Megaprojects and risk: An anatomy of ambition.* Cambridge: Cambridge University Press.

Flyvbjerg, Bent, Carsten Glenting, and Anne Kvist Rønnest. 2004. *Procedures for dealing with optimism bias in transport planning: Guidance document.* London: British Department for Transport.

Frankena, William K. 1973. *Ethics.* 2nd ed. Englewood Cliffs, N.J.: Prentice-Hall.

Howe, Elizabeth. 1994. *Acting on ethics in city planning.* New Brunswick, N.J.: Center for Urban Policy Research, Rutgers University.

Kaufman, Jerome. 1990. American codes of planning ethics: Content, development, and after-effects. *Plan Canada* 30: 29–34.

Lawton, Alan. 2003. Developing and implementing codes of ethics. Presented at conference of European Group of Public Administration, Oeris.

Lempert, Robert J., Steven W. Popper, and Steven C. Bankes. 2003. *Shaping the next one hundred years: New methods for quantitative, long-term policy analysis.* Santa Monica, Calif.: RAND Pardee Center.

Lindblom, Charles E., and David K. Cohen. 1979. *Usable knowledge: Social science and social problem solving.* New Haven, Conn.: Yale University Press.

MacIntyre, Alisdair. 1977. Utilitarianism and cost-benefit analysis: An essay on the relevance of moral philosophy to bureaucratic theory. In *Values in the Electric Power Industry,* ed. Kenneth Sayre. South Bend, Ind.: Notre Dame University Press.

Marcuse, Peter. 1976. Professional ethics and beyond: Values in planning. *Journal of the American Institute of Planners* 42: 264–74.

———. 2009. Social justice and power in planning history and theory. Paper submitted to Planning with People Workshop. http://p-p-workshop.net.technion.ac.il.

———. 2011. The three historic currents of city planning. In *The New Blackwell Companion to the City,* ed. Gary Bridge and Sophie Watson, 643–55. Oxford: Wiley-Blackwell.

Pickrell, Don H. 1992. A desire named streetcar: Fantasy and fact in rail transit planning. *Journal of the American Planning Association* 58: 158–76.

Rawls, John. 1971. *A theory of justice.* Cambridge, Mass.: Harvard University Press.

Richmond, Jonathan. 2005. *Transport of delight: The mythical conception of rail transit in Los Angeles.* Akron, Ohio: University of Akron Press.

Silva, Carlos Nunes. 2006. Urban planning and ethics. In *Encyclopedia of Public Administration and Public Policy.* 2nd ed., ed. Evan M. Berman.

Thatcher, David. 2004. The casuistical turn in planning ethics: Lessons learned from law and medicine. *Journal of Planning Education and Research* 23: 269-85.

Wachs, Martin. 1990. Ethics and advocacy in forecasting for public policy. *Business and Professional Ethics Journal* 9: 141–57.

PART II

Equity-Oriented Planning

Chapter 6

Toward an Equity-Oriented Planning Practice in the United States

Norman Krumholz

Over the past sixty years almost all older industrial cities in the United States have been losing population, jobs, and economic investment. As a consequence, most are becoming locations of concentrated poverty and unemployment. Global economic changes have eliminated employment and income opportunities for many lower- and moderate-income people, with minority populations in center cities being particularly affected (Wilson 1987). Many of the people remaining in these places live in areas that provide poor education, have high crime rates, and in every respect offer a sharply lower quality of life than that enjoyed by other Americans.

Both local and national leadership have responded to this crisis by attempting to stimulate new investment, bring the middle class back to the city, and develop heavily subsidized real estate projects in downtown areas, hoping that the benefits of these efforts would somehow "trickle down" to those in the lower reaches.

To an extent, these efforts have succeeded: new offices, hotels, and sports stadiums have been built in many cities, physically changing their skylines. None, however, has succeeded in reducing poverty, unemployment, or dependency among their resident populations, nor have they lowered rates of negative socioeconomic outcomes associated with concentrated poverty. Moreover, these efforts have left unimproved most of the neighborhoods of the working class and poor, leaving virtually untouched the ever-widening economic disparity between neighborhoods in central cities and between central cities and their suburbs.

Verification of these trends can be found in a study of 302 American cities. Of these, researchers identified some 65 older industrial cities that, based on eight economic indicators, have been lagging behind the others in the survey in job loss, unemployment rates, median household income, poverty rates, and other economic indicators (Vey 2007). The economic disparities between these cities and their suburbs were also increasing as jobs and incomes were shown to be growing much faster (on average) in the suburbs than in the central cities.

In other words, the "trickle-down" policy in American cities—which took the form on the ground of programs such as urban renewal, urban development action grants, and empowerment zones—has produced few benefits for increasingly destitute residents. Instead, it has exacerbated geographical disparities and created a more divided metropolitan area, split between downtown, wealthy suburbs, and other zones of relative affluence, on one hand, and low-income neighborhoods in and outside the central city, on the other.

Planning practitioners working in the mainstream of their profession have contributed to these changes partly as a result of their striking success in serving the needs of growth. This was particularly true in the post-World War II period. Growth advocates and coalitions required major land use modifications and changes in the structure of local government, and city planners were important actors in both efforts. Planners often played significant roles in designing and authorizing urban renewal redevelopment schemes, highway projects, downtown renovations, and suburban developments.

Mainstream professional practice in city planning adapted—perhaps too well—to the needs of growth coalitions. In the process, concerns for redistribution and broader participation were pushed to the margins of the profession. But an alternative practice, more oriented toward equity concerns, with roots that go back to the turn of the last century, was also at work during this period; one can find connections between that movement and the emerging constituencies of recent decades, as well as those seeking to address the needs of the present.

Equity-Oriented Planning in the United States and Its Lessons for Planning and Planners

The early history of city planning is marked by many well-known equity-oriented initiatives. These include the planned, socially owned garden cities proposed by Ebenezer Howard and the work of the "material feminists" like Alice Constance Austin, who sought housing and community arrangements to form a planned and egalitarian social landscape. Patrick Geddes, a Scottish biologist, drew up dozens of town plans in India and elsewhere based on a cooperative model of city evolution; the Regional Planning Association of America led by Clarence Stein sought to build housing to achieve social objectives; and Lawrence Veiller, the New York housing reformer, endeavored to improve slum conditions by regulating ventilation, sanitation, and density standards. Housing reformers like Mary K. Simkhovitch carried their determination to improve neighborhoods into the struggle for public housing, while Robert A. Wood, Edith Elmer Wood, and Catherine Bauer linked housing reforms with planning and neighborhood improvement (Scott 1995; Hayden 1976).

A wide range of progressive planning initiatives also emerged during the New Deal of the 1930s. The public housing movement was one, as was the work of the National Resources Planning Board under Frederic A. Delano and Charles W. Elliott, II, and the Greenbelt Program of planned communities under Rexford G. Tugwell's Resettlement Administration. Later, in the 1960s and 1970s, Paul Davidoff, Chester Hartman, Herbert Gans, and others developed the concept they called advocacy planning. Planners, they said, did not have to support the "growth machine" (Logan and Molotch 1988), but could use their training and talents to aid populations and groups victimized by those city policies. Their work and the ferment of the 1960s showed planners how to fight racial segregation and reduce poverty.

By the 1970s, the American Planning Association Code of Ethics reflected a new concern for vulnerable populations. It read: "A planner shall seek to expand choice and opportunity for all persons, recognizing a special responsibility to plan for the needs of disadvantaged groups and persons, and shall urge the alteration of policies, institutions, and decisions which militate against such objectives" (AICP/APA 1991). And this concern took hold at least within some part of the profession. By 1993, 30 to 40 percent of the APA annual conference sessions focused on social equity issues, and APA Planner's Press published a book of papers on social equity (APA 1994). How deep the commitment was to rank-and-file planning practitioners is still to be determined.. In 2005 AICP/APA amended its Code of Ethics and Professional Conduct by moving its clause on "special responsibility to plan for disadvantaged groups" from rules of conduct for which planners can be held accountable and subject to disciplinary action to a merely aspirational principle that cannot be the subject of an ethical misconduct charge (APA/AICP 2005; Marcuse; Wachs, this volume).

Advocacy or equity planners not only concern themselves with the physical aspects of the community but, in their day-to-day practice, also deliberately try to move resources, political power, and political participation toward the lower-income, disadvantaged populations of their cities. Where the work of most city planners is rarely consciously redistributive, equity planners often understand the potential contribution of planners in broad economic and social terms and try to provide for a downward redistribution of resources and political participation to create a more just and democratic society.

This approach has been documented in a number of American cities including Chicago, Cleveland, Jersey City, Santa Monica, and others, where planners have pressed for regional low-income housing schemes, increased mobility for those without cars, broadened citizen participation, rent control, linkage arrangements, and other programs designed to aid lower-income residents. Minority or liberal mayors are more likely to provide equity planners with essential support, but progressive planning ideas have also been implemented under more conservative political leadership (Krumholz and Clavel 1994).

It should be noted, though, that these progressive ideas are often difficult to implement. A scheme to distribute low-income housing on a "fair share" basis across a region, for example, counters long-established policies deliberately designed to concentrate low-income households, especially minority ones, in poor inner-city neighborhoods by excluding them from most other neighborhoods through zoning and building codes.

This is not to suggest that urban planners, no matter how expert their practice, can reverse industrial decline or change the political economy of their cities. Only broad social and political movements can accomplish that. But urban planners can make a substantial difference to the quality of life of their cities if they focus less on large-scale downtown redevelopment projects like convention centers, stadiums, and the like than on fixing the basics—safe streets, good schools, competitive taxes, efficient services—and give highest priority to improving the lives of the poor and near-poor residents who make up a larger and larger proportion of their population. This is not a radical proposal; it is simply providing appropriate service in keeping with the reality of conditions in the city and the inherently exploitative nature of the American metropolitan development process, which sorts out people by economic class and consigns the poorest and the darkest to the central city or first-ring suburbs. Such a proposal is also in accordance with the aspirations of the code of ethics of the American Planning Association and the American Institute of Certified Planners. On a more pragmatic level, it is acceptance of the fact that until the social and economic problems of the poor are abated, older industrial cities are unlikely to attract much new private investment.

A work program for an equity planning agency assumes that the agency will broaden its activities beyond zoning, land use planning, and urban design; use the full range of the training and talents of its staff; and become a more important and visible operator in local affairs. Planners, bolstered by planning legislation and their ability to set agenda, frame issues, and initiate public discourse, already have a substantial amount of power that can be expanded in the future.

Moreover, planners have certain advantages that they can call on to expand their influence. First, as Alan Altshuler (1965) has pointed out, planning is an extreme example of administrative discretion. There is no national planning, little mandated state planning, and little uniformity of planning practice in the United States by law or custom; within limits, planners can design their own work programs. Second, because they have a responsibility to prepare general land use plans and support capital improvement programs, planners are sitting on top of more data and information (most of which now goes unused) than anyone else in local government. Third, many planners, particularly the younger ones, are well-versed in powerful computer and geographic information systems (GIS) techniques. Finally, more than other participants in local government, planners think comprehensively and are endowed by their training with a greater ability to see the relationships among programs and quantify the costs and benefits of alternative programs.

Having access to all this information and placing the data in a cogent analysis should convey increased political power to the hands of the planning officials. As this expertise grows, mayors and city managers will begin turning to their planners as key advisors on nearly all government activities and resource uses. For some planners, this opportunity for greater responsibility and status will go unnoticed and unexploited; they will decline to assume the risks involved. For bolder planners ready to seize these opportunities and the institutional openings offered, the change in importance will project them into the highest rank of responsibility in government and administration. Unfortunately, it will also make planners much more vulnerable when administrations change. (A challenge for professors who teach planners will be how to change risk avoiders into bolder risk takers.)

There are ample opportunities for bold city planners to expand their role in local government. The bureaucratic structure of local government that looks like a monolith to those outside is, in fact, a good deal more porous than generally imagined. Broad areas of public policy exist often outside the domain of any specific agency, and other areas of responsibility are handled casually by agencies that would prefer not to deal with them. An activist planning agency with objectives, competence, and willingness to seize opportunities for greater responsibility can take on new roles, become recognized as the city's expert on certain issues, and influence both politicians and the policies of other city agencies.

Experience-Based Proposals
for Equity-Oriented Planning Practitioners

Equity-oriented roles for planners can be classified into five categories: (1) imposition of restraints, (2) creative investment proposals, (3) policies for constructive shrinkage, (4) strengthening of community organizations, and (5) regional collaboration. In many respects, most of these activities are more closely related to planning-based management than to traditional notions of long-range, comprehensive land use planning.

Imposition of Equity-Oriented Restrictions

The first category is the imposition of restraints. In most cities, hardly a month goes by without headlines proclaiming a new scheme to "turn the city around." Some of these schemes amount to little more than large-scale construction projects—a mall, a stadium, a convention center. Others involve proposals for major residential, commercial, or industrial development. All promise to attract jobs and people back to the city; all demand a massive commitment of public subsidies before construction. But all these proposals will also come before planners for evaluation and approval. When planners review these proposals, they should ask three overriding questions:

- What is being produced?
- For whose benefit?
- At whose cost?

In those cases where analysis indicates that the public costs will likely outweigh the public benefits or where the benefits are likely to accrue to those least in need of public support, planners should reject the proposal outright, modify the proposal to make it more suitable, or publicly question the proposal and attempt to engage the public and politicians in mutual learning. If what is being proposed is a sports stadium, for example, planners can frame the issue not as it is usually framed—build the stadium or lose the team—but as a series of questions: How will the subsidies for the stadium proposal affect the city's ability to provide basic services? How will they affect the capital investments needed in city neighborhoods? How will they affect the city's bond rating? Such questions, based on analysis that has been practically and ethically thought through, may provide important information to the public at large and may strengthen the hand of sympathetic politicians and lead to a more successful negotiation.

Indeed, sports stadiums provide a substantial example of public funds being used for nonproductive purposes. From 1989 to 2003, American cities built 20 new stadiums for football, 18 new stadiums for baseball, and 26 new arenas for basketball or ice hockey, at an estimated cost of $20 to $25 billion. One wonders how cities, counties, and states can justify throwing money at sports teams, which, after all, are successful private enterprises, earning large returns for their owners. Their proponents allege that stadiums are important vehicles for economic development, but planners could point out that careful research makes clear that these facilities rarely meet their inflated expectations (Euchner 1993; Rosentraub 1997).

If sports stadiums must be built, planners could be arguing with team owners for a better deal on cost-sharing, pointing out that the public's share of the 18 new baseball stadiums constructed from 1989 to 2003 has ranged from 5 percent (San Francisco) to 100 percent (Baltimore and Chicago). The 20 new stadiums for professional football offer similar distributions, from zero (Carolina and New England) to 100 percent (Tampa Bay, St. Louis, Tennessee, Buffalo, and Atlanta) (Sandy, Sloan, and Rosentraub 2004). In the interests of greater equity, planners can argue that owners should pick up most of the construction costs for new stadiums that benefit their interests.

If cities and their planners must yield and provide what seem to be inappropriate subsidies for sports stadiums and other megaprojects in which public support is involved, they can argue for linkage deals or Community Benefits Agreements (CBAs). In a linkage deal, the subsidies or special rights granted by the city are offset by special contributions by developers for neighborhood investments, low-income housing, child care, public transportation, or job training (Keating 1986). CBAs are similar to linkage arrangements. They are legally binding, documented bargains between the developer, the city, unions, and often community groups that ensure, as a condition of development, the provision by the developer of affordable housing, educational initiatives, job training, and jobs for minorities and women (Wolf-Powers 2010).

Signatories to CBAs are generally neighborhood-based organizations from the neighborhood affected by the development and city officials. Planners are more likely now than in the past to work with project developers as the pattern of public-private co-investment has become the norm in American urban development. As of 2009, there were 27 CBAs in effect and nine ongoing negotiations that had not yet resulted in agreements (Levine 2009). Reflecting real estate market conditions, only three of the CBA agreements are in older industrial cities. Given the tragic legacy of Title I Urban Renewal in inner-city neighborhoods, planners have the particular responsibility to ensure that inner-city residents gain jobs, job training, affordable housing, and other economic opportunities through CBAs and similar public-private investments. If developers offer little in return for public subsidies or special privileges, planners and other officials should try to re-frame the project or argue against it.

Developing Proposals for Creative Investments

Arguing against the commitment of resources to projects that offer few returns implies that there are more productive investments that the city should be making. That leads to the second category: developing creative investment proposals.

In this category of activities, planners can seek opportunities to direct the city's resources toward programs and projects that will result in long-term savings, make existing systems work more efficiently, or direct private resources toward the fulfillment of public objectives. They can also try to improve the operations of other public or private agencies that lack internal planning capability. In addition, planners can take part in efforts to insist that commercial banks and savings and loans make loans in poor neighborhoods and maintain regular branches there to provide banking services at lower rates than same-day lending and check-cashing businesses. They can also try to improve management of local government functions.

Two young planners accomplished such management reform by over-hauling Cleveland's Capital Improvement Program (CIP) in the early 1980s. During the 1970s and earlier, Cleveland's CIP, assigned by charter to the City Planning Commission, was scorned as a bad joke because of a chronic short-age of city funds and intensely political competition for available resources. As a result, the city's roads, bridges, and public buildings fell into disrepair. The city's default on its fiscal obligations in 1978 seemed to cap the infrastruc-ture problems; there was no comprehensive strategy for capital spending and, in a bankrupt city, no money to spend in any event. Yet, during the 1980s, with support from the administration, the business community, and the in-novations of a small group of dedicated and bold urban planners, the CIP was restructured, existing resources heavily leveraged, and hundreds of mil-lions of dollars systematically invested in public infrastructure with highly visible results (Hoffmann and Krumholz 2000).

Another example of creative investment is the Cleveland Land Bank, which emerged as a response to widespread tax delinquency and property abandonment of inner-city land. Cleveland's planners executed a detailed study that measured the extent of the problem in 1972 (Olson and Lachmann 1976). Then the planners helped draft a new state law modeled on a similar law in the state of Missouri and organized a successful lobbying effort with the Ohio General Assembly to pass the law. Once passed, the new law short-ened and streamlined the foreclosure procedure dealing with tax-delinquent land and enabled Ohio cities to set up land banks to receive such parcels, clear their titles and liens, and dispose of the land for reuse. From 1976, when the new bill was signed into law, until 2000, the Cleveland Land Bank ac-quired, cleared, and sold more than 8,000 parcels and returned most of them to productive use by individuals and community development corporations. As many of Cleveland's community development corporations will attest, parcels from the land bank have become essential building blocks in neigh-borhood revitalization efforts (Linner 1977; Bright 2000; Dewar 2006).

Although helpful for recovering and redeveloping abandoned parcels, these local efforts to manage tax-delinquent and abandoned land have not been enough to counteract the huge subprime mortgage disaster. By 2008, Cleveland neighborhood developers, funding sources, and city of-ficials were becoming aware that predatory lending, Wall Street greed, and fraudulent home financing were undermining their neighborhood revital-ization programs and causing damage that will probably take decades to correct. Thousands of mortgages were failing in inner-city neighborhoods, foreclosures were increasing, and abandonment was spreading to the sub-urbs. By 2008, many Ohio counties were fighting for state legislation that would establish countywide land banks with authority to manage the sub-prime mortgage crisis (Lind 2008).

Equity planners can also become involved in more contemporary social justice issues by participating in attempts to raise the incomes of workers in their communities. This can be done by providing support for local living wage ordinances and by trying to make sure that all eligible workers in their communities file for the Earned Income Tax Credit.

Two points should be clear from these examples. First, the proposals for ways the city should invest its resources are very modest and in many ways not as politically appealing as the big real estate proposals they seek to re-strain. They do not promise to transform the city completely. Rather, they promise only to help the city program and invest its resources in meaningful ways. Second, efforts to influence the investment of the city's resources in-volve time-consuming commitments and political participation by the plan-ners. The cases make clear that it is *not* enough for planners to present their findings to the planning commission, to articulate broad policy statements, to run regressions, prepare studies, or testify at budget hearings, and then stop. Much more is needed. It is essential to set up coalitions with other in-terested participants and work closely over long periods with other public and private entities to develop and help implement very specific program and project ideas. Ends and means interact: if planners are truly interested in beneficial outcomes and better futures for their cities (and what else is urban planning all about?), they must be prepared for protracted participation and some political risk.

Promoting Policies for Constructive Shrinkage

The third category, policies for constructive shrinkage, involves recognition of the fact that as the population and economic base of a city decline, the city may have to divest itself of certain responsibilities. Planners can play an active role in negotiating the terms and conditions under which the city can trans-fer some of its facilities to higher levels of government that can then draw on a broader base for their tax and political support. However, before engaging in such transfers, the city should obtain guarantees of improved service for its residents—especially those city residents who are most vulnerable.

In Cleveland, as an example, city planners worked over a five-year period with other local, county, and state officials to transfer the city's transit system to a regional transit authority (RTA). But RTA was set up only after the city got guarantees of better service and lower fares for its elderly and those riders who depend on RTA for their entire mobility around the metropolitan area. The planners also led successful efforts to lease Cleveland's three lakefront parks to the state of Ohio (Krumholz and Forester 1990). The effort resulted in the state's spending approximately $50 million from 1980 to 2000 in capital improvements and another $40 million on maintenance and staffing. These formerly neglected and underfunded city parks are now the finest, most popular parks in the state park system.

Strengthening Neighborhood-Based Community Development Corporations (CDCs)

My fourth category of useful things planners can do to improve the quality of life in their cities is strengthening neighborhood-based community organizations. CDCs are grassroots nonprofit groups that sponsor and promote housing, commercial development, and neighborhood revitalization in lower-class, inner-city neighborhoods. Why are these groups natural allies for urban planners interested in greater equity? The answer is simple. They often speak for the poor, provide a countervailing political force to the constant demands by downtown interests for capital improvements, and, through their advocacy, may have a major, long-term beneficial impact on efficient delivery of public services to the city's neighborhoods.

Given the many constraints in their operations, CDCs have been quite successful. According to a 2005 report, there are about 4,600 CDCs in American cities, and since 1980, they have developed more than 1.2 million housing units and 125 million square feet of commercial and industrial space (National Congress for Community Economic Development 2005). At present, CDCs are the core of the below-market housing system in the United States (Vidal 1995; Bratt 2006).

Their advocacy for inner-city neighborhoods has also been important and has produced important results. Noting the success of the Community Reinvestment Act (CRA) in encouraging bank lending in urban neighborhoods, Grogan and Proscio (2000) comment, "Not only have community based organizations found it easier to line-up financing and equity investments for their projects, but millions of individual borrowers and home buyers have found credit where for decades there had been only rejections." CRA has generated over $1 trillion in 390 CRA agreements between CDCs and lenders (Squires 2003). Both CRA and its companion legislation, the Home Mortgage Disclosure Act, are direct results of the anti-redlining and anti-predatory lending activities carried out by CDCs in the 1960s and 1970s.

CDCs build projects in sections of old industrial cities marked by abandoned and contaminated properties. These areas hold little interest for profit-seeking private developers. CDCs remain committed to their neighborhoods because their boards are made up of area residents and business people. They lobby continually for their areas and execute residential and commercial projects that improve their neighborhoods while encouraging still remaining residents. Their work can demonstrate that projects are financially viable and create markets for other developments, executed by other agencies, that might not have taken place otherwise. In some cities, official planning agencies in city hall assign their planners to neighborhoods to work on planning projects and land use changes with the CDCs. The resulting plans are then folded into the city's official long-range comprehensive plan. This often results in an easy back-and-forth between official planners and neighborhood development professionals. Sometimes, through direct contact with the most disadvantaged populations, official planners form bonds with them, adding to the pressure for progressive change from within the city administration.

At the local level, this interaction and cooperation can be extremely effective as indicated by the experience of the Cleveland Housing Network (CHN). CHN was formed as an intermediary in 1981 by six CDCs with staff assistance from a group of city planners at Cleveland State University. Its mission was to develop affordable housing for the low- and moderate-income residents of Cleveland, stabilize neighborhoods, promote neighborhood-controlled development, and create assets for poor families. At present, CHN has 15 affiliated CDCs whose territories cover most of the city. CHN directs fund raising and coordinates affordable housing production among its members. It also functions as a developer in arranging financing and partners with the CDCs in deciding which projects to undertake. After construction is completed, CHN manages the properties.

As of 2006, CHN had produced 2,400 lease purchase homes for very low-income families, 1,350 for-sale homes, and 71,000 energy conservation jobs (CHN 2007). It has also developed hundreds of units of permanently supportive housing for the homeless. Ninety percent of the lease purchase households took title at advantageous prices after expiration of the fifteen-year lease. In response to Cleveland's foreclosure crisis and the collapse of financial markets, the organization has adjusted quickly, cutting back or dropping non-productive projects, developing new programs, finding new partners and sources of support like the Cleveland Housing Authority, state and federal energy programs, and the community college, and continuing to package highly complex financial deals. CHN employs a staff of 105 with a high level of skills in affordable housing production and housing management, and successfully manages an annual budget of about $60 million.

Cleveland's CDCs have enjoyed the support of banks and the philanthropic community, but their most important source of support is the city of Cleveland, which has supplied a steady stream of funding through the Community Development Block Grant (CDBG). Each council member (all of whom are elected by ward) is allocated about $400,000 per year from the CDBG. Most of them give significant amounts of their allocation to the CDCs in their own wards for housing and neighborhood improvement. This funding, which amounts to about $200,000 per year per CDC, and other support from the city's community development department, means that about 25 percent of the city's CDBG allocation goes to nonprofit developers for expenses, including operating costs. This arrangement raises questions about CDC independence, but it assures stable staffing and program continuity and helps produce a cadre of highly competent housing professionals, some of whom now occupy important positions in local intermediaries and the city planning and development departments.

CDCs in American cities represent a new institutional force that, in many cities, was nurtured into being by urban planners. Although still evolving, this force has an unusual combination of entrepreneurial, management, and political skills and the perseverance to carry forward their programs. It deserves the wholehearted support of urban planners interested in more equitable futures for their cities. It is possible that CDCs will provide the leadership, not only to rebuild the housing stock of troubled neighborhoods, but to also rebuild the shattered social and economic infrastructure of declining communities (Krumholz 1997).

Regional Collaboration

My final recommendation for equity planners is to work toward regional collaboration. In this struggle for regional equity, planners should promote four strategies: (1) manage regional growth and investment to restrict suburban sprawl; (2) require "fair-share" affordable housing in the suburbs;

(3) use federal programs in transportation to connect inner-city poor to sub-urban opportunities; and (4) link regional economic development programs to anti-poverty goals. The issue of urban sprawl, which has recently ener-gized many planners, involves much more than the loss of green space and farmland or increased air and water pollution; it involves significant issues of equity. The way we sprawl traps the minority poor in obsolete inner-city and first-ring suburban neighborhoods and prevents most low-income city residents from gaining access to the better housing, jobs, and schools in the suburbs. This is the result of local zoning regulations, government policies, and market forces (Jackson, 2000). Suburbs are not interested in opening their borders to low-income housing. Even if they were, they could not do so without major federal housing subsidies that are now in short supply. As a result, whole regions of many metropolitan areas in the United States are barred to most low-income families (Rusk 1999; Downs 1994)

The worst result of this economic segregation or sorting out of economic classes is our continuing failure to provide a decent education to millions of young students. At this moment more than 25 percent of all U.S. children under sixteen are black or Hispanic. Most come from low-income families, and most go to school in big-city systems that provide very low-quality edu-cation. Without the opportunity for education, these children will find it very difficult to rise above their circumstances. Their lack of proper education blights their young lives and threatens America's future standard of living; in a global economy they will be unable to compete with better-educated chil-dren from other countries.

The present system of economic segregation and sprawl is fundamentally unfair and undemocratic. Decentralization of islands of concentrated pov-erty and relocation of their occupants to affordable housing in better envi-ronments should produce many benefits including access to better jobs and schools (Downs 1973). Elsewhere in this book, Vale and Keating both discuss the possibilities and problems of Hope VI. Here it is sufficient to note that urban planners have been working toward regional solutions to concentrated poverty since the passage of the 1968 Open Housing Act. The cities of Dayton, Chicago, San Francisco, and Washington, D.C., conducted brief experiments with regional fair-share, low-income housing schemes in the 1970s (Keating 1997). However, HUD withdrew its support for the program, and fair-share housing became a local initiative and survives almost nowhere, beaten back by the political power of suburban jurisdictions.

A second phase of efforts to deconcentrate poverty began with the 1974

Housing Act, which began the movement away from traditional "hard" public housing units owned and operated by a local housing authority and contained a tenant-based rent certificate called Section 8 to help pay rent for
private units within a local jurisdiction. This was followed in 1983, when
Congress broadened the geographic area where rent-supplement housing
vouchers could be used, and in 1998, when Congress merged the Section
8 and Voucher programs into what are now known as Housing Choice
Vouchers. A third phase of deconcentration was undertaken in the 1992
Moving to Opportunity (MTO) program in five demonstration cities: New
York, Los Angeles, Chicago, Boston, and Baltimore. Ultimately, under pressure from suburbs, funding for MTO was restricted by Congress.

In the past, urban planners actually contributed to economic and racial
segregation through large-lot zoning laws, restrictions on the construction
of multi-family apartments, and other regulatory devices (Pendall 2000).
Instead, planners must work with many others to tear down restrictive racial
walls and redirect public investment in infrastructure, housing, and schools
away from exclusion and toward collaboration. They should never use zoning
or other land use regulations for discriminatory purposes.

Planners must try to ensure that growth management and affordable
housing do not conflict. When properly implemented through increasing
residential densities, mixing uses and housing types, and implementing inclusionary zoning schemes within the region, growth management can improve housing affordability, preserve open space, and lower transportation
and energy costs (Nelson et al. 2004).

Concluding Comments:
The Future of Older Industrial Cities in the United States

Most of these recommendations for effectively planning America's older,
industrial cities may strike some as modest, not the kind of visionary proposals—the gleaming new towers in the park-like setting, the megablocks
of architectural innovations—that citizens are accustomed to hearing from
urban planners. In fact, the whole idea of aging and shrinking strikes some
people as an admission of defeat. This is to be expected in a society that is
preoccupied with newness and youth as is the case in the United States.
However, the aging analogy cannot be carried to its ultimate conclusion. No
city is going to disappear from the map. Older industrial cities may be smaller

in the future; they may look somewhat different; but they will still be places where major museums and other cultural venues exist along with hospitals and institutions of higher education, where important things are happening and hundreds of thousands of people work and live. The question for urban planners is How can we help make the best of our situation?

America's older industrial cities need not be less desirable places to live than our rapidly growing cities. If growth were an unqualified blessing, there would not be so many people opposing it in various parts of the country. And, of course, if politicians and planners are successful in the modest tasks I have set out, our cities will be run more competently, public services will improve, and our neighborhoods will become more desirable residential locations and so better able to compete with other locations in our regions.

While decline does present huge problems—the difficulty of matching municipal revenues with expenditures, the thinning out and abandonment of parts of the inner city, the reduction in economic opportunities for disadvantaged groups—all of them can be addressed and mitigated through wise public policy if we have the vision and political will.

Neither planners nor politicians should fall into either of two opposite traps concerning the future of older industrial central cities. One is the trap of hopelessness, giving up because the city seems to be declining in so many ways, as giving up creates its own tragic fulfillment.

The other trap is pretending there are easy and glitzy solutions by accepting some comfortable delusion that glosses over the reality of the situation. Cities cannot go back to the past, nor can they expect the federal government to bail them out. There are no grand and simple solutions, and pretending there are no serious problems is one means of never improving anything.

References

AICP. 2005. Code of ethics and professional conduct. http://www.planning.org/ethics/ethicscode.htm, accessed 7 July 2010.

AICP/APA. 1991. *Code of ethics and professional conduct*, Section A, 5. Chicago: American Planning Association.

APA. 1994. *Planning and community equity.* Chicago: APA Planning Press.

Altshuler, Alan. 1965. *The city planning process: A political analysis*. Chicago: University of Chicago Press.

Bratt, Rachel G. 2006. Community development corporations: Challenges in supporting a right to housing. In *A right to housing: Foundations for new social agenda*, ed. Rachel G. Bratt, Michael E. Stone, and Chester Hartman, 340–60. Philadelphia: Temple University Press.

Briggs, Xavier de Souza, ed. 2005. *The geography of opportunity: Race and housing choice in metropolitan America*, 318–41. Washington, D.C.: Brookings Institution.

Bright, Elise M. 2000. *Reviving America's forgotten neighborhoods*, 139–56. New York: Garland.

Cleveland Housing Network. 2007. Annual report. Cleveland: Cleveland Housing Network.

Dewar, Margaret. 2006. Selling tax-reverted land in cities: Lessons from Cleveland and Detroit. *Journal of the American Planning Association* 72(2): 167–80.

Downs, Anthony. 1973. *Opening up the suburbs: An urban strategy for America*. New Haven, Conn.: Yale University Press.

———. 1997. *New visions for metropolitan America*, 95–120. Washington, D.C.: Brookings Institution.

Euchner, Charles. 1993. *Playing the field: Why sports teams move and cities fight to keep them*. Baltimore: Johns Hopkins University Press.

Grogan, Paul, and Tony Proscio. 2000. *Comeback cities: A blueprint for urban neighborhood revival*. Boulder, Colo.: Westview Press.

Hayden, Delores. 1976. *Seven American Utopias*, 300–301. Cambridge, Mass.: MIT Press.

Hoffmann, Susan, and Norman Krumholz, with Kevin O'Brien and Billie Geyer. 2000. How capital budgeting helped a sick city: Thirty years of capital improvement planning in Cleveland. *Public Budgeting and Finance* 20(1) (Spring): 24–37.

Jackson, Kenneth, T. 2000. Gentleman's agreement: Discrimination in metropolitan America. In *Reflections on Regionalism*, ed. Bruce Katz, 185–217. Washington, D.C.: Brookings Institution.

Keating, W. Dennis. 1986. Linking downtown development to broader community goals: An analysis of three cities. *Journal of the American Planning Association* 52(2) (Spring): 133–41.

———. 1997. *The suburban racial dilemma: Housing and neighborhoods*. Philadelphia: Temple University Press.

Krumholz, Norman. 1997. The provision of affordable housing in Cleveland: Patterns of organizational and financial support. In *Affordable housing and urban redevelopment in the United States*, ed. Willem van Vliet, 52–72. Thousand Oaks, Calif.: Sage.

Krumholz, Norman, and Pierre Clavel. 1994. *Reinventing cities: Equity planners tell their stories*. Philadelphia: Temple University Press.

Krumholz, Norman, and John Forester. 1990. *Making equity planning work: Leadership in the public sector*. Philadelphia: Temple University Press.

Levine, Amy. 2009. Community benefits agreements. http://www.communitybenefits. blogspot.com, accessed 19 October 2009.

Lind, Kermit J. 2008. The perfect storm: An eyewitness report from Ground Zero in Cleveland's neighborhoods. *Journal of Affordable Housing & Community Development Law* 17: 237–58.

Linner, John. 1977. Cleveland is banking tax delinquent land. *Practicing Planner* 7(2).

Logan, John R., and Harvey L. Molotch. 1988. *Urban fortunes*. Berkeley: University of California Press.

National Congress for Community Economic Development. 2005. *Reaching new heights*. Washington, D.C.: NCCED.

Nelson, Arthur C., Rolf Pendall, Casey J. Dawkins, and Gerrit J. Knapp. 2004. The link between growth management and housing affordability: The academic evidence. In *Growth management and affordable housing: Do they conflict?* ed. Anthony Downs, 117–58. Washington, D.C.: Brookings Institution.

Olson, Susan, and Leanne Lachmann. 1976. *Tax delinquency in the inner city*. Lexington, Mass.: Lexington Books.

Pendall, Rolf. 2000. Local land use regulations and the chain of exclusion. *Journal of the American Planning Association* 66(2): 125–42.

Rosentraub, Mark S. 1997. *Major league losers: The real costs of professional sports and who's paying for it*. New York: Basic Books.

Rusk, David. 1999. *Inside game/outside game: Winning strategies for saving urban America*, 178–200. Washington, D.C.: Brookings Institution.

Sandy, Robert, Peter J. Sloane, and Mark S. Rosentraub. 2004. *The economics of sport*. London: Palgrave Macmillan.

Scott, Mel. 1995. *American city planning since 1890*. Chicago: APA Planners Press.

Squires, Gregory D, ed. 2003. *Organizing access to capital: Advocacy and the democratization of financial institutions*. Philadelphia: Temple University Press.

Vey, Jennifer S. 2007. *Restoring prosperity: The state role in revitalizing America's older cities*. Washington, D.C.: Brookings Institution.

Vidal, Avis C. 1995. Reintegrating disadvantaged communities into the fabric of urban life: The role of community development. *Housing Policy Debate* 6: 169–230.

Wilson, William Julius. 1987. *The truly disadvantaged: The inner city, the underclass, and public policy*. Chicago: University of Chicago Press.

Wolf-Powers, Laura. 2010. Community Benefits Agreements and local government. *Journal of the American Planning Association* 76(2): 141–59.

Chapter 7

Urban Transportation and Social Equity: Transportation-Planning Paradigms That Impede Policy Reform

Jonathan Levine

To the casual observer, transportation may seem to be an egalitarian aspect of metropolitan life. The vehicles of the wealthy travel in traffic jams at the same speed as those of the poor. An overcrowded rapid transit system leaves all passengers uncomfortable regardless of social class. But access to the means of transportation and to the destinations they connect is distributed highly unequally in cities of the developed and developing world—an inequality that affects nearly all aspects of the lives of people with limited ability to reach their destinations. This presents a particular challenge for equity-based planning. Views on social equity in general can be divided between an expansive view that focuses on equity in outcome, and a more constrained view that seeks to limit itself to equality of opportunity (Litman 2002). Under the former view, severe societal inequities are a problem per se; under the latter, they are a problem only to the extent that they stem from unequal opportunities. In the more constrained view, the planning approach to societal inequity is presumably the treatment of unequal opportunity as a root cause of unequal outcomes.

In this connection, transportation ought to be an especially promising venue for equity-based planning. This stems from the view that transportation, or movement, is not an end in itself, but only means to provide access to one's destinations. If access to destinations is a prerequisite for economic and social opportunity, then some level of equality in transportation would

easily fit both the more expansive and more constrained definitions of societal equity. Moreover, given the pervasive involvement of planning in the
transportation realm and the intimate connection with equality of opportunity, one might expect the practice of transportation planning and policy to
be a significant force for promotion of transportation equity, or at minimum
provision of an equitable baseline.

In many areas, transportation planning has lived up to this challenge.
Innovative polices have sought to expand poor people's access using a variety
of means, including public provision and expansion of markets; conventional
mass transit and innovative flexible services; and approaches based in technology, land use, and attention to the human dimension of social exclusion.
Exemplars of equitable transportation planning seem to be the exception,
however. In many regions worldwide, auto-oriented transportation planning
leaves the nondriving minority—or often majority—with ever-deteriorating
accessibility (Sanchez et al. 2003). Even public transit investment and pricing
structures frequently favor commutes by the affluent in both the developed
(Grengs 2005) and developing worlds (Laquian 2004).

Given these documented inequities, this essay considers the capacity of
transportation policy to reform itself for a more equitable practice. It argues
that three paradigms of transportation planning have impeded the equity
of its practice. The first is a focus on mobility as an end in itself, rather than
as one means to the greater purpose of accessibility. The second is an implicit equation of policy changes to the status quo with interventions into
the free market. In this framework, policy reform ostensibly hinges on
demonstration of market failure—even when the shifts considered are the
reform of existing exclusionary governmental practices. Finally, transportation planning has treated revealed willingness to pay as definitive evidence
of the value of a trip. This framework sheds little light on the role of transportation in the lives of the poor and even less on needs that are unmet in
the present.

Reform of these paradigms is not a sufficient condition for the improvement of transportation equity. To a great extent, transportation inequities
emerge from the imbalances of political power that inevitably find their expression in the planning process in general and the transportation planning
process in particular. But the three paradigms in combination constitute an
obstacle to the reform of transportation planning into a more equitable practice. Such reform will not rest on the improvement of the technical methods
that emerged from these worldviews; rather, fundamental reforms for a more

equitable transportation planning practice need to be grounded in a change in the worldviews themselves.

A search for those elements of the transportation planning process that have led to inequities differs from analyses of transportation equity that gauge the extent of inequity in land use and transportation systems and then conceive of possible planning responses. For example, Schweitzer and Valenzuela (2004: 392) write: "For practicing planners, the research on cost distribution raises questions about what, if anything, planning can do to address the local, regional, and global costs associated with transport in the United States." This latter approach conceives of a status quo that is not fundamentally shaped by planning; within that framework, the question of whether and how planning ought to intervene is a logical one. But if one conceives of a world in which planning is ubiquitous, then surely the inequities of transportation would have their roots partly in planning per se. In this world, the question becomes not whether planning ought to intervene—because it already has—but rather what are the elements of transportation planning practice that have exacerbated transportation inequities and impeded planning's capacity to overcome them?

The following sections consider the three paradigms: mobility versus accessibility; construction of free markets; and use of revealed willingness to pay. The final section interprets the arguments presented for transportation planning practice.

Mobility-Oriented Transportation Planning Practice

"An experienced Australian traveler once said that on business trips to Australian cities he could reckon to make four meetings in a day," writes Thomson (1977: 48). "In Europe he could manage five; in the United States he could manage only three." The reason behind the variations in this traveler's itineraries was not an American propensity for long meetings, or the speed of travel in American cities, which is in any case faster than in Western Europe or Australia (Kenworthy and Laube 2002). Instead, his schedules were determined by the great distances—and hence long travel times—separating his contacts in metropolitan areas of the United States. The speed at which he was able to travel was relatively unimportant; much more central was the amount of interaction he could accomplish in a given time.

This traveler was unwittingly expressing a view of transportation policy based in accessibility, in contrast to the mobility-centered view so dominantly reflected in current policy and in the physical form of the built environment in North American metropolitan areas and increasingly worldwide. Accessibility can be defined as the "ease of reaching destinations" (Hansen 1959; Handy and Niemeier 1997; Kwok and Yeh 2004), as opposed to mobility, the "ease of movement." Where destinations are nearby, high accessibility can be provided even with low mobility (as the Australian business traveler found in the compact cities of Europe); conversely, where origins and destinations are spread broadly, even great mobility does not ensure high accessibility.

The primacy of accessibility stems directly from the understanding of transportation demand as derived from the demand to reach destinations. If reaching destinations (or more broadly, filling needs) is the goal, then movement must be seen as one *means* to reach that goal, but not the only one. Where one's destinations are nearby, one can reach them without much movement; hence proximity is another means toward the ends of accessibility. And with rapidly expanding digital technology, remote connectivity is a third means to improve accessibility (Kenyon et al. 2002). The three means—mobility, proximity, and connectivity—interact in important ways. For example, high levels of connectivity—e.g., broadband Internet access—can be difficult to provide in areas of low population density and hence low proximity (Stenberg et al. 2009). The relationship between proximity and mobility is somewhat more complex: in areas where travel origins and destinations are near each other, travel tends to be slow; in areas of rapid surface travel, origins and destinations tend to be farther apart. In this way, a tension exists between mobility and proximity in generating accessibility: more mobile areas are not necessarily more accessible, because of the intervening variable of distance. It may be that in some areas of rapid travel, distances between origins and destinations are so great that accessibility is degraded.

Notwithstanding the understanding of the derived nature of travel demand, the transportation professions in the United States and elsewhere have frequently understood their mission as facilitating mobility, or even automobilty. This is reflected in most conventional measures to evaluate transportation outcomes. For example, the *Highway Capacity Manual* (Transportation Research Board 2000) defines the concept "Level of Service" as a function of the freedom of a stretch of roadway from congestion. The Texas Transportation Institute compares transportation outcomes between metropolitan regions in the United States with its Annual Mobility Study, which focuses on roadway delay per capita, or dollar value wasted while stuck in traffic (Schrank and Lomax 2007). Standard transportation planning methodology seeks to forecast future traffic volumes in order to size transportation links accordingly—informed by the view that the proper function of the transportation planning field is the facilitation of unimpeded movement.

In a policy environment in which movement is treated as an end and not as a means, it is not surprising that even transportation equity is analyzed in this light. This issue applies in much of both the developed and developing world. For example, South Africa suffers from continuing segregated patterns of living, as a legacy from the apartheid era in which Blacks most commonly resided in townships remote from the urban job centers. In the apartheid era this exclusion necessitated lengthy commutes, a pattern that persists to this day, as new low-cost housing is located far from existing urban centers and transportation infrastructure (Vanderschuren 2003). Yet methods of transportation analysis in that country remain drawn from American models rooted in the problem of developing and sizing freeways (Behrens 2004). Even a move to "customer-based" passenger transport in the post-apartheid era still focused dominantly on the issue of moving workers from peripheral townships to employment centers, largely neglecting other approaches to improving access. A recent analysis of the equity of South Africa's current transportation policies focuses on its effort in "access management" (Page 2003). This tool is a set of policies designed to limit the number of intersections and curb cuts onto a roadway with the concept of maintaining regular and safe traffic flow.

One way these approaches systematically underrepresent the transportation needs of the poor is by focusing on peak-period travel under the implicit assumption that this is the time of the greatest transportation challenges (Behrens 2004). This view comes from a congestion mitigation paradigm under which travel in uncongested periods is relatively problem free—a view that applies particularly poorly to people without cars (Behrens 2004). In the environment of post-apartheid South Africa with its continuing legacy of residential segregation, a transportation equity perspective might analyze the various dimensions of access. For example, it might research obstacles to proximity in the form of continuing barriers that lower-income Black populations face in locating closer to urban job centers. It might examine policies and investments that can assist these populations in overcoming these great distances to give them access to work and other destinations. It might view transportation to overcome the great travel distances that are the legacy of the apartheid regime as a pragmatic "second best" solution to allow people to improve their lives in the face of continuing market and policy obstacles to closer-in living. It might consider the possibility of remote connectivity as a means to augment their access (Kenyon and Rafferty 2002). But where traffic movement per se is seen as the proper end of transportation policy, questions of transportation equity will focus on the fairness or lack of fairness of more narrowly circumscribed traffic management policies.

The tension between movement-based solutions and proximity-based solutions to transportation equity problems is evident in the United States as well. U.S. suburbs are notable for enacting policies to restrict development densities, often in response to local home-owning constituencies determined to preserve the low-density, land use separated environments to which they have become accustomed. Where these municipalities are also important job centers, significant spatial separation between jobs and housing arise, since the capacity of people employed locally to make commute-reducing residential choices is constrained (Cervero 1996; Levine 2006). In this environment, mobility is an approach to overcoming the inequities in accessibility generated by poor proximity. It has been said that the U.S. affordable housing policy is "drive until you qualify" (Leinberger 2008): that is, where exclusionary regulations limit the supply of close-in affordable housing, people find housing sufficiently far from their destinations that the lower prices allow them to qualify for a mortgage. Clearly, this approach is relevant only to the share of the population that can afford to own and operate private vehicles over great distances. In this environment, the transportation planner's focus on movement as the solution is comfortable because it avoids challenging the exclusionary status quo even as it seeks to make it functional by providing a certain level of mobility-based access. But several notable failings are associated with this solution. First are the evident external costs of congestion, pollution, global warming, and traffic accidents. In addition, people who make these locational decisions bear the internal costs of excess time spent in travel. Finally, a definition of the problem as inherently one of equitable movement short-circuits the policy debate and limits potential avenues of accessibility enhancement, notably the reduction of exclusionary barriers that prevent close-in living.

This is illustrated well in the debate over spatial mismatch in the United States. Standard analyses of the employment impact of separation between urban minority populations and suburban job centers effectively seek to model the effect of distance on job outcomes (Ihlanfeldt and Sjoquist 1998).

Yet the effects of center city job loss go well beyond the simple variables of proximity and mobility, and enter the range of cultural transformations that deprive people of the ability to seek and hold jobs (Wilson 1996). This suggests an approach to accessibility that would transcend a narrow focus on mobility—or even mobility plus proximity—to reach into the multidimensional barriers that exclude people from full participation in society. This broad view of accessibility is at the heart of an emerging approach in Europe termed "social exclusion" (Hine and Mitchell 2001). "Social exclusion" was a term-of-art of French social policy in the 1980s and later spread throughout much of Europe (Gaffron et al. 2001). Sanchez et al. (2003: 10) write: "The British effort to combat 'social exclusion' is a more wide-ranging approach than the American battle against spatial mismatch. Efforts to eradicate social exclusion address communities that are isolated from or marginalized by general society." The British government defines social exclusion as "a shorthand term for what can happen when people or areas suffer from a combination of linked problems such as unemployment, poor skills, low incomes, poor housing, high crime, bad health and family breakdown." That mobility is only part of the answer is inherent to this school of thought: "too often access to services has been seen as merely a transport issue rather than one that can be solved by, for example, better land use planning, or through policies to enable safer streets and stations" (Social Exclusion Unit 2003: 40, reported in Farrington and Farrington 2005). But still, in a range of contexts worldwide, mobility-based problem definitions remain politically attractive because of their capacity to obscure more fundamental and vexing societal problems.

Construction of Free Market in Transportation and Land Use Planning

The second reform-impeding element of transportation planning tradition—the construction of a free market in transportation and land use planning—is intimately related to the first. This phenomenon is most apparent in the United States where two elements of the planning environment are especially salient: a relatively strong ideological preference for market or market-like approaches to public problems and a decentralized approach to land use planning deferential to municipal regulatory prerogative. In many circumstances decentralization policies are associated with market-based approaches to societal ordering. But the two can be on a collision course when

decentralized planning seeks to exclude market-driven denser and more accessible development in close-in suburban municipalities. Transportation
and land use analysis in the United States frequently seeks to resolve this tension by implicitly treating the highly regulated status quo as a more-or-less
free market.

Planners informed by a public economics tradition are taught to look for
evidence of significant market failures as a basis for their intervention into
the marketplace. Thus, zoning is often justified by the externalities that one
land use can impose on its neighbor, open space provision by its presumed
"public goods" nature, or reporting and disclosure requirements by imper-
fect information. Under this formulation, market ordering (as opposed to
direct public provision or regulation) becomes a default state of affairs, or the
way things are done in absence of a reasonably conclusive demonstration of a
market failure of significant magnitude. No area of planning has in principle
adopted this framework more than transportation planning, as a professional
area steeped in the economics tradition.

One expression of this is the nearly four-decade search for the travel
behavior impact of different land use patterns. Starting with Lansing et al.
(1970), researchers have scrutinized the extent of walking, transit use, driving, and cycling in ranges of urban settings, with an eye toward potential
land use policy approaches to mitigate transportation problems. On the one
hand, travel patterns differ significantly between areas, with more central,
dense, and mixed use neighborhoods generally demonstrating less automotive travel and greater transit and nonmotorized travel per capita. But as
numerous researchers have noted (and sought to control for), observed differences in travel behavior may be a function of demographics and neighborhood self-selection, rather than a pure neighborhood-design effect. Thus,
if dense neighborhoods exhibit fewer vehicle kilometers traveled per capita,
this may be a product of the presence there of (for example) lower-income
people, who tend to drive less overall, rather than a direct influence of urban
design on travel behavior. Even more complex, observed differences in travel
behavior between pedestrian- and auto-oriented neighborhoods may be a
product of neighborhood self-selection unaccounted for in the measured
variables.

The result of this long search has been largely indeterminacy and controversy, with numerous authors reporting significant effects of urban form on
travel behavior (e.g., Ewing and Cervero 2001; Frank and Engelke 2001) and
others finding more modest effects (e.g., Boarnet and Crane 2001; Kitamura

et al. 1997), or attributing observed effects to self-selection. Yet the sides of this controversy seem to be in agreement about the policy implications of potential findings: significant travel behavior impact would tend to justify government intervention into markets on behalf of walkability and compactness; lack of travel behavior impact would tend to undermine the claim for such intervention. The unspoken implication is that the status quo is a more or less free market in which one could choose to intervene or not. In this way, the travel behavior research amounts to an investigation into the extent to which compact, walkable development constitutes a remedy for the externalities of the automobile, notably pollution, greenhouse gas emissions, and impacts on energy dependence. Strong linkages between land use and travel behavior (with compact development causing less driving and more walking, cycling, and transit use) would presumably support the view that urban density constitutes a remedy worthy of governmental intervention.

Such a presumption neglects the web of already existing governmental interventions that continue to shape the status quo. These include transportation and parking standards that ensure that large proportions of developed land area will be devoted to the automobile, subdivision requirements that specify minimum lot sizes, and most notably zoning and other land use regulatory techniques that specify limits on development densities. If these regulations are binding—that is, if the private market in some high-accessibility locations seeks to develop more densely than regulations allow—then policy reform would depend in large measure on the liberalization of existing regulations. For example, reforms might allow greater floor-area ratio, building height, or lot density than previously permitted, particularly in areas of high accessibility (notably high-quality transit accessibility).

Apart from allowing greater compactness of development, these reforms would remove significant obstacles to the development of housing supplies where they are needed most: in areas of high accessibility to work and non-work destinations. In this way the affordable housing goals of overcoming exclusionary zoning and other regulatory barriers are consistent with the pursuit of metropolitan compactness. The inaccurate designation of the status quo as a more or less free market (into which one intervenes only with justification) simultaneously constitutes a barrier to a more compact urban form and to greater inclusiveness in housing and land development policy.

One case (of many) that clearly demonstrates regulatory obstacles to compact and more affordable development was observed in West Bloomfield Township, Michigan. The site is at the growing edge of the Detroit region.

West Bloomfield Township had identified the site for development as part of its master plan review process and called for consolidation of preexisting lots and minimization of curb cuts to promote free-flowing traffic. The original zoning on the 20-acre site, R-15, was the largest lot zoning in the township and would have allowed for only 30 single family homes on 15,000-square-foot, 100-foot-wide lots. Given the high visibility and accessibility of the site, the developer sought to respond to a perceived market of childless young professionals and seniors with development considerably denser than that allowed by existing regulations. The initial proposal entailed 122 units of attached condominiums. The developer proposed a rezoning to RM-6, the only zoning that would have allowed condominium development on this site. Such a rezoning would have permitted 6 dwellings to the acre, close to enabling the 122 proposed units on the 20-acre site. Thus the developer proposed something considerably denser than what the township had in mind.

The proposed development would not have qualified as a transit-oriented development or as a mixed use, pedestrian-oriented neighborhood—and would not have housed low-income households in any case. But as a neighborhood considerably denser than its surroundings in a relatively high-accessibility location, the development would have offered a number of attributes to its target population that were otherwise unavailable. The density and shared-wall construction would have lowered development costs and yielded a more affordable and energy-efficient product. Although the location offered no high-quality transit, it was closer to high-employment areas of suburban Detroit than many of its alternatives and could have offered its occupants a shorter and less expensive commute.

Interaction with the township's planning commission led to significant modification of the project; from the initial proposal, the concept was reduced to 110, then 100 attached units, then finally to 61 detached units, or 3.2 units to the acre. Yet even the modified proposal generated significant public opposition and a close vote when it was considered by the township's board of trustees. About 100 vocal opponents from neighborhoods up to three miles away from the site attended the hearing. Concerns centered predictably on traffic, noise, property values, and the existing single-family character of the neighborhood. The reduced project was ultimately approved by a 4-3 vote of the trustees. There is little doubt that the modification imposed by the planning process reduced the development's affordability, together with its compactness; the process led to a doubling of zoned densities but only half the units the developer sought.

Although some argue that increasing market pressures for compact development ultimately would lead to revised land use regulations, the project's developer sees things differently. "A lot of communities [such as West Bloomfield] don't have the tools set up to react to, respond, review and approve the kind of development that is now being proposed," he explained. "As the market changes, as the demand for certain product types change, residential development demand changes. Unfortunately, many of the communities that have established planning and zoning have very traditional tools" (Inam et al. 2002: 531). The developer's perception that land use regulations failed to accommodate growing demands for this type of housing seems correct, but the fault may not lie with the "traditional tools." In fact, a zoning designation existed in the township that would have allowed the development to go forward. Rather than unavailability of tools, the lack of will to employ them in this particular circumstance appeared to be the bottleneck; in the process both housing affordability and the potential for relatively close-in living for 61 households in metropolitan Detroit were reduced.

In an environment of draconian intervention *against* development density on the part of land use authorities, transportation and land use analysis persist in asking implicitly whether or not governmental intervention *on behalf* of density is justified as a remedy to the externalities of transportation. Reform of this paradigm would be based on the understanding that the status quo is highly shaped and maintained through government action—including regulatory action.

Treatment of Revealed Preference as a Definitive Indicator of Transportation Needs

In its most classic version, the transportation planning method is based on a logic of "predict and supply." That is, travel volumes at some future time are extrapolated from current travel behavior and a forecast of future land use (itself an extrapolation of current development patterns). These forecasts are developed to anticipate likely metropolitan growth and to ensure that it enjoys sufficient transportation capacity. In most cases in the United States, this often means building or widening roads to attempt to provide ample room for free-flow traffic. The approach has been adopted in many locales worldwide.

This standard means of transportation planning has been widely criticized. It imagines a world in which provision of transportation infrastructure serves but does not fundamentally shape demand for transportation. In this framework, growth—particularly low-density, auto-oriented growth at the metropolitan fringe—occurs independently of any planning action, and transportation planning merely serves the mobility needs of the inhabitants of the newly developing areas. In this it neglects the role of highway infrastructure provision in generating or accelerating metropolitan sprawl.

But this approach has significant negative side effects in addition to its capacity to accelerate metropolitan sprawl and reinforce automobile dependence, first identified by Wachs and Kumagai (1973). Under this approach, future transportation plans are based primarily on the extrapolation of current revealed demand. But extrapolation requires a baseline observation from which estimates of future trips are derived. Demand that is unrevealed in the present will not be reflected in future extrapolations. Where predict-and-supply transportation planning methodology rules, needs that are unfulfilled in the present will be unaccounted for in the future.

Those needs would most likely lie with the lower-income travelers. A high income enables one to translate one's needs into consumption of goods and services. By contrast, low-income people—especially from among the non-car owning households—may have many desired trips that are not served by the current transportation system, notably based on the configuration of public transit lines. Where these needs are revealed, they would get "picked up" by a system based on extrapolation; where they are not, revealed-preference methodologies will not include them in future forecasts that form the basis of plans. In this way, standard transportation planning methodology will systematically neglect currently unserved transportation needs. In many cases, transportation planners are aware of this and often study the transportation needs of the poor as an input to the transportation planning process. But where the core of the process is predict-and-supply in character, these analyses tend to be marginalized.

There is another means by which assumptions about revealed preference systematically bias transportation plans against the needs of the poor. Following neoclassical microeconomics, transportation planning methodology views willingness to pay to save time as the measure of the value of a trip. This perspective has distinct implications for the fundability of different transportation options. In standard cost-benefit analysis in transportation, project costs are analyzed in comparison to benefits, largely found in terms of travel time savings. The value of travel time tends to be evaluated as a percentage of the prevailing wage rate; a higher value of time would tend to make a project more worthwhile.

The problem comes when different transportation investments are used by groups with significantly different incomes. In that case, the differences in values of time would tend to make improvements to the mode used by the more affluent more worthwhile. For example, in 2003 the U.S. Department of Transportation recommended that the following figures be used for value of an hour of travel time for intercity business travel: $21.20 for surface modes and $40.10 for air travel. The implication is that an intercity bus or rail improvement would need to save almost twice as much time as an air travel improvement of similar cost before it would be viewed as equally worthwhile.

The Department of Transportation memorandum was quite aware of the controversy that would surround this procedure:

> Objections are sometimes raised against adoption of empirical estimates of the value of time that are a smaller percentage of wages for travel on transport modes used disproportionately by lower-income individuals. On grounds of distributional equity, it is often argued that emphasizing strictly monetary measures of benefits to the public will cause these modes to receive a smaller share of investments that improve travel speeds or conditions, even if the psychological satisfaction derived from time savings is just as great for low-income as for high-income travelers.

But the memorandum dismissed these arguments in the name of economic efficiency:

> Although this argument may be attractive, it is difficult to justify in the context of evaluating public investment choices. First, the primary purpose of conducting economic evaluations of government decisions is to improve the efficiency of resource allocation within the nation's economy. Influencing the distribution of income among individuals or groups is an explicit goal of certain government programs (such as those that provide services directly to low-income groups), but the central purpose of public investments is to deliver maximum benefits to society as a whole from the resources withdrawn from the private economy to finance them. Measuring the travel time savings

and other benefits from government expenditures by the dollar values their recipients attach to them is the only way to ensure that the
investments chosen make the largest possible improvement to econ-
omy-wide welfare. (U.S. Department of Transportation 1997: 3)

In addition to the core idea—willingness to pay as a definitive measure of
societal value—the Department of Transportation memo illustrates several
facets of the worldview of standard transportation planning. First is the presumption that efficiency is the primary goal of economic analysis of public
policy. This is taken as self-evidently true even though "equity" has at least an
equally plausible claim on analysis. For example, in a situation where lower-
income individuals suffer poor levels of service in intercity travel, equity-in-
formed policy may choose to spend *more* resources per hour saved on their
travel than on that of the affluent, who already receive reasonable levels of
service. By contrast, the radical conclusion of this study—it's worth spending
nearly twice as much to save an airline traveler one hour compared to a bus
or train rider—is presented as something akin to fact. "Maximum benefits
to society as a whole" are taken implicitly to refer to actions judged efficient
under the utilitarian Kaldor-Hicks criterion whereby an action is desirable if
the winners can afford to compensate the losers and still come out ahead. The
principle consciously rejects distributional concerns: an action that benefits
the rich and costs the poor is still desirable as long as it generates more overall benefits than costs.

The second idea implicit in the language above is that technical, neutral
transportation planning ought not to be in the business of altering resource
distributions in society. In this worldview, while there may be programs that
are legitimately geared at putting more resources in the hands of poor people,
transportation planning is not one of them. Implicit in this notion is the idea
that there is an externally generated distribution of resources in society, a
kind of neutral default backdrop. This framework does not acknowledge the
possibility that transportation planning itself unavoidably alters resource allocations in society by changing the distribution of accessibility among societal sectors. Based on transportation planning practices, destinations can
be closer or more remote, accessible broadly or only to those who drive cars.
If transportation planning itself helps determine societal resource distributions, then it cannot with integrity offload any distributional considerations
to (non-transportation) programs explicitly oriented toward social welfare.
Yet as the quotes above illustrate, the fiction of a neutral default distribution

of resources in society—and in particular accessibility resources—has become a cornerstone of transportation planning.

Finally, the Department of Transportation statement incorporates deeper notions about the relationship between the government and the private sector. The phrase "the central purpose of public investments is to deliver maximum benefits to society as a whole from the resources withdrawn from the private economy to finance them" reflects a view that the public sector exists as a necessary intrusion into the private sector. In this view, the resources the public extracts from the private sector are not inherently the legitimate foundations of society as a whole and the private sector itself in particular. Rather, they are deviations from market ordering that demand legitimation—a grounding found not in the societal vision implemented with these resources, but in the extent to which their allocation logic matches that of the private sector from which they were extracted in the first place.

The assumption that willingness to pay is a definitive measure of societal value has other far-reaching implications in transportation planning. For example, when rationing roadway space, does one prefer vehicles willing to pay a toll, or high-occupancy vehicles? If the goal of operating the facility is maximization of person throughput, there will be cases where the high-occupancy vehicles should receive preference even over toll-paying single occupancy vehicles. Under a willingness-to-pay approach, a high-occupancy vehicle that is unwilling or unable to pay the toll provides prima facie evidence that its trip is of sufficiently low value that should not receive priority for roadway space. Like the other approaches described in this section, the broad acceptance among transportation planners and researchers of congestion pricing is based on the notion that willingness to pay for a trip is a definitive measure of societal value.

Conclusion

Like urban planning in general, transportation planning exists in a societal set of power relationships that condition its functioning. Privileged groups seek to use transportation planning to augment their accessibility, a process that can leave less-privileged populations worse off in relative or even absolute terms. But transportation planning methodology does not operate through politics directly. Rather, it establishes its legitimacy through an internal logic that lends its analyses and policy recommendations an aura of objectivity. For this reason, the assumptions and frameworks of transportation planning—whether implicit or explicit—are relevant to its capacity to plan for equitable access. Promoting equity in transportation demands first that transportation planning reform its own practices that have impeded such equity over the decades.

Much effort in transportation planning in recent years has focused on refining predictive models of traffic and metropolitan movement more generally. But more equitable forms of transportation planning will not emerge from improvements in the accuracy of forecasts of traffic flows, better quantification of people's willingness to pay for transportation improvements, or capacity increases in transportation systems. Instead, reform of the profession depends on its serious consideration of a more fundamental set of challenges to core ideas to which it has adhered for decades.

The perspectives referred to here—a focus on mobility, adherence for criteria to justify intervention into markets, and reliance on revealed preference to demonstrate value—have in many cases served the transportation planning profession well. A focus on getting people from point A to point B is frequently a useful simplification of the complex task of the transportation planner. Some trips are certainly more valuable than others, and in many circumstances, revealed preference can be a reliable guide for distinguishing and prioritizing different kinds of travel. And most planning traditions entail, to a significant extent, a respect for the capacity of markets to deliver a range of goods and services efficiently—and hence rely on criteria for which functions are left to markets and which to public planning. Transportation planning has in many ways benefited from these core ideas, and equity-based policy reform does not require their wholesale abandonment.

But reform is in order. Mobility-based evaluation has long guided both transportation and land use planning in many regions in the form of roadway level-of-service standards that tend both to constrain development densities and accelerate roadway construction—all in an often-futile attempt to keep cars moving. The replacement of this mode with accessibility-based evaluation would fundamentally alter transportation planning (and perhaps land use planning as well). For example, roadway construction on the metropolitan periphery would be evaluated not just for its capacity to speed up the traffic, but simultaneously for its potential to induce accessibility-degrading growth in distances between origins and destinations. Similarly, a proposal for dense infill development would be assessed not just for its danger of degrading traffic beyond some threshold, but also for the improvement in proximity it would offer its residents. Accessibility-based evaluation does not imply abandonment of mobility metrics; to the contrary, mobility is a necessary component. But under the reformed approach, mobility would not be evaluated as a desirable end in isolation; rather, impacts of transportation infrastructure or land development on mobility and proximity would be analyzed jointly within an accessibility framework.

The second paradigm is the fiction of the free market in land development, where uncertainty in travel behavior studies is construed as evidence against the desirability of government intervention. Reform of this paradigm demands the abandonment of the fallacious equation of policy *reform* with governmental *intervention*. With the status quo in land development already one of ubiquitous governmental intervention on behalf of low densities and land use separation, the question is not whether to intervene into markets; that has already occurred. The question is the *form* that intervention should take; uncertainty in travel behavior science ought not to be construed as an obstacle in choosing more sensible regulations over less sensible ones. That formulation has been paralyzing in transportation and land use policy, and its abandonment is a prerequisite to significant reform.

Under the third paradigm, revealed preference is taken as the definitive indicator of the value of a trip. "Willingness to pay" can be a good guide for selection among transportation investments when there is little difference between the income groups they serve. The guidance this criterion provides degrades with increasing socioeconomic differences between the constituencies relevant to the transportation decision at hand, and is certainly undermined when trips of one mode are treated as inherently more valuable because its passengers are affluent. Unless "willingness to pay" is adjusted for "ability to pay," this paradigm will remain an obstacle to equity-based transportation planning. And a "predict-and-supply" mode of planning—which in its focus on extrapolation lacks the classic planning element of conceiving desired futures—can be supplanted by a "backcasting" approach. Under this framework, desired future states of accessibility and its distribution are envisioned, and transportation planning's quantitative toolkit is employed to infer necessary paths toward that goal.

One can conceive of a hierarchy of approaches to transportation inequity. At the lowest level, only mobility-based solutions are considered. The second includes approaches that enhance mobility and connectivity and remove barriers to proximity. The third and most comprehensive approach includes lower-level strategies, together with approaches to treat the social dimension that can generate exclusion even in the face of physical accessibility. Choice among these approaches is an intricate affair. On the one hand, policy reform might aspire to the most comprehensive approaches. Under this perspective, limiting one's tool kit to mobility improvements alone restricts policy effectiveness and obscures the more nettlesome problems of physical and social exclusion. In this way, defining the problem as one of poor mobility alone can be an overly convenient and nonthreatening approach to transportation equity. Even the second stage—mobility, proximity, and connectivity together—can be hopelessly partial in the face of the full range of barriers to full participation in society.

At the same time, policy reform may seek a pragmatic adaptation to a particular policy environment. Where the more comprehensive approaches based on proximity or overcoming social exclusion are politically infeasible, pragmatic planning may focus on enhanced mobility as a near-term fix. This would be the case with proposals to distribute used automobiles free to carless households able to maintain and operate them, or with effective transport services to locales that are job-rich but housing-poor because of exclusionary regulations or a history or racial segregation. Pragmatic proposals for enhanced mobility need not be rejected because they fail to address social exclusion comprehensively. In most cases current planning institutions lack the tools or authority to pursue a higher-level accessibility vision because of the functional division of realms; transportation agencies are separate by organization and mandate from both land use regulators and social welfare bodies. This environment calls for a dual-level approach whereby lower-level solutions are pursued tactically even as the planner seeks strategic institutional reform that would support the more comprehensive vision of expanding accessibility over all its dimensions.

References

Behrens, Roger. 2004. Understanding travel needs of the poor: Towards improved travel analysis practices in South Africa. *Transport Reviews* 24(3): 317–36.

Boarnet, Marlon, and Randall Crane. 2001. *Travel by design: The influence of urban form on travel.* New York: Oxford University Press.

Cervero, Robert. 1996. Jobs-housing balance revisited: Trends and impacts in the San Francisco Bay Area. *Journal of the American Planning Association* 62(4): 492–511.

Ewing, Reid, and Robert Cervero. 2001. Travel and the built environment: A synthesis. *Transportation Research Record* 1780: 87–114.

Farrington, John, and Conor Farrington. 2005. Rural accessibility, social inclusion and social justice: Towards conceptualization. *Journal of Transport Geography* 13(1): 1–12.

Frank, Lawrence, and Peter Engelke. 2001. The built environment and human activity patterns: Exploring the impacts of urban form on public health. *Journal of Planning Literature* 16(2): 202-18.

Gaffron, Philine, Julian P. Hine, and Fiona Mitchell. 2001. The role of transport on social exclusion in urban Scotland: Literature review. Transport Research Institute, Scottish Executive Central Research Unit, Napier University.

Grengs, Joe. 2005. The abandoned social goals of public transit in the neoliberal city of the USA. *City* 9(1): 51–66.

Handy, Susan L., and Deborah A. Niemeier. 1997. Measuring accessibility: An exploration of issues and alternatives. *Environment and Planning A* 29: 1175–94.

Hansen, Walter G. 1959. How accessibility shapes land use. *Journal of the American Institute of Planners* 25(2): 73–76.

Hine, Julian, and Fiona Mitchell. 2001. Better for everyone? Travel experiences and transport exclusion. *Urban Studies* 38(2): 319–32.

Ihlanfeldt, Keith R., and David L. Sjoquist. 1998. The spatial mismatch hypothesis: A review of recent studies and their implications for welfare reform. *Housing Policy Debate* 9(4): 849–92.

Inam, Aseem, Jonathan Levine, and Richard Werbel. 2002. Developer-planner interaction in transportation and land use sustainability. MTI Report 01-21, Mineta Transportation Institute, College of Business, San Jose State University.

Kenworthy, Jeff, and Felix Laube. 2002. Urban transport patterns in a global sample of cites and their linkages to transport infrastructure, land use, economics, and environment. *World Transport Policy and Practice* 8(3): 5–19.

Kenyon, Susan, Glenn Lyons, and Jackie Rafferty. 2002. Transport and social exclusion: Investigating the possibility of promoting inclusion through virtual mobility. *Journal of Transport Geography* 10(3): 207–19.

Kitamura, Ryuichi, Patricia Mokhtarian, and Laura Laidet. 1997. A micro-analysis of land use and travel in five neighborhoods in the San Francisco Bay Area. *Transportation* 24: 125–58.

Lansing, John B., Robert W. Marans, and Robert B. Zehner. 1970. *Planned residential environments.* Survey Research Center, Institute for Social Research, Ann Arbor, Mich. Prepared for U.S. Department of Transportation, Bureau of Public Roads.

Laquian, Aprodicio A. 2004. Who are the poor and how are they being served in Asian cities? Paper presented at Forum on Urban Infrastructure and Public Service Delivery for the Urban Poor, Regional Focus: Asia, Woodrow Wilson International Center for Scholars and National Institute of Urban Affairs, India Habitat Centre, New Delhi.

Leinberger, Christopher B. 2008. *The option of urbanism: Investing in a new American dream.* Washington, D.C.: Island Press.

Levine, Jonathan. 2006. *Zoned out: Regulation, markets, and choices in transportation and metropolitan land use*. Washington, D.C.: Resources for the Future.

Litman, Todd. 2002. Evaluating transportation equity. *World Transport Policy & Practice* 8(2): 50–65.

Page, Oliver. 2004. Equity impacts and challenges of highway access management in an emerging economy—South Africa at the crossroads. Center for Urban Transportation Research, Tampa. Presented at Sixth Access Management Conference, Kansas City.

Sanchez, Thomas W., Rich Stolz, and Lacinta S. Ma. 2003. Moving to equity: Addressing inequitable effects of transportation policies on minorities. Joint report of the Center for Community Change and the Civil Rights Project, Harvard University.

Schrank, David, and Tim Lomax. 2007. *The 2007 urban mobility report*. College Station: Texas Transportation Institute.

Schweitzer, Lisa, and Abel Valenzuela, Jr. 2004. Environmental injustice and transportation: The claims and the evidence. *Journal of Planning Literature* 18(4): 383–98.

Social Exclusion Unit. 2003. Making the connections: Transport and social exclusion. Interim Findings from the Social Exclusion Unit. London. http://mtcwatch.com/pdfiles/3819-CO.pdf, accessed July 18, 2012.

Thomson, J. Michael. 1977. *Great cities and their traffic*. London: Gollancz.

Stenberg, Peter, Mitch Morehart, Stephen Vogel, John Cromartie, Vince Breneman, and Dennis Brown. 2009. Broadband internet's value for rural America. Economic Research Report (ERR-78), U.S. Department of Agriculture Economic Research Service.

Transportation Research Board. 2000. *Highway Capacity Manual*. Washington, D.C.

U.S. Department of Transportation. Office of the Secretary of Transportation. 1997. Departmental Guidance for the Valuation of Travel Time in Economic Analysis. Memo from Frank E. Kreusi, Assistant Secretary for Transportation Policy. http://ostpxweb.dot.gov/policy/Data/VOT97guid.pdf. Accessed May 2011.

———. 2003. Revised departmental guidance for the valuation of travel time in economic analysis. Memo from Emil H. Frankel, Assistant Secretary for Transportation Policy. http://ostpxweb.dot.gov/policy/Data/VOTrevision1_2-11-03.pdf. Accessed May 2011.

Vanderschuren, Marianne J. W. A., and Sirin Galaria. 2003. Can the post-apartheid South African city move towards accessibility, equity and sustainablity? *International Social Science Journal* 55: 265–77.

Wachs, Martin, and T. Gordon Kumagai. 1973. Physical accessibility as a social indicator. *Socio-Economic Planning Sciences* 7(5): 437–56.

Wilson, William Julius. 1996. *When work disappears: The world of the new urban poor*. New York: Random House.

Chapter 8

Social Equity in the Network Society: Implications for Communities

Penny Gurstein

Digital networks are increasingly replacing or complementing social networks of face-to-face communication, furthering the formation of globally interdependent relationships within the economy, state, and society. The "network society" typified by Castells (1996) and van Dijk (1996) created by these new relationships is the result of a shift in spatial and temporal patterns that undermine the importance of local, regional, and national boundaries in many facets of social life.

The consequences of this fraying of boundaries are still unfolding. What is and will be the impact of networked relationships on just and equitable resource allocation globally, nationally, regionally, within communities, and between households? Who are the winners and losers in this global phenomenon? What are the opportunities and uncertainties? What are the implications for regional and community development as well as for localized place-based communities? What role can policy and planning play in encouraging equity?

This chapter addresses these questions in light of research that reveals the complexity of the spatially diffuse relationships that are forming, and the impact these relationships are having on people's lives, communities, and regions. While some of the research reports positive outcomes and promises new opportunities for inclusion, many of the findings point to troubling consequences that link the network society to increasing disparities in income distribution, fragmentation in workplaces and communities, and the blurring of boundaries between public and private space and time. Other studies point to new barriers to social inclusion for some social groups, as well as a declining quality of working life for many workers.

To understand this phenomenon will be a four-step process. The first defines the network society and situates inequalities that are perpetuated in this society in terms of a "digital divide." The next makes sense of the workforce that is being created through these processes and the implications for regional and community development. We then move from the question of workforce to broader issues of governance and democratic processes in the network society. The chapter concludes with a discussion of how the network society can be harnessed to provide equitable benefits in planning and policy-making.

Exclusion in the Network Society

The Logic of the Network Society

The concept of the network society evolved from a recognition of the importance of the creation, distribution, diffusion, use, integration, and manipulation of information as a significant driver of the economy, as well as the role these processes play in shaping political and cultural activities. The network society has been portrayed as one where the social structure is open and decentralized, with people and organizations involved in several networks concurrently; activities are "footloose," free from spatial barriers; and physical spaces are replaced by virtual spaces (Albrechts and Mandelbaum 2005). Van Dijk defines the network society as a "social formation with an infrastructure of social and media networks enabling its prime mode of organization at all levels (individual, group/organizational, and societal)" (2006: 20). For Van Dijk, networks have become the nervous system of society. As one moves through and interacts in a network society, just as in a web, the center is continually shifting relative to reference points, what Derrida (1978) described as "decentering" in an analysis of the deconstruction of Western European hegemony.

New networked forms of organization and network logic—and with this pervasiveness, flexibility, and convergence—are transforming capitalism and replacing vertically integrated hierarchies as the dominant form of social organization. As economic and social activities increasingly organize around hubs and networks, what Castells (1996) called the "space of flows," the established understanding of the role of social, ethnic and national entities in providing societal structure and meaning is being diminished.

The Digital Divide

In this new informational environment, those who have control of information technologies and their use are the "haves" in this "network" society, and those who don't, or must rely on those who do to provide access and work opportunities, are the "have nots." This "digital divide" (Norris 2001; van Dijk 2005) is a gap between people with access to digital and information technologies, as well as the resources and skills needed to use those technologies, and those with very limited or no access. Schon, Sanyal, and Mitchell (1999) tied the problem of access to a lack of available technology, skills, and financial resources. Mitchell (1999a) argued that the divide would lessen over time and that digital technologies would be an equalizing force, providing opportunities for those who would be otherwise excluded, and creating tools at low cost. While this has proved true to some extent, there is still a digital gap, with inequities globally, within regions, and within societies.

Technological determinism obscures any analysis grounded in the material conditions in which technologies are embedded (Thrift 1996). In other words, it is the social relations, based on class, gender, race/ethnicity, ability and point in lifecycle, an individual's economic and information resources, as well as temporal and spatial constraints imposed by their household responsibilities, that affect access to technologies and the information society.

At the global scale, the gap is narrowing between rich and poor nations (and the rich and poor within nations) when it comes to access to communication tools such as cellular telephones. But it remains wide in terms of high-speed Internet connectivity, which is needed for participation in information-rich industries. Of the 6.85 billion people in the world as of 2010, 4.88 billion were without Internet access and excluded from the "network" society because of lack of resources, infrastructure, and expertise (Internet World Statistics 2010).

Trends are, nevertheless, changing quite profoundly, reflecting emerging new economic powers. As Table 8.1 illustrates, from 2000 to 2010 the growth in Internet usage rose dramatically in Asia, Africa, the Middle East, and Latin America. Asia now constitutes 42 percent of the world's usage, far surpassing North America and Europe.

The table is less able to reveal the different forms of unequal access to these resources. Only 11 percent of the African population has Internet usage in contrast to over three-quarters of North Americans. Developing

Table 8.1. Internet Usage (1999 and 2010)

2010 % population (penetration)	Usage % of growth 2000–2010	2010[b] Usage % of world	1999[a] Usage % of world	Region
10.9	2,357.3	5.6	0.75	Africa
21.5	621.8	42.0	17.0	Asia
58.4	352.0	24.2	21.0	Europe
29.8	1,825.3	3.2	0.5	Middle East
77.4	146.3	13.5	57.0	North America
34.5	1,032.8	10.4	3.0	Latin American/Caribbean
61.3	170.0	1.1	0.75	Oceania/Australia
28.7	444.8	100.0	100.0	World total

(a) From NUA Surveys, "Internet Users by Location," http://www.nua.net/surveys Sept. 1999
(b) From Internet World Statistics: Usage and Population Statistics, http://www.internetworld
stats.com/stats.htm June 30, 2010.

countries often have prohibitive communication costs rendering connectivity unaffordable for the majority of the population, and access is mainly in urban areas, not the rural countryside. In Vietnam, for example, almost all the telephone lines are in the five major cities. This further exacerbates the disparity between the rich and poor, and between genders, as often in rural areas poor women form the majority because they have fewer opportunities to migrate to urban areas. While gender differences in Internet use in the U.S. have lessened (78 percent of males and 75 percent of females are connected), there are still significant disparities in many countries and often those differences are predicated on cultural factors which inhibit women's access.

Politics, too, can inhibit the use of new technologies. In China and Iran, for example, there are restrictions on use of the Internet because political leaders are concerned about its use to ferment dissent. Socioeconomic, political, and cultural realities in particular locales challenge the notion of the openness of the network society and reinforce disparities between, and within, countries. To counter this, France and Finland are the first countries to make Internet access a human right (CNet 2009). While only a few governments recognize access as a citizen's right, Internet access is fostering the globally interconnected economy and the work patterns that follow from it.

A Mobile, Flexible Workforce

Telework

Globally networked workplaces, not bound by geographical distance and place-based imperatives, are emerging, driven by technologies that permit both traditional office work and production to be separated into parts undertaken in different locations. In this restructuring of business models, "telework" has become a prominent strategy for employers and policy-makers aiming to address the globalization of the economy and the need to be competitive (Barfield, Heiduk, and Welfens 2003). This strategy has created a two-tiered workforce of core and peripheral workers (Cornfield, Campbell, and McCammon 2001). While a core of full-time salaried workers remain in companies, temporary workers are hired on a contingency basis, or the work is outsourced, creating precarious employment.

Telework (or "telecommuting" as it is sometimes called in the United States) is defined as work-related substitutions of telecommunications and related information technologies (ICTs) for travel (Huws, Korte, and Robinson 1990). Definitions differ according to the amount and proportion of time spent off the employer's premises; the location of the work; the contractual relationship with the employer; the nature of the technology used; and the nature of the relationship with the employer (Illegems and Verbeke 2003). Telework includes a range of working relationships: employees connected to corporate networks while working from their homes or other remote locations, such as telecenters or client offices; self-employed consultants or business operators usually working from home; independent contractors or self-employed subcontractors who rely on digital media to carry out their work; and workers, whether directly employed or outsourced, located in back-offices or call centers, who are linked to employers' central offices.

Determining the magnitude of telework is problematic. Accurate statistics are hard to find because telework is often included in statistics with other forms of flexible employment (Gurstein 2001; Mokhtarian et al. 2005). A WorldatWork report (2006) estimated that approximately 5 percent of the total workforce in the United States—12.4 million full- or part-time employee teleworkers and 16.2 million contract (self-employed)—are teleworkers, 60 percent of them men. The growth in the number of teleworkers is attributed to widespread home computer ownership and low-cost Internet access rates.

Telework came into prominence in the 1970s as a work option that reduces dependence on transportation (Mokhtarian 1991; Nilles et al. 1976), but has been of continuing interest to both the private and public sectors because it produces a mobile, flexible labor force and reduces overhead costs (Huws 1991). Telework and home-based employment was lauded by futurists in the 1970s as a strategy to conserve energy (Nilles et al. 1976; Harkness 1977), and was also recognized as a way to humanize corporations (Bell 1973; Schumacher 1973) and achieve greater personal fulfillment at work (Toffler 1980). In certain circumstances, it was also found to allow work to be balanced with domestic responsibilities and to provide a presence in neighborhoods during the day.

In the late 1980s the arguments supporting telework became driven by corporations that, recognizing that to survive they had to be leaner, were looking for a way to reduce overhead costs and increase organizational adaptability. Governments saw entrepreneurship and self-employment through outsourced telework as a viable strategy in a stagnant economy. Telework also fit into the quest for urban sustainability by allowing efficient use of urban space (e.g., live/work) and reduction in consumption of material and energy resources (e.g., less travel for work). During the 1990s and now in the twenty-first century, we have seen a significant increase in jobs conducted entirely online, from website designers, computer graphic artists, systems analysts, and programmers to online stock traders.

How are we to understand the meaning and consequences of telework? The current impetus for flexible employment driven by the need for global competitiveness while making telework attractive as a survival mechanism has left a far less secure workforce. In both the UK and North America, as well as globally, it has resulted in a trend toward social polarization, with a bifurcated workforce made up of highly skilled, highly paid knowledge workers (often men) and low-skilled, low-paid piece workers (predominantly women, immigrants, and visible minorities), the latter often made redundant by new technological capabilities (Rowbotham 1993; Gurstein 2001; Switter 2005). While employed teleworkers may have some security depending on the benefits in the organization in which they are employed, independent contractors are part of a vulnerable labor force with no union protection, few benefits, and little long-term security.

Global Outsourcing

A second phenomenon that has become increasingly consequential as the result of the implementation of new technologies is outsourcing. Global outsourcing is the "process of identifying, evaluating, negotiating and configuring supply across multiple geographies in order to reduce costs, maximize performance and mitigate risks" (Aberdeen Group 2003). It allows the relocation of non-core internal operations or jobs to an external entity (such as a subcontractor) that specializes in that operation and is a strategy which allows businesses to focus on their core competencies. While outsourcing of manufacturing and back office employment has occurred since the 1970s, the Internet has allowed the proliferation of the current wave of outsourced tele-mediated work ranging from data processing, customer services, and software development to design functions and radiology viewing.

Outsourcing can manifest itself in a variety of work relationships. For example, a U.S. company may decide to restructure so as to provide only a core set of services, with the rest is handled by, for example, an onsite company contracted to be in charge of human resources ("in-sourcing"), by offsite sourcing to another out-of-state branch of the company providing training and staff development, by near-shoring to a Canadian company of customer support and telesales, and by off-shoring software development to India. The value chain, however, does not stop there. The software developer in India may outsource part of its work to one of its subsidiaries in China and the company where customer support and telesales are being handled may be subcontracting its work to home-based workers ("home-shoring") (Gurstein 2007).

As one example of the growth in outsourcing of services, remote customer service work (call and technology support centers), in the United States grew 20 percent annually in the 1990s and first years of the twenty-first century, accounting for approximately 4 percent of total employment, or about 4 million people, 100,000 of them home-based (O'Toole and Lawler 2006).[1] In 2008, only 2.3 million people were in this employment, the decline being attributed to the shrinking of the economy and off-shoring (U.S. Department of Labor 2008). The growth in call center jobs in Britain was almost three times greater than that for overall employment in the early twenty-first century (Keating 2005). With computer-telephone integration (CTI), the growth of contact centers globally has increased by double digits with India, the Philippines, and Jamaica some of the prime benefactors (Rohde 2003), although this trend has slowed recently due to the economic downturn.

In this geographically dispersed workforce, outsourced workers are expected to strive for "seamlessness" and "synchronicity," which has consequences for workers' livelihood, job security, and working conditions (Gurstein 2007). These consequences are both temporal (such as working to a timeframe imposed by another global region "in-sync") and a-spatial, in the need to integrate work activities "seamlessly" with those of clients and the need to make invisible the location and culture of the global region and company where the outsourced worker works. These jobs, typified as "emotion work" (Mirchandani 2003), require not only a sophisticated understanding of both technological and interpersonal skills, but also an ability to work under stress, none of which is rewarded by the relatively low wages workers receive.

Despite recent specialization of companies and regions in fields where they hold a competitive advantage, the reliance on advanced technology and global expertise means that they are in a situation of highly unstable employment. The reasons for locating work in a particular region may vanish. Economic processes and corporate strategies that led to restructuring and relocation may lead to further reorganization which threatens the employment created through relocation. The organizational and technological change necessary for relocating work may result in work organizations and information systems that make employment easy to relocate again, resulting in regional employment disparities.

Regional and Community Impact of the Networked Society

While some predict that the network society and tele-mediated work created from this connectivity will "flatten" the unequal division of labor between developed and lesser developed countries (Friedman 2005), as well as between regions within countries, others argue that the existing balance of power between transnational corporations and their workers, and between developed and lesser developed countries, has only reinforced the centralization of control and technologies (Huws 2003).

Conditions may look bleak in many marginalized regions, and media reports in North America are widespread about job loss and workers made redundant, but global sourcing does not always necessarily have an adverse impact on local economies. In a study from better economic times, Huws, Dahlmann, and Flecker (2004) reported that EU employment trends in the "computer and related" sectors revealed no evidence of net job loss between

2000 and 2003. With the exception of Denmark, there was net growth in all European Union member states in this sector, one where jobs are most likely to be affected by offshore outsourcing. No state lost employment in "other business activities," and some experienced very rapid growth, most dramatically the Czech Republic. While there are disparate corporate cultures, and global sourcing has accelerated in the last few years, what can be learned from the EU research is that there may be job loss in one part of the supply chain but growth in other parts.

Case studies from across Canada (Gurstein and Tate 2009) describe global outsourcing as having mixed impacts on regional economic development, especially in regions attracting low-paying work. The effects vary by community location (rural versus urban, more remote or near/within a large metropolitan center; community size; and the type of business activities a community wants to attract or retain). For example, companies are finding it attractive to locate contact centers in Canada in urban areas where they can find a skilled, multilingual labor force. Other companies are relocating business functions in remote regions where the regulatory climate and benefits support their activities.

Urban theorists raise important questions regarding the potential of employment delocalization to affect urban hierarchies at a variety of scales. Cities occupying primary positions in a given hierarchy (whether national or international) tend to receive a different type of economic development from those at lower levels. Once highly centralized, this structure has begun to disintegrate through broad macro-processes such as the rise of global city systems (Friedmann 1986), an increasing globalized division of labor (Castells 1989; Hall 1998), the changing industrial base, the rise of the service sector, and shifting inner-city demographics (Hutton 2009). Graham and Marvin (1996) and Graham (2001) identify contemporary cities as socio-technical complexes of infrastructural power and mobility. Sassen (2001) has acknowledged a seemingly contradictory pattern of centralization of some economic functions (especially related to higher level management activities) coupled with a dispersal of others.

While outlying communities are seeking call centers to enhance employment or compensate for declining local industries, it has yet to be determined whether these new jobs have helped local economies. An Australian study showed mixed experiences with rural call centers (Standen and Sinclair-Jones 2003). The same mobility that enabled new rural jobs increased their vulnerability to offshore relocation or replacement through technology advances like automated voice recognition. The call center jobs that are less vulnerable to quick relocation are often centrally located, out of a need for a specific type of expertise or language capability, with nearly 70 percent of all call center jobs in Australia concentrated in and around the two largest cities, Melbourne and Sydney.

The locational decisions of new enterprises point to employment relocations that are reinforcing the growth of suburban communities, where land values allow more flexibility in land uses. Delocalization results in fragmentation in certain locales and re-concentration in other locales evidenced by the proliferation of technology parks for off-shored work in India. What is occurring is a network model of urban growth (Castells 1996; Sassen 1998).

Castells (1989) argues that the trend toward the "telecommunicated city" has increased the functional zoning of time and space, creating a concentration of activities around workplaces, homes, and leisure. "Electronic zoning" further segregates the mix of people and activities that land use zoning has tried to regulate. The consequence of such zoning is that the city is evolving into a dual society of haves and have-nots based on access to digital technologies. Certainly, there is a very clear pattern in Canadian cities of highly paid knowledge workers clustering in expensive inner city neighborhoods that offer a high quality of life as well as cultural and social amenities, what Florida (2005) terms the "creative city," while lower-paid service workers are forced to seek more affordable housing in the suburbs, precipitating long commutes and challenging the notion that the network society will reduce the need for travel. A fluid employment market with little expectation of job security does reinforce the idea that people choose their housing location not by proximity to their employment (as that might change a number of times during their career) but by affordability, access to good education for their children, and other household-based factors.

In addition, the network society is intensifying the expansion of the private domestic sphere and the corresponding abandonment of uses and functions of the public sphere. Mitchell (1999b) contends that digital networks selectively loosen place-to-place and person-to-place relationships producing fragmentation and recombination of urban patterns. There is now a hybrid of physical/virtual places as the role of the body in space is transformed. Menzies (2000), among others, addresses the serious consequences of this transformation and the subsequent weakening of the importance of place-based communities. The expansion of digital public space is occurring at the same time as budgetary cutbacks for public and social spaces such as libraries, schools, and universities.[2] Physical public space is disappearing as more spaces fall under the control of corporate interests, limiting their use.

In response to these trends and varied analyses, Graham and Healey (1999) argue that both planning theory and practice must better consider how dynamics in places are changing. In terms of practice, this means moving beyond problem-solving approaches that assume the city is a single place, or even a collection of smaller, physically integrated districts. Rather, cities are nodes in interdependent and interrelated webs at the regional, national, and transnational levels. More specifically, it means recognizing that a particular normative approach, such as promoting compact urban form or New Urbanism principles, will be less likely to produce the desired social, economic, and environmental responses.

While place-based communities are not necessarily losing their importance, what is occurring in the network society is a fragmentation and re-combination of place-based and non-place-based spaces that transform the role of physical spaces; a dispersal of activities away from traditional nodes and forms of activities; a re-concentration in other nodes in other ways; and a schism based on those who are included or marginalized. In addition, as the private sphere increasingly embodies public functions, the public/private distinction is being challenged.

Governance and Democratic Processes

It is widely reported that there is a crisis of representative democracy emerging from mistrust of political institutions and disillusionment with elected officials and bureaucrats (Dear 1999; Coleman and Wright 2008). Online governance strategies purport to create more openness and transparency by providing citizens easier access to government institutions. Many cities, states/provinces, and countries have some form of "e-governance," delivering government services online, including access to information electronically, and opportunities for citizen to interact with government online such as paying bills.

An overarching impetus for governments to institute organizational change is in response to neoliberal political and economic policies within nations and globally. Governments are seeking to maintain a competitive edge in the "new economy" by shifting the delivery of services online and adapting work to new technologies. These strategies are linked to broader,

international and national projects promoted by the Organization for
Economic Cooperation and Development (OECD) (2003) and the World
Bank (2005) that place importance on private sector organizational and
management models for governmental reform, including privatization and
outsourcing. Yet, by these last measures governments could become less accountable to citizens, increasingly blurring the distinction between public
and private delivery of services.

Nevertheless, governments are recognizing the importance of providing
conduits for digital access. For example, a Canadian initiative, Connecting
Canadians Agenda, established in 1997 by the federal government, consists
of six aspects or pillars: Canada Online; Smart Communities; Canadian
Content On-line; Electronic Commerce; Canadian Government On-line;
and Connecting Canada to the World (Connecting Canadians Agenda
2003). One program, the Broadband for Rural and Northern Development
Pilot Program, seeks to enhance broadband access for rural and remote communities. Microwave links and wireless cellular systems provide access and
services to these communities, effectively breaking down part of the digital
divide between the city and the countryside.

Digital Public Space

The Internet is becoming a virtual space for multiple voices to be involved
in the public arena and for citizen engagement. "E-democracy" is typically
defined as the use of digital technologies to create strategies to enable more
active citizen participation within political and governance processes of local
communities, nations, and globally (Clift 2004). Using as their starting point
Habermas's call for "communicative action" (1984) which allows an equal opportunity for all participants in a social discourse to initiate and sustain communication, and "bourgeois public space" (1991) as a locale where citizens
can engage in debate and bridge the state and civil society and the dynamics of power and powerlessness, Heng and de Moor (2003) contend that the
Internet has the potential to provide users with a platform for open discussion and "communicative empowerment" (336).

What digital public space could provide is the opportunity for social
learning and an open process that provides critical feedback and reflection,
and a strong institutional memory (Friedmann 1987). The challenge is how
to enrich the process of deliberative engagement and how to establish new

modes of interaction between citizens and remote institutions of governance through digital tools. Applications have been explored for planning and governance that draw on information and interactive technologies. These include uses such as analysis (GIS: Geographical Information Systems); modeling and visualization (CAD: Computer-Aided Design); communication (teleconferencing); online activism to foster community linkages and civil society (websites such as moveon.org); public participation and decision-making (online voting); service delivery; information dissemination; public access (community online networks); collaborative research; and technology transfer, both locally and internationally.

Carr (2008) describes how Barack Obama's election campaign for the U.S. presidency harnessed the power of social networking's communication capabilities through Facebook and other sites with aggressive database development. Using freely available online applications they created a social movement that raised money for the campaign, organized locally, and got out the vote that led to Obama's election. While potentially this network could be used to govern, going directly to citizens rather than delivering a message through media outlets, this has not materialized.

Others have also recognized the potential of the network society for mobilization. Rheingold (2002) describes "smart mobs," a form of technology-mediated self-structuring social organization, as an indication of the evolving use of digital media for activist purposes. Now that communication tools such as the cellular phone are converging in their ability to receive and transmit information wirelessly (text-messaging; digital photography and video), new forms of instantaneous mobilization are occurring. The fax machine was indispensable for disseminating information and mobilizing dissent during the Tiananmen Square Demonstrations in Beijing in 1990; text messaging and video feeds off cell phones were the preferred communication during the riots in the suburbs of Paris and other French cities in 2005; twitter messages were indispensable to connect anti-government demonstrators in Iran in 2009; and a Facebook page has been credited with sparking the overthrow of the Egyptian president in 2011.

While online networking is being used to mobilize collective action, it has also created opportunities for manipulation and control. Since its inception, the Internet has been a blend of military strategy, corporate power, and countercultural innovation (Hafner and Markoff 1991). This has resulted in the proliferation of both bottom-up initiatives and commercial enterprises. For example, online social networking and open-source technologies are promoted by companies to solicit innovations and build brand loyalty (Tapscott and Williams 2008). While I was writing this chapter, a social networking site promoted "Kick a Ginger Day" (*Vancouver Sun* 2008), resulting in attacks all over North America on red-headed children and youth; the suicide of a youth in the U.S. was viewed and encouraged by his online audience (Stelter 2008); and there were numerous accounts of teenagers lured from their homes by online predators.

Swyngedouw (1997) and Hampton (2003) point to a form of "glocalization" whereby citizens are globally connected and locally involved. This is neither weakening nor radically transforming community; instead, it is adding another form of communication, whose use and implications are intertwined with other forms of community activity. Certainly, research on community organizing after the Hurricane Katrina disaster in New Orleans, Louisiana, points to the importance of Internet-based strategies as a way to reach and inform the scattered New Orleans population, and to engage that population in neighborhood planning and disaster recovery (Wagner 2010).

While the network society can foster better communication and allow increased access to information, thereby increasing opportunities for involvement and calls for public accountability, it does not mean that this will occur. The organizational structure created can perpetuate existing power hierarchies, impeding the opportunity for any meaningful discourse to occur. Online involvement widens the range of potential connections, but those connections can be ethereal and lessen privacy as the global network gathers all forms of data on individuals.

Menzies (2000) sees digital public space as a threat to community-building in physical places. She identifies the power of mass media in promoting fear of public spaces, and use of the Internet furthering isolation, social fragmentation, and polarization, leading to atrophy of social habits such as trust and cooperation. As public spaces become more anonymous, fearful places, our expanded private spaces, and our online interactions within those spaces, accentuate our atomization.

Implications for Planning and Policy-Making

The growing complexity in society that accompanies the rise of new technologies, changes in production processes, globalization of culture and economy, and the ensuing problems of fragmentation, uneven development, and the crisis in representative democracy are making for real challenges in planning and policy-making. Governments at all levels are finding that to be relevant they need to adopt strategies that reflect the networked societies in which they are embedded.

The task ahead is about community building to mitigate and reverse inequities. As societies increasingly function in a networked manner, multiple nodal attachments resulting from grassroots mobilization, across national borders, with broad social agendas and alliances may help to frame more empowered responses to current trends. An example of this is how labor organizations are developing new strategies for enhancing worker agency in a networked world to avoid the negative impact on employees of failed or badly managed outsourcing. The European white-collar unions discussed by Ramioul and De Bruyen (2008) have opted for a partnership approach that attempts to make work more "sustainable" at both ends of the global value chain. In the United States, Wash Tech, originally an alliance of Seattle high-tech workers, has grown in influence as it has advanced the issues facing its "precarious workforce," including challenging offshoring by government and employers, and by linking to other unions and supporting the organization of IT workers in India (Rodino-Colocino 2008). UNISON, the UK Public Service Union, is working with the East London Communities Organisation (TELCO), a large, diverse alliance of nearly forty independent grassroots institutions, on the Living Wage Campaign, to raise awareness of the problems of poverty pay in public services, privatization, and the two-tier workforce. Through organizing in local community, religious, and voluntary organizations, they have created visibility and support from policy-makers and the predominantly female, immigrant, and visible minority low-waged workers, successfully negotiating new contracts that have improved the conditions of their workers (UNISON nd).

While global networks are important in this work, it is still the relationships sustained and nurtured at the local level that will endure. In a world where people are increasingly likely to have multiple place affinities, new efforts could be directed at helping to more firmly anchor local relationships. Policy responses to inequities in urban hierarchies are challenging, particularly for regional and municipal level planning. To have any meaningful influence, they must go beyond rhetoric and be embedded in an understanding of both the evolving nature of network structures and the spatial rootedness of community interests. Planners will thus require greater awareness of the specific local ways new fragmented urban patterns are evolving. For example, choices in economic development strategies need to consider local economic conditions, quality of life issues, and global forces as well. Footloose industries may not be appropriate for locales that need to build a stable employment base.

"Community Informatics" is a community-based approach that links economic and social development at the community level to electronic commerce, flexible networks, and telework by integrating participatory design of information technology resources, popular education, and asset-based development to enhance citizen empowerment and quality of life. An example of such an approach is the proliferation of community networks in the United States, Canada, and elsewhere, which not only provide community- and civic-oriented public access to the Internet while gathering information and communication resources related to their community and organizing them consistently, but also promote community-oriented discussion forums (Schuler 2003). Gurstein, O'Neill, and Petersen (2009) also document the power of social entrepreneurship linked to the global network in furthering poverty alleviation in developing countries such as Cambodia and Laos.

Still, it may be erroneous to assume that the concept of networks benefits all people who lack resources (Fainstein 2005). Gurstein and Vilches (2009), in a study of lone mothers on income assistance, found that when women were directed by government institutions to lean on their private social networks as a means of lessening government responsibilities, it put women and their children in an even more precarious situation because of the fragile nature of their complex webs of support. In addition, not all locales benefit in the network society. There is a growing disparity between urban and rural areas as poor infrastructure for telecommunications impedes rural development opportunities.

However, people living in remote and rural communities are quick to imagine the infinite possibilities access to online services will provide them in education, entertainment, networking, health, employment opportunities, and a market for their commerce, and when access is available they are heavy users. In Nunavut Territory in northern Canada, a local service provider serves all twenty-five communities with wireless broadband Internet services, delivered via satellite.[3] The private company, initiated by a Nunavut-based nonprofit broadband corporation with a membership of community and private sector representatives, has a penetration of 3,700 subscribers servicing a population of 29,000 people dispersed over 2 million square miles. In this model, each community has a trained local person, called a

Community Service Provider, who can install wireless modems, handle basic troubleshooting, and collect payment for services.

The examples in this chapter illustrate the range of policies and planning initiatives that need to be developed to optimize opportunities in the network society and support individuals and groups who use technologies to overcome disadvantages such as physical isolation, lack of skills, or poverty. Digital networks can provide opportunities for participation in deliberative engagement, but inequalities will not necessarily be diminished. These networks need to be accessible and reflect users' priorities. Of equal importance is the process of community building that has to occur to build confidence in participatory processes and allow for genuine public dialogue (Bohman 2004).

The network society reinforces the delocalization that alters material and social patterns, creating new options for, and constraints on, individual and collective action. While global access to information technologies is growing dramatically, this has not necessarily ensured a lessening of inequality. The inequities generated are at a number of levels. Competition for employment creates disparities at the country, regional, and city levels. Household access to digital technologies results in a social divide. Networked employment practices redefine the workplace, and flexibility and control within it, changing employment and contractual relations, creating new risks to well-being and a demarcation between "core" positions with secure job tenure and good pay and "periphery" employment with uncertain remuneration, benefits, and job security. E-governance affects the quality of public service and blurs the distinction between public and private delivery of those services. Digital public space can further societal fragmentation. The social and spatial relations that emerge describe dispersal of activities away from traditional nodes and forms of activities, re-concentration in other nodes in other ways, and polarization and disparity within and between societies.

While disparities are widening, this does not mean that they are irreversible. Reimagining how networks, and the resources they bring, can be for the benefit of all is crucial. This is not a naïve belief in the power of technologies to transform society but recognition that societal responsibilities to ensure equity should be at the core of any policy framework for the network society.

Social inclusion can only be furthered by open and democratic planning and policy-making. To encourage the development of social networks and enhance the range of choices for workers as well as their employers, social policies must allow greater balance and further the available options in working life. Re-imagining the household as an essential support system that is part of larger community and government support networks would offer an alternative to neoliberal models focused on individualism, free markets, and free trade. Although this might seem utopian in the present policy context, it is utterly achievable with a different understanding of what constitutes societal responsibilities and a recognition that social infrastructure is equally, if not more, important than the physical and technological.

Notes

1. Home-based customer service employment has not grown significantly because of companies' concerns about lack of managerial control, privacy issues, and the need for expensive equipment in workers' homes.

2. The one area of library funding actively supported is in the area of new technologies.

3. See Qiniq website, http://www.qiniq.com/.

References

Aberdeen Group. 2003. Global sourcing: What you need to know to make it work. http://searchcio.techtarget.com/generic/0,295582,sid19_gci1049457,00.html?bucket=REF, accessed May 2011.

Albrechts, Louis, and Seymour J. Mandelbaum, eds. 2005. *The network society: A new context for planning.* Abingdon, N.Y.: Routledge.

Barfield, Claude E., Günter Heiduk, and Paul J. J. Welfens, eds. 2003. *Internet, economic growth and globalization: Perspectives on the new economy in Europe, Japan and the U.S.* Berlin: Springer.

Bell, Daniel. 1973. *The coming of post-industrial society.* New York: Basic Books.

Bohman, James. 2004. Expanding dialogue: The Internet, the public sphere and the prospects for transnational democracy. *Sociological Review* 52(S1) (June): 131–55.

Canadian Telework Association. 2008. Canadian telework scene includes Canadian organizations that telework. http://www.gdsourcing.com/works/Telework.htm.

Carr, David. 2008. Obama's social networking was the real revolution. *New York Times*, October 9.

Castells, Manuel. 1989. *The informational city: Information technology, economic restructuring, and the urban-regional process.* Oxford: Blackwell.

———. 1996. *The information age: Economy, society and culture.* Vol. 1, *The rise of the network society.* Cambridge, Mass.: Blackwell.

Clift, Steven. 2004. E-Democracy resource links. http://www.publicus.net/articles/edemresources.html, accessed May 2011.

CNet. 2009. Finland makes 1Mb broadband access a legal right. http://news.cnet.com/8301-17939_109-10374831-2.html., accessed October 14, 2010.

Coleman, Stephen, and Scott Wright. 2008. Political blogs and representative democracy. *Information Polity: The International Journal of Government & Democracy in the Information Age* 13(1/2): 1–5.

Connecting Canadians Agenda. 2003. Connecting to the Connecting Canadians Agenda: Rural Internet use for government information. Working paper, August. http://www.mta.ca/research/rstp/pdf/govcontact-paper.pdf.

Cornfield, Daniel B., Karen Campbell, and Holly J. McCammon, eds. 2001. *Working in restructured workplaces: Challenges and new directions for the sociology of work.* Thousand Oaks, Calif.: Sage.

Dear, Michael. 1999. Telecommunications, gangster nations and the crisis of representative democracy: An editorial comment. *Political Geography* 18(1): 81–83.

Derrida, Jacques. 1978. Structure, sign, and play in the discourse of the human sciences. In *Writing and difference*, trans. Alan Bass, 278–94. London: Routledge.

Fainstein, Susan S. 2005. Commentary: Local networks and capital building. In *The network society: A new context for planning*, ed. Louis Albrechts and Seymour J. Mandelbaum, 222–25. Abingdon, N.Y.: Routledge.

Florida, Richard. 2005. *Cities and the creative class.* New York: Routledge.

Friedman, Thomas I. 2005. *The world is flat: A brief history of the twenty-first century.* New York: Farrar, Straus and Giroux.

Friedmann, John. 1986. The world city hypothesis. *Development and Change* 17(1): 69–84.

———. 1987. *Planning in the public domain: From knowledge to action.* Princeton, N.J.: Princeton University Press.

Graham, Stephen. 2001. The city as sociotechnical process: Networked mobilities and urban social inequalities. *City* 5(3): 339–49.

Graham, Stephen, and Patsy Healey. 1999. Relational concepts of space and place: Issues for planning theory and practice. *European Planning Studies* 7(5): 623–46.

Graham, Stephen, and Simon Marvin. 1996. *Telecommunications and the city: Electronic spaces, urban places.* London: Routledge.

Gurstein, Penny. 2001. *Wired to the world, chained to the home: Telework in daily life.* Vancouver: University of British Columbia Press.

———. 2007. Navigating the seamless environment in the global supply chain: Implications for Canadian regions and workers. *Work Organisation, Labor and Globalisation* 1(2): 76–97.

Gurstein, Penny, James O'Neill, and Marisol Petersen. 2009. Outsourcing to further human development: The case of a social enterprise in Cambodia and Laos. In Special Theme Issue, *Work Beyond Boundaries, Journal of Architectural and Planning Research—JAPR* 26(4) (Winter): 276–86.

Gurstein, Penny, and Laura Tate. 2009. Global sourcing and community change. *Work beyond boundaries*. Theme issue, *Journal of Architectural and Planning Research—JAPR* 26(4) (Winter): 287–300.

Gurstein, Penny, and Silvia Vilches. 2009. Re-visioning the environment of support for lone mothers in extreme poverty. In *Public policy for women: The state, income security, and labour*, ed. Marjorie Griffith Cohen and Jane Pulkingham, 226–47. Toronto: University of Toronto Press.

Habermas, Jürgen. 1984. *The theory of communicative action*. Trans. Thomas McCarthy. Boston: Beacon Press.

———. 1991. *The structural transformation of the public sphere: An inquiry into a category of bourgeois society*, trans. Thomas McCarthy. Cambridge, Mass.: MIT Press.

Hafner, Katie, and John Markoff. 1991. *Cyberpunk, outlaws and hackers in the computer frontier*. New York: Touchstone.

Hall, Peter. 1998. Globalization and the world of cities. In *Globalization and the world of large cities*, ed. Fu-chen Lo and Yue-man Yeung, 17–36. Tokyo: United Nations University Press.

Hampton, Keith. 2003. Grieving for a lost network: Collective action in a wired suburb. *Information Society* 19: 417–28.

Harkness, Richard C. 1977. *Technology assessment of telecommunications/transportation interactions*. Stanford Calif.: Stanford Research Institute.

Heng, Michael S. H., and Aldo de Moor. 2003. From Habermas's communicative theory to practice on the Internet. *Information Systems Journal* 13: 331–52.

Hutton, Thomas A. 2009. Trajectories of the new economy: Regeneration and dislocation in the inner city. *Urban Studies* 46(5&6): 987–1001.

Huws, Ursula. 1991 Telework: Projections. *Futures* (January/February): 19–31.

———. 2003. *The Making of a cybertariat: Virtual work in a real world*. New York: Monthly Review Press.

Huws, Ursula, Simone Dahlmann, and Jörg Flecker. 2004. *Outsourcing of ICT and related services in the EU*. Dublin: European Foundation for the Improvement of Living and Working Conditions.

Huws, Ursula, Werner B. Korte, and Simon Robinson. 1990. *Telework: Towards the elusive office*. Chichester: John Wiley.

Illegems, Viviane, and Alain Verbeke. 2003. *Moving towards the virtual workplace: Managerial and societal perspectives on telework*. Cheltenham: Edward Elgar.

Internet World Statistics. 2010. Internet usage statistics, June 30, 2010. http://www.Internetworldstats.com/stats.htm, accessed May 2011.

Keating, Matt. 2005. Phone Home: Could the alternative to overseas call centres be found in the UK's living rooms? *The Guardian*, October 15.

Menzies, Heather. 1996. *Whose brave new world: The information highway and the new economy*. Toronto: Between the Lines.

———. 2000. Postscript: On digital public space and the real tragedy of the commons. In *E-commerce vs. e-commons: communications in the public interest*, ed. Marita Moll and Leslie Rita Shade. Ottawa: Canadian Centre for Policy Alternatives.

Mirchandani, Kiran. 2003. Challenging racial silences in studies of emotion work: Contributions from anti-racist feminist theory. *Organization Studies* 24(5): 721–42.

Mitchell, William J. 1999a. Equitable access to the online world. In *High technology and low income communities: Prospects for the positive use of advanced information technology,* ed. Donald A. Schon, Bish Sanyal, and William J. Mitchell, 151–62. Cambridge, Mass.: MIT Press.

———. 1999b. *E-Topia: "Urban life, Jim—but not as we know it."* Cambridge, Mass.: MIT Press.

Mitter, Swasti. 2005. Globalization, ICTs and economic empowerment: A feminist critique. In *Gender and the Digital Economy: Perspectives from the Developing World,* ed. Cecelia Ng and Swasti Mitter, 29–53. New Delhi: Sage.

Mokhtarian, Patricia L. 1991. Defining telecommuting. *Transportation Research Record* 1305: 273–81.

Mokhtarian, Patricia L., Ilan Salomon, and Sangho Choo. 2005. Measuring the measurable: Why can't we agree on the number of telecommuters in the U.S.? *Quality & Quantity* 39: 423–52.

Nilles, Jack M., with F. Roy Carlson, Jr., Paul Gray, and Gerhard J. Hanneman. 1976. *The telecommunications-transportation tradeoff.* New York: Wiley.

Norris, Pippa. 2001. *Digital divide: Civic engagement, information poverty, and the Internet worldwide.* New York: Cambridge University Press.

OECD. 2003. The e-Government imperative: Main findings. http://www.oecd.org/dataoecd/60/60/2502539.pdf, accessed February 29, 2012.

O'Toole, James, and Edward E. Lawler, III. 2006. *The new American workplace.* New York: Palgrave Macmillan.

Ramioul, Monique, and Tom De Bruyn. 2008. Towards strategies for making offshore outsourcing economically and socially sustainable. *Work Organisation, Labour and Globalisation* 2(1): 117–32.

Rheingold, Howard 2002. *Smart mobs: The next social revolution.* Cambridge, Mass.: Perseus.

Rodino-Colocino, Michelle. 2008. Technomadic work: From promotional vision to Washtech's opposition. *Work Organisation, Labour and Globalisation* 2(1): 104–16.

Rohde, Gerhard. 2003. Jobs with no frontiers—Global mobility: A challenge to unions and researchers. http://www.boeckler.de/pdf/wsimit_eng_2003_10_rohde.pdf, accessed May 2011.

Rowbotham, Sheila. 1993. *Homeworkers worldwide.* London: Merlin Press.

Sassen, Saskia. 1994. *Cities in the world economy.* Thousand Oaks, Calif.: Pine Forge Press.

———. 1998. *Globalization and its discontents.* New York: New Press.

———. 2001. *The global city: New York, London, Tokyo.* 2nd ed. Princeton, N.J.: Princeton University Press.

Schön, Donald A., Bish Sanyal and William J. Mitchell, eds. 1999. *High technology and low income communities: Prospects for the positive use of advanced information technology.* Cambridge, Mass.: MIT Press.

Schumacher, E. F. 1973. *Small is beautiful: Economics as if people mattered*. London: Blond and Briggs.

Schuler, Douglas. 2003. Digital cities and digital citizens. In *Community networking and community informatics: Prospects, approaches and instruments*, ed. Michael Gurstein, Michel Menou, and Sergei Stafeev, 194–215. St. Petersburg: Centre of Community Networking and Information Policy Studies.

Standen, Peter, and Jan Sinclair-Jones. 2003. eWork in regional Australia. Rural Industries Research and Development Corporation, Australian Government. https://rirdc.infoservices.com.au/downloads/04-045, accessed February 29, 2012.

Stelter, Brian. 2008. Web suicide viewed live and reaction spur a debate. *New York Times*, November 24.

Swyngedouw, Erik. 1997. Neither global nor local: Glocalization and the politics of scale. In *Spaces of globalization: Reasserting the power of the local*, ed. Kevin R. Cox, 137–66. New York: Guilford.

Tapscott, Don, and Anthony Williams. 2008. *Wikinomics: How mass collaboration changes everything*. London: Atlantic.

Thrift, Nigel. 1996. New urban eras and old technological fears: Reconfiguring the good-will of electronic things. *Urban Studies* 33(8): 1463–93.

Toffler, Alvin. 1980. *The third wave*. New York: William Morrow.

UNISON website. n.d.. Bargaining for fair wages. http://www.unison.org.uk/bargaining/doc_view.asp?did=377&pid=193.

Vancouver Sun. 2008. No suspensions after "Kick a Ginger Day" incites problems. November 25.

Van Dijk, Jan A. G. M. 2005. *The deepening divide: inequality in the information society*. London: Sage.

———. 2006. *The network society*. London: Sage.

Wagner, Jacob A. 2010. Digital media and the politics of disaster recovery in New Orleans. In *Multimedia explorations in urban policy and planning: Beyond the flat-lands*, ed. Leonie Sandercock and Giovanni Attilli, 105–28. London: Springer.

World Bank Group. 2005. Administrative and civil service reform: Alternative service delivery mechanisms. http://web.worldbank.org/wbsite/external/topics/ extpublicsectorandgovernance/extadministrativeandcivilservicereform/0,contentMDK: 20134061~menuPK:286372~pagePK:148956~piPK:216618~theSitePK:286367,00. html#1, accessed February 29, 2012.

U.S. Department of Labor. 2008. Customer service representatives. http://www.bls.gov/oco/pdf/ocos280.pdf, accessed February 29, 2012.

Chapter 9

The Center-Periphery Dilemma:
Spatial Inequality and Regional Development

Daniel Shefer and Amnon Frenkel

Variations exist among regions. These variations manifest themselves in the levels of the *population*'s economic and social well-being. Different regions are endowed with production factors and characteristics that offer different opportunities for specialization, which can be exploited to gain regional comparative advantage. They then may add to the region's aggregate income and well-being. It is of paramount importance, then, first to identify a region's comparative advantages and then to devise policies that exploit those advantages. Many outlying regions (peripheral regions) suffer from a high rate of unemployment, a low level of per capita income, and net out-migration. Most often the out-migrants come from the highly educated and highly motivated population. Among them, we can find a high percentage of potential entrepreneurs. Outlying areas attract less investment than do central regions because of the low marginal productivity of factors of production in the former. In order to alleviate these hardships and prevent them from being further inflicted on outlying regions, central governments often devise incentive and investment programs whose main objective is to reduce gaps among regions and, thus, to reduce regional inequalities.

Over the past three decades, high-technology industries have expanded worldwide at a tremendous pace. Attracting high-tech firms to outlying regions is now in vogue, due in part to the image they project as magnets for highly educated and highly paid employees. Public/private investment in large-scale facilities, such as highways and railways, technological incubators,

universities, and hospitals, are among the projects proposed in order to facilitate economic growth in outlying areas

The principal objective of this chapter is to critically review the spatial
implications of alternative public investment programs designed to facilitate
the growth of peripheral regions, reducing the disparities between central regions and outlying (peripheral regions). We begin with the economic growth
model and the Conversion-Diversion hypothesis, followed by Krugman's
New Economic Geography model. This is followed by a discussion of the
spatial concentration of economic activities—agglomeration economies,
clustering, and networking—that spawn innovations, entrepreneurships, and
start-ups, and in turn result in creation of new enterprises. All this activity
contributes to regional growth. We then turn to a recently employed policy
instrument—the technological incubator—and an extensive assessment of
the impact of investment in transport infrastructure on regional development, particularly in a peripheral region.

Economic Growth: Conversion-Diversion and the NEG Model

The restrictive assumptions embedded in the neoclassical growth model—
exogenous technology, constant returns to scale, and diminishing marginal
productivity of capital in a perfect competition situation—do not provide a
good explanation for the observed process of continuous growth in per capita income and, thus, in the standard of living (Solow 1956). The endogenous
economic growth models that emerged in the 1980s prompted by the seminal
work of Romer (1986) and Lucas (1988) brought to the fore the importance of
endogenous technological progress (Aghion and Howitt 1998; Romer 1994;
Grossman and Helpman 1991; Nijkamp and Poot 1997). Thus, technological
progress could explain the persistent growth in income and, consequently, in
income per capita or standard of living.

In recent years, researchers have become increasingly aware of the role of
technological progress and innovation on regional development and economic
growth. Regions with a high level of innovation have become a destination for
highly skilled labor and an impetus for improved social and physical infrastructures. These regions enjoy at times unique opportunities for development
of new firms, expansion of market share, profitability, and employment growth.

Industries that are heavily engaged in technological innovation usually possess a high market value resulting from a comparative advantage, at least during the first stage of the diffusion process. Open economies can take advantage of an expanded market and, through increasing returns to scale, have the benefit of greater production efficiency and a higher rate of economic growth. Greater production efficiency enables industries to expand their domestic market share through import substitution and increases in local consumption and, at the same time, to penetrate new foreign markets and raise their export share (Porter 1990; Krugman 1979, 1991, 1995).

In a classic article published in 1955, Simon Kuznets hypothesized that the relationship between economic growth and inequality follows an inverted U-shaped curve. In the early development stage, regional income differentials increase and subsequently stabilize; then, when the economy matures, personal income inequality among regions diminishes.

Kuznets's hypothesis suggests that poor economies tend to grow faster than rich ones, thus decreasing disparities among regions. Indeed, empirical studies in general support this hypothesis (Barro and Sala-i-Martin 1991, 1995: chap. 11). Convergence is further reinforced by the phenomena of increased globalization, trade liberalization, and treaties among countries like the EU and NAFTA that enable the flow of production factors—labor mobility, products (export), and direct foreign investment (DFI). It is facilitated by specialization and increasing returns to scale. Nevertheless, although disparities among countries decrease, a widening gap may be observed between regions within countries. This divergence phenomenon originates from a greater concentration of economic activity in a few central areas, enabling the agglomeration economies fueled by technological progress and pecuniary externalities. Central areas enjoy greater efficiency in production of goods and services than do outlying areas. Consequently, economies of agglomeration are the principal force that exacerbates inequalities among regions in a given country (Kanbur and Venables 2005).

In China, for example, although the economy was growing at an astonishing rate in the last decades, a significant differential annual rate of growth was observed between the booming coastal regions and the interior, and these gaps were increasing rapidly (Fujita and Hu 2001). Similarly, in counties of the European Union, disparities in per capita income levels between countries have narrowed; at the same time, regional disparities within countries have widened (Geppert and Stephan 2008; Fan et al. 2009).

In 1991, Paul Krugman published his seminal paper, "Increasing Returns and Economic Geography," which presented a synthesis of the core-periphery model and the neo-classical endogenous growth model. It was the basic framework for the New Economic Geography (NEG) model. The NEG model explains the formation of large varieties of agglomeration economies in geographical space in a general equilibrium framework. It treats simultaneously trade, economic growth (increasing returns to scale), and economic geography (i.e., the location of people and economic activities in space). In order to reduce the cost of transporting goods and to benefit from increasing returns to scale, firms and workers are pulled together toward selected places where agglomeration economies prevail.

Krugman showed how in equilibrium, inequality in per capita income exists between regions. He alluded to centripetal and centrifugal forces that shape the economic landscape (see also Losch 1954). The former, centripetal forces, pull economic activities together to form the spatial concentration of economic activities in a few selected points in space and in locations where agglomeration economies are in existence. The latter, centrifugal forces, push them apart (Fujita and Thisse 1996; Fujita and Krugman 2004; Fujita and Mori 2005). Krugman lists under centripetal forces market size, pool of labor markets, and external economies (knowledge spillovers) and under centrifugal forces immobile factors of production, land rents (commuting costs), and external diseconomies (congestion and environmental pollution) (Krugman 1998: 8).

Agglomeration, Innovation, and the Location of High-Tech Industries

Profit-maximizing location decisions made by individual entrepreneurs cause firms to cluster together in select discrete locations (Ellison and Glaeser 1997, 1999; Malmberg and Power 2005). Different regions offer different opportunities for specialization, which when exploited may add to the aggregate income and well-being of a region. Since entrepreneurs strive to maximize profits, they are motivated to invest in regions where the greatest profits can be attained, given some pre-specified level of probabilities of risk owing to uncertainties. Profit will be maximized in regions where there is comparatively higher productivity of inputs, such as labor, capital, and efficiency, in the network of transport and other systems of communication.

Agglomeration Economies and Industrial Clustering

Theoretical and empirical studies support the effect of agglomeration economies and clustering of industries on production efficiency (see, for example,
Shefer 1973; Fujita and Thisse, 1996 2002; Graham 2008). Modern location
theory demonstrates the significant role that agglomeration and localization
economies play in explaining the growth of cities as hubs generating new
ideas and technological progress (Jacobs 1969). Agglomeration economies,
localization economies (measured by the size of industries in a given location), and the economies of scale of the single firm are the principal forces
fostering the continuous concentration of people and economic activities in
a selected point in space. Agglomeration economies, though, are not a very
tangible concept, since they encompass several loosely defined factors. They
can be measured by the number of employees in a particular industry (localization economies) or by the diversity of workers residing in a given locality
(Shefer 1973).

Two major groups of variables affect the rate of innovation by firms. The
first is *internal* to the firm; the second is *external* (Davelaar and Nijkamp
1989). The first refers to the firm's structural attributes, and includes the following characteristics: size, age, ownership type, and location of firm, as well
as the type of industry to which it belongs and the extent of technological
change and innovation in R&D activities taking place in the firm. R&D activities can be measured either by the number of employees engaged in R&D
or by the total expenditure allocated to it. The second, external group of variables creates the *local innovation milieu* (Shefer and Frenkel 1998).

Local Innovation Milieu

The local innovation milieu includes the degree of local innovation, the degree of cooperation and collaboration among firms (*networking*), and the
degree of economies of industrial localization and urban agglomeration.
Spillovers between firms are very important in enhancing a firm's productivity and innovation capabilities. Agglomeration economies play a significant part in the increase in the rate of a high-tech firm's innovation potential
(Fujita and Thisse 1996, 2002).

One methodological framework for analyzing local innovation milieu is
depicted in the two-dimensional diagrams in Figure 9.1. In both diagrams,
the vertical axis represents the degree of local innovativeness: the rate of

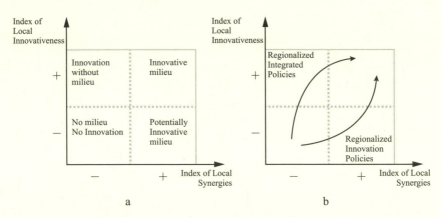

Figure 9.1. Sub-areas of an innovative milieu. Daniel Shefer and Amnon Frenkel, "Local Milieu and Innovativeness: Some Empirical Results," *Annals of Regional Science* 32 (1998): 188.

innovation in a specific locality. The horizontal axis measures local synergies: the degree of socioeconomic interaction among firms in a cluster—*networking*. Such interaction is considered a cost-reducing factor that diminishes uncertainty and increases production efficiency (Camagni 1995; Kleinknecht and Poot 1992; Shefer and Frenkel 1998). The diagram on the right shows that there are two ways to reach the innovative milieu (the upper right quadrant), through regionalized integrated policies or regional innovation polices. Most central regions are expected to be found on the upper right-hand quadrant, and most peripheral regions on the lower left-hand quadrant of the diagrams (Shefer and Frenkel 1998).

A production milieu becomes attractive when companies cluster within it, creating economies of scale and agglomeration economies (Davelaar 1991; Audretsch and Feldman 1996; Porter 1998; McCann and Shefer 2004). A region's comparative advantage is manifested in its technology level, developed infrastructures, social capitals (quality of personnel, etc.), and institutional framework, compared to other regions (Frenkel 2000).

Spatial Diffusion of Innovation

Diffusion of innovation is a complex process involving changes in the behavior of economic agents. The diffusion process may be understood by integrating three basic elements: companies, environment, and technology. The integration of these elements creates the early necessary conditions for adopting innovation. Development regions are able to adopt technologies associated with production processes; however, they may face severe difficulties in adopting advanced product innovation. Process innovation usually can be bought "off the shelf" on the open market. Product innovation, on the other hand, is not as readily available. The reason is that innovation is the means by which a firm can maintain a competitive edge over its rivals. Therefore, product innovation is less transferable in terms of diffusion.

In space, we can presume that a greater amount of uncertainty and limited bits of information are being transmitted to a location at a distance from the concentration of people and economic activities—the metropolis. Thus, we can hypothesize that the process of diffusion of innovation in space follows the form depicted in Figure 9.2a. Two major processes can be distinguished: the first is movement from the center to the boundaries, or the periphery (suburbs), of the metropolitan area; the second is the strong connection, in spite of the distance separating them, between centers of activities—metropolitan areas. These affinities between centers traverse intermediate areas that could be considered peripheral to the metropolis. Thus, the spatial diffusion of innovation from the center to the periphery follows the pattern depicted in Figure 9.2b. That pattern portrays a sequential process that gradually declines in intensity from the heart of the metropolis outward. Given these diffusion processes, we would expect that the rate of innovation will follow similar spatial patterns: a gradual decline in the rate of innovation as one proceeds from the center toward the periphery.

Agglomeration and localization economies affect positively and significantly the rate of innovation in high-tech industries, but their effect on low-tech industries is much less pronounced (Audretsch 1998; Shefer and Frenkel 1998). The electronics industry is affected positively and significantly by the high concentration of people and economic activities. Its rate of innovation rapidly increases with the prevalence of agglomeration. Agglomeration economies, on the other hand, do not significantly affect the rate of innovation in low-tech industries.

Consistent results have been obtained in various empirical studies of the effects of agglomeration. One obvious conclusion that can be drawn from this consistency is that it would be counterproductive to push electronics firms away from the core. On the other hand, the rate of innovation in firms

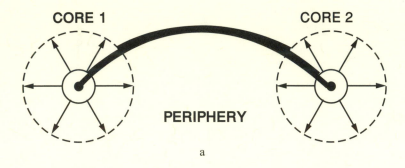

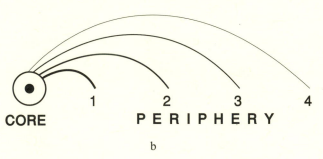

Figure 9.2. Spatial diffusion of innovation. Shefer and Frenkel, "Local Milieu and Innovativeness," 190.

belonging to the low-tech sector, such as plastics and metals, will be affected only marginally and insignificantly by a move from the core toward the intermediate and peripheral regions. These conclusions suggest that public policies designed to promote regional growth and development should be industry-specific (Shefer et al. 2001).

Entrepreneurship and Innovation

A major element in building new markets, invigorating business sectors, and furthering economic growth in general is entrepreneurship (Schumpeter 1934; Acs and Armington, 2004; Audretsch and Keilbach 2004, 2005).

Regions that traditionally encourage entrepreneurship and innovative activities have a higher probability of growth. Absence of entrepreneurship will lead to insufficient resource utilization, which may retard the growth of firms, cities, and regions (Acs and Storey 2004).

Entrepreneurial development of technological innovation depends mainly on a production milieu that encourages a high level of local innovation and the synergy of different factors to create regional comparative advantages. The existence of entrepreneurship capital is one way to define a region's ability to create and attract new firms.

Technological Incubators in Peripheral Areas

The aim of a technological incubator program, as a development program "from below," is to foster entrepreneurial activities from the very beginning of a project's initiation. Not surprisingly, the incubator has the advantages and drawbacks typical of this kind of program. On the one hand, it can help create a healthy entrepreneurial culture by empowering local people and encouraging them to develop their own firms. On the other hand, it works very slowly: at least ten or fifteen years is needed to assess the actual impact on employment and economic development. Then again, a technological incubator in a peripheral region may be able to provide functions that are seldom found in these areas, such as venture capital supply, business and legal services, and the filtering of valuable ideas.

The idea of the technological incubator program emanated from the desire to encourage and support budding start-ups in their critical years before reaching maturity. The incubator increases a small firm's chances of graduating from the incubator—and therefore of survival—by supplying them with such basic services as assistance and consultation in outlying areas, thereby helping to accelerate their rate of growth. Enterprises that began life in an incubator have been found to have a higher rate of success than those that did not.

At a national level, the technological incubator program may be seen as a tool for filtering and developing new ideas and for providing seed capital. At a local level, the incubator may be viewed as a means of local economic development, since it can induce the creation and development of new firms in a specific location. A good example is the award-winning Austin Technology Incubator, which generated more than $1.4 billion and created some 3,000 jobs (Wiggins and Gibson 2003). Hannon and Chaplin (2003) reported, on the basis of a literature survey, that evidence from the United States and the UK strongly suggested that most incubator tenants came from the immediate locality and that most of the firms that graduated from an incubator stayed in the same locality.

Technological incubators are not limited to the industrialized world. They now can be found in such countries as China, Turkey, Brazil, South Korea, and Indonesia, where the economy has passed through structural changes. Among the developing countries, the largest technological incubator program exists in China and Brazil. In China, there were 131 technological incubators in operation in 2000, consisting of 7,693 companies and 128,776 employees. By 2000, a total of 836 companies had graduated from the program (Harwit 2002; Xu 2010). In Brazil, 107 high-tech-based incubators and 40 mixed (traditional and high technology) incubators were in operation in 2003 (Etzkowitz and Klofsten 2005).

The Israeli Technological Incubator Program was initiated by the Chief Scientist's Office (CSO) in the Ministry of Industry and Trade in the early 1990s. The program was designed, among other things, to help with the absorption of new immigrants from the former Soviet Union and assimilating the vast technological knowledge and experience they brought with them (Shefer and Frenkel 2003). Ten years after the establishment of this program, it was discovered that incubators were capable of enlarging their budget from nongovernmental sources, mostly in the form of royalties, sale of shares, dividends, and strategic partnerships. These new sources of funding suggest that the government's large-scale support, needed at the initial stage, can gradually be withdrawn over time, once outside private funding sources are developed and attained. Still, technological incubators in peripheral regions require more public support, for a longer period of time, than do those in the central regions of the country (Frenkel et al. 2008).

Following a universal trend in the developed world, Israel moved to privatize some of its publicly run technological incubators. A recent study by Frenkel et al. (2008) examined this process. The main conclusion was that private incubators cannot substitute fully for the Public Incubator Program. Israel's Public Technological Incubator Program was founded to meet national objectives, such as geographical distribution, which includes rural and peripheral areas, as well as special incentives for populations like minorities and new immigrants, for whom such activities would otherwise be out of reach. In other words, the basic justification for public incubators still stands:

they promote not only an economic and a business interest but also a national and social interest, such as helping minority entrepreneurs and new immigrants, increasing exports, and developing peripheral areas.

Investment in Transportation Infrastructure and Economic Integration

Economic Impact of Transport Investment

Using a simple model of a regional economy, it may be seen that transportation investments can affect the regional economy in two significant ways. First, the transport system affects the movement of goods and people within a region, largely shaping how various components of the regional economy relate to one another. Second, investments in the transportation system can affect economic ties between a region and the outside world. In this regard, it can either inject additional income into the regional economy (stimulus) or cause income to leak out of the region (dampening).

Firms may also experience changes brought about by transportation investments from the demand side, benefiting from increased flows of visitors into the region or from an increase in the overall population base of the area. However, the impacts on regional firms are not all necessarily positive. Firms from outside the region may compete more intensely within the region because of lower distribution costs. Furthermore, increased sales by one firm may be offset by decreased sales by other firms in the region that did not directly benefit from the transportation improvements.

The impact on households is reflected mainly in the income and employment status of individuals. Households also are major consumers of products produced within the region. When regional firms change their output—and hence their derived demand for labor—the income and employment of individuals are affected. Transportation investments can also lower costs of locally produced goods by increasing competition from firms that import into the region.

This traditional economic analysis ignores the benefits to individuals of reduced travel times to work and commercial centers, since it considers households merely as inputs into the production process of a region or as consumers of regionally produced products. It does not incorporate the time saved by individuals (as opposed to firms) directly into projected economic benefits of transportation improvements, nor does it look at the potential tax base increases brought about by an influx of population stemming from the greater accessibility and reliability of travel means within the region. Moreover, the effect on local government of transportation improvements will be seen in revenues generated from changes in land value and land use in the vicinity of the improvements.

From the neoclassical economic perspective, it is logical to expect that reductions in production costs produced by investments in transportation will lead to increased market shares for firms whose accessibility is improved. These increased market shares will translate into increased production by the affected firms, leading to enhanced employment and income for the region. However, profits may leak from the region or result in little net impact, especially when most firms sell to the same market or purchase inputs from a fully employed economy.

Export income accrues to a regional economy when goods are shipped out via the transportation system or when tourists visit a region and make nonresident purchases. At the same time, transportation impacts are quickly dampened when regional importation increases. The money then injected into the economy is spent and re-spent. In each cycle of spending, a certain amount leaves the region as payments for imports and other leakages, the net change in the local or regional economy being called the multiplier effect.

The influence of improvements in the transportation system on the regional economy involves the impact of transportation infrastructure on the operation of the economy. Users, both providers (truck lines, etc.) and users (firms, households) of transportation services, are the initial benefactors. The beneficial aspects are reflected in either lower production costs or increased demand for outputs. Ultimately, user impacts are transferred to non-users. Cost saving by firms may be capitalized into new investment in the region, resulting in direct and indirect impacts on output, employment, and income in the economy. Alternatively, the cost saving may be passed on directly to consumers as lower prices or higher wages, leading to higher local consumption. Non-users who own land may also benefit from a rise in land values. These non-user benefits go together with benefits to the revenue streams of local governments.

Investment in Transportation Infrastructure

New transportation infrastructure may clearly reduce travel times and, hence, the cost of doing business in a specific region; however, its larger effect on the regional economy is much more complicated to predict. Other relevant economic factors that can influence a region's overall economic performance must obtain in order to attract economic activities to the region. Without the necessary regional business climate, a new transportation link may actually hinder growth by making it more cost-effective to move resources, including human and physical factors of production, from that region to more developed areas (Blum 1982; Rietveld and Bruinsma 1998; Biehl 1991; Rietveld and Nijkamp 2000).

New transportation infrastructure is not by itself a driving force for regional development; rather, it can induce growth when used in conjunction with complementary private investment and other public initiatives and policies designed to raise the region's relative competitive advantage. As a factor of production, the transportation infrastructure has a value that can vary from sector to sector and industry to industry. Thus, to predict the outcome of a given investment in transport infrastructure, the industries in that region must be checked for sensitivity to transportation costs (Batten and Karlsson 1996; Banister and Berechman 2000). Investment in infrastructure may encourage development in underdeveloped regions, but its construction alone is not enough to bring about the desired economic changes. Other factors, such as the economic climate in the relevant region, the relative price of factors of production (labor, capital, and materials), and agglomeration economies, tend to determine the viability of a region more than does its basic infrastructure (Vickerman 1991; McCann and Shefer 2004).

Adequate transportation infrastructure is a necessary, but not a sufficient, factor for the economic development of a region. On the other hand, the undersupply of transport infrastructure can severely hinder growth. The impact of a new transportation link, such as the Cross-Israel Highway (a north-south toll road, Route 6, farther inland and parallel to the main coastal road), on core versus periphery development trends should be carefully studied. In Europe, for example, the Channel Tunnel has had great impact, both short and long-term, on development patterns in northwest Europe. However, as Vickerman (1987: 188) points out, "the crucial question is whether such infrastructural investment can be the driving force in regional development, independently of other factors, or whether it has only an enabling role."

The case of the Channel Tunnel, as well as other examples of corridor development in Europe, show that a new link that improves access to major metropolitan areas may have the potential to either encourage or hinder development of areas peripheral to those metropolitan centers. A further analysis of the users of these new links in their respective regional economic contexts is needed to better understand and predict net economic outcomes.

Transport and Regional Development

The outcomes of transportation investments on the regional economy manifest themselves through observable and measurable changes in the relative *accessibility* of the region affected. It has been shown empirically that public capital infrastructure plays an important complementary role in the productivity of the private sector. Other studies suggest that heavy infrastructure investment during the 1950s and 1960s may have been a key, previously underrated factor in the strong economic performance of the United States in that period (Aschauer 1989).

Investment in transportation contributes to economic development if it significantly reduces transportation costs, thereby improving the net return on mobile resources in the area. Mobile resources can be attracted to the impact area of a new facility by providing this area with a better return than competing locations. If any economic activity is attracted from other sites within the defined region, then it cannot be viewed as new economic development. Therefore, how an affected area is defined can play a significant role in the corresponding net impact of a particular investment. Uncertainty about future demand for the transport facility makes an accurate benefit-cost analysis very difficult.

Rather than seeking economic efficiency, an alternative criterion for guiding investments in transport infrastructure is income redistribution. If the goal of government policy is to influence investment patterns in a particular area, then infrastructure investment may not be efficient in the traditional sense. It could be said that the government is aiming at "place prosperity" rather than "people prosperity." A government may wish to spread out economic development, with the hope that improved accessibility will lead to the attraction of economic activity, possibly balancing development across the country. However, trying to distribute development evenly may diminish countrywide growth, leaving residents possibly worse off than if there had been no such policy objective.

Good transportation facilities are not enough to ensure that economic development will occur. The area must be able to attract the necessary factors of production, labor, capital, and materials. Without these factors, even a good transportation facility will accomplish little. The safest way to generate economic development is to focus on cost savings for users and consumers.

Inefficient or insufficient investment in capital infrastructure precipitates urban decay. The efficiency of capital investment is greatest during a period of sustainable growth and development. When the level of public and private investment falls below that required for the satisfactory maintenance and replacement of infrastructure in a certain area, the competitive advantages of that area will gradually decline as its productivity erodes. The amounts as well as the mix of public and private investment, with a positive input required from both sectors, are crucial for sustainable development.

Conclusions

The center-periphery dilemma has long occupied researchers and policy-makers. Krugman's New Economic Geography model (1991a, b), along with the work of scholars such as Fujita et al. (2001), showed how trade theory, comparative advantage, trade liberalization, and globalization together induced greater economic concentration. Because of the inherent advantages of centers, disparities among regions—like inequalities in per capita income—do not vanish over time. On the contrary, centripetal forces exacerbate inequalities across space, particularly within countries. In order to reduce regional disparities between central and peripheral regions, government agencies devise policies and initiate programs whose main objectives are to increase population, employment levels, per capita income, and, in general, the welfare of outlying regions.

In the past few decades, high-tech industries have undergone tremendous expansion worldwide. Policy-makers view these industries as an important component of regional economic growth and, increasingly, as a crucial part of a region's export base. Attempts to attract high-tech industry to peripheral regions that appear at a disadvantage because of their distance from the urban center often encounter problems. Yet, policy-makers often remain optimistic that high-tech industrial development is possible anywhere because of the expanding communication technology which continues to increase the freedom of footloose firms (Shefer and Bar-El 1993). Mass production, which mostly demands semi-skilled and unskilled manual labor, is a more footloose activity than R&D, and hence it is more likely to locate in, or move to, peripheral areas. R&D activities, on the other hand, require agglomeration economies and clustering of economic activities for formal and informal networking and knowledge spillovers. R&D activity, which spurs innovation by its very nature, demands a local milieu, which can be found primarily in central areas where a large pool of human, social, and creative capital is offered (Shefer and Frenkel 1998; Florida 2002).

Competitive markets, motivated by private investors, usually lead to a high concentration of economic activities in central regions. However, this "private equilibrium" may deviate from the "social optimum" that takes into account costs borne and benefits enjoyed by the entire society (Charlot et al. 2006). In such instances of market failure government intervention is necessary, which could take the form of investment in transport infrastructure and/or labor force training (in order to upgrade the labor force). These steps could reduce the gap between private and social optimums and enhance the competitiveness of at least some peripheral regions (Malul and Bar-El 2009). It is of paramount importance to thoroughly evaluate the cost-effectiveness of alternative incentive programs that are intended to reduce inequalities among regions, while accommodating societal objectives such as equity and justice in addition to economic efficiency.

Investment in transportation infrastructures through improving and expanding roads, railways, and other transport networks, for instance, could make peripheral regions more competitive. These investments improve accessibility, regional competitiveness, and the range of both employment and social opportunities, and, in doing so, contribute to the economic integration of outlying areas. However, it is essential to identify the missing, or weak, links in the transportation networks so as to ensure that the investment program will effectively advance regional growth and reduce inter-regional disparities. Of course, there is no universal policy that can be applied to yield successful results. In fact, the most appropriate policies are *region specific*, based on the special circumstances associated with a region's location, endowments, comparative advantages, and disadvantages relative to other regions.

In addition to short-term public policy programs that include investment in institution building, infrastructure, and incentive programs for outlying areas, it is important to initiate long-term education and training programs that will build up and enhance the region's human capital. The hope, of course, is that improving the skill level of local labor will attract both entrepreneurs and capital to these peripheral regions.

What is the lesson to be learned by planners and decision-makers who are working to advance the status of peripheral regions? First, they should remember that the complex and dynamic nature of the planning process requires a high level of both proficiency and perseverance, as well as the ability to implement. Second, spatial strategic planning will permit the integration of disjointed parts of a region into a comprehensive whole, a whole that is able to very efficiently harness the existing resources and, in doing so, strengthening the tie between all parts of the region as necessary.

Using spatial strategic planning will help change peripheral regions that are fragmented, physical, cultural, social and economic entities into a comprehensive unified whole. Doing so is of the utmost importance, but also a complicated task. Yet, even in the face of great difficulties, it must be undertaken, as this task will determine the ability of peripheral regions to develop and grow and, as a consequence, provide a decent standard of living and a higher quality of life for their inhabitants.

References

Acs, Zoltan J., and Catherine Armington. 2004. Employment growth and entrepreneurial cities. *Regional Studies* 38(8): 911–27.

Acs, Zoltan J., and David J. Storey. 2004. Entrepreneurship and economic development. *Regional Studies* 38(8): 871–77.

Aghion, Philippe, and Peter Howitt. 1988. *Endogenous growth theory*. Cambridge Mass.: MIT Press.

Aschauer, David Alan. 1989. Is public expenditure productive? *Journal of Monetary Economics* 23: 177–200.

Audretsch, David B. 1998. Agglomeration and the location of innovative activity. *Oxford Review of Economic Policy* 14: 18–29.

Audretsch, David B., and Maryann P. Feldman. 1996. R&D spillovers and the geography of innovation and production. *American Economic Review* 86: 630–40.

Audretsch, David B., and Max Keilbach. 2004. Entrepreneurship, capital, and economic performance. *Regional Studies* 38(8): 949–59.

———. 2005. Entrepreneurship capital and regional growth. *Annals of Regional Science* 39(3): 457–69.

Banister, David, and Joseph Berechman. 2000. *Transport investment and economic development*. London: UCL Press.

Barro, Robert J., and Xavier Sala-i-Matin. 1991. Convergence across states and regions. *Brookings Papers on Economic Activity* 22(1): 107–82.

———. 1995. *Economic growth*. New York: McGraw-Hill.

Batten, David F., and Charles Karlsson, eds. 1996. *Infrastructure and the complexity of economic development*. Berlin: Springer.

Biehl, Dieter. 1991.The role of infrastructure in regional development. In *Infrastructure and regional development*, ed. Roger W. Vickerman, 9–35. London: Pion.

Blum, Ulrich. 1982. Effects of transportation investment on regional growth: A theoretical and empirical investigation. *Papers and Proceedings of the Regional Science Association* 49(2): 169–84.

Camagni, Roberto P. 1995. The concept of innovative milieu and its relevance for public policies in European lagging regions. *Papers in Regional Science* 74: 317–40.

Charlot, Sylvie, Carl Gaigné, Frédéric Robert-Nicoud, and Jacques-François Thisse. 2006. Agglomeration and welfare: the core-periphery model in the light of Bentham, Kaldor, and Rawls. *Journal of Public Economics* 90: 325–47.

Davelaar, Evert Jan, and Peter Nijkamp. 1989. The role of the metropolitan milieu as an incubation centre for technological innovation: A Dutch case study. *Urban Studies* 26: 517–25.

Ellison, Glenn, and Edward L. Glaeser. 1997. Geographic concentration in U.S. manufacturing industries: A dartboard approach. *Journal of Political Economy* 105(5): 889–927.

———. 1999. The geographic concentration of industries: Does natural advantages explain agglomeration? *American Economic Review* 89(5): 311–16.

Etzkowitz, Henry, and Magnus Klofsten. 2005. The innovating region: Toward a theory of knowledge-based regional development. *R&D Management* 35: 243–55.

Fan, Shenngen, Ravi Kanbur, and Xiaobo Zhang. 2009. *Regional inequality in China: Trends, explanations and policy responses*. London: Routledge.

Florida, Richard. 2002. *The rise of the creative class*. New York: Basic Books.

Frenkel, Amnon. 2000. Can regional policy affect firms' innovation potential in lagging regions? *Annals of Regional Science* 34(3): 315–41.

Frenkel, Amnon, Daniel Shefer, and Michal Miller. 2008. Public vs. private technological incubator programs: Privatizing the technological incubators in Israel. *European Regional Studies* 16(2): 189–210.

Fujita, Masahita, and Dapeng Hu. 2001. Regional disparity in China 1985–1994: The effects of globalization and economic liberalization. *Annals of Regional Science* 35: 3–37.

Fujita, Masahita, Paul Krugman, and Anthony Venables. 2001. *The spatial economy: Cities, regions, and international trade*. Cambridge, Mass.: MIT Press.

———. 2004. The new economic geography: Past, present, and future. *Papers in Regional Science* 83: 139–64.

Fujita, Masahita, and Tomoya Mori. 2005. Frontiers of the new economic geography. *Papers in Regional Science* 84(3): 377–405.

Fujita, Masahita, and Jean-François Thisse. 1996. Economics of agglomeration. *Journal of the Japanese and International Economies* 10: 339–78.

———. 2002. *Economics of agglomeration, cities, industrial location, and regional growth*. Cambridge: Cambridge University Press.

Geppert, Kurt, and Andreas Stephan. 2008. Regional disparities in the European Union: Convergence and agglomeration. *Papers in Regional Science* 87(2): 93–217.

Glaeser, Edward L. 2008. *Cities, agglomeration, and spatial equilibrium*. Oxford: Oxford University Press.

Graham, Daniel J. 2008. An empirical analytical framework for agglomeration economies. *Annals of Regional Science* 42: 267–89.

Grossman, Gene M., and Elhanan Helpman. 1991. *Innovation and growth in the global economy*. Cambridge, Mass.: MIT Press.

Hannon, Paul D., and Paul Chaplin. 2003. Are incubators good for business? Understanding incubation practice—the challenges for policy. *Environment and Planning C: Government and Policy* 21: 861–81.

Harwit, Eric. 2002. High-technology incubators: Fuel for China's new entrepreneurship? *China Business Review* 29(4): 26–29.

Jacobs, Jane. 1969. *The economy of cities*. New York: Random House.

Kanbur, Ravi, and Anthony Venables, eds. 2005. *Spatial inequality and development*. Oxford: Oxford University Press.

Krugman, Paul R. 1979. A model of innovation, technology transfer, and trade. *Journal of Political Economy* 83: 253–66.

———. 1991. Increasing returns and economic geography. *Journal of Political Economy* 91: 483–99.

———. 1998. What's new about the new economic geography? *Oxford Review of Economic Policy* 14(2): 7–17.

Kuznets, Simon. 1955. Economic growth and income inequality. *American Economic Review* 45: 1–28.

Losch, August. 1954. *The economics of location*. New Haven, Conn.: Yale University Press.

Malmberg, Anders, and Dominic Power. 2005. (How) do (firms in) clusters create knowledge? *Industry and Innovation* 12(4): 409–31.

Malul, Miki, and Raphael Bar-El. 1999. The gap between free market and social optimum in the location decision of economic activity. *Urban Studies* 46(10): 2045–59.

McCann, Philip, and Daniel Shefer. 2004. Location, agglomeration, and infrastructure. In *Fifty years of regional science*, ed. Raymond J. G. M. Florax and David. A. Plane, 177–96. Berlin: Springer.

Nijkamp, Peter, and Jacques Poot. 1997. Endogenous technological change, long run growth, and spatial interdependence: A survey. In *Innovative Behaviour in Space and Time*, ed. Cristoforo Sergio Bertuglia, Silvana Lombardo, and Peter Nijkamp. Berlin: Springer.

Porter, M. E. 1998. Clusters and the new economics of competition. *Harvard Business Review* 76(6): 77–90.

———. 1990. *The competitive advantage of nations*. New York: Free Press.

Rietveld, Piet, and Frank Reinier Bruinsma. 1998. *Is transport infrastructure effective?* Berlin: Springer.

Rietveld, Piet, and Peter Nijkamp. 2000. Transport infrastructure and regional development. In *Analytical Transport Economics*, ed. Jacob B. Polak and Arnold Heertje, 208–32. Cheltenham: Edward Edgar.

Romer, Paul M. 1986. Increasing returns and long-run growth. *Journal of Political Economy* 94(5): 1002–37.

———. 1994. The origins of endogenous growth. *Journal of Economic Perspective* 8(1): 3–22.

Schumpeter, Joseph A. 1934. *The theory of economic development*. Cambridge, Mass.: Harvard University Press.

Shefer, Daniel. 1973. Localization economies in SMSA's: A production function analysis. *Journal of Regional Science* 13(1): 55–64.

Shefer, Daniel, and E. Lambert Bar-El. 1993. High technology industries as a vehicle for regional growth in Israel's peripheral regions. *Environment & Planning C* 11: 245–61.

Shefer, Daniel, and Amnon Frenkel. 1999. Agglomeration and Industrial Innovation in Space. In *Regional development in an age of structural economic change*, ed. Piet Rietveld and Daniel Shefer, 53–71. Aldershot: Ashgate.

———. 2003. Evaluation of the Israeli incubators program and projects within them. Haifa: S. Neaman Institute for Advanced Science and Technology, Technion-Israel Institute of Technology.

———. 1998. Local milieu and innovations: some empirical results. *Annals of Regional Science* 32(1): 185–200.

Solow, Robert M. 1956. A contribution to the theory and economic growth. *Quarterly Journal of Economics* 70: 65–94.

Venables, Anthony J. 1998. The assessment: Trade and location. *Oxford Review of Economic Policy* 14: 1–6.

Vickerman, Roger W. 1987. The Channel Tunnel: Consequences for regional growth and development. *Regional Studies* 21(3): 187–97.

———, ed. 1991. *Infrastructure and regional development*, London: Pion.

Wiggins, Joel, and David V. Gibson 2003. Overview of U.S. incubators and the case of the Austin Technological Incubator. *International Journal of Entrepreneurship and Innovation Management* 3(1/2): 56–66.

Xu, Lilai. 2010. Business incubation in China: Effectiveness and perceived contributions to tenant enterprises. *Management Research Review* 33(1): 90–99.

PART III

Planning and Excluded Groups

Chapter 10

Planning and Poverty:
An Uneasy Relationship

Michael B. Teitz and Karen Chapple

Do planners hate the poor? The evidence of history suggests that at best they have been indifferent, especially if offered the opportunity to plan on a massive scale. From the clearance of Roman *insulae* for imperial palaces in the first century C.E., to Haussmann's boulevards in the 1850s, to urban renewal in U.S. cities in the 1960s and the current destruction of old Beijing, the possibility of grandiose projects has seemingly blinded planners, urban designers, and architects to the consequences of their actions for people in the path of change. Despite the variety of idealistic rationales for planners' actions, the lure of building large seems irresistible, no matter what the cost in human suffering: even in smaller development or beautification projects, planning for the poor is usually an afterthought.

Yet, there is another side to this picture. Some grand civic engineering projects have brought benefits to poor as well as rich urban dwellers, especially as the risks to health of urban life became clear. Roman aqueducts brought clean water; Parisian sewers carried off waste; the urban parks of New York and London provided space to breathe. Institutionally, too, the application of science to health in the nineteenth century ushered in public health movements in both Europe and the United States. Not far behind came a new awareness of the plight of the poor, embodied in nascent efforts at social amelioration, such as the Chicago settlement house movement, or housing reform efforts, such as those in New York and London. Together with the socialist impulse of the times, these initiatives laid the foundation for explicit public policies to raise incomes and aid the poor and disadvantaged, which found expression later in the New Deal of the 1930s in the U.S., the reforms of the Labor government in Britain after 1945, the creation of welfare states in Germany and Scandinavia, the rise of development and concern for incomes in developing countries, and the Great Society attempts at social planning in the U.S. in the 1960s. Planners played different parts in all of these, depending on the particular social and political institution. This has left the field with a largely unquestioned belief that planning does indeed have a social mission without a clear sense of how planning can affect it. Perhaps this is best exemplified in the emphasis on the importance of social equity manifested in the often quoted adherence of plans to the "three Es"—economy, environment, and equity.

This contrast between the willingness of planners to serve power in the pursuit of grand visions, and the relatively recent sense that there should be limits to that power as it affects people in its path, or that planning should actively seek to reduce poverty, creates a profound tension within the field itself. In its modern form, planning has been full of good intentions. Few among its practitioners, though not among its critics, are so cynical as to claim that the role of planning is simply to serve the powerful. Yet, to be effective in a public role, planners must have access to power, albeit often limited. How they seek that access and employ the resulting power is a central story in planning, whether an individual such as Robert Moses, an organization such as the London Development Agency, or even a community group such as ACORN. This chapter seeks to interpret the history of how planning affects the poor by examining the power exercised by planners not for, but in spite of, the poor.

Four pivotal moments reveal the schism between planners and the poor, each in a new light. The first moment in the United States was the split between the Public Health/Progressive movement and the City Beautiful/City Efficient movements at the turn of the twentieth century. The second is the recognition of poverty in the collapse of colonial regimes after World War II, and the rise of development as a sociopolitical objective on a world scale. A third is the social upheaval and social movements of the 1960s and 1970s in the U.S. and Europe, which highlighted the flaws of the physical planning approach in addressing urban poverty and resulted in a series of well meaning but marginalized attempts to plan for the poor. The fourth moment, now occurring, is the crisis of global urbanization, which faces poverty on a hitherto unimaginable scale and arguably shifts the focus back to economic development planning and sustainability. Currently popular formulations of the sustainability problem almost invariably cite the three Es, attempting to close the historic circle. However, it may not be that easy.

Planning and Poverty: The First Divide

We begin with an overview of what might be called the emergence of a planning conscience in Britain, the U.S. and Europe—the attempt to understand the impact of planning on the poor and the level of poverty in society, coupled with the rise of critical voices in the field. Throughout its history, planning has tried to reconcile the harsh realities of poverty with the affluence that has been the mark of successful capitalist cities. One major stream of planning finds its origins in the socialist and progressive efforts to ameliorate conditions of life in nineteenth-century industrial cities. At the same time, planners and landscape architects invented and designed new forms of urban development suited to the needs and predilections of the wealthy and rising middle class.

The roots of modern concern with poverty and planners' engagement with it lie in the nineteenth-century industrial city. The industrial revolution and the rise of the industrial cities frame the emergence of urban planning (Benevolo 1967; Hall 2002). How this occurred resembles a historical ballet, in which different impulses attract a variety of actors to planning activities. The new industrial cities, first in Britain, then later in the nineteenth century in Europe, the U.S., Russia, and Japan, were dangerous, dirty, unhealthy, congested, and ill governed, but they were also very rich. The emerging bourgeois middle class sought ways to solve these problems. They professionalized the police, built sewers and water systems, created public health and hospitals, and drove new street systems through old urban fabrics. Industrialists and their associates, too, remade the city, mostly in their own interest, but also with reformist impulses. Think of Andrew Carnegie and the Homestead steel plant, Robert Owen and New Lanark, and George Pullman and the town of Pullman.

But it is only in the latter half of the nineteenth century that we see the origins of urban planning, as we know it, emerging from this welter of urbanization and reform, and connecting itself to the problem of poverty, at least for a time. Again, there are many strands—progressive reformers seeking to improve housing, counter poverty, assimilate new immigrants, and decongest the city; designers and developers such as the Olmsteds, creating new forms of suburban living; industrialists and architects creating grand visions in the City Beautiful of Chicago's 1909 Plan; and, of course, the socialists and utopians, from Ebenezer Howard to Edward Bellamy, seeking ways, albeit often impractical, to ameliorate or transform capitalism. What an amazing time it was, though city planning was still institutionally nascent.

Conventionally, we ascribe the direct linkage between planning and poverty in the U.S. to the pioneers, mainly women, who sought to tackle poverty directly in the slums of New York and Chicago in the last quarter of the nineteenth century (Wirka 1996). The settlement house movement, led by the formidable Jane Addams, and reinforced by Mary Simkhovitch and Florence Kelly, sought to assuage the worst excesses of urban industrial capitalism, acting directly to alleviate poverty by bringing new immigrants into the American mainstream. That their efforts were ultimately insufficient to address the scale of the problem in no way diminishes the significance of their actions or the sincerity of their intentions. They created what came to be known as social welfare, the only branch of government that explicitly sees its constituency as the poor, and they left behind a rich tradition of guided social philanthropy. Other progressives saw the problem of poverty in more physical terms, focusing on the role of inadequate housing in its perpetuation (Lubove 1962). Whether, they saw the solution, like Lawrence Veiller, in the form of regulation of rental housing, or like Edith Elmer Wood and later Catherine Bauer, in direct public provision of low-income housing, they were intent on changing the living standards and conditions of the poor; and some of these progressives were connected to the emergence of urban planning as a public function in its own right. For the most part, however, housing advocates differentiated themselves sharply from the institutional form that planning would take.

To understand why this was so, we need to look at another critical aspect of thought about society in the late nineteenth century: the question of socialism. Both in its revolutionary form, communism, and in its more moderate forms, socialism exerted a powerful influence on those opposing and those advocating reform. Socialism lurked as a threat to property and stability in Europe and the U.S., particularly after the revolutions of 1848 onward, leading its opponents, such as Bismarck in Germany, to advocate welfare reforms. At the same time, socialist thought inspired those who sought an alternative to (or modification of capitalism) that would be equally productive while providing greater equity in the distribution of income and wealth. In Europe, notably the Scandinavian countries, this led to the welfare state, where the notion of urban planning became almost seamlessly embedded. In the U.S., however, the powerful belief in private property, together with a deep strain of anti-communism, especially at times of crisis, inhibited such reforms, except in a few states like Minnesota, where a socialist political tradition took weak hold. Even in such a stronghold of progressivism as California, the political outcome was more populist than socialist. The 1917 revolution in Russia, and the resulting creation of the communist Soviet Union, simply enhanced these tendencies, with socialists and reformers projecting onto it their own beliefs and fears.

For planning in the U.S., at its critical moment of institutional formation, the outcome was a decisive turn away from social goals toward a role in support of the market, albeit informed by a distinct ideology of improving the physical setting in which people would live. The institutional birth of planning in the U.S. can be seen as having taken place at the first National Conference on City Planning, convened in New York City in 1909. Planning turned out to be not so much planning of ideals and visions, but rather more practical concerns such as regulation, zoning, and subdivision control (Boyer 1983). A very different group of innovators were at work. Men such as Benjamin Marsh, who had traveled to Germany and returned to advocate regulation of urban development, served as secretary to a new Commission on the Congestion of Population that would advocate urban decentralization to relieve traffic and overcrowding. In 1913, the Peoples Institute of New York City invited a German planner, Werner Hegeman, to visit the U.S. He toured the country, visiting cities, lecturing, and producing a plan for Oakland and Berkeley. His report comprised four chapters—harbors, railroads, and streets; parks; and civic centers. Its prefatory language is revealing:

CITY PLANNING IS INSURANCE
AGAINST WASTE OF PUBLIC FUNDS

City-planning means coordination of the activities that make for the growth of the city, especially the activities of railroad and harbor engineers, landscape architects, street-building and civil engineers, builders of factories, of offices, of public buildings, and dwelling houses. Without this pre-planning coordination, clashes between these different activities, unsatisfactory results and most expensive rearrangements, become unavoidable. City-planning therefore does not mean additional expenditure of money, but it means an INSURANCE AGAINST INEFFICIENT EXPENDITURE of the enormous sums that go—in the regular course of events—into the development of a progressive city. (Hegemann 1915: Preface)

This kind of planning seems to be driven by the market and by the need to establish norms and standards for public intervention that could stand the test of constitutionality while making the world safer for development by preventing excesses, whether of high buildings canceling each other's light in New York, or of subdividers threatening neighboring investments. Its heroes were a different breed: lawyers such as Alfred Bettmann, who would devise the strategy for securing zoning in the 1923 Euclid decision of the Supreme Court, at the price of detaching zoning from an active planning function at the local level; planning professionals, notably Harland Bartholomew, who became both the first city planner, named as such, to be hired by an American city, Newark, and founded the most successful planning consulting firm in the first half of the twentieth century; and, later, theorist/practitioners such as T. J. Kent (Kent 1964). In other words, these were planners who, though they had visions of a "better" city, sought to understand and shape its physical form, with little concern for how their interventions would affect poverty.

Many planners, especially those who saw themselves as intellectuals and reformers, such as Lewis Mumford and Catherine Bauer, were socialists and concerned with planning for the poor, but they had modest influence on the emerging field. Even the Great Depression and the New Deal, which elicited direct action to alleviate poverty among the unemployed, and led to major innovations in housing policy and regional planning, did not fundamentally reorient planning in the United States. However, planners did become involved in new economic and social initiatives, from Robert Moses using federal money to create jobs rebuilding Central Park in Manhattan, to Rexford Tugwell advocating for new towns, to the creation of the Tennessee Valley Authority with the avowed intent of raising farm incomes and industrializing through hydroelectric power. The years of the New Deal were stirring ones for planning, but the underlying presumption of direct government intervention in the economy would not survive World War II. Instead, World War II and its aftermath led to even more profound changes, especially in the form of new public programs that would deeply affect the role of planning in relation to poverty, both in the U.S. and on a world scale.

For American planning, the decades following World War II witnessed both the worst and the best of its engagement with poverty. The worst was urban renewal, the federal government-funded effort to restore the viability of the central business districts in older, declining cities by demolishing older residential and commercial areas, while providing incentives to business to redevelop the land with viable, primarily commercial, projects or housing. In cities across the U.S., tens of thousands of older residential units, primarily rentals, were demolished, with little or no compensation for displaced residents. The process was exacerbated by the simultaneous building of major freeways designed to connect downtowns to suburbs and the Interstate Freeway System.

One way to look at this effort is to see it as the logical continuation of a view of planning as the process of making a "better" city, allied with a view of the city as the product of competition in real estate markets that would ensure efficiency in land use. Thus, land economists and real estate advocates, such as the Urban Land Institute, together with the support of some, but not all, urban planners, first worked to justify and then implement the program of remaking substantial portions of America's cities (Weiss 1980).

In part, the objectives of urban renewal were admirable. Older central cities were losing employment, population, and commercial and industrial activity, and seemed to be sinking into obsolescence and decay. City governments were becoming financially unviable, losing tax base, even as costs were rising with new demands from increasingly impoverished populations. The fundamental error from its inception, however, was moral blindness to the real consequences of the program for poor and minority, primarily African American populations that were being displaced. The expectation that these populations would be able to find new housing through the working of the market, or through the construction of replacement housing, was a profound misjudgment, even though some housing would be freed up by the exodus of more affluent groups. Just as important to understand is the absence of awareness of or concern for the destruction of low-income communities that provided support for their populations using intricate, place-based strategies (Gans 1962). As a result, communities were dispersed or herded into high-rise public housing projects that were now the preferred form of low-income, subsidized housing development in major cities.

There can be little doubt that the outcomes of urban renewal were negative for the poor in American cities. A case can be made that without the large-scale clearance and rebuilding, the current renaissance of many downtown areas in U.S. cities would have been much more difficult. However, many older industrial cities have not experienced much regeneration and the question is speculative. The financial cost and emotional damage to thousands of displaced low-income families is a matter of record in U.S. planning's worst hour.

The Rise of Development

Even as urban renewal was marking the nadir of American planning's relationship with the poor, another, more hopeful moment was unfolding. After World War II, a multinational effort, supported by new international organizations, was created to promote economic growth and stability. For the first time in history, a truly international goal of raising living standards in the new post-colonial nations was set forth in the United Nations Charter. Obstacles and failures have beset the way forward from that moment, but the commitment was made and it continues.

For planners in Europe and the U.S., the implications of this change were powerful. For the first time, the possibility of planning for international development presented itself outside the historic domain of empire. This is not to say that national interests were absent in the emergent field of development planning; the rivalry between the U.S. and the USSR was a driving force of the process as each struggled for power and influence in the formerly colonial countries, with agencies such as U.S.AID funding many development projects. And the process of decolonization, itself, was painful. Even where the hand-over of power was peaceful, as in British India, the aftermath saw widespread intergroup violence. Elsewhere, as in Vietnam and Algeria, wars of liberation broke out, or, as in Kenya and South Africa, liberation struggles would go on for decades. The Japanese empire, too, left a legacy of great bitterness in Korea and China. Furthermore, in time, the postcolonial countries themselves sought paths to development that would be alternatives to market capitalism or Soviet communism, giving rise to the idea of a Third World beyond the major ideologies.

The actual task of inducing development proved to be far more complex than initially contemplated. In contrast to the Keynesian ideas that emerged from the Great Depression, informing and shaping the new financial order embodied in the IMF, there was no equivalent theory of economic development. Building on the insights of thinkers like Colin Clark, economists such as Sir Arthur Lewis began to build an intellectual framework around the idea of modernization (Clark 1939; Lewis 1955). In the absence of a theory of development, the choices seemed to fall between forced industrialization, more or less in the Soviet image, or infrastructure and resource development and agriculture, serving world markets. Although building dams on the TVA model was very popular, given the history of colonial exploitation, many countries were unwilling to rely on agriculture, turning instead to export-led industrialization, as in Korea, or to efforts at endogenous development based on a socialist model, as in India.

However, it was in the cities that the consequences of decolonization for planning became most pronounced. By the early 1950s, it was becoming evident that urbanization on an unprecedented scale was occurring along with development. The developing countries had little in the way of resources to cope with the huge number of rural-to-urban migrants, whose survival was being enhanced by improvements in epidemiology and health care. Observers such as Gunnar Myrdal and Albert Hirschman called attention to the apparent polarization of growth, which far from leading to development across a nation's territory, actually seemed to make poverty worse in the periphery (Myrdal 1968; Hirschman 1958). This led some advocates to call for measures to stem migration, or at least to reduce its scale, while others who saw urbanization as inevitable looked for ways to meet its challenges.

Advocates of curbing urbanization looked toward large-scale regional planning as the way to achieve balanced growth, a position adopted by planners in some countries, notably India, that were looking for a third path to development (Friedmann and Weaver 1979). It was hoped that by supporting development of intermediate-sized cities, together with rural development, planners could reduce the rate of growth in the new nations' primary cities. Given the absence of a full spectrum of city sizes, and the evident problems of the largest cities, this appeared to be a reasonable approach. To make it work required effective regional planning to create the economic base for regional centers. A great many planners' efforts were devoted to this regional strategy, but in the end it was not effective (Friedmann and Weaver 1979). However, regional development has not entirely disappeared. Rather, it is now expressed primarily in sectoral rather than spatial terms, especially in relation to rural and agricultural development, which continue to be vital concerns in the field.

The issue was how to manage growth in ways that would ameliorate the deplorable conditions in which the poor were living. Conventional planning doctrine called for slum elimination and construction of modern housing affordable to the population. While this worked in Hong Kong, it was politically and financially disastrous in most developing countries, providing only a small amount of housing for the relatively well-off or politically connected at the cost of displacing poor people living in what were perceived as slums. The proliferation of informal settlements—favelas, barrios, or shantytowns—seemed impervious to policy, so planners turned toward efforts at their improvement. Efforts such as the Ford Foundation Project in Calcutta, or the work of individuals, notably John Turner, focused on development of basic services, especially clean water and sanitation, together with modest housing improvements and changes in land titling so that occupants could make their own improvements with security of tenure over time (CMPO 1966; Kingsley and Kristof 1971; Turner 1968). The resulting improvement projects and programs scattered around the world, with international and national funding, created a new body of international development planners working for organizations from international aid sponsors and nongovernmental organizations to local self-help groups.

The complete history of international development planning remains to be written, the full implications of which are not yet visible. Nonetheless, it seems likely that the efforts of planners, often working at a very local scale, did have positive outcomes for the poor. The recognition that informal settlements could be viable, self-supporting communities has helped to fend off the continuing attempts by governments and their planners to destroy them when profit or national policy—often indistinguishable—finds their land desirable (Perlman 1976). Nonetheless, the evolution of development over the past two decades suggests that outcomes for the poor have been determined by factors other than development planning as it emerged after 1950. In particular, export-led development strategies, combining old recipes, such as low-cost manufacturing, with neoliberal trading regimes, and technological advances, have enabled countries such as China and India to make great gains in productivity and income. As in all mass industrialization episodes, the cost to the very poor has been great, even though they may have benefited from new employment opportunities. Governments and their planners have created new global cities at a speed inconceivable in earlier eras. In the face of power, the powerless are removed, often with little or no compensation. At the other end of the spectrum, some countries, especially in Africa, seem to have benefited little from decades of development efforts. In part, this is due to continuing population growth, but it is now generally recognized that without economic improvement population growth will not slacken.

Upheaval and Adjustment:
The Twentieth Century Concludes

In the United States, the 1960s essentially sanctified the right of planners to be indifferent to the poor. By linking income support programs to infrastructure and other construction projects, the New Deal had begun to integrate planning for the poor into development, while planning itself did not change course dramatically. But largely in response to the social upheavals of the mid-1960s, Lyndon Johnson broadened the New Deal menu of programs to expand the government role in social welfare from education to health care and economic opportunity more generally. In the process, the War on Poverty essentially reassigned responsibility for the poor from mainstream planning to a revitalized subfield of community development.

Community development in the 1960s had its roots in the settlement house movement but broadened under the Great Society through Model Cities and the Economic Opportunity Act (Halpern 1994). A reconception of the relationship between the federal government and cities stimulated the development of new local institutional capacity and leadership to deal with poverty. As cities targeted particular neighborhoods for poverty alleviation efforts, and community development corporations emerged to provide economic opportunity (and soon, housing), the field took on a place-based focus. Scholar-advocates, notably Paul Davidoff (1965) and later Norman Krumholz (1983), provided intellectual leadership for the new advocacy and equity planning movements.

Meanwhile, American planning went on its way into the 1970s. The expiration of the 1949 Housing Act meant the end of traditional urban renewal, culminating in the demolition of high-rise public housing. Freed of the obligation to house the poor, urban redevelopment programs evolved into public-private partnerships that focused on new market demand for entertainment, retail, and tourist facilities in downtowns and waterfronts (Frieden and Sagalyn 1989). A burst of spending on mass transit resulted in heavy and light rail lines geared toward the suburban-downtown commuter, with little concern for the mobility of the poor. As planners adjusted their gaze from inner cities to entire metropolitan areas, they increasingly revisited the efficiency rationales for planning so popular in the beginning of the century. *The Costs of Sprawl* (Real Estate Research Corporation 1974) and similar works pushed for planning that acknowledged and mitigated the government role in facilitating the market's unsustainable development patterns. In much of this work, the poor were not even an afterthought. Instead, it was assumed that the voice of the poor would be represented via institutionalized mechanisms for citizen participation, like the National Environmental Policy Act (Arnstein 1969).

We can credit Ronald Reagan for inadvertently bringing the poor back to planning. By accelerating the destruction of the safety net of social programs, and gradually undermining the array of federal anti-discrimination programs, the Reagan revolution abandoned the poor. In response, planners mobilized. Across planning subfields from transportation to land use to urban design, there was an increasing consciousness of how power affects the poor—as well as a sense of obligation to incorporate the poor into planning. Although mainstream planning may have remained untouched for the most part, a social equity agenda began to be embedded in many plans, policies, and programs.

Transportation planning, for example, paid increasing attention to issues of job accessibility, mobility, and quality of life for the urban poor. Ironically, many programs gained funding with the advent of welfare reform legislation, which mandated not only the transition to work but also provision of work supports such as transportation assistance. In the 1990s, experimental programs in reverse commuting, linking low-income urban residents to suburban jobs expanded, while hundreds of nonprofit, low-income car ownership or loan programs also emerged. Around the same time, new concerns about urban health and quality of life contributed to freeway demolitions around the country, including San Francisco, Portland, New York, Milwaukee, and Boston.

With old-style urban renewal now politically impossible, publicly funded megaprojects (especially in strong market regions) began to offer mitigation for impact on poor communities through community benefits agreements. Best known are the two agreements negotiated by a labor-community-faith coalition led by the Los Angeles Alliance for a New Economy, around the Staples Center and LAX Airport construction projects. The Staples agreement forced the developer to target job opportunities locally, pay living wages, and provide affordable housing. Many large-scale projects, from stadiums to university expansions to freeways, followed suit.

Although the large-scale public housing construction enabled by the Housing Acts of 1937 and 1949 came to an end, multiple smaller housing programs emerged (Schwartz 2006). While housing choice vouchers sent many of the poor to look for housing in the private market, the tradition of direct provision continued first through community development corporations and then through a scaled-up nonprofit development industry. Cities, counties, and even metropolitan planning organizations worked alongside these organizations to legislate programs, from regional fair share to inclusionary housing that would obligate private developers to provide some housing for the poor alongside market-rate units. Federal housing policy also became enamored of mixed-income development, facilitating the demolition and reconstruction of some 50,000 units of older public housing in the HOPE VI program. Though many of these new developments are considered design successes, they often fail to house all of the original public housing occupants, raising serious questions about whether planners are again failing to plan for the poor.

As a field, land use planning also saw shifts toward addressing poverty through more equitable land use patterns. The New Urbanist and smart growth movements of the early 1990s gradually changed the discipline's focus, from a purely physical approach to one that promoted the densifying of neighborhoods to incorporate social concerns, particularly the need for affordable housing (Talen 2005). Still, despite a growing awareness that planning smart was not necessarily planning for the poor, the seemingly inexorable increase of land values near the urban core in most regions meant that most dense new developments remained unable to support housing for low- and moderate-income families.

More generally, neighborhood planning became more inclusive, addressing more of the concerns of the poor, if not poverty itself. Some cities legitimized community-originated plans, such as the charter-enabled community planning process in New York City, while others expanded general planning to include more specific plans with extensive community participation. Environmental justice concerns led to a new focus on the potential health impacts of development, with a health assessment added to environment review in some cities. Through this, the original schism between public health and planning began to mend (Corburn 2004).

By the 1990s, the community development movement of the 1960s had matured into a community economic development machine (Giloth 2007). In large part leaving behind the earlier goals of community empowerment, the new generation focused instead on building assets for the poor, refueling small business entrepreneurship, and revitalizing commercial corridors through business improvement districts and similar programs. The implied poverty policy partly mirrored the national shift toward sectorally based anti-poverty efforts that were grounded in research on the importance of education and human capital development that favored people over place, but even these were ineffectual in the context of rising income inequality and the lack of wage gains by low income workers (Danziger 2007). The well-documented failures of job training led to the reform of workforce development systems, which, though unsuccessful in making a significant impact on work opportunities for low-income populations, at least could connect the disadvantaged to employers at a small scale. Despite this progress, it remains unclear how to understand these economic development efforts and whether they are to be considered planning or a separate descendant of the social welfare movement.

Though these policy innovations add up to a remarkable menu of improvements for the poor, they keep poverty at the margin of planning. The day-to-day business of planners proceeds apace: plans are made and updated, new highways and subdivisions appear in the suburbs, public facilities are allocated, and cities get rebuilt without any strategic or comprehensive thinking about how physical planning can help alleviate poverty—and near frightening naïveté about how power shapes these planning processes and reinforces the exclusion of the poor.

If anything, the last few decades have exposed the larger difficulty of planning adopting a social mission. With the exception of a few years in the 1990s, income inequality has grown steadily. Poverty itself has escalated into broad-based economic insecurity, as the middle class and working poor increasingly experience declining incomes, inability to obtain health insurance, and, most recently, home foreclosure. It is easy to point a finger at the neoliberal state for enabling the continued immiseration of the poor. But it is perhaps even less appropriate to point to planning as the magic bullet that can substitute for the welfare state in a state founded on a belief in private property. Even in Europe, social democracies have struggled with how planning can address poverty, as the difficult experience of these states with the social inclusion of newcomers testifies.

Examples from international development continue to be instructive. In particular, many Latin American governments have proved much more effective at taking care of their poor than the U.S., with near universal public health care and generous access to higher education. Yet, with the possible exception of community participation in Brazilian cities, planning there remains far from progressive (Caldeira and Holston 2005). Pro-growth forces and grandiose visions, though slowed (and made more incremental) by community movements, continue to win the day, and the schism remains.

Global Urbanization and Beyond

At the turn of the twenty-first century, the world planners face is beyond anything they have addressed in the previous 200 years. Global population has reached 7 billion, with the prospect of 9 billion by 2040. Of the current world population, 50 percent live on less than $2.50 per day—in other words, in deep poverty (World Bank 2008). Poverty levels have fallen over the past twenty years, yet all but 10 percent of the decrease can be accounted for by China's extraordinary rise as the greatest manufacturing nation in history. At the same time, China's industrialization exemplifies the new problem of global climate change, which is now a universal issue. Both of these, in turn, reflect the globalization of economic and social life that appears to be the defining characteristic of the twenty-first century. Whether growth is sustainable is profoundly in question (Worldwatch Institute 2009).

The greatest planning challenge remains in the fact that development means urbanization, which, in turn, has both positive and negative consequences for the poor. About half the world's population now live in urban areas, one-third in slum conditions. Rapid urban growth, even when associated with gains in productivity and income, has implied the development of informal settlements that require immense investments in water, sewer systems, and other public facilities. That was the principal task faced by planners from the 1960s onward. However, with the rise of export-led development, exemplified by China, the construction of modern global city centers, such as Beijing and Shanghai, has come at the expense of poor residents in the areas subject to this most recent manifestation of urban renewal. Although new housing is being constructed, it is often too costly and too distant to be affordable. And, of course, as in the U.S. case, communities are shattered. Relatively little has been documented about this issue, in contrast to the numerous studies of favela redevelopment in Latin America. These are not recent settlements, but old, long-established communities that embody important cultural history, as in the case of the Hutong-Siheyuan neighborhoods in Beijing (Zhang and Fang 2004). It may seem that in the march to development, such costs are unavoidable and necessary, but the moral blindness of this new march is the same as before, and the cost to the poor is no less.

Planning has not been slow to respond to globalization, especially global warming. Planners in Europe, and at the state and local levels in the U.S., have been among the leaders in bringing global issues to the local level through efforts to achieve sustainable development. Yet, at the same time, the stark fact is that the world's wealthiest countries, with about 1 billion people, account for 76 percent of world GDP, while the poorest countries, with 2.4 billion people, account for only 3.3 percent. Although there is some debate about the trend in overall distribution of income, in both rich and poor countries, income inequality continues to grow; the U.S., the world's wealthiest nation, also has the widest distribution of income. The choices that must be made by the wealthiest countries, as well as by the industrializing countries, in order to stave off the worst consequences of global warming are so difficult that it is hard to see how they can be politically possible, other than in the presence of massive environmental disasters, which will strike the poor hardest.

One must also ask whether urbanization is sustainable in the light of global warming. At this time, this question is barely being addressed, though it is clear that even with massive reductions in greenhouse gas emissions by the developed countries, industrialization based on manufacturing in developing countries would overwhelm such efforts in a few decades. Here, then, is the paradox for policy in planning and development. Alleviation of poverty by the most likely means, given the experience of recent decades, will generate an enhanced greenhouse effect, the consequences of which are unknowable but likely to be disastrous. Some hope that innovations in technology will permit development with poverty reduction and sustainability, but more than technology will be needed.

Although the language of sustainability now explicitly addresses poverty, it is hard to imagine cities and states adopting sustainable practices that actually help the poor in the absence of national income redistribution. Even if regions spawned denser development patterns supported by transit systems, the ever increasing land prices would continue to push the poor to the periphery, where jobs, services, and support networks are less accessible. The push for sustainability is likely to result in the strategic downsizing or "shrinking" of some regions, as is already happening in the U.S. Rustbelt, in Germany, and in other advanced industrial countries. What this planned decline will mean for the poor is unclear. Are sustainable regions yet another vain, grandiose vision of planners? There is a real risk that planners dazzled by the emerald city will once again lose sight of its favelas.

Conclusion

What can we learn from this history? Perhaps most striking is the continuing tension and ambivalence with which planners address poverty. Although concern for the poor has manifested itself throughout the history of planning, it is frequently pushed aside by other considerations to the point of invisibility, resulting in outcomes that have often been antithetical to the needs of the poor. Although much has been learned about policies for addressing poverty, there is little evidence that planning is an effective tool for that purpose. Old debates about people versus place remain unresolved, while the scale of problems expands. Globalization and development are raising incomes, but at a high cost for the very poor. Climate change and the need for sustainable growth are evoking new responses, but the commitment to equity is shaky. Over the past 150 years, the domain within which people call themselves planners has expanded dramatically, so it may be that we must step away from the idea of a universal agenda for fighting poverty within the field and instead speak of specific commitments to address poverty within planning's many worlds. There are many points of such commitment, but it may no longer be possible to speak of planning's commitment and impact as unitary, any more than we might of medicine or law. In a world of 7 billion people, that may not be a bad thing. It should be clear by now that there are no simple answers.

What might the next generation of planners do? First, if history tells us anything, it says that we should always question grand schemes because, more likely than not, they will hurt the weakest in society. Second, working locally has more potential for global impact than ever before because all localities are now interconnected. There is no escape from the world. Third, industrialization in the nineteenth and twentieth centuries required powerful government intervention to bring its benefits to the poor. While the social democratic model may remain the most effective way of curbing the excesses of capitalism, in the twenty-first century, community empowerment will be even more important in countries undergoing industrialization. Planners can help, but even more, should not lose sight of their moral obligations.

References

Arnstein, Sherry R. 1969. A ladder of citizen participation. *Journal of the American Planning Association* 35(4): 216–24.

Benevolo, Leonardo. 1967. *The origins of modern town planning*. Trans. Judith Landry. Cambridge, Mass.: MIT Press.

Boyer, Christine. 1983. *Dreaming the rational city*. Cambridge, Mass.: MIT Press.

Calcutta Metropolitan Planning Organisation. 1966. *Basic development plan for CMD 1968–86*. Calcutta: Calcutta Metropolitan Planning Organisation.

Caldeira, Teresa, and James Holston. 2005. State and urban space in Brazil: From modernist planning to democratic interventions. In *Global assemblages: Technology, politics, and ethics as anthropological problems*, ed. Aihwa Ong and Stephen Collier, 354–72. Malden, Mass.: Blackwell.

Clark, Colin. 1939. *Conditions of economic progress*. London: Macmillan.

Corburn, Jason. 2004. Confronting the challenges in reconnecting urban planning and public health. *American Journal of Public Health* 94(4): 541–46.

Davidoff, Paul. 1965. Advocacy and pluralism in planning. *Journal of the American Institute of Planners* 31(4): 331–38.

Danziger, Sheldon H. 2007. Fighting poverty revisited: What did researchers know 40 years ago? What do we know today? *Focus* 25(1): 3–11.

Frieden, Bernard J., and Lynne B. Sagalyn. 1989. *Downtown, Inc.: How America rebuilds cities*. Cambridge, Mass.: MIT Press.

Friedmann, John, and Clyde Weaver. 1979. *Territory and function: The evolution of regional planning*. Berkeley and Los Angeles: University of California Press.

Gans, Herbert J. 1962. *The urban villagers*. New York: Free Press.

Giloth, Robert P. 2007. Investing in equity: Targeted economic development for neighborhoods and cities. In *Economic development in American cities: The Pursuit of an equity agenda*, ed. Michael I. J. Bennett and Robert Giloth, 23–42. Albany: State University of New York Press.

Hegemann, Werner. 1915. *Report on a City plan for the municipalities of Oakland and Berkeley*. Berkeley, Calif.: Municipal Governments of Oakland and Berkeley et al.

Hall, Peter. 2002. *Cities of tomorrow: An Intellectual history of urban planning and design in the Twentieth Century*. 3rd ed. New York: Blackwell.

Halpern, Robert. 1994. *Rebuilding the inner city: A history of neighborhood initiatives to address poverty in the United States*. New York: Columbia University Press.

Hirschman, Albert O. 1958. *The strategy of economic development*. New Haven, Conn.: Yale University Press.

Kent, T. J., Jr. 1964. *The urban general plan*. San Francisco: Chandler.

Kingsley, G., Thomas and Frank S. Kristof. 1971. A housing programme for Metropolitan Calcutta. Calcutta: Ford Foundation.

Krumholz, Norman. 1983. A retrospective view of equity planning, Cleveland 1969–79.

In *Introduction to planning history in the United States*, ed. Donald A. Krueckeberg. New Brunswick, N.J.: Center for Urban Policy Research.

Lewis, W. Arthur. 1955. *Theory of economic growth.* London: George Allen and Unwin.

Lubove, Roy. 1962. *The progressives and the slums: Tenement house reform in New York City, 1890–1917.* Westport, Conn.: Greenwood Press.

Myrdal, Gunnar. 1968. *Asian drama: An inquiry into the poverty of nations.* New York: Twentieth Century Fund.

Perlman, Janice. 1976. *Myth and marginality: Urban poverty and politics in Rio de Janeiro.* Berkeley: University of California Press.

Real Estate Research Corporation. 1974. *The costs of sprawl: Detailed cost analysis.* Washington, D.C.: U.S. Government Printing Office.

Schwartz, Alex F. 2006. *Housing policy in the United States: An introduction.* New York: CRC Press.

Talen, Emily. 2005. *New urbanism and American planning: The conflict of cultures.* New York: Routledge.

Turner, John. 1968. Housing priorities, settlement patterns and urban development in modernizing countries. *Journal of the American Institute of Planners* 34(6): 354–63.

Weiss, Marc A. 1980. The origins and legacy of urban renewal. In *Urban and regional planning in an age of austerity*, ed. Pierre Clavel and John Forester, 53–80. New York: Pergamon.

Wirka, Susan. 1996. The city social movement: Progressive women reformers and early social planning. In *Planning the twentieth-century American city*, ed. Mary Corbin Sies and Christopher Silver, 55–75. Baltimore: Johns Hopkins University Press.

World Bank. 2008. *World Bank development indicators, 2008.* Washington, D.C.: World Bank.

Worldwatch Institute. 2009. *State of the world, 2009: Into a warming world.* Washington, D.C.: Worldwatch.

Zhang, Li, and Ke Fang. 2004. Is history repeating itself? From urban renewal in the United States to inner-city redevelopment in China. *Journal of Planning Education and Research* 23(3): 286–98.

Chapter 11

The City as Local Welfare System

Alberta Andreotti and Enzo Mingione

Since the 1960s, economic, demographic, social, and political change has been reshaping individual and institutional life throughout the industrialized world. These changes have brought back to the fore the crucial role played by local context in both economic development and social welfare programs. This new importance of the local has only been strengthened by a tendency toward territorialization of policies through devolution of programs and provisions at different territorial levels and contexts.

Policies regarding welfare provision are increasingly planned and implemented at the local level, as are other urban policies—as one might expect when considered through a lens of vertical subsidiarity.[1] At the local level, moreover, the number of actors participating in the definition of policies and provision of services has risen, giving way to partnerships between public and private actors as well as between nonprofit and for-profit organizations, thereby increasing horizontal subsidiarity. The renewed importance of the local and the multiplication of actors have led to a significant expansion of the range of policies and their modes of implementation and outcomes. Urban scholars and planning professionals should give serious consideration to the impact of welfare rescaling on urban development as it plays out in different cities, each with its own requirements and features, its unique social and historical contexts. In what follows we frame the main lines of this emerging issue, with particular reference to European cities. Alongside the local context,[2] with its ability to act as a collective social actor (Bagnasco and Le Galès 2000), the nation-state is still the main arbiter of policy, but in an increasingly diverse frame. The push toward decentralization and rescaling has been widespread even as the overarching regulatory framework remains in the hands of the central states—certain countries excepted, like Italy and Spain, where it has shifted to regional authorities (Kazepov 2010). Even in these places, the nation-state still shapes the possibilities and limits of freedom in local contexts. In Europe, a further element adds to the complexity of the picture: the ever-increasing role of the European Union. Thanks to its directives, funding programs (e.g., the European Social Fund, target programs like URBAN), and the omnipresent possibility of appealing to the Court of Justice, the EU enhances the process of vertical subsidiarization, and in doing so is increasing the importance of local contexts (Ferrera 2005, 2008).

The presence of these processes has led to the formation, within and beyond the field of social policy, of local welfare systems, defined here as "dynamic arrangements in which the specific local socio-economic and cultural conditions give rise to different mixes of formal and informal actors, public or not, involved in the provision of welfare resources" (Andreotti, Mingione, and Polizzi 2012). By "local welfare system," we mean not only the local government but also the complex combination of social and political institutions and actors who comprise the system, shaped differently by cultural and historical factors and processes. This view of local welfare systems challenges traditional models of *welfare capitalism* that assume national homogeneity. The diverse range of local welfare systems and the richness of their configurations make understanding their multiple changes in direction more difficult than in the past. This problem is compounded by traditional analytical tools, which while useful for understanding national welfare capitalisms are less so for local dimensions.

In what follows we discuss local welfare in comparative terms. Our hope is that this will prove useful to urban planners who are confronting local contexts in their practice, where the capacity to provide social services and welfare support to a very heterogeneous and unstable urban population is increasingly important for promotion of social cohesion and a high standard of urban life. The chapter is organized in two parts. The first discusses the shift from national to local welfare systems and highlights some of the processes that have led to increasing reliance on local provision. The second suggests ways to integrate analysis of the traditional parameters of welfare systems with analysis of the population's needs and the way the public good is institutionalized. This approach can help planners and others make sense of local variety and support them in the process of identifying local change, which we hope will be useful in planning and implementation of social and urban policies.

The National Welfare Capitalisms

The *national welfare capitalisms* were established between the postwar period and the beginning of the 1970s. They were based on three fundamental pillars: (1) spread of stable, high-wage employment for male breadwinners; (2) social and demographic homogeneity of nuclear families with a strong gender division of labor; (3) national welfare programs aimed at protecting individuals and families from risks in the areas where the combined contribution of family and salary was insufficient (Esping-Andersen 1990)—mainly education and vocational training, health and pensions, housing, and transportation networks. These social assistance programs were relatively meager, although it should be acknowledged that there were significant differences among national systems. Welfare programs everywhere had two basic objectives: to produce a nationally homogeneous system of social citizenship rights in spite of social and territorial inequalities, and to distance the autonomy of individuals from the traditional protection offered by family, relatives, and community networks.[3]

What this meant for socio-spatial organization is that nearly all capitalist welfare states foresaw the need for national regulation of territorial inequalities. The nation-state's goal was to keep internal territorial inequalities under control and, if possible, promote stable growth with positive effects for the entire territory (Brenner 2004). Although local governments maintained various degrees of autonomy, they were considered mere transmission belts for centrally defined policies. The degree of local autonomy depended on specific national features. Overall, however, two main features help explain local welfare system autonomy: (1) the presence of a centralized state (as in France) rather than a locally articulated one (as in the federal or regional states of Germany or Switzerland); (2) the presence of a strong state (as in Britain, France, and Germany) rather than a weak one (as in Italy), a state unable to promote high levels of national identity, cultural homogeneity, and prestige and efficiency of its own bureaucracy.

The key words defining welfare capitalisms are centralization, homogenization, and standardization. These tendencies, however, give different outcomes depending on combinations of historical, socioeconomic, and spatial factors. This can be made clear through a brief review of national welfare conditions prior to the rescaling processes of the last thirty years.

The study of the diversification of national welfare systems comprises a substantial body of literature that has become mainstream in welfare analysis.

Drawing on Esping-Andersen's classification (1990), the analytical categories adopted by these studies are state, market, and family and civil society, with the related principles of redistribution, market, and reciprocity. These studies rarely take into account the spatial dimension or discuss outcomes in terms of spatial exclusion and poverty concentration at a lower level, such as the neighborhood (Musterd et al. 2006 is an exception).

The welfare literature identifies at least four welfare regime models: social-democratic, liberal, corporatist conservative, and Mediterranean familistic (Ferrera 1996; Mingione 1991, 1997; Liebfried 1993). Rather than this familiar literature, we will address their spatial ramifications. In the *social-democratic model*, found in the Scandinavian countries, Denmark, and to some extent the Netherlands, the state ensures protection and social services to citizens on a universalistic basis. From the point of view of spatial organization, the state is central but leaves some room for local autonomy. The rescaling process has involved strong rationalization aimed at reshaping local authority by reducing the number of local authorities while allowing more local provision of services and protection, all the while not affecting the fundamental principles of equity and universalism. In this model, spatial segregation at the neighborhood level is kept under control. Indeed, there are almost no sources of inequality deriving from the neighborhood, due to the strength of the welfare state that sufficiently moderates these differences (Musterd et al. 2006). In the *liberal model*, private services and insurance are more widespread and the state intervenes only in a residual way with people who can prove the lack of other forms of protection (means-tested programs). The growth of inequality from a spatial perspective, particularly in the British case, was partly controlled by a weaker shift of autonomy in favor of local authorities, as means-tested programs and public services remained under control of the central state. In this model, greater variation in neighborhood circumstances and spatial concentration exists, some of it reflecting neighborhood history and city-level influences.

The *corporatist model* (most countries of central Western Europe) requires strong family responsibility in providing welfare resources, accompanied by relatively limited development of public social services, especially in the social care area. This model calls for a range of spatial articulation and segregation, with varying degrees of autonomy in different local contexts. There are cases of strong centralized states with standard benefits and services (France) and states with a long tradition of local autonomy balanced by a strong central power that ensures minimum welfare assistance standards nationwide (Germany and Belgium). In these countries we can find relatively high spatial segregation (e.g., Paris, Berlin, Brussels) and less pronounced segregation with neighborhood effects kept under control (e.g., Hamburg) (Musterd et al. 2006).

The familial South European model exacerbates the features of the previous one. There is an overall low degree of development of public welfare services, national measures, or last-resort safety net, and high local fragmentation of social assistance programs. The weakness of public institutional support is compensated for by the persistently strong role of the family in both monetary and material support and care. From the spatial dimension, these cases are characterized by longstanding local autonomy and a weak central state (Italy, Greece, and Spain), lower standardization power and a locally fragmented citizenship system, and differentiated minimum standards for welfare assistance and social protection. Italy, a striking example of this model, has been characterized in the last ten years by strong decentralization of regulatory political power toward regional authorities (Kazepov 2008, 2010).

At the neighborhood level spatial segregation assumes various forms, depending on local resources and history.[4] That some main features of the national welfare capitalism models can be found in current local welfare systems makes clear that path dependency and national policies remain significant. It can be generically hypothesized that the growing importance of the local level is not in itself sufficient to overturn preexisting configurations of welfare capitalism. Sweden, for instance, retains its strong universalistic character even as privatization is bringing about new forms of local differentiation, differentiated cooperation with local agencies and third sector actors, and direct involvement of citizens in the realization of welfare services (Khakee 2005). France has also retained its strongly centralized character, despite formal recognition of the role of local jurisdictions as holders of specific social responsibilities. It should be noted, however, that in a given national context and system of regulation, a local welfare system will most likely diversify to favor social inclusion and cohesion in a way that recognizes the presence of different risks and resources available locally (on this point see also Musterd et al. 2006).

The New Importance of the Local

The post-industrial transition, which began in the 1970s, has promoted three interconnected processes that have enhanced the importance of the local level while reducing the strength and legitimization[5] of continued expansion of welfare capitalism: (1) individualization; (2) destandardization; and (3) fragmentation, particularly at the urban level.

Individualization is the process of bringing about and increasing the freedom of individuals from traditional social belongings and their constraints (Paci 2005: 59). It is a long-term structural process that certainly did not start in the 1970s, but rather came (once again) to the foreground with the decline of Fordism. Beck (1992) suggests two analytical dimensions of individualization: the break from historically preexisting social forms and constraints, and the loss of traditional certainties (in many ways a process of disillusionment). In other words, it brings about a loss of the capacity of traditional collective organizations (family, kinship network, political parties, trade unions) to protect the individual *and* a decrease in the social control of these organizations with a corresponding increase in individual choice, freedom, and responsibility. The individual's *empowerment* (to use a fashionable term) is seen to be enhanced, bringing both advantages and, as noted, risks. This can be seen in the new flexible professional paths of highly qualified youth: they gain high autonomy and potential for personal fulfillment, but they are less protected, lacking the stability, pension schemes, health care, professional training, trade union representation, and so on of their elders.

When traditional social organizations (familial, community, or professional) no longer offer protection to their members, social assistance becomes crucial. In welfare capitalism cases, assistance is traditionally organized and implemented at the local level. Tied to the process of individualization is the process of *destandardization*—personalization of social risks. We see social risks as the outcome of economic, social, and demographic changes that make needs less standardized and more likely to be the result of individual biographies, that is, more dependent on the specific situation and available personal and contextual resources (e.g., being single or in a partnership, having or not having dependent children, being an immigrant or member of an ethnic minority, stage of life). In this environment, needs can no longer be met by general standardized social services, but require targeted interventions that can be realized only at the local level. This process of (vertical) rescaling has also been boosted by the fiscal and political crisis of the national welfare states.[6]

The combination of individualization and destandardization calls into question the ability of local welfare systems (defined rather broadly here as the mix of local government agencies and other local actors) to expand social service provision and promote forms of context-specific adaptation, that is, to encourage diversity both in the types of services and in the actors providing those services, thus giving way to innovative partnerships between public and private (market and third sector) actors or to the privatization of opportunities. Local capacity to increase and diversify the nature of welfare provision and involve new private providers will, as noted above, increase an individual's freedom from traditional belongings and, at least theoretically, broaden an individual's opportunities, with the idea that doing so will lead to further empowerment. Toward that end, when considering the crucial factors of successful urban development, urban planners should now be sure to consider how local conditions could promote a city's or region's capacity as an efficient welfare provider.

Finally, *fragmentation* is an effect of individualization and destandardization. It is, however, more problematic because of the difficulty of keeping the various pieces/fragments of urban society together. Fragmentation takes place at different levels. At the individual level, it leads to a growing fragmentation of personal biographies: the variety of working experiences risks not leading to a coherent professional career, if individuals are not able to coordinate all the pieces and build them around some solid identity reference. Similar forms of fragmentation can be traced in the sphere of personal and family relationships: increase in separations and divorces, decrease in marriages, and lengthening the periods in life when one lives alone.

As a form of urban spatial organization, fragmentation can be spotted in the territorial distribution of the population and the overlap between areas of social risk and specific population groups. This articulation leads to a city divided into spaces (neighborhoods) which do not communicate, which do not connect, creating tensions that must be taken into account when planning social or urban policies (Musterd et al. 2006). We see this in the territorial distribution of new immigration flows, which reflect different migratory aims (short, medium, or long-term stay with or without family reunion) and professional conditions: the map of micro-segregations is becoming increasingly complex and, even more than older forms of ghettoization and spatial segregation, it raises new problems for local governments (Mingione 2009).

In social policy, fragmentation is visible in the establishment of locally based systems of citizenship that ensure different rights and quality standards according to place of residence. Clearly, this threatens the universalism principle which is the basis of welfare capitalism systems (although not realized in all of them).

These three processes all contribute to the increasing importance of local context and the recent prevalence of local welfare systems. Also, albeit in different ways, these processes affect all models of *welfare capitalism*. Before addressing the parameters for understanding local welfare systems, we should make clear what we mean by local welfare system.

Parameters for the Analysis of Local Welfare Systems

From both a theoretical and a methodological point of view the concept of a local welfare system is poorly established. Its boundaries are both blurred and controversial. As far as territorial borders are concerned, there is no agreement as to what constitutes the "local" level. Studies generically refer to an unspecified "local context": region, province or county, metropolitan area, city, or neighborhood. The choice of territorial level depends on the object of analysis and is strongly influenced by the institutional regulation of policies, that is, by the institutions responsible for planning and implementation, as well as by the degree of autonomy, potential for mobilization, and collective action of each territorial level.[7]

Maurizio Ferrera's analysis of the spatial reconfiguration of social protection in Europe (2005), for instance, focuses attention on regions. Analyzing the rescaling of social policies in different welfare capitalism models, Yuri Kazepov (2008) focuses on municipalities for Scandinavian and Southern European countries, but for continental Europe prefers to discuss the intermediate bodies at the provincial or regional level. Kazepov (2010) focuses mainly on the local, by which he means the municipal level, and suggests a division between welfare systems that remain centrally framed (with more or less local/municipal autonomy) and those where power to frame policies is shifting to regions.

These studies refer to the rescaling of social policies and spatial rearrangement of responsibilities as a matter of political-institutional level. However, city planners and urban scholars tend to have a larger focus, where that level is only one of the elements that need to be taken into account.

Understanding a local welfare system must start from its socioeconomic conditions, as well as the social structures in which it is embedded; each local context has its distinctive cultural, economic, and social resources, all contributing to the creation of a unique mix of actors who, in turn, affect the resources. It is precisely this mix and interplay that must be examined. The municipal territory or metropolitan area appears the most suitable proxy for this purpose. Every city, even in the same regional context, has its own history, during which specific features have emerged in economic organization, but also in sociodemographic structure, organization of "civil society," and political-institutional traditions, all of which shape different local systems and the "vision" they express through social and urban policies.

The primary challenge for understanding local welfare systems is the need to go beyond descriptive information of local diversity and identify interpretive parameters that enable comparison and evaluation of different contexts. The analysis of local systems, in fact, makes sense only in a comparative framework. Comparison, by similarity or contrast, allows useful elements to emerge for the interpretation of local conditions of change, specifically the needs and resources for local welfare and, consequently, for the development of urban and planning-based perspectives.

The analytical categories of state, market, and family/civil society (Esping-Andersen 1990) are only somewhat useful for the construction of comparative typologies of local welfare systems. As a matter of fact, these categories are far less homogeneous and standardized when comparing local systems, as they assume different meanings in different contexts. The national level has lost its centrality in favor of other (local) levels of government (regions, provinces, counties, municipalities) as well as the other actors providing welfare interventions. For this last reason, considering family and community networks (informal protection, within a limited system, of the micro-redistribution of resources and responsibilities) together with the third sector and civil society in general no longer holds, not even at the national level.

The analysis of these three categories can be efficiently integrated by looking at how public welfare is institutionalized, that is, how it is provided through welfare resources and how it is legitimized. We strongly stress that in this complexity it is important to look at, on the one hand, the population and its specific needs in the local context (local articulation of welfare needs) and, on the other hand, the institutional provision, by which we mean the set of the different providers of services.

The analysis of needs and their growing differentiation and destandardization is based in the specific social and economic conditions in the local context. Figure 11.1 shows which factors play particularly relevant roles, especially occupational, demographic, and socio-territorial factors.

The analysis of these factors will produce information about the various population groups and their demand for services, while also giving us a sense of the degree of the social context's homogeneity and heterogeneity, which has strong consequences for planning and implementation of social and urban policies.

The analysis of institutional provision focuses primarily on two aspects: (1) the characteristics of the local providers: for example, private for-profit, third sector, and public actors, as well as the different partnerships and their forms; (2) the capacity of public actors to promote and coordinate forms of cooperation and participation/empowerment of citizens. These aspects recall the *governance* narrative and its relationship with *government*.

Paths of an In-Depth Study

A few examples may be useful for understanding how to interpret demand and supply in the analysis of local welfare systems. They also bring to the fore potentially different research paths. We first turn to some that demonstrate the current emphasis on social inclusion and individual responsibility that is at the heart of today's welfare policies. In the social assistance field, this emphasis is evident in the Revenu Minimum d'Insertion[8] (minimum income), introduced first in France, later in Spain (Renta Minima) and Portugal (Rendimento Mínimo Garantido), and as a short-term experiment in Italy (Reddito Minimo d'Inserimento).[9] Almost all European countries (with the exception of Italy, Greece, and a number of countries that recently joined the EU) currently have national minimum income programs (Immervol 2009). In most cases[10] the policy is decided at the national level with national standards. But it is implemented locally and assumes different features in different contexts. This differentiation is the result of the specific profiles of people at risk of poverty and their eligibility in different contexts (single adults, families, unemployed youths, immigrants, etc.), local actors such as private providers (employers, industries, professional guilds, etc.), and third sector partners involved in programs.

The measure makes explicit reference to the responsibility of the citizen (in particular the social service recipient). In the case of the Revenu Minimum d'Insertion the recipient had to sign a contract with the social service when he or she took part in a suggested activity, such as vocational training, social jobs, social and psychological counseling, and the like.

Although these measures include a coercive element, they tend to take a comprehensive approach. They often set in motion a process of negotiation between recipients and social workers, who decide together which actions

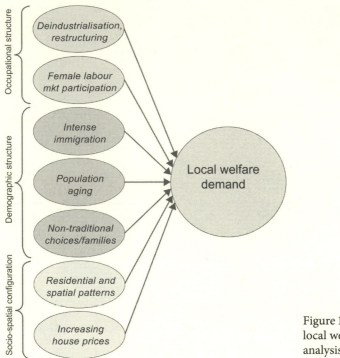

Figure 11.1. Factors of local welfare systems analysis.

have to be taken, thus enhancing the responsibility and the power of the recipient.[11]

There are many possible modes of implementation for these social inclusion programs. The testing of the Reddito Minimo d'Inserimento in Naples offers an interesting example of the demand and supply of local welfare being set in motion. Naples has very a low rate of female employment (24.4 percent; Istat 2007), and early child care services cover only 2 percent of children. Among the few children enrolled in public or private services, the majority are children of female college graduates, the few double-income households, and some richer families that do not fall into the other two categories. Empirical studies underline the importance of early access to collective care and pre-education systems; such access partly neutralizes the unequal distribution of human capital among households (see Esping-Andersen and Mestres 2003). In this context the Reddito Minimo di Inserimento allowed a few mothers to organize into social cooperatives to start a micro-crèche, after receiving some professional training. This experiment took into account the local need for child care; the need of poor mothers to find employment; the children's needs and their right to care and education; the role of third sector agencies; and the empowerment of recipients. This measure was centrally adopted (and funded), but locally used, exploiting the specific context and its conditions, thus activating a small virtuous circle. The same program would not have had the same meaning in contexts characterized by high female employment, though other similarly innovative experiments are possible. In Turin, a city in northern Italy with high female employment, a similar project has been implemented for immigrant women, many of whom experience greater discrimination in the labor market, in terms of both access to and position within it.

As our examples show, the capacity to produce innovative forms of local welfare provision is connected, on one hand, to a proper understanding of the specificity of the local demand and, on the other hand, to a process of governance, participation, and activation that can valorize the best local resources. In this sense the problems of local welfare are becoming a crucial part of planning analysis and debates over governance, empowerment, and participation.

The emphasis on empowerment and activation also has a collective dimension, as when it refers to active involvement of citizens' associations or organizations. This is an old question, particularly evident in the processes of urban renewal and again today in the local planning of welfare provision. Citizens' associations are asked to take on responsibilities through active participation in civic governance and to cooperate with local administrators and other local actors as they plan projects to be realized. Projects are therefore not imposed on the local context (e.g., the neighborhood), and institutions have to listen to citizens' opinions. In this type of welfare planning process, the citizens' needs, the relations between the different third sector agencies, the relations between the latter and market actors, as well as the coordination strategy of the public sector (municipality or neighborhood) have to be taken into account. The question to be raised here, however, is whether simply looking at the activist side of the coin risks over-estimating the capability and responsibility of active and empowered citizens. Citizens' associations, in fact, can also be of the NIMBY (not in my back yard) type, whereby the interest of a particular group can become a priority with respect to the public interest of the whole area (or neighborhood) in question, creating even more conflicts.[12] Looking at the issue from this point of view, moreover, there are problems with other forms of commitment on behalf of the citizen. We see this in the case of movements that entail protest, search for political change, or opposition to the local administration (insurgent citizenship). Who decides which associations of citizens can take part in the round-table on planning? And who are the citizens taking part? Are they all disadvantaged citizens, whose *civicness* needs to be awakened by local administrators? Or are they the most integrated citizens, who have their interests to defend? Attention to local welfare systems means considering these types of questions, taking into account the needs and interests of the various civil society groups.

The mobilization of a broader spectrum of local actors deserves further attention. On the one hand, it reflects the destandardization of needs and answers that originate with different providers and services. On the other hand, it calls into question the relationship between government and governance as well as that between national or regional actors and those at the local level, as well as the capacity to coordinate between the two. Indeed, diversification can be seen as Janus-faced. Bringing collective action and welfare provision closer to the people by enabling greater empowerment to citizens creates opportunities for participation and democratic decision-making, but at the same time it bears important risks of fragmentation and can disingenuously disguise the retrenchment of public responsibility for welfare provision.

The increase in, and diversification of, local actors can be an important resource for citizens, and it can improve democratic participation. It must, however, be regulated and coordinated, or it can end up fragmented, and thus reduce citizens' opportunities for choice. Returning once again to the earlier example of child care policies, for instance, making such a program work requires both coordination among various providers and establishment of national minimum standard rules for quality of services that must be respected in local contexts. This is possible only if the preconditions of cooperation between local public and private actors, as well as of constant exchange between central and local levels, are fulfilled.

Concluding Remarks: Understanding Local Welfare Is Necessary but Difficult

An emphasis on the differentiation of local welfare systems is crucial for urban planners today, for it allows identification of the needs and risks of the populations concerned and is able to involve them at the decision-making level. Furthermore, it offers a way to overcome the limitations of the ideological debate on privatization. Privatization could be fundamental to increasing margins of choice, competitive rationalization, and maximization of the resources at stake, but it also drastically diminishes protection for citizens in more marginalized situations. We started by showing that an accurate local analysis can highlight the conditions that give a more rational and possibly optimal amount of protection for individuals, but also the conditions that lead to a dangerous broadening of what might be called a protection deficit.

Comparative analysis of local welfare systems (with the obvious ambition of being able to generalize a few parameters to have at least a rudimentary operations manual on which to count) is, however, extremely difficult. It requires a focus on the dynamics (in relatively fast processes of change[13]) of risks and protection needs, in contexts that are increasingly individualized and unstable. It also demands a focus on what formal and informal resources can be mobilized to ensure protection, as well as an assessment of the potential impact of different protection arrangements. The examples here show a number of critical areas that are ripe for further analysis: the contexts of hierarchic configuration of public responsibility; the new meaning of empowerment and of enhancing recipients' responsibility under different conditions; and ways of constructing and coordinating partnerships between public and private institutions.

The analytical and comparative framework must remain focused on ensuring that social cohesion and social inclusion are public goods, that is, providing adequate social protection for the most vulnerable individuals. The European debate on social exclusion has made progress in this direction, by identifying and analyzing the typologies of individuals principally at risk of being penalized by protection deficits on different local scales. Among those who face the greatest risk are immigrants and minorities, large families supported by a single low-wage breadwinner, and the long-term unemployed—particularly those with low professional and educational qualifications—single parents, and the lone elderly who are not self-sufficient. This list does not include the most severe cases such as the homeless or the chronically ill with no family protection. Identification of the different mechanisms that result in situations of poverty and/or social exclusion and the profiles of those who are at risk of poverty are helpful starting points. In addition, however, the local and territorial conditions in which those situations of risk develop must be explored in detail, along with the personal and institutional resources that can be called on in the each context. As we have indicated, the transformative processes—increased heterogeneity, instability, individualization—may be similar, but they are found among different populations, each more or less segregated, with formal and informal resources that can vary significantly even in similar cities.[14]

We have argued here that planners and urban scholars should devote greater attention to local welfare problems, as local welfare provision is an increasingly crucial part of the urban development process. It is not easy to develop comparative tools on this subject, but we have at least suggested an initial framework for understanding local welfare systems based on two foci: increasingly diversified and changing population needs, and local welfare provision as an asset that produces empowerment, participation, and involvement of local agencies as well as developing the coordination capacity of local authorities. This process of understanding is not dissimilar to the traditional questions city planners considered when working on housing. But here, in addition to the various residential needs of different social groups, an increasingly diversified demand for social support and welfare services is also at stake. Moreover, both new welfare needs and forms of provision are increasingly at the local level.

By way of concluding, we ask what the impact of the current crisis might be in various local welfare contexts. This opens new questions for debate. It is evident that some profiles will suffer more, including young entrants into the labor market, workers with low professional qualifications, immigrants, and disadvantaged minorities. It will, however, require great analytical initiative and interpretive imagination to rapidly identify the impact. It will likely need to be understood in terms of social inclusion and social cohesion in different contexts, characterized by diversified population selection processes, social mixes, and protection capacities. The new unemployed, as they are locally articulated in different social profiles (young, women, adults with obsolete qualifications, migrants, etc.), will become a local problem in the places they tend to concentrate. There are broad discussions today about national and European programs to end the crisis, but it is already clear that local impact will be strongly diversified (like the geographically uneven effects of deindustrialization, but perhaps stronger). Therefore, urban scholars and planners need to invest greater analytical and interpretative resources in understanding the diversified role of local welfare in the process of urban development. Such an investment is crucial if we are to engage the current crisis at the local level and for the long term, to make the planning process more efficient in general.

Notes

1. Subsidiarity is usually defined as the principle that policies ought to be handled by the institutions or agencies best positioned to get the most immediate and efficient results. This implies that a central authority should have a subsidiary function, performing only those tasks that cannot be performed effectively at a more immediate or local level (Kazepov 2008).

2. The centrality of the local dimension, cities in particular, is not something new, at least not in the European context. It has played a leading role in economic and social development for a long time (Poggi 1990; Le Galès 2002).

3. In some countries (e.g., Italy and Germany), the familial obligation to support members is even declared in the Civil Code. This principle remains operational for local service agencies, which can decide to apply it on a discretionary basis (see Millar and Warman 1996).

4. Again, the case of Italy is illuminating. In Milan, a relatively wealthy city in the north, the neighborhood effect is very low, i.e., the neighborhood is not a source of inequality per se (Andreotti 2006). In Naples, in the south with few employment opportunities and poor resources, the neighborhood effect is much higher (Morlicchio and Pugliese 2006).

5. The national welfare apparatuses are more or less—depending on the cultural and historical configuration of different national and local cases—kept alive by strong bureaucratic and trade unionist interests.

6. These processes can also encourage a shift from structural to individual factors as the cause of poverty or marginal situations, and end up blaming the victims, as if it is their fault for not being able to "choose" the "right options." This tendency to blame must be kept under control in the analysis and in planning social and urban policies.

7. There is also a problem with regard to the availability of homogeneous, comparable data. Even within the EU Nuts 2 and Nuts 3, data representing regional and provincial/county levels are not always homogeneous from country to country in terms of territory/population represented—and they are not always available. The level more important for city planners and urban scholars—the city/metropolitan city level—has to be, most of the time, drawn in greater detail, something that can only be done with great difficulty.

8. The RMI was introduced in 1988 as a universal (and differential) benefit. It created a new, universal entitlement to state provision of services and activities (*droit d'insertion*), and was designed to help individuals integrate into society and actually enjoy full-fledged citizenship. Although *normatively* universal in principle (either the benefit or the right to activities and services), RMI catered to the poor and the "socially excluded," once eligibility for other benefits was exhausted (Barbier 2001: 15). In 2008, the RMI was replaced by the Revenu de Solidarité Active (RSA), which has a more work-oriented approach.

9. The Reddito Minimo di Inserimento was tested in Italy over a three-year period (1998–2001), involving 39 municipalities throughout the country.

10. The Spanish case is exceptional. The Renta Minima was first introduced by the government of the Basque country and adopted with very different characteristics and benefit levels by other Autonomous Communities at a later stage.

11. The comprehensive approach and ability of recipients to negotiate their activities make the real difference between workfare policies and the work-first approaches typical of Anglo-Saxon contexts (see Barbier 2001).

12. This can also be seen in the work of scholars who, following Putnam, have introduced the distinction between bridging and bonding social capital, where NIMBY movements represent bonding social capital.

13. See, e.g., immigration flows in the cities of Southern Europe: not only have they increased greatly, since 1990, in an unpredictable way, but within relatively short periods of time the origins of the most significant flows have also changed. In the span of three years the presence of Romanians in Italian and Spanish cities shifted from extremely modest to one million and one and a half million respectively.

14. The comparison between Milan and Turin in Italy is interesting, as it has highlighted significant differences in ways of providing assistance (Mingione and Oberti 2003). Today, moreover, Turin is often cited as an example of good practice and positive adaptation, despite the fact that the city was one of the most dramatically hit by deindustrialization.

References

Andreotti, Alberta. 2006. Coping strategies in a wealthy city of northern Italy. International Journal of Urban and Regional Research 30(2): 328–45.

Andreotti, Alberta, Enzo Mingione, and Emanuele Polizzi. 2012. Local welfare systems and social cohesion. In Urban Studies 49(9): 1925–40.

Bagnasco, Arnaldo, and Patrick Le Galès, eds. 2000. *Cities in contemporary Europe*. Cambridge: Cambridge University Press.

Balbo, Laura, ed. 1978. *Tempi di vita*. Milano: Feltrinelli.

Barbier, Jean-Claude. 2001. Welfare to work policies in Europe: The current challenges of activation policies. Document de Travail 11. Paris: Centre d'Études de l'Emploi.

Beck, Ulrich. 1992. Risk society: *Towards a new modernity*. London: Sage.

Brenner, Neil. 2004. *New state spaces: Urban governance and the rescaling of statehood*. Oxford: Oxford University Press.

Esping-Andersen, Gøsta. 1990. *The three worlds of welfare capitalism*. Cambridge: Polity Press.

———. 1999. *Social foundations of post-industrial economies*. Oxford: Oxford University Press.

Esping-Andersen, Gøsta, and J. Mestrers. 2003. Ineguaglianza delle opportunità ed eredità sociale. *Stato e Mercato* 67(4): 123–51.

Ferrera, Maurizio. 1996. The Southern model of the welfare state in social Europe. *Journal of European Social Policy* 6(1): 17–37.

———. 2005. *The boundaries of* welfare. Oxford: Oxford University Press.

———. 2008. Dal welfare state alle welfare regions: La riconfigurazione spaziale della protezione sociale in Europa. *Rivista delle Politiche Sociali* 3: 17–49.

Khakee, Abdul. 2005. Transformation of some aspects of the local mode of regulation in Sweden. *Planning Theory* 4(1): 67–86.

Kazepov, Yuri. 2008. The subsidiarization of social policies: Actors, processes and impacts. *European Societies* 10: 247–73.

———, ed. 2010. *Rescaling social policies: Towards multilevel governance in Europe*. Aldershot: Ashgate.

Le Galès, Patrick. 2002. *European cities: Social conflicts and governance*. Oxford: Oxford University Press.

Leibfried, Stephan. 1993. Towards a European welfare state? In *New perspectives on the welfare state in Europe*, ed. Catherine Jones, 135–56. London: Routledge.

Lewis, Jane. 1992. Gender and the development of welfare regimes. *Journal of European Social Policy* 2(3): 159–73.

Millar, Jane, and Andrea Warman. 1996. *Family obligations in Europe: The family, the state and social policy*. York: Joseph Rowntree Foundation.

Mingione, Enzo. 1991. *Fragmented societies: A sociology of economic life beyond the market paradigm*. Oxford: Blackwell.

———. 1997. *Sociologia della vita economica*. Roma: Carocci.

———. 2009. Family, welfare and districts: The local impact of new migrants in Italy. *European Urban and Regional Studies* 16(3): 225–36.

Mingione, Enzo and Marco Oberti. 2003. The struggle against social exclusion. *European Journal of* Spatial *Development* 1: 1–23.

Morlicchio, Enrica, and Enrico Pugliese. 2006. Naples: Unemployment and spatial exclusion. In *Neighbourhoods of poverty: Urban social exclusion and integration in Europe*, ed. Sako Musterd, Alan Murie, and Christian Kesteloot, 180–97. Bristol: Palgrave Macmillan.

Musterd Sako, Alan Murie, and Christian Kesteloot, eds. 2006. *Neighbourhoods of poverty: Urban social exclusion and integration in Europe*. Bristol: Palgrave Macmillan.

Paci, Massimo. 2005. *Nuovi lavori, nuovo welfare,* Bologna: Mulino.

Poggi, Gianfranco. 1990. *The state: Its nature, development and prospects*. Stanford, Calif.: Stanford University Press.

Putnam, Robert 2000. *Bowling Alone: The collapse and revival of American community*. New York: Simon & Schuster.

Saraceno, Chiara, ed. 2002. *Social assistance dynamics in Europe: National and local poverty*. Bristol: Policy Press.

Chapter 12

Policies Toward Migrant Workers

Izhak Schnell

Transnational worker migration is a complex and variable phenomenon. As such, it should command the full attention of the various disciplines that influence planning strategies for migrant workers. Any attempt to evaluate plans for migrant worker absorption must take a multidisciplinary perspective in order to capture the wider structural context in which planning decisions are made.

Transnational migration in recent decades is but one symptom of the crystallization of a global economic system that has adopted neoliberal ideologies, global economic regulations, international agreements, and the like. This current wave of global migration can be characterized by five features: (1) globalization of migration: Israel, for example, absorbs migrants from more than 50 countries on four continents; (2) magnitude: in numbers of immigrants, far larger than any previously experienced; (3) the multitude of migration routes has been institutionalized; (4) women are included on a greater scale than in the past; (5) politicization of migration on the international and national level is deeper than ever (Castles and Miller 1998). The mobilization of labor on a global scale, particularly of low-skilled, second labor market workers from less developed to highly developed countries and, alternatively, of highly skilled workers among developed countries, has become an essential characteristic of our era (Levitt, DeWind, and Vertovec 2003). The main goal of this chapter is to unravel the ideological and structural context in which policies toward second labor market migrant workers are formulated. Doing so will make clear the context in which planners are planning for migrant workers.

Main Principles

Any analysis of migrant worker policies must relate to three scales of impact on absorption: migrants' daily practices as performed in local communities; state and institutional policies toward migrant workers; and global political economy (Guarnizo and Smith 2001). While neoliberal views are hegemonic in the world system at large, imposed and enforced by a small group of highly developed countries, at the national level, nationalist ideologies and political interests still compete with economic interests when decisions are made (Hix and Noury 2007). In addition, discrepancies often exist between national and urban policies, as can be seen in several recent case studies of European countries along with Tel Aviv, Israel (Schnell and Alexander 2002; Alexander 2003). In other words, at each scale a separate policy has been developed based on different ideologies and interests, despite the fact that municipalities in Israel, for instance, are highly dependent on national institutions.

A second point to be stressed is that the array of interests represented by established institutions, political parties, and organizations are the main agents active in policy formulation. These interests and, more important, the institutions that function as their advocate, are not monolithic at any of the three scales, particularly at the nation-state and urban levels. They operate differently in each country because of differences in political structure along with divergent political, social, and cultural histories (Boswell 2007). Planners in each country and even in each city operate in a unique ideological and institutional context that ought to shape policies toward migrant workers in a unique way; planners consequently, in my view, should adopt different means to achieve different goals. In this chapter, some of the main dimensions of these policies are highlighted in order to supply planners with a better understanding of the main forces that shape the incorporation and integration of migrants into society.

In what follows, the issue of migrant workers is conceptualized in terms of host-stranger relations. By host-stranger relations I refer to the relationships between a dominant local community and a particular type of other—newcomers—who must confront the exclusionary strategies implemented by a dominant host community (Schnell and Alexander 2002; Alexander 2003). This definition stresses the role of power relations since the identity of the other and the choice of exclusionary strategies used against them, including economic ones, are determined by the hosts. According to modernist perspectives, hosts tend to feel threatened by the ambivalent character of strangers in a reality where collective identity is nurtured by clear borders between similar "we"s and different others (Bauman 1995). In the drive to reduce ambivalence, hosts may seek either to assimilate strangers, to make the different similar, or to exclude and marginalize them, to demarcate clear borders for the purpose of representing the superiority of "us" over "them." According to postmodernist theory, otherness may nevertheless be valued as a source of inspiration by allowing for differences (Bauman 1995; Levinas 2004). These models set the range of alternative forms of host-stranger relations to be discussed later.

In what follows, I take the wave of migrants as given and discuss the milieu in which policies toward migrant workers are formulated while trying to identify the main factors that explain such policies. This line of argument is based on the assumption that any planning for the absorption of migrant workers cannot transcend these structural conditions. Instead, any planning project has to be rooted in the power structure and the ethos of society both of which should be used to promote stated goals. No common set of principles for planning for migrant workers will emerge from this essay, but readers should finish with an understanding of the main characteristics of the milieu in which planners act.

Theoretical Debates

Among the three levels of analysis, global, national, and urban, the nation-state is the key level for understanding differences in policies. The most prominent theory of migration policy is Freeman's (1995) political-economic theory, which argues that policies are determined by organized interest groups, with politicians serving as major brokers who represent as well as mediate these interests. In many cases, groups directly affected by migration policies organize to influence policy decisions while the general public, which essentially takes the associated risks, remains diffuse, unorganized, and therefore ineffective in making its claims. Lobbies for employers and migrant workers consequently succeed in persuading political leaders to adopt liberal policies toward the absorption of migrant workers, even though these policies may work against the interests of the local working class.

The principal critique of this theory is that it oversimplifies human agency and treats agents as if they are all driven by common interests and motivations. This critique focuses on the salience of the ideologies adopted by different social groups in the public debates that frame public discourses (Hammar 2001). Political parties, civil society organizations, and so forth participate in debates along with interest groups; each brings nationalist and/or other values that influence how attitudes toward migrant workers are framed. Brubaker (1995) has commented that European societies are more corporatist and stress social democratic values more than is typical in the United States, and that as a result we find greater politicization of migrant access to social services and rights and, consequently, greater involvement of nationalist and other ideologies in the framing of the respective policies. This theory also challenges views of the autonomic power of the nation-state, which are assumed to be actively wielded in order to influence policies based on considerations beyond the typical liberal considerations of interest groups, or the global system (Hollifield 1992).

The state is a complex entity and migrant worker policies are just one issue in a wider debate conducted along a set of ideological and institutional cleavages. The state itself may be torn between contrasting constituencies such as economic, neoliberal interests that demand the import of cheap labor in contrast to other national, religious, and class interests, which call to close the country to immigration. For example, the Israeli state made special efforts to reduce inflation and simultaneously block the flood of migrant workers into Israel during the 1990s. Whereas the Ministry of Finance feared the loss of cheap labor in the construction sector (housing prices have a tremendous impact on inflation rates), the religious parties put pressure on the government to expel the migrant workers to secure a Jewish character for the state.

Boswell (2007) explains the role of the state as motivated by its need for public legitimacy along four criteria: securing the territorial integrity of the state; supplying physical security to its residents; securing the conditions for well-being; and securing human rights. I tend to stress yet another role, that of consolidating national identity and cohesiveness. While allowing entrance to migrant workers is motivated by an economic rationale, migration policies must relate first to a state's responsibility for creating a better environment for the accumulation of wealth. However, if this goal negates any of the state's other goals, several strategies may be activated, one of which involves altering the ranking of the other sources of state legitimacy. Boswell's contribution is important for understanding migrant worker policies in the complex global, national, and local realities characterizing most developed states. His model is, however, less sensitive to the impact of national ideologies on state policies. What is needed is a model that stresses the importance

of cultural and national identity considerations in formulating national policies toward migrant workers (Brubaker 1992; Hollifield 1994; Meyers 2000;
Money 1999).

Such models tend to view immigration policies as one dimension of
nation-building (Schnapper 1992); states in the throes of nation-building
tend to develop immigration regimes that serve this purpose by defining citizenship policies and control apparatuses (Hammar 1985). A frequently referenced model of this kind is suggested by Castles (1995), who identifies three
different strategies for defining "us" as opposed to "strangers." According to
Castles, nations that emphasize ethnicity as a major criterion for belonging
tend to exclude immigrants other than members of the same ethnic group intent on repatriation. Nations that adopt a republican ideology, in which membership is based on communal solidarity, tend to accept multiculturalism. In
many cases, settlers' societies, but also some more homogeneous states, tend
to adopt multicultural policies. An alternative model can be constructed in
which different policies are deduced from answers to two considerations that
pertain to the national level: whether the migrants are perceived as temporary visitors or permanent residents; and in what ways they are expected to
integrate into society (Schnell and Alexander 2002; Alexander 2003).

National Policies

Our model distinguishes among five types of national policies toward migrant workers (Figure 12.1).

(1) *Absorption of transient migrants* occurs mainly in "secondary labor
markets," with hosts and migrants sharing expectations of a short stay in the
host country. Workers of this type are intent on saving capital in order to
improve their standard of living in their home country, whereas host interest
groups are seeking cheap labor (Piore 1979). According to Piore, delays in
migrants' return to their home countries represent the failure to save sufficient capital for their original purposes. A more significant characteristic
of this policy is state refusal to take responsibility for the migrant workers'
well-being and civil rights. In extreme cases like Israel during the 1990s, the
state privatized the import of migrant workers, thereby freeing itself from
any responsibility for the migrants' well-being. Furthermore, the deportation
policy adopted by the Israeli government did not reduce the number of migrant workers in the country but did undermine the workers' willingness to

stand up for their rights according to the law. They were constantly afraid of being deported once their employer, who retained their documents, decided to stop employing them or they were caught by the police as undocumented workers. The fact that importing an alternative worker enables the employer to reap additional profits encourages employers to fire and deport "disobedient" workers (Rozenhek 2000; Schnell 2001).

The result is a state policy that provides an umbrella permitting harsh exploitation of migrant workers by employers. In Israel, the NGO Workers' Hot Line estimated that more than 70 percent of the migrant workers in Israel were cheated by their employers; most of these workers were afraid to complain to avoid deportation. In California, more than an estimated 12 million undocumented Mexican workers who work under even more radical forms of exploitation have been documented (Schnell 2001). Although such a policy tends to be adopted by most receiving countries during the initial decades of importing migrant workers, it remains in place in almost all countries that employ significant numbers of undocumented workers.

(2) *Guest worker policies* represent the state's understanding that public policies defining migrant workers' rights and establishing control mechanisms to protect those rights are required. This stage is based on the realization that irrespective of the migrant workers' exclusion from the host society with the accompanying denial of civil rights and eligibility for citizenship, the state has to take responsibility for their well-being. Guest workers are not represented in any way in public organizations, although informal dialogue with the entry of migrants' organizations into the vacuum left by the state may develop. Social rights have been legislated to define migrants' rights, although those rights are usually more limited than for local workers. For instance, the rights to education, implementation of labor laws, and limited social security and health programs have been specially legislated for migrant workers. In implementing guest worker policies, the state attempts to maintain the homogeneity of the national society while securing those basic rights for migrant workers that are perceived to be necessary for securing economic wealth. Under such circumstances, the state may have to confront contradictions arising between its role as a facilitator of economic wealth and as a protector of the national identity.

In Europe, guest worker policies often replace transient policies either because of fear of riots and instability initiated by exploited migrant workers or as a result of growing pressure from progressive segments in the host society who are working to eliminate the harsh exploitation of migrant workers in their country. Soysal (1994) has shown how when the global system stresses civil rights, it creates pressure to extend civil rights to migrant workers in individual states. Others have shown how intrastate institutions tend to campaign for granting migrant workers civil rights in the name of ethical values as well as the continued securing of economic wealth (Favel 2001; Guiraudon 2002, 2003). Guest worker policies are more likely to characterize states stressing ethnicity-based national identity since these countries perceive migrant workers as threats to national identity. In many of these countries, the issue of migrant workers has been made a security issue to legitimate restrictions on the entrance of migrant workers and retain segregation of strangers from migrant workers who have been made nationalized (Bigo 2002; Rudolph 2003). The result of these policies is mass absorption of migrant workers to meet the labor demands of the secondary labor market together with marginalization of those same workers. The formerly homogeneous society is transformed into a heterogeneous one with a privileged local working class and a new underclass of immigrants. The privileged rights of the host working class are marked by differential access to social security programs and by deportation policies that undermine migrant workers' motivation to struggle for access to their limited rights.

(3) *Assimilationist policies* characterize states that are sensitive to the needs of a stable national identity but are stressed by the deprivation of large numbers of migrant workers for a long period of time. Assimilationist policies seek to integrate migrant workers into the host society on a permanent basis by opening routes for adoption of the host's culture and values. Such policies are based on the assumption that migrant workers will readily take the opportunity to assimilate in a way that makes their "strangerness" temporary. Others who prefer to retain their cultural otherness are sanctioned formally and informally through marginalization and segregation. Although the process may take as long as three generations, the migrants' communities will be transformed, with the host communities free to remain immune from any change in response to their encounters with migrant communities.

In such circumstance, any deviation of the migrant from the dominant host culture is perceived as a social problem that must be remedied through resocialization. Civil democracies like France, which allow any stranger to adopt French citizenship if he/she is willing to adopt French culture, are more likely to adopt assimilationist policies. Yet, ethnic democracies like Germany have also replaced guest worker policies with assimilationist ones following internal pressures to reduce the deprivation of minority migrant

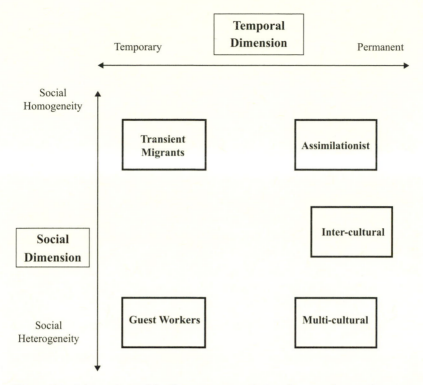

Figure 12.1. Schematic model of host-stranger relations between host and migrant worker communities.

worker communities. Policies in assimilationist countries are universally oriented toward disregarding ethnic diversity. No policies oriented toward the migrants' otherness are legitimized, except those helping migrants assimilate and acculturate in the host society (euphemistically called the "melting pot"). Such policies are likely to include a requirement to learn the local language, perceived as the main lever for integration in the labor market and through it into society at large.

(4) *Multicultural policies* assume the permanence of migrant workers in the host society but also the right of migrant workers to maintain their otherness for the long term. Integration is not achieved by transforming the newcomers, by promoting their adoption of the host values and culture, but by mutual adjustments. Differences are perceived as positive values, rooted in what Levinas referred to as the ethics of taking responsibility for the others'

otherness. Cultural diversity is also perceived as an enriching experience that may positively reflect on creativity and economic development. Multicultural policies tend to select different means, as appropriate for different groups, based on ethnic, racial, or religious foundations. Policies, therefore, are more oriented toward the community level, with the aim of developing partnerships among communal leaders. In a related manner, empowerment of ethnic institutions is perceived as a process supporting social integration. Such policies are therefore expected to be implemented according to a general ethics that appreciates cultural difference together with mutual tolerance. We should be aware, though, that in many cases, multicultural worldviews have been replaced by communitarianism (Bauman 1995).

(5) *Intercultural policies* are one response to the failure of multicultural policies. The recognition that some migrant social groups refuse to adopt basic values associated with respect for civil rights and tolerance, values that are held in common by other groups, has focused attention on the need for the state to promote these values, primarily through education. Only by cultivating respect for the otherness of migrant communities will these shared values be respected by all. Therefore, intercultural policies emphasize the need to unite society at large around common values, usually focused on citizenship and national ethos as much as around the acceptance of cultural differences among groups.

Many European countries first adopted a transient policy toward migrant workers, and replaced it with a guest worker policy in the second stage. In the third stage some countries adopted assimilationist policies while others adopted multicultural policies. Since the year 2000 several countries have tended to replace either the assimilationist or multicultural policies with intercultural policies.

Local Policies

Despite the fact that the migration literature focuses on global and national factors, with national policies perceived as the primary regulators of migration policy, local authorities and large cities have a tremendous impact on immigrants' life conditions. The city is the arena in which hosts and strangers interact in the course of daily life; local policies have the power to regulate living conditions on the level of daily practice (Vernez 1993). Most migrants meet members of host societies in the centers of the larger metropolises of the more developed countries. In many of these cities, migrant workers make up as much as one-quarter of the local population. It is in the cities that migrants seek to develop communal visibility by opening ethnic markets, conducting festivals, establishing places of worship, and so forth. Many migrant workers became permanent residents of these cities, where they contribute to the local economy as one of the more active segments of society, despite their continued vulnerability, which results from their legal inferiority on the national level.

Municipalities, as political institutions, have much to do with regulating the nature of these intercommunal encounters. Local policies, in their focus on municipal and other local institutions, enable the exercise of local discretion with respect to the interpretation of decisions and actions channeled from upper levels of government down to migrant workers. Several studies have focused on local policies, but only a few have compared different cities in the same nation to test the possibility of evaluating the power of cities to distance themselves from national policies (Rex and Samad 1996). Friedmann and Lehrer (1997) and Schnell and Alexander (2002) focused their studies in Frankfurt and Tel Aviv respectively, on the ways municipalities have challenged national policies to promote more open and liberal policies. The two municipalities observed were backed by progressive host citizens who revolted against national exclusionary policies. The municipality of Frankfurt pioneered adoption of a multicultural policy calling for a process of *zusamenwachsen* (growing together) while respecting differences (Wolf-Almanasreh 1993). Policy measures—for example, reducing fear of strangers among local residents, transforming the educational system into a multicultural system, promoting public debate over ethnic discrimination, and securing universal religious freedom—were directed at the city's entire population. Additional measures were directed specifically toward migrant populations: social work with delinquent boys, empowering migrants' organizations, providing social services to migrants irrespective of their official status, among others (Friedmann and Lehrer 1997). Tel Aviv adopted a much less ambitious policy. By means of a series of conferences that brought together municipal administrators, government administrators, and academics, pressure was put on the government to adopt measures aimed at securing minimal rights for migrant workers (Schnell and Alexander 2002).

It seems that municipalities act mainly through supplying services, either incorporating migrant workers into the service system, even, as in Tel Aviv, including undocumented migrant workers, or by supplying targeted services to migrant workers. These services may include many dimensions, starting from educational and health services and even social or public housing. Several municipalities cooperated with migrant workers' organizations in adapting services to the unique needs of migrant workers.

Conversely, municipalities also tend to challenge national policies that seek to legalize migrant workers who are seen as a burden on the municipal budget. Some municipalities have also sought to make migrant workers visible in the urban space in order to load their places with symbolic meanings. Finally, many municipalities have attempted to desegregate migrant workers as a way to increase assimilation and acculturation, thereby reducing inter-ethnic stereotyping and antagonizing of the migrants (Schnell and Ostendorf 2002; Alexander 2003).

Explaining Differences in Policies

While nation-states remain the main actors in determining policy, global regulations and norms of conduct do influence government decisions and public debates in host countries. Civil rights discourses have also infiltrated public debate and led to gradual expansion of civil rights in many host countries (Soysal 1994). By the same token, as noted above, municipalities have proved willing to challenge national policies (Schnell and Alexander 2002). Numerous large cities in highly developed countries have led campaigns in favor of expanding migrant workers' access to human services and civil rights (Alexander 2003).

While at the global scale, a set of neoliberal modes of conduct are dominant, national and local policies have been shown to be more diverse. The five alternative worldviews I have identified—transient, guest workers, assimilationists, multicultural, and intercultural—in effect guide national and local policies. Historical accounts of the absorption of migrant workers in host societies reveal that transient and guest worker policies are temporary and that most states tend to gradually adopt either assimilationist, multicultural, or intercultural policies. The route of this development is influenced by the state's sensitivity to the balance of power among interest groups in addition to the various sources of its legitimization. Three issues are at the core of the associated debate: control of the flow of immigrants into the state, extension of civil rights and citizenship to migrant workers, and inclusion in the welfare state. States differ in their orientation toward the three aspects of policy.

According to Hix and Noury (2007), the main debates take place between potential employers and the host working class (economic interests) and between political and ideological interest groups tied to different sources of legitimization. Several theoretical inputs may help us understand each society's orientation concerning the aforementioned types of policies. Here I present them in the form of an explanatory model that combines political, social, economic, and ideological factors (Figure 12.2).

The ideological component predicts that conservative governments will tend to adopt more restrictive policies toward migrant workers' civil rights and welfare benefits, while liberal and social-democratic governments will tend to adopt more hospitable policies. Several empirical studies in the U.S. have confirmed this generalization (Berry et al. 1998; Graefe et al. 2008; Lieberman and Shaw 2000; Zylan and Soule 2000). These studies show that liberal and conservative parties remain highly consistent when introducing policies toward migrant workers as part of their more general welfare and citizenship schemes. While liberal governments tend to search for innovative ideas in order to integrate migrant workers into society, conservative governments tend to minimize distribution of rights and benefits to migrant workers (Graefe et al. 2008; Plotnich and Witness 1985). In the European context, inclusionist policies toward migrant workers are institutionalized in the agenda of social-democratic parties (Kitschelt 1995), whereas rightist parties tend to support exclusionary policies. Both political blocks demonstrate that ideological factors are considered before economic ones. The social democrats represent the host working class who may feel economically threatened by the inclusion of migrant workers, while the rightists represent the economic elites who may suffer losses by not allowing for importation of cheap labor into the host economy (Brubaker 1992; Neumayer 2005). Changes in policies, therefore, are the result of strains in one or more aspects of the model. A typical example might be an economic recession or imbalanced growth in needy populations among migrant workers to a degree that strains the national economy.

Introduction of welfare programs for migrant workers may become the main trigger for the rise of racist attitudes toward migrant workers. In the same way, increasing numbers of migrant workers, if they threaten the dominance of host cultures and identities, may unintentionally provoke a racist backlash (Lieberman 1995; Quadagno 1990). (A similar example, not involving migrants, can be seen in U.S. states with a large black population, that tend to impose strict welfare policies, with voters less willing to support welfare programs; see Plotnick and Winters 1985; Soss et al. 2001; Zylan and Soule 2000.) The rise in demand for welfare funds among migrant workers kindles conservative ideologies that blame the welfare system for producing a culture of poverty. This argument rests on the principle that services produce the needs they are meant to meet, as is demonstrated by the case of young migrant mothers in the United States whose number increased significantly following the introduction of social security programs aimed at this group (Bachu and O'Connell 2001). Recognition of this process, which is more likely to occur during economic crises, motivates governments to restrict welfare programs aimed at migrant workers, as is the case in the United States. Beyond that, high concentrations of migrant worker communities with high visibility that represents their otherness in the public space tend to threaten host communities and increase racist attitudes among the local population. Nauck (1988) has shown that segregated neighborhoods of ethnic minorities caused deeper resentment among Germans than did mixed neighborhoods.

The idea that the state's economic situation has a significant effect on policies toward migrant workers has already been demonstrated. Scholars like Lieberman and Shaw (2000), Soss et al. (2001) and Rector (2006) have all provided evidence that welfare programs that strained the national economy led to both increased stereotyping of needy populations and criticism of the welfare system that produced the so-called culture of poverty. These steps created the climate for adoption of stricter policies toward migrant workers by reducing their eligibility for welfare benefits. Some studies have shown that in the United States, the states with higher average incomes tend to adopt more liberal policies toward migrant workers, mainly in terms of welfare policies, than do states with lower average incomes (Howard 1999)

Political aspects of the model relate to the ways competition between parties is handled. When the political system is dominated by one large party that is, in most cases, also backed by members of the elite, elitist interests tend to dictate policies toward migrant workers, which means support for policies that supply a cheap labor force to the labor markets. In cases where several parties strongly compete for popular support, their policies tend to be more responsive to popular attitudes. This trend is particularly strong when the populations affected by these policies are permanent state residents who actively participate in elections. In the North American political context, greater electoral competition is associated with adoption of more liberal policies toward migrant workers; when one party dominates, this leads to more

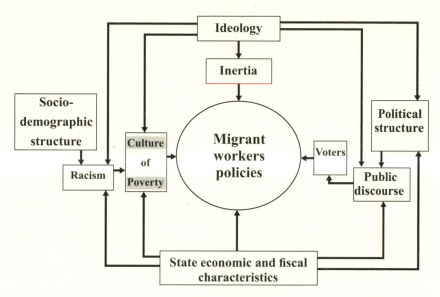

Figure 12.2. General model explaining differences in migration policies between states.

conservative policies (Brace and Jewett 1995; Graefe et al. 2008; Peterson and Rom 1989).

In general, ideology, economy, sociodemography, and political structure simultaneously influence the formulation of policies toward migrant workers. Their combined effects may lead to different policies that are nonetheless rooted in unique state histories and characteristics. Furthermore, the interplay among these features can culminate in controversy, as the European case demonstrates. In Europe, the major parties advocate policies that place the economic interests of their voters at risk for the sake of ideology, thereby demonstrating the privileged status of ideological considerations in party decision-making. Economic considerations come to the fore when the financial burden of funding welfare programs becomes too stressful, due to economic crises or an increasing number of welfare recipients among the migrant workers. The impact of economic considerations is frequently associated with shifts in ideology, as happened with the adoption of a worldview that accepted the existence of a culture of poverty, or when racist ideologies blame rising welfare expenditures on the welfare system or welfare populations. Sociodemographic balances between hosts and migrants become essential once the demographic or cultural dominance of the hosts is threatened. Such situations may degenerate into intolerance toward migrant workers, in the form of both growing fears and racist behavior. Finally, the structure of the political system and the dynamics of the public debate on the issue may provide platforms for the expression of different interests, with stronger influence attributed to the wider public once it becomes a major factor in public debates and party competition.

It appears that the matrix of structural preconditions for intervention in host-migrant relations is complex. It has to take into consideration political, economic, social, and ideological aspects in the level of the state as described above. The same model can be developed to understand the forces that shape urban policies toward migrants at the municipality scale as well. Different types of gaps between municipal and national policies may add complexity to the matrix and different historical memories will have an impact on public debates about policies, leading to even further complexity. Even at the most local level, local communities and family involvement have a significant impact on the realm of migrants' integration in society. As a consequence, I believe that it is impossible to arrive at any generalized principles of engineering host-migrant relations by a predefined set of instructions and regulations for action. Rather, planners should expect to relate to the forces in society that shape host-migrant relations in order to improve the social well-being in terms of their stated value system.

Policies tend to use a wide range of means. Alexander (2003) identified four domains: Juridical-political, socioeconomic, cultural, and spatial. Some planners devote special attention to the distribution of migrant residents in space, their access to services, and their visibility in space. Such an approach assumes an oversimplified isomorphism between society and space in which residential segregation is automatically associated with social exclusion and spatial desegregation is expected to stimulate assimilation and acculturation. In response these planners tend to promote housing policies that desegregate migrant workers and minority groups in residential space, believing this act will integrate them in society (Domburg-De Rooij and Mustard 2002). I would argue that this set of tools is rooted in the Newtonian container conception of space that dominated planning thinking in the 1960s and 1970s. Studies on segregation in the era of globalization show that direct association between residential segregation and social exclusion has broken down (Schnell and Benjamini 2001, 2005; Schnell 2002), leading to the conclusion that new strategies have to be adopted by planners.

I believe that the two basic types of action needed are opening up more possibilities for migrant worker networks and removing the structural barriers that envelop migrants on their route to integration. Migrants need to maintain networks with their ethnic mates in home and host societies, and at the same time they need to join key networks in the host society. These networks can be open or closed, marginalizing or empowering, enslaving or enabling. Planners need strategies to channel these networks to the service of their goals—goals that may change from one social context to another. At the same time planners have to analyze the enveloping structural characteristics of both host and ethnic milieus in order to identify and act on barriers to the achievement of their stated goals for interaction. Simplified models of isomorphism between space and society are not relevant any more, but a deep understanding of the structures of migrants' everyday routines and networks, and the structural characteristics of the hosting envelope, may lead to effective intervention.

Planners must act through the political system, using the structured forces in society, to promote tendencies toward the integration of migrant workers in societies and to break down barriers to integration. They should act in order to change laws and formal regulations in order to in collaboration with NGOs to supply migrant workers with equal opportunities in society. The planner is one actor in a complex system. She needs to understand the system and to find creative routes to influence the operation of the system with its different interest groups, in order to achieve a set of stated objectives.

Epilogue

Monitoring the development of public policies toward migrant workers and the worldviews that guide them led to the conclusion that in the early stages of migration, nation-states tend to avoid dealing with the human aspects of the absorption of migrant workers by treating them as an economic resource. Growing public pressure then leads to the adoption of guest worker policies that view migrants as temporary residents who need to be treated humanely and decently as long as they stay in the country. From that point on, countries split in their responses to the realization that migrant workers have become permanent residents of the host state. Some develop assimilation policies, directed toward acculturation of migrants while integrating them into society at large. The lack of migrant openness to acculturation may nonetheless leave them socially marginalized and spatially segregated (De Rooij and Mustard 2002; Farwick et al. 2002). Other states develop multicultural policies in which both host and migrant communities are expected to change, replacing the common ground based on cultural homogeneity with one of cultural heterogeneity. Both groups of countries experienced difficulties implementing these policies, difficulties that moved them to introduce new intercultural policies. The development of worldviews that guide policies therefore depends on the political, sociodemographic, ideological, and economic histories of each country. Overall, five types of policies have been identified by states.

In addition, the world system, which is dominated by global economic interest groups who have lost their dependency and their care for places, and by neoliberal ideology, promotes two alternative reactions to migrant workers as strangers in host societies: avoidance of their social needs or adaptation of a communitarian world view that treats them as economic resources. The result is the rise of a new underclass characterized by reduced social and human rights, as well as a large group of undocumented workers, who lack human rights. The opposing strategy, grounded in human rights, has primarily been adopted by civil society NGOs and social democratic parties that transcend national belonging. On the local level, a multitude of strategies may be adopted by hosts and strangers, which may gain autonomous power from the state in shaping host-stranger relations.

The overall conclusion that may be drawn from this analysis is that planners are functioning in complex political milieus in a way that makes it difficult to reach any simple set of generalizations. Instead, planners ought to analyze migrants' networks and the structural milieu that envelops their daily lives, in order to act on structures of opportunities and barriers necessary for their integration into society at large.

References

Alexander, Michael. 2003. Host-stranger relations in Rome, Tel Aviv, Paris and Amsterdam: A comparison of local policies toward labor migrants. Ph.D. thesis, Universitat van Amsterdam.

Bachu, Amara, and Martin O'Connell. 2001. *Fertility of American women*. Report P20-543RV. Washington, D.C.: U.S. Census Bureau.

Bauman, Zygmunt 1995. *Life in fragments: Essays in postmodern morality*. Oxford: Blackwell.

Berry, William D., Evan J. Ringquist, Richard C. Fording, and Russell L. Hanson. 1998.

Measuring citizens' and governments' ideology in the American states. *American Journal of Political Science* 42(1): 327–48.

Bigo, Didier. 2002. Security and immigration: On the critique of the governmentality of unease. *Alternatives* 27: 63–92.

Brace, Paul, and Aubrey Jewett. 1995. The state of state politics research. *Political Research Quarterly* 48(3): 643–81.

Boswell, Christina. 2007. Theorizing migration policy: Is there a third way? *International Migration Review* 41(1): 75–100.

Brubaker, Rogers. 1992. *Citizenship and nationhood in France and Germany.* Cambridge, Mass.: Harvard University Press.

———. 1995. Comments on "Modes of immigration policies in liberal democratic states." *International Migration Review* 29(4): 903–8.

Castles, Stephen. 1995. How nation-states respond to immigration and ethnic diversity. *New Community* 21(3): 218–30.

Castles, Stephen, and Mark J. Miller. 1998. *The age of migration: International population models in the modern world.* New York: Guilford Press.

Domburg-De Rooij, Tineke, and Sako Musterd. 2002. Segregation and state polices: Ethnic segregation and the welfare state. In *Studies in segregation and desegregation,* ed. Izhak Schnell and Wim Ostendorf. Aldershot: Ashgate.

Farwick, Andreas, Britte Klagge, and Wolfgang Taubmann. 2002. Urban poverty in Germany. In *Studies in segregation and desegregation,* ed. Izhak Schnell and Wim Ostendorf. Aldershot: Ashgate.

Favell, Adrian. 2001. *Philosophies of integration.* Basingstoke: Palgrave.

Freeman, Gary P. 1995. Modes of immigration policies in liberal democratic states. *International Migration Review* 24(4) 881–902.

Friedmann, John, and Ute Angelika Lehrer. 1997. Urban policy responses to foreign in-migration. *APA Journal* 63(1): 61–78.

Graefe, Deborah R., Gordon F. De Jong, and Shelley K. Irving. 2008. The whole is the sum of its parts: Theory, technique and measurement applied to TANF rules. *Social Science Quarterly* 87(4): 818–27.

Guarnizo, Luis Eduardo, and Michael Peter Smith. 2001. The locations of transnational-ism. In *Transnationalism from below,* ed. Michael Reter Smith and Luis Eduardo Guarnizo, 3–34. Edison, N.J.: Transaction Books.

Guiraudon, Virginie. 2002. The Marshallian tryptich re-ordered: The role of court and bureaucracies in furthering migrants' social rights. In *Immigration and welfare: Challenging the borders of the welfare state,* ed. Michael Bommes and Andrew Geddes, 72–89. London: Routledge.

———. 2003. The constitution of an immigration policy domain: A political sociology approach. *Journal of European Public Policy* 10(2): 263–82.

Hammar, Tomas. 1985. *European immigration policy: A comparative study.* London: Cambridge University Press.

———. 2001. Politics of immigration control and politicisation of international migration. In *International migration into the 21st century: Essays in honour of Reginald Appleyard*, ed. M. A. B. Siddique, 15–28. New York: Edward Elgar.

Hix, Simon and Abul Noury. 2007. Policies, not economic interests: Determinants of migration policies in the European Union. *International Migration Review* 41(1): 182–205.

Hollifield, James F. 1992. *Immigrants, markets and states: The political economy of postwar Europe.* Cambridge, Mass.: Harvard University Press.

———. 1994. Immigration and Republicanism in France: The hidden consensus. In *Controlling Immigration: A global perspective*, ed. Wayne A. Cornelius, Philip L. Martin, and James F. Hollifield, 143–75. Stanford, Calif.: Stanford University Press.

Howard, Christopher. 1999. *The hidden welfare state: Tax expenditures and social policy in the United States.* Princeton, N.J.: Princeton University Press.

Kitschelt, Herbert. 1995. *The Radical right in Western Europe: A comparative analysis.* Ann Arbor: University of Michigan Press.

Levinas, Emmanuel. 2004. *The humanism of the Other Man.* Jerusalem: Bustan. [In Hebrew].

Levitt, Peggy, Josh DeWind, and Steven Vertovec. 2003. International perspectives on transnational migration: An introduction. *International Migration Review* 37: 567–75.

Lieberman, Robert C. 1995. Race, institutions and the administration of social policy. *Social Science History* 19(4): 511–42.

Lieberman, Robert C., and Greg M. Shaw. 2000. Looking inward, looking outward: The politics of state welfare innovation under devolution. *Political Research Quarterly* 3(2): 215–40.

Meyers, Eytan. 2000 Theories of international immigration policy: A comparative analysis. *International Journal of Migration* 34(4): 1245–82.

Money, Jeannette. 1999. *Fences and neighbors: The political geography of immigration control.* Ithaca, N.Y.: Cornell University Press.

Nauck, Bernhard 1988. Sozial-ökologischer Kontext und außerfamiliäre Beziehungen. *Sonderheft* 29: 139–78.

Neumayer, Eric. 2005. Bogus refugees? The determinant of asylum migration to Western Europe. *International Studies Quarterly* 49(3): 389–410.

Peterson, Paul E., and Mark Rom. 1989. American federalism, welfare policy and residential choice. *American Political Science Review* 83(3): 711–28.

Piore, Michael J. 1979. *Birds of passage: Migrant labor and industrial societies.* Cambridge: Cambridge University Press.

Plotnick, Robert D., and Richard F. Winters. 1985. A politico–economic theory of income redistribution. *American Political Science Review* 79(2): 458–73.

Quadagno, Jill. 1990. Race, class and gender in the U.S. welfare state: Nixon's failed Family Assistance Plan. *American Sociological Review* 55(1): 11–28.

Rector, Robert. 2006. Amnesty and continued low-skill immigration will substantially raise welfare costs and poverty. Heritage Foundation Backgrounder 1936, May 16.

Rex, John, and Yunas Samad. 1996. Multiculturalism and political integration in Birmingham and Bradford. *Innovation* 9(1): 11–31.

Rozenhek, Ze'ev. 2000. Migration regimes, intrastate conflicts and the politics of exclusion and inclusion in the Israeli welfare state. *Social Problems* 47(1): 49–67.

Rudolph, Christopher. 2003. Security and the political economy of international migration. *American Political Science Review* 97(4): 603–20.

Schnapper, Dominique. 1992. *L'Europe des immigrés*. Paris: François Bourin.

Schnell, Izhak. 2001. *Directions for migrant workers policy in Israel*. Jerusalem: Center for the Study of Social Policy in Israel.

———. 2002. Segregation in everyday life spaces: A conceptual model. In *Studies in segregation and desegregation*, ed. Izhak Schnell and Wim Ostendorf. Aldershot: Ashgate.

Schnell, Izhak, and Michael Alexander. 2002. *Municipal policy toward migrant workers: Lessons from Tel-Aviv-Jafo*. Jerusalem: Floresheimer Institute for Policy Studies.

Schnell, Izhak, and Yoav Benjamini. 2001. The socio-spatial isolation of agents in everyday life spaces as an aspect of segregation. *Annals of the Association of American Geographers* 91(4): 622–33.

———. 2005. Globalization and the structure of urban social space: The lesson from Tel Aviv. *Urban Studies* 42(13): 1–22.

Schnell, Izhak, and Wim Ostendorf, eds. 2002. *Studies in segregation and desegregation*. Aldershot: Ashgate.

Soss, Joe, Sanford F. Schram, Thomas P. Vartanian, and Erin O'Brien. 2001. Setting the terms of relief: Explaining state policy choices in the devolution revolution. *American Journal of Political Science* 45(2): 378–95.

Soysal, Yasemin Nuhoğlu. 1994 *The limits of citizenship*. Chicago: University of Chicago Press.

Vernez, George. 1993. *Needed: A federal role in helping communities cope with immigration*. Santa Monica, Calif.: Rand Corporation.

Wolf-Almanasreh, Rosi. 1993. *Zweieinhalb Jahre amt für multikulturelle Angelegenheiten*. Frankfurt: AMKA.

Zylan, Yvonne, and Sarah A. Soule. 2000. Welfare as we know it: Welfare state retrenchment, 1989–1995. *Social Forces* 79(2): 623–52.

Chapter 13

Planning for Aging Involves Planning for Life

Deborah Howe

We are in the midst of profound demographic changes taking place on a global scale. Society is aging, the result of declining fertility rates and increasing longevity. The number of older people and their increasing share of the population have significant implications for the extent to which society can provide necessary levels of support to ensure their quality of life.

Public policy has historically sought to meet elders' needs through pensions and health care. At the same time, there has been systematic neglect of the role the built environment plays in framing alternatives for individuals as they age. We live our daily lives at the local level, and thus land use and development standards frame the environment that will hinder or support our ability to meet needs that can change significantly with age. Planners have a particular responsibility to view communities through an aging lens in order to identify ways in which the environment can be improved. This is an issue with elements of both equity and efficiency in that a supportive environment will enable older people to maintain their independence and health, thus reducing societal costs and lessening the impact on other generations of meeting the needs of elders. It is also an issue of humanity in that society can be judged on the basis of how it treats those who are most vulnerable.

This chapter is a call to planners to appreciate the implications and opportunities inherent in an aging society in order to guide the development of communities to create environments that support people of all ages. While the discussion will emphasize experiences in the United States, the issues raised are relevant throughout the world. The bottom line is the importance of valuing older people and understanding how they experience the environment. We will begin by considering the range of changes that can occur as a person ages. This will be followed with data on global demographic trends that give a sense of the magnitude of the challenges ahead. We will then discuss aging and the built environment, highlighting various ways in which the environment can be a constraint to independence. We will discuss why planners have historically ignored aging issues, describe a range of planning frameworks that have incorporated an aging perspective (or could do so) and present specific land use approaches that can be aging supportive. We will conclude with consideration of what it will take to make communities aging supportive.

The Aging Experience

Aging is an intensely personal experience typically defined by a decline in a range of capacities affecting one's ability to maintain independence. While each of us hopes to have good health to a ripe old age followed by a peaceful, easy death, the inevitability of decline is the norm. Age-related losses in strength, agility, and fine motor control, and a decline in bone density can contribute to problems with balance and an increased risk of injuries from falls. With age, the lens of the eye becomes harder, less flexible, more yellow and more opaque, contributing to myriad problems including difficulty in depth perception, increased sensitivity to glare, and inability to focus on near objects such as written material. Losses in hearing, taste, smell, and skin sensitivity create challenges in daily life. Dementia affects half of all people aged 85 and older with impairments including loss of orientation, short- and long-term memory, and ability to carry out sequential tasks, along with slowed reaction time.

The consequence of these changes is an increasing need for assistance in carrying out the activities of everyday life along with medically oriented care. Nine percent of those aged 65-69 need assistance with daily activities, rising to nearly one third for those aged 80-84 and half of those 85 and older (U.S. Census Bureau 1996). Health care costs for older adults are substantial; in the United States those 65 and older constituted 13 percent of the population in 2002 and 36 percent of personal health care expenses with average annual expenses over three times those of working age people, ages 19-64 (Stanton 2006).

Demographic Trends

According to a United Nations report (UN 2009),

- In 2009, there were over 737 million older people (defined as age 60 and above) with projections of 2 billion by 2050.
- Older people constituted 11 percent of the global population in 2009, with this proportion projected to double by 2050, reaching 33 percent in developed regions and 20 percent in less developed regions. The overall median age will increase from 28 to 38 years during this period.
- By 2050, nearly 80 percent of older people will be found in developing countries.
- The older population is itself aging. Currently one in seven older people are age 80 and above. By 2050 this number will nearly quadruple (from 102 to 395 million) resulting in a ratio of one in five. The number of centenarians is expected to increase ninefold from 455,000 in 2009 to 4.1 million in 2050.
- Due to women's greater longevity, they are the majority among older people; this proportion increases with age. Worldwide, there are 83 males per 100 females aged 60 and above, with women outnumbering men by 66 million. Given historic discrimination in access to education, employment, and other resources, women are more likely than men to be poor and suffer disabilities in older age (WHO 2002).

Elder support has traditionally been provided by families and friends supplemented by social and professional services. The aging of society will place enormous stress on this system. Declining fertility and thus smaller family sizes mean fewer adult children to provide care. For example, in 2002, 18 percent of U.S. women aged 40 to 44 had never had a child compared to 10 percent in 1976. This cohort averaged 1.9 children in 2002 versus 3.1 in 1976 (Downs 2003).

There are also fewer workers paying into pension systems. The potential support ratio (PSR), defined as the number of people aged 15 to 64 compared to the number aged 65 and older, decreased globally from 12 to 9 between 1950 and 2009. By 2050 the PSR is projected to decline to 4 (UN 2009). This is not only a pension issue. Since there will be relatively fewer professional caregivers, their pay scale and thus the overall cost of care will be correspondingly higher.

The global economic downturn of 2007-2009 provided a focus to the challenges ahead. Dramatic declines in the value of pension funds and significant losses in property equity have compromised older people throughout the world and negatively affected the capacity of families to provide intergenerational support. The implication of this might be less if more people lived in extended families, but cultural norms worldwide favor independent living with older people and their adult children maintaining separate households.

Aging and the Built Environment

As a result, many older people live independently in communities that do not meet their needs. Low density communities can be particularly problematic as they are defined by the automobile and favor healthy, middle aged people who can drive and have the financial means and physical capacity to maintain large homes. These location decisions may have made sense for young families with children, but when the children grow up and move away, their parents remain, choosing to "age in place."

In the United States, those aged 65 and older have home ownership rates of 80 percent and a median duration of owner occupancy in their current unit of 25 years. Three fourths of these dwellings average over 1700 square feet on one-third acre lots (U.S. Census Bureau 2005). Long tenure in a house raises the likelihood that the mortgage will be paid off resulting in a reduced monthly housing expenditure which is helpful for retirees on fixed income. For many older people, it makes economic sense to remain in their home. Not surprisingly, eight out of ten respondents in an American Association of Retired Persons (AARP) survey expressed the desire to age in place in their existing home (Matthew Greenwald and Associates 2003).

But problems can emerge when physical, emotional, and cognitive changes associated with aging contribute to a misfit between older people's needs and the housing environment in which they live, compromising their independence, creating personal hardships, and placing additional stress on caregivers. The steps to the entrances of homes or the internal stairs to the second floor bedrooms may present insurmountable obstacles to people with physical limitations. Adaptations to accommodate wheelchairs with ramps, wider doorways and accessible bathrooms can be costly if they are in fact feasible. Ongoing maintenance responsibilities such as shoveling snow, moving trash cans, or cleaning out gutters can be difficult and dangerous.

Making a move as one's needs change is costly, emotionally draining, and difficult. It often involves selling the current house for less than full potential value since older adults on fixed incomes may not have the financial resources or energy to make needed improvements before selling. At the same time, they have to pay full market price for another dwelling. Those who live in areas with low housing values such as an older industrial city may not even consider moving, as the sale of their home would not give them sufficient resources to relocate.

As a further twist on the long-term implications of aging in the United States, some researchers are forecasting a sell-off among baby boomer owner-occupants that will depress housing prices and reduce their equity. Myers and Ryu (2008) have raised concerns about this and what they define as the "crossover point"—when the amount of housing put on the market will exceed the number of buyers.

The built environment can also pose significant constraints on mobility, especially in the suburbs where the absence of sidewalks and transit services forces continuing reliance on the personal automobile. The level of driving licensure among older adults in the United States has increased dramatically over the past 25 years from 61 percent in 1980 to 80 percent in 2003 (Houser 2005). Those who have spent decades driving a car may find this an increasingly difficult and dangerous task due to vision difficulties associated with poor lighting, shadows and glare, and a natural decline in reaction time. While some older people voluntarily restrict their own driving, others have to be forced to give up their keys. The notion that those who no longer drive would use transit or walk is unrealistic (Rosenbloom and Stahl 2002). Destinations may be too far and unsafe to walk. Older pedestrians are vulnerable to injuries and death; while only one fifth of road users, they represent over half of all pedestrian deaths. Transit services, if available, are often difficult for older people to use. Another concern with the reliance on the automobile for transportation is an associated decline in physical activity and rising rates of obesity. Over the long run, obesity can contribute to a decrease in longevity and an increase in the length of time that older people live with disabilities (Preston 2005; Reynolds, Saito, and Crimmons 2005; Visscher and Seidell 2001).

The Reasons for a Lack of Attention to Aging

Given the extraordinary implications of aging for society's current and future capacity to meet anticipated needs, one would assume that a focus on aging would be in the forefront of community planning issues. Unfortunately, community planners have given little attention to aging despite efforts to raise awareness over the past twenty years (see Howe, Chapman and Baggett 1989). There are several reasons for this.

1. The needs of older adults are viewed predominately as a social service/ caregiving issue and thus not under the purview of mainstream community planning.
2. The housing market is driven by buyers who are healthy and have adequate financial resources. There is a prevailing notion that people will move to more appropriate living situations when their needs change.
3. Older adults are overlooked due to discrimination and society-wide lack of respect.

Social service agencies clearly play a front line role in meeting the needs of older adults. Those working in this field, however, do not necessarily have the resources, time, and capacity to actively articulate their perspective within the community planning process. The same can be said of families and friends serving as caregivers who find that an enormous amount of time and emotional energy is involved in just coping with daily needs and crises. These people are in survival mode and do not have the wherewithal to consider their experience in the context of community planning. Thus, planners are not hearing about the challenges caregivers face that are directly attributable to problems posed by the built environment.

The idea that people will move when their needs change is in large part an implicit recognition that most housing fails to meet the needs of older people. Consumers are not demanding that the housing they are buying will be appropriate for their future needs as they age, and builders are not offering such a product. The cost and difficulty of a hypothetical future move may be unfathomable to a young or middle-aged adult in the midst of a home purchase. For older adults, however, a move involves relinquishing cherished possessions, comprehending a new environment at a point when one's abilities may be in decline, difficulties in orchestrating the logistics of a move, and high costs when one is on a fixed income. All this assumes, of course, that affordable housing alternatives are available. It is not surprising, then, that so many older people prefer to remain in their homes, refusing to move until a precipitating event such as a medical crisis forces a move. While the challenges they face may be a direct result of their individual choices, the responsibility for meeting their needs falls to families, friends, and service providers.

Age discrimination in the United States remains socially acceptable with societal norms that devalue older people expressed in numerous ways. Age-based job discrimination and negative media images are two common complaints. Terms such as "sweet little old lady" and that "old curmudgeon" are considered to be endearing but in fact devalue older adults. Researchers are documenting "links between ageist language and reported health outcomes as broad as reduced life satisfaction, lowered self-esteem, and even depression" (Anti-Aging Task Force 2008). The media portrays older people as "dependent, helpless, unproductive and demanding rather than deserving" (Dittman 2003). Seniors engaged in local planning processes are often perceived as self-serving, focused solely on their own interests to the exclusion of others. They may be viewed as anti-children, especially in terms of supporting school taxes.

The reasons why aging is not in the forefront of community planning concerns are at the same time the very reasons why planners need to get involved—and need to do so now. Planners have a particular obligation to give voice to those who are not adequately represented in public decision making. The implications of aging are complex and multifaceted, requiring the long range and comprehensive perspective that planners can offer. There are the immediate and profound needs of people who are already facing the challenges of old age. Then there is the question of how we can do a better job of preparing our communities over the course of the next twenty to thirty years to be more aging supportive.

Frameworks for Community Planning
with an Aging Focus

Thus far, leadership on behalf of community planning for aging is coming out of the social service field primarily through a range of governmental and academic initiatives. Advocacy organizations are also playing key roles. In the United States, at the state level, the Minnesota Department of Health

Services sponsored a five year planning effort to examine the implications of aging for their state. Project 2030 (2002) had a three-pronged approach that considered aging needs in terms of their impact on local and state government; opportunities for businesses and economic development; and individual responsibilities to adequately prepare. In Florida, the Department of Elder Affairs sponsors the Communities for a Lifetime program, which provides technical assistance to support developing partnerships that promote senior-friendly community amenities.[1] The Kansas Department on Aging offers a Lifelong Communities program involving state certification of communities on the basis of a self-study, action plan and implementation achievements.[2] Michigan's Commission on Services to the Aging and the Texas Department of Aging and Disability Services sponsor comparable programs.

The Center of Home Care Policy and Research of the Visiting Nurse Service of New York sponsors the AdvantAge Initiative which involves working with communities to plan for aging using detailed survey data that focuses on defining the needs of older adults.[3] The Center for the Advanced Study of Aging Services at the University of California, Berkeley, hosted an innovative online Creating Aging-Friendly Communities conference in early 2008 involving 750 participants from 17 countries.[4] Presentations covered the unique characteristics of aging-friendly communities, strategies for their creation, and best practices. The conference was followed by the creation of the Community of Practice which provides monthly programs and technical assistance to promote the notion of planning for aging. The Sustainable Communities for All Ages Program is coordinated by Temple University's Center for Intergenerational Learning and offers a community-based framework for developing opportunities for inter-generational benefit.[5] Their explicit purpose is to transform "varied age groups and organizations from competitors to allies."

In the U.S. nonprofit sector, examples include the AARP, which has made livable communities for older adults a program priority, developing support materials including community self-assessment protocols.[6] Another effort that provides technical assistance for community planning efforts is Partners for Livable Communities, a nonprofit organization that focuses on community renewal, and co-sponsors the Aging in Place Initiative with the National Association of Area Agencies on Aging.[7]

On a global scale, the UN World Health Organization (WHO) has established the Global Network of Age-friendly Cities building on a study of

33 cities that confirmed "the importance for older people of access to public transport and outdoor spaces, as well as appropriate housing, community support and health services." WHO is calling on participating cities to "continuously assess and implement steps to improve the environment for their older residents" (UN News Centre 2010: 1).

All f these programs devote explicit attention to alternatives for improving the aging experience at the local level. As such, they emphasize self-assessments that serve to identify the issues that are specific to each community. This is important because it speaks to the notion of aging as it is experienced by real people within the context of everyday life in existing communities. The range of initiatives that have resulted from these planning processes are impressive, including development of community centers, caregiver training and support, exercise programs, housing rehabilitation, enhanced 911 services, recruitment of medical personnel, senior millage devoted to developing community resources, transit services, and leadership and community awareness programs.

Many communities are giving some attention to improving the built environment with curb cuts and sidewalk improvements to serve people with disabilities and facilitate pedestrian activity. At the same time, there is an impressive lack of urgency to undertaking the challenge of transforming the built environment specifically in support of aging. This is not an easy task because of the extent to which land use practices are framed by locally-controlled zoning regulations and conservative building codes. Given that by 2030, "about half of the buildings in which Americans live, work, and shop will have been built after 2000" (Nelson 2004: v), there are considerable opportunities for transforming the built environment. The same can be said for countries throughout the world.

Various planning movements that are laying the groundwork for innovative planning and development practices offer significant opportunities for creating more aging supportive built environments. For example, New Urbanism calls for infill and new development to create pedestrian-oriented, compact neighborhoods. Transit-Oriented Development involves high density, mixed uses near transit stops associated with pedestrian amenities and reduced parking to encourage transit use. Smart Growth emphasizes creation of livable communities and protection of natural resources through mixed uses, compact development, transportation alternatives, and investment in existing communities. Complete Streets calls for redesigning roads for multiple users, including pedestrians, transit, bicyclists, and motorists. Particular attention is given to safety, environmental impacts, and aesthetics.

While these initiatives call for community design features that support aging, including housing diversity, pedestrian amenities, and transit access, more is needed. For example, the Smart Growth Network's two implementation primers (n.d., 2003) give little attention to aging as a planning framework and do not provide specifics as to how one would focus planning efforts on this issue. New Urbanism has been effective in encouraging pedestrian scale, mixed-use developments with a range of housing alternatives. But New Urbanism does not seek to influence the internal design of dwellings by calling for first floor bedrooms and bathrooms, for instance. None of these planning movements give much attention to the availability of clean, safe, and accessible public restrooms—very important to older adults who often have to plan their daily travels with the availability of public restrooms in mind.

While there is a compelling need to articulate a public interest in effecting a transformation of the built environment in support of aging, it is not necessary to develop a discrete movement with aging as a focus. From a planning perspective, it makes more sense to articulate an aging perspective within the context of these various reform efforts. This avoids pitting one interest against another and enables connections with existing constituencies with compatible goals. At the same time it is essential that the case be made for immediate and profound changes in land use and development standards in order to create more aging supportive communities.

An aging focus in planning needs to begin with an intimate understanding of the aging experience both as lived by the individual and supported by families and caregivers. This means putting the focus on people. The goal should be fostering the creation of an environment that supports needs throughout one's lifespan, offering both opportunities and alternatives. Thus, a stairway is an environmental stressor that can enable one to improve and maintain health whereas a ramp may be essential if one has or develops physical limitations. The built environment should offer both.

Specific Land Use Alternatives: Housing

Visitability

It is abundantly clear that home is important to older adults and they need the option of remaining in their home, aging in place. Public policy should be supportive. At the most basic level, new housing should be built to be usable by people with a range of abilities. Smith, Rayer, and Smith (2008) considered the lifespan of a newly constructed single family detached dwelling in light of changing American demographics. They estimate a 25 percent probability that a new dwelling will ultimately house a resident with a self-care limitation and a 60 percent probability of a resident with a physical limitation. These estimates rise to 53 and 91 percent respectively for disabled visitors.

A grassroots effort led by Concrete Change, an Atlanta-based advocacy group, is successfully promoting the concept of "visitability" as a new construction requirement.[8] The basic premise is that all houses should be accessible to a visitor with a disability. This involves one zero-step entrance, doorways at least 32 inches wide, and at least a half bathroom on the first floor. These requirements add on average $100 for concrete slab houses and $300–600 for houses with basements and crawl spaces. Fewer than 5 percent of houses need to be exempted from the entrance requirement due to topography constraints. Proponents see the requirements as reasonable, simple, and cost effective, making the idea of visitability requirements more acceptable to local jurisdictions. Pima County in Arizona adopted visitability requirements in 2002 that resulted in 15,000 new, visitable housing units within five years. Mandatory visitability requirements have been adopted in San Antonio and Austin, Texas, as well as Bolingbrook, Illinois (AARP 2008). Requirements are established either by ordinance or by building code amendment.

Universal Design

Visitability requirements do not mandate full accessibility. Universal design takes the next step by approaching design in terms of ensuring that needs of people with varying abilities are addressed. A bedroom on the first floor is essential for someone with a physical limitation. Features such as non-skid floor surfaces, lever door knobs, and electrical outlets reachable by someone in a wheelchair add little if any cost to housing construction. A grab bar is less expensive to install in a bathroom with reinforced walls. Considerable resources are available demonstrating the principles and application of universal design including technical guide books, training programs, and a home plans book.[9] Examples of housing using universal design can be found throughout the United States, including a Habitat for Humanity project in North Carolina and a Milwaukee Housing Authority Hope VI project.

Maryland's Howard County requires universal design for single family detached dwellings in age-restricted housing (Taylor 2007).

Widespread adoption of mandatory requirements for universal design is resisted by home builders because of the additional costs for construction. The National Homebuilders Association feels that accessibility features should be voluntary and offered in response to demand (NAHB 2003). It may be time, however, for planners to assert leadership in articulating the idea of universal design as a matter of public interest and an imperative for achieving the public health goals which are among the rationales behind building code requirements.

Shared Housing

The extent to which people have a right to most effectively use the space in their own home is delimited by local zoning requirements that set development and land use standards. One common constraint is the definition of "household" in cases where a zoning code is used to restrict the number of unrelated people living together. Reflecting conservative values about who should have a right to live in a community, restrictive definitions can limit alternatives such as shared housing arrangements which may be particularly helpful to older adults who are single or whose spouses have died.

Accessory Apartments

In the United States, zoning codes typically do not allow creation of accessory apartments in the excess space of a single family house. The basis for this restriction is the preservation of the single family home as the most revered land use. The irony is that an increase in the average size of new single family homes from a median of about 1,500 square feet in the mid-1970s to over 2,200 square feet in 2005 (Gupta 2006) has corresponded to a decrease in the average size of American households. The average household size declined from 3.11 in 1970 to 2.59 in 2000; single-person households rose from 17.6 to 25.8 percent during the same time period (Hobbs and Stoops 2002). American households are in general over-housed with a considerable amount of excess space.

Local restrictions on creation of accessory apartments place significant limitations on people of all ages. Accessory apartments give homeowners options in providing rental income and/or living quarters for family members or caregivers. This could make a huge difference in enabling seniors to age in place because they could afford to pay the property taxes or have live-in assistance in maintaining their property. An accessory apartment might be ideal for an elderly parent coming to live with his daughter in that it would provide some measure of privacy and separation from the nuclear family. Accessory apartments also represent a method of enabling younger adults to purchase the large houses being vacated by seniors, strengthening the local housing market and addressing the aformentioned concerns raised by Myers and Ryu (2008).

It should be noted that some jurisdictions allow accessory apartments with the intent of supporting seniors by restricting them to occupancy by family members or in some cases allowing their installation only by older adults. These restrictions can significantly limit the value of this housing alternative. A study of accessory apartment owners in Seattle found that only 14 percent of owners and 11 percent of tenants were over sixty-five, although there was evidence that the units would serve a higher proportion of older people over time. The conclusion of this study was that age restrictions in zoning codes could be counterproductive, prohibiting development by owners who have the energy and resources to undertake such a task (Chapman and Howe 2001).

One alternative is to allow flexible housing in which a single family house is designed for easy incorporation and removal of an accessory apartment. In this way a house can be easily adapted to changing household needs with the structure designed to work well in terms of privacy with and without an accessory apartment (Howe 1990). If this idea were combined with Universal Design, a particular house would be able to meet a range of household needs both now and in the future.

ECHO Housing

An elder cottage housing opportunity (ECHO) dwelling is a small, apartment-sized unit that can be temporarily located in the backyard of a single family house. It uses the water, electric, and sewer systems of the primary home. An ECHO unit facilitates familial-based care in the context of privacy and independence for an older person. The units can be leased and ultimately removed and reused, thus reducing overall costs. The concept originated in Australia and has been strongly advocated by AARP and senior services agencies for adoption in the United States. Zoning restrictions and lack of available units have constrained the widespread adoption of ECHO housing, but new concepts are being developed. A 12 by 24 foot MedCottage is a mobile, modular unit: in essence, a medical home that includes a kitchen, bath, and bedroom along with extensive remote medical monitoring services. At a rental rate of U.S. $2,000 per month, it is less costly than assisted living facilities, which can cost twice as much or more.[10]

Active Living Communities

Despite the fact that older adults on average have lived in their homes for a long time, many do move. There is a strong national market for age-restricted Active Living Communities. Originating in the south and southwest, they are now found throughout the United States. A 2005 study in Massachusetts identified over 150 developments with more than 10,000 units either existing or under construction; an additional 14,000 units have been proposed or permitted (Hendorfer 2005). These communities typically offer a maintenance free, amenity rich lifestyle with single family housing. This tends to be a suburban phenomenon with local jurisdictions embracing the concept because it can bring in much-needed tax revenues without putting pressure on school districts. Some zoning ordinances prohibit development when schools are overcapacity but exempt age-restricted housing. Thus, there is the very real potential for overbuilt markets. This could result in pressure to remove age restrictions.

Active living communities are not necessarily supportive of aging in place. In the extent to which they are located and designed so as to require a car for transportation, they impose a long-term limitation on people when they can no longer drive. Some of these communities in Arizona explicitly do not offer aging supportive infrastructure, such as accessible housing, transportation, or social services because the developers want to attract young, healthy retirees, and images of frail seniors with walkers could be a deterrent in marketing the community. The expectation is that people will move away when their needs change.[11]

Given the significant role retirement communities play in housing older adults, community planners should ensure that the relevant land use and development standards require location, design, and infrastructure elements that support aging in place. These might include universal design for the dwellings, provisions for transit services, and sidewalks. The issue of encouraging age-restricted housing should be carefully evaluated with respect to the potential of overbuilding as well as long-range needs of younger households.

This type of housing market may not be sustainable in light of changing demographics and changing values regarding age segregation.

Naturally Occurring Retirement Communities

The dominant preference to age in place can result in high concentrations of older people in specific buildings, developments, and neighborhoods. These are called "Naturally Occurring Retirement Communities" or NORCs. These communities were not purpose-built for older people, and there may be various physical constraints for those who are aging. However, the high concentrations of older people create opportunities to promote healthy aging and independence through the targeted and coordinated provision of services such as case management, health care, recreational activities, and volunteer opportunities. The Jewish Federations of North America, a leader in developing the concept of NORC-Supported Special Services, sponsors the NORC Aging in Place Initiative, which secured federal demonstration grants in 45 communities within 25 states serving over 20,000 older people. While the emphasis has been on supportive services, Masotti et al. (2006) draw attention to the opportunities for creating "healthy NORCs" through improvements in the built environment that support pedestrian comfort and safety, provide amenities such as parks, and change zoning to encourage proximate land uses enabling older people to walk to needed services.

Mixed Use Development

The increasing prevalence nationwide of mixed use and high density downtown residential developments is a positive step in the creation of aging-friendly communities. This land use form raises the possibility of less reliance on the automobile with a corresponding increase in transit use and walking. Cutting-edge examples such as rental and condominium housing above branch libraries in Portland, Oregon, and housing above major grocery stores in Portland, San Francisco, and Bellingham, Washington (Pryne 2008; White, Gellen and Williams 2004) offer viable alternatives to the traditional single family house and as such may inspire more people in the long run to consider residential moves when their housing needs change. Planning and zoning reform efforts should specifically encourage this type of development.

Specific Land Use Alternatives: Mobility

Driving

Outside the home, the greatest challenge in the built environment for aging is mobility. Planners need to acknowledge the continuing role that cars play for older adults and give particular attention to ensuring road design and improvements that reflect the unique needs of older adults.[12] This means, for example, legible signs in advance of intersections, turning lanes that provide a refuge from oncoming traffic, and clearly demarcated entrances to the land uses along a road. Speed limits may need to be lowered, street lighting enhanced, and fog lines regularly maintained to improve safety and visibility at night time.

Pedestrians

For the older pedestrian, sidewalks should be designed to accommodate walkers by adjusting widths and avoiding potential hazards such as cracks and gaps in tree well grates. Hand railings may be appropriate in certain locations. Walk signal times may need to be lengthened and, if necessary, a pedestrian refuge provided in the middle of the street. Low-level lighting can remove shadows cast by street lights. Appropriately designed benches are needed with armrests to facilitate getting up and down; a right angle in the seat design enables easier conversation with another person in comparison to sitting side by side, as twisting can be painful for an older person.

Transit Use

Transit stops need adequate shelter and comfortable seating; the stops should be close to homes and destinations. Transit schedules need to be legible and routes and stops should be clearly announced by drivers to assist those with vision and hearing problems. Timing and frequency of service along with destinations and routes must be attentive to the needs of older people.

Transportation as a System

The specific transportation improvements that are needed to support aging in any given community will vary according to the condition of the existing transportation system and the specific needs of the community. It is imperative to undertake community-level assessments and to fully engage residents in planning initiatives in a way that elucidates individual experiences in moving through the environment. It is important to think in terms of linkages and details. Thus the value of well-designed sidewalks is limited if intersections are not safe. A gravel parking lot can be a huge barrier to someone in a wheelchair. Absence of accessible and safe public restrooms may preclude some older adults from using public transit.

Transitioning to Aging Supportive Environments

Clearly, every one of us has a vested interest in meeting the needs of older people. We are all affected whether through caregiving responsibilities to family members and friends, concerns about meeting societal needs with limited resources, or the reality that someday we ourselves will be old. The transformation of the built environment to support aging could go a long way toward reducing living expenses, enhancing independence, easing difficulties in caregiving, and improving quality of life. Ultimately community planning for aging involves a broader imperative of creating a built environment that is user friendly, one that is supportive of human dignity and independence. An aging focus highlights the imperative of providing affordable housing choices, improved driving conditions, and alternative means of transportation, along with safe environments for physical activity, so that people can maintain their health and independence.

We need a sense of urgency, recognition that the aging of society is a powerful dynamic that must be explicitly addressed where we live our daily lives. Aging provides a powerful lens for assessing and transforming the built environment. Given the unique characteristics of each community, it is essential to identify locally specific aging issues and on that basis develop and implement relevant solutions. We also need to establish a system for, and a commitment to, continuously identifying opportunities for improving the environment for all users. For example, painting a curb so that it is more visible can mask the presence of a surface change for someone wearing dark glasses or bifocals. This author witnessed a serious injury to an older person who missed such a cue. Planners need this type of anecdotal experience and observation to solicit, interpret, and translate into changes in standards and practices. To that end, planners need to fully engage older people in community planning processes. This involves giving attention to constraints that might limit involvement, such as evening meetings, uninteresting agendas, or inaccessible locations. On the other hand, for many, retirement age offers opportunities to focus on service, and community planning could be very compelling.[13]

We must also take advantage of every opportunity to make needed improvements, like requiring new sidewalks as a condition of land use approvals or replacing signage during road repairs. Aging-oriented initiatives can also be done on a voluntary basis. For example, Elders in Action of Portland, Oregon, sponsors an elder friendly business certification program acknowledging establishments that meet specified standards of accessibility, customer service, and building layout.[14] While consumers can make more informed housing choices, and developers can respond to a perceived market niche, public policy can acknowledge a longer term public interest in mandating visitability or universal design. Community planning initiatives can provide the framework for encouraging such multifaceted responses.

Of course, communities have the option of doing nothing, in which case older people will have to fend for themselves. The actual impact would be immeasurable but would likely include compromised health, social isolation, high levels of stress for care givers and even early death. The legacy would be more of the same aging experience for subsequent generations. Alternatively, we can collectively embrace aging as a compelling perspective that enables us to define who and what we are as a society and in doing so create an alternative legacy. Planners can and should provide leadership in ensuring that every community offers the type of environment that gives all of us choices throughout our lifespan and enables a high quality of life as we age.

Notes

1. www.communitiesforalifetime.org/.
2. www.agingkansas.org/SeniorSupport/LifeLong/lifelongcommunity.htm.
3. www.vnsny.org/advantage/.
4. www.icohere.com/agingfriendly/.
5. http://communitiesforallages.org/.
6. For example, http://assets.aarp.org/rgcenter/il/d18311_communities.pdf.
7. www.aginginplaceinitiative.org.
8. www.concretechange.org.
9. For more information, http://www.universaldesign.org/ and http://www.universaldesignonline.com/.

10. www.medcottage.com.

11. Sandra Rosenbloom, e-mail message to author, December 8, 2008.

12. For detailed recommendations see Staphlin, Lococo and Byington 1998.

13. One in four of those 65 and over in the U.S. works as a volunteer. These people give nearly 100 hours of service annually, twice the national average (Corporation for National and Community Service 2006). Various organizations creatively match seniors with community needs. Experience Corps works in 22 cities nationwide, engaging over 2,000 older adults in service to inner city schools (www.experiencecorps.org). Senior Corps facilitates engagement of over 500,000 Americans age 55 and older, providing well over 100 million hours of service. www.seniorcorps.org/.

14. http://www.eldersinaction.org/whatwedo/elderfriendly/, accessed August 29, 2010. This program has been replicated in 11 states.

References

AARP Public Policy Institute. 2008. Increasing home access: Designing for visitability. In Brief 163. Washington, D.C.: AARP.

Anti-Aging Task Force. 2008. Words that hurt—In more ways than one. New York: International Longevity Center. http://www.ilcusa.org/pages/media_items/words-that-hurtE28094-in-more-ways-than-one194.php?p=12, accessed August 29, 2010.

Chapman, Nancy J., and Deborah A. Howe. 2001. Accessory apartments: Are they a realistic alternative for aging in place? *Housing Studies* 16: 637–50.

Corporation for National and Community Service, Office of Research and Policy Development. 2006. *Volunteering in America: State trends and rankings: 2002–2005*. Washington, D.C.: Corporation for National and Community Service.

Dittman, Melisssa. 2003. Fighting ageism. *Monitor on Psychology* 34(5): 50.

Downs, Barbara. 2003. Fertility of American women: June 2002. *Current population reports P20-548*. Washington, D.C.: U.S. Census Bureau. http://www.census.gov/prod/2003pubs/p20-548.pdf, accessed August 29, 2010.

Gupta, Sanchi. 2006. Characteristics of new single family homes: In-depth analysis, September 11. Washington, D.C.: National Association of Home Builders. http://www.nahb.org/generic.aspx?genericContentID=64030, accessed August 29. 2010.

Hendorfer, Bonnie. 2005. *Age restricted active adult housing in Massachusetts: A review of the factors fueling its explosive growth and the public policy issues it raises*. Boston: Citizens Housing and Planning Association. http://www.chapa.org/sites/default/files/f_122952789640BUpdateDec2008_4.pdf., accessed August 29, 2010.

Hobbs, Frank, and Nicole Stoops. 2002. Demographic trends in the 20th century. U.S. Census Bureau, Census 2000 Special Reports, Series CENSR-4. Washington, D.C.: Government Printing Office. http://www.census.gov/prod/2002pubs/censr-4.pdf, accessed August 29, 2010.

Houser, Ari. 2005. *Older drivers and automobile safety: Fact sheet.* Washington, D.C.: AARP Policy Institute.

Howe, Deborah A. 1990. The flexible house: Designing for changing needs. *Journal of the American Planning Association* 56: 69–79.

Howe, Deborah A., Nancy J. Chapman, and Sharon A. Baggett. 1989. *Creating livable environments for older adults: Training physical planners, Final Report AOA Grant No. IOAT0019/01.* Portland, Ore.: Portland State University, Institute on Aging.

Masotti, Paul J., Robert Fick, Ana Johnson-Masotti, and Stuart MacLeod. 2006. Healthy naturally occurring retirement communities: A low-cost approach to facilitating healthy aging. *American Journal of Public Health* 96: 1164–70.

Matthew Greenwald and Associates. 2003. *These four walls: Americans 45+ talk about home and community.* Washington, D.C.: AARP. http://assets.aarp.org/rgcenter/il/four_walls.pdf, accessed August 29, 2010.

Minnesota Department of Health Services. 2002. Project 2030. St. Paul: Minnesota Department of Health Services. http://www.dhs.state.mn.us/main/idcplg?Idc Service=GET_DYNAMIC_CONVERSION&RevisionSelectionMethod=LatestRele ased&dDocName=id_005426#, accessed May 2011.

Myers, Dowell, and SungHo Ryu. 2008. Aging baby boomers and the generational bubble: Foresight and mitigation of an epic transition. *Journal of the American Planning Association* 74: 17–33.

National Association of Home Builders (NAHB). 2003. *NAHB Resolution: Single family accessibility.* Washington, D.C.: National Association of Home Builders. http://www.nahb.org/assets/docs/files/Res7_SFAccessibility_521200341404PM.pdf, accessed August 29, 2010.

Nelson, Arthur C. 2004. *Toward a new metropolis: The opportunity to rebuild America.* Washington, D.C.: Brookings Institution.

Preston, Samuel H. 2005. Deadweight? The influence of obesity on longevity. *New England Journal of Medicine* 352: 1135–37.

Pryne, Eric. 2008. New Bellevue Safeway caters to urban dwellers. *Seattle Times,* June 27.

Reynolds, Sandra L., Yasuhiko Saito, and Eileen Crimmins. 2005. The impact of obesity on active life expectancy in older American men and women. *Gerontologist* 45: 438–44.

Rosenbloom, Sandra, and Agneta Stahl. 2002. Automobility among the elderly: The convergence of environmental, safety, mobility and community design issues. *European Journal of Transport and Infrastructure Research* 2: 197–213.

Smart Growth Network. 2003. Getting to Smart Growth II: 100 more policies for implementation. Washington, DC: International City/County Management Association http://www.smartgrowth.org/pdf/gettosg2.pdf, accessed August 29, 2010.

Smart Growth Network and International City/County Management Association. n.d. *Getting to Smart Growth: 100 policies for implementation.* Washington, D.C.: International City/County Management Association http://www.smartgrowth.org/pdf/gettosg.pdf, accessed 29 August 29, 2010.

Smith, Stanley K., Stefan Rayer, and Eleanor A Smith. 2008. Aging and disability: Implications for the housing industry and housing policy in the United States. *Journal of the American Planning Association* 74(3): 289–306.

Stanton, Mark W. 2006. The high concentration of U.S. health care expenditures. Research in Action Issue 19. Rockville, Md.: Agency for Healthcare Research and Quality. http://www.ahrq.gov/research/ria19/expendria.pdf, accessed August 29, 2010.

Suchan, Trudy A., Marc J. Perry, James D. Fitzsimmons, Anika E. Juhn, Alexander M. Tait, and Cynthia A. Brewer. 2007. Census atlas of the United States: Series CENSR-29. Washington, D.C.: U.S. Census Bureau. http://www.census.gov/population/www/cen2000/censusatlas/, accessed August 29, 2010.

Staphlin, Loren, Kathy H. Lococo, and Stanley R. Byington. 1998. *Older driver highway design handbook.* FHWA-RD-97-135. Washington, D.C.: U.S. Department of Transportation, Federal Highway Administration. http://www.fhwa.dot.gov/publications/research/safety/97135/index.cfm, accessed August 29, 2010.

Taylor, Charles. 2007. Aging populations inspire "Universal Design" housing. *NACO County News,* January 15, 2007.

UN Department of Economic and Social Affairs. 2009. *World Population Aging 2009.* New York: United Nations.

UN News Centre. 2010. UN launches new scheme to make cities friendlier to elderly people. New York: UN News Service, June 29. http://www.un.org/apps/news/story.asp?NewsID=35176&Cr=elderly&Cr, accessed August 29, 2010.

U.S. Census Bureau. 1996. 65+ in the United States. *Current Population Reports, Special Studies, P23-190.* Washington, D.C.: Government Printing Office. http://www.census.gov/prod/1/pop/p23-190/p23-190.pdf, accessed August 29, 2010.

———. 2005. American housing survey for the United States 2005. *Current Housing Reports Series H150/05.* Washington, D.C.: U.S. Census Bureau. http://www.census.gov/prod/2006pubs/h150-05.pdf.

Visscher, Tommy L. S., and Jacob C. Seidell. 2001. The public health impact of obesity. *Annual Review of Public Health* 22: 355–75.

White, Kate, Martin Gellen, and George Williams. 2004. *Housing above retail: Creating incentives for the replacement of single-story retail sites with mixed-use projects.* San Francisco: San Francisco Planning and Urban Research Association, February 18. http://www.spur.org/publications/library/report/housingaboveretail_050104.

WHO. 2002. *Health and ageing: A discussion paper.* Geneva: World Health Organization.

PART IV

Housing and Community

Chapter 14

Public Housing in the United States: Neighborhood Renewal and the Poor

Lawrence J. Vale

Overview: The Meanings of Public Housing

The tortuous and tortured saga of public housing in the United States is a kind of double social experiment: first when it was built—under the high modernist hopes of the mid-twentieth century—and again, as the century closed, when it was redeveloped as a nostalgia-riddled effort that mimicked a pre-modernist urbanism. In both phases, planners and designers promised new and improved housing for low-income households, clearing slums the first time and, in the second iteration, clearing public housing itself. In both cases, planners and designers used physical design and development processes to substitute a new kind of community for one judged to be less desirable, leading to a kind of double gentrification. I situate my own work, which has mostly focused on Boston, in the context of those who have written extensively about public housing in other American cities, such as Chicago, St. Louis, San Francisco, Philadelphia, Baltimore, Los Angeles, and New York. To do so is to examine the relationship between design ideals and larger sociopolitical processes, with a focus on understanding why it has been so difficult for planners and policy-makers in the United States to address the housing needs of the least advantaged.

In what follows, I trace both the evolution of public housing as conceived, designed, and managed, and the corresponding ways scholars and practicing planners have responded to this housing. This means (1) coming to terms with the initial enthusiasm for public housing by dissecting the rationales of its proponents; (2) contending with the "rise and fall" critiques that soon followed; and (3) assessing more contemporary efforts to defend, reinvent, replace, or simply eliminate this form of deeply subsidized housing.

The saga of public housing in the United States since the 1930s provides a window into not just the relationship between planning and people, but a much broader and deeper set of social relations. Public housing, as both a reflection of other trends and as a causal force in its own right, makes visible the strains of race and ethnic relations. It clarifies the struggles over class and how self-definitions of "poor" and "middle class" get constructed. Public housing decisions reveal distinctive choices about land use and zoning in the American city (and, by extension, show ways that Americans operate rather differently from those in many other countries). Ultimately, public housing forces contentious discussions about the role and limits of the state in providing shelter to the poorest citizens. In the context of the United States, public housing has demonstrated the power of private markets to influence even that which is explicitly termed "public."

Initial High Hopes: Public Housing as a Reward

The struggle to produce and sustain public housing in the United States is rooted in multiple, shifting, and mixed motives for supplying low-rent dwellings in a country that has an ideological veneration for the owned single-family private house. Support for public housing has always been partial and reluctant, cloaked in ongoing suspicion about which of the poor are deserving of government subsidy and which are not. Housing subsidies have come more easily to the non-poor, especially those who own homes and who have received preferential tax treatment for more than a century (Vale 2000; Bratt, Stone, and Hartman 2006; Bauman, Biles, and Szylvian 2000). Even before that, the owned home gained national ideological support through such federal government mechanisms as the Homestead Act of 1862 (which gave tracts of western lands away as long as there was a commitment to build a home on them). By the 1920s, the federal government and local real estate interests worked in carefully orchestrated concert to enshrine expanded homeownership as both an ideological and a material reality. From the "Own Your Own Home" movement to the "Better Homes in America" initiatives, both public and private sectors worked assiduously to support the moral supremacy of the homeowner over the renter (Vale 2007). By contrast, even as

Western European democracies were embarking on extensive social housing building programs in the aftermath of the First World War (Bauer 1934), U.S. government policy-makers resolutely resisted such moves, viewing housing as a private sector, market-driven realm. The chief exception to this aversion to housing subsidy benefited homeowners through the mechanism of tax deductions targeted solely at those who owned their own home. As a consequence, even after the Great Depression made large-scale government intervention to support low-rent housing almost inevitable, the embrace of non-market mechanisms took place in an atmosphere of profound ambivalence.

Public housing, as it emerged as a New Deal program in 1934 and subsequently with the Housing Act of 1937, was often rationalized as a byproduct of other priorities. As Peter Marcuse points out, the concept of "public housing" has used the same name over many decades to conflate multiple programs with different purposes (Marcuse 1995). Far from a program of unabashed humanitarian support for the least advantaged, public housing aimed in the first instance to be a kind of reward system for the temporarily submerged middle class (Friedman 1968), while also providing a needed boost to the construction industry, primarily through provision of jobs. In this context, the earliest iterations of public housing emerged as heir to a much longer tradition of using public sector largesse to reward only those among the poor judged to be the most "worthy" (Vale 2000). Similarly, many Western European countries also chose to avoid targeting the least-advantaged poor when tenanting their social housing (Carmon 1981). Despite the calculatedly benign nature of the people chosen to live in these places, their planners faced constant criticism and responded by doing everything possible to make public intervention in housing as unthreatening as possible to private real estate interests.

The Housing Act of 1937 linked all new low-rent housing to slum clearance by mandating an "equivalent elimination agreement": public housing construction must be accompanied by the "elimination by demolition, condemnation, and effective closing, or the compulsory repair and improvement of unsafe or insanitary dwellings situated in the locality or metropolitan area, substantially equal in number to the number of newly constructed dwellings provided by the project." This provision effectively ensured that public housing would not contribute to any significant gains in the low-rent housing stock, since even if "elimination" was accomplished through rehabilitation rather than demolition, the resultant improved properties would probably demand substantially higher monthly rentals. The required link to slum clearance efforts also encouraged public housing construction in inner city neighborhoods, rather than in more affluent peripheral areas (Friedman 1968). In this way, public housing itself constituted a form of neighborhood renewal in the form of replacement housing, even as many other neighborhoods were cleared for other purposes, many of which served private purposes much more than public ones.

The Housing Act of 1949 promised a dramatic upsurge in public housing construction, but this was soon undercut by subsequent legislation even more favorable to the private sector (von Hoffman 2000). The Housing Acts of 1954 and 1956 permitted cities to use public housing as part of a "Workable Program" for the elimination and prevention of slums and blight, but gave it secondary emphasis. In the attempt to encourage private investment, policymakers relegated public housing to the category of "other aids that can be used for urban renewal purposes," and the Housing and Home Finance Agency explained that federal support for it would come only "where wanted and needed" (Housing and Home Finance Agency 1955). Beginning with these programs of urban redevelopment and urban renewal that rewarded savvy developers for tackling inner-city sites, Congress continued to devise new roles for the private sector in the attempt to make development of low-income housing commercially profitable. This growing privatization movement began with a program providing private nonprofit developers with direct below-market interest-rate loans intended to spur construction of housing for the elderly (Section 202 of the Housing Act of 1959) and continued with other programs (in 1961, 1968, and 1974) inviting sponsorship of multifamily subsidized housing by private for-profit groups. Critics charged, however, that subsidizing the private market in such ways produced "not only too little housing, but housing invariably aimed at the not-so-poor"—just as the housing philanthropists of a century earlier had also discovered (Bratt 1986: 341-42). In short, a public housing program initiated over the staunch opposition of private real estate interests underwent a gradual privatizing transformation, first by the inclusion of private developers in urban renewal ventures and subsequently by more than four decades of programs that spurred the homebuilding industry and provided many new investment opportunities (Vale 2000).

Much of the early public housing, however spare in ornament and amenity, enjoyed high standards of construction, making it surprisingly durable despite a checkered history of deferred maintenance. Many cities still have usable buildings constructed during the 1930s, 1940s, and early 1950s—the times of highest enthusiasm for the program. In addition to the lingering buildings themselves, the documentary remains of early public housing history comes down to us in two forms: as triumphalist public sector propaganda carefully crafted to evade or outflank the charges that such housing was socialist, and as more sober assessments from insiders, again championing the successes of the first auspicious decades of construction when buildings were new, residents were carefully vetted, management was eager, and tenants had the financial resources to cover the operating costs of the complexes through their rent payments.

Over time, however, public housing lost its intended clientele and, with that, some of the principal rationales for building it. Although some large housing authorities, such as New York's, resisted efforts by the federal government and made special efforts to retain middle-income households in their developments (Bloom 2008), in most U.S. cities by the 1960s, public housing occupancy shifted dramatically. As the white working class prospered and gained new housing options in the suburbs, the population seeking entry to public housing rapidly became both much poorer and disproportionately non-white. No longer a reward, by the late 1950s or 1960s, it had gradually become housing of last resort.

The "Decline and Fall" of Public Housing

Catherine Bauer's classic essay "The Dreary Deadlock of Public Housing" (Bauer 1957) ushered in a second phase of public housing assessment, but this was just a warning shot across the bow compared to the vast literature that would soon follow and turn "Decline and Fall" narratives into a small industry. This tradition of work began in St. Louis with *Behind Ghetto Walls: Black Families in a Federal Slum* (Rainwater 1970), an ethnographic account by Lee Rainwater detailing black family life in Pruitt-Igoe during the mid-1960s. Rainwater and his team assembled 30,000 pages of notes between 1963 and 1966 with the aim of providing a "basic analysis of the conditions underlying the pathological behavior currently found in urban public housing," as well as "hopefully" offering "new proposals for social remedies for these pathologies" (1970: 9). As seems always the case in sensitive matters of housing, public perceptions about failing public housing conflated management failures, architectural failures, and human failures.

Many books offered up intimate portraits of project life including vivid works of journalism such as Alex Kotlowitz's *There Are No Children Here* (1991), which explores the impossibility of childhood in Chicago's Henry Horner Homes project, and Daniel Coyle's *Hardball: A Season in the Projects* (1993), which chronicles the travails of a Little League baseball team in Chicago's Cabrini-Green development. Additional accounts pointing to the intractability of project life include two books about the institutional collapse of public housing in St. Louis (Meehan 1975, 1979). Still other accounts, based on the experience of cities such as Chicago, attested to the design deficiencies of the developments, with titles such as *Vertical Ghetto* (Moore 1969) and *The Poorhouse* (Bowly 1978), or to systemic fiscal desperation (de Leeuw 1970; Hunt 2009). As the worst large projects descended into social chaos and gang-dominated violence, researchers continued to assess the distress, perhaps nowhere more graphically than in *The Hidden War: Crime and the Tragedy of Public Housing in Chicago* (Popkin et al. 2000), an account of high rise public housing in Chicago.

Racial politics have been central to the saga of public housing in nearly every city, whether in cases where whites clung to a few project strongholds and resisted integration, as in Boston (Vale 2000, 2002) or in cities such as Chicago (Hirsch 1983), Philadelphia (Bauman 1987), Baltimore (Williams 2004), Detroit (Thomas 1997; Sugrue 1998), Cincinnati (Fairbanks 1988), San Francisco (Baranski 2004), or Birmingham (Connerly 2005) where public housing targeted to blacks served as a bulwark of segregation. Arnold Hirsch's account of the way Chicago's City Council sited and politically manipulated public housing to consolidate the city's "Second Ghetto" remains the classic of this genre, but each city has its own sad and cautionary tale. The title of Jack Bauman's review essay in *Journal of Planning Literature* sums up the dark view of this era of public housing—and public housing scholarship— quite succinctly: "Public Housing: The Dreadful Saga of a Durable Policy" (Bauman 1994).

Beyond Public Housing Failure: Revisionist Lenses

What I am calling the "revisionist" literature on public housing has staked out three principal challenges to the conventional wisdom about persistent, widespread abject failure. This revisionism has questioned the ubiquity of failure, rediscovered the powerful voices and influences of the people who inhabit the projects, and reconsidered the role of design in both the decline and the recovery of public housing neighborhoods.

Refining and Redefining Success

First, scholars have taken particular note of the early successes of public housing, including very large, high-rise projects in big cities. Even the notorious Pruitt-Igoe project enjoyed initial popularity among residents, though this fact is now largely forgotten (Rainwater 1970; Heathcott forthcoming). Similarly, Sudhir Venkatesh's account of the "rise and fall" of Chicago's most infamous public housing development makes clear that "in its first three years, Robert Taylor was a success by any definition"—despite housing 27,000 low-income people (20,000 of them children) in high-rises (Venkatesh 2000: 22, 276). One book examining public housing in Chicago takes such early successes as its focus. *When Public Housing Was Paradise* is a kind of collective memoir compiled by early Chicago public housing official J. S. Fuerst, who served as director of research and statistics for the Chicago Housing Authority (CHA) from 1946 to 1953. His "paradise" is conveyed through oral histories of dozens of Chicago public housing residents who "consistently remember their public housing developments as clean and well run, with vigilantly made repairs and enthusiastically provided tenant services" (Fuerst 2003).

Nicholas Dagen Bloom's *Public Housing That Worked: New York in the Twentieth Century* makes a bolder, more surprising claim. He not only praises the well-built and carefully tenanted communities of the early "paradise" years, but also contends that, by and large, New York City Housing Authority (NYCHA) housing can be considered a success that lasted throughout the twentieth century, despite having the nation's largest program, much of it in high-rises. For Bloom, this success is rooted in effective management, which included careful tenant selection and concerted efforts to attract and retain families with stable jobs. Similarly, he gives high marks to NYCHA for attention to maintenance and efforts to enhance landscape design. Still, it is worth noting that he cast the book's title in the past tense, implying that NYCHA housing "worked" for a long time, but may not be working so well in the present. The caution is well taken, given the budgetary squeeze and management shortfalls in recent years.

For Bloom, as for Fuerst and many others, the key variable has been management. D. Bradford Hunt's *Blueprint for Disaster: The Unraveling of Chicago Public Housing* also stresses management issues, but focuses on the internal financial challenges of the Chicago Housing Authority (Hunt 2009). Much of the early public housing that was built and tenanted before the mid-1950s met its management challenges quite well. Since then, however, few big city public housing authorities in the United States have been able to sustain their successes. And, all too frequently, the tenants themselves have borne the brunt of the blame for the systemic failures that engulfed them.

Revaluing Tenant Activism

A second major strand of the revisionist literature on public housing reverses the conventional direction of the analyst's lens. Instead of focusing on the institutional challenges of managing the projects and their tenants, the view has shifted towards examination of the ways that these tenants have, in effect, attempted to manage their managers. In this view, public housing is seen less as a story of management failure or design failure than as a tale of resident activism. Rather than passive victims of misguided policies or, worse, as perpetrators of destructive behaviors that make projects unmanageable and un-maintainable, scholars since the 1990s have emphasized the powerful and positive roles of tenant leaders, especially women. Tenants, in this view, are not policy-receiving, but are effectively policy-makers themselves. Some of this emerged through the early activism of tenant leaders in St. Louis, Boston, Chicago, and Washington, D.C., who sought to take on unprecedented management roles, although those successes have been mixed at best (Peterman 1993).

More positively, revisionist scholarship on public housing has found greater examples of success in the actions of tenants who worked in concert with existing public sector and private sector managers. The result has been a series of more community-centered articles and books that have delved into the complex dynamics of neighborhood transformation, not simply management reform or design innovation (although these other dimensions are often co-present). This newer scholarship on public housing has highlighted the power of residents to take action on their own behalf, forge coalitions, and do all they can to make sure the more trouble-mongering portions of their community and in the neighborhoods beyond it are not permitted to stop progressive change. Such struggles do not always yield wholly satisfactory outcomes, but they make clear that public housing communities, however impoverished and marginalized, can sometimes be effective advocates for their own future.

In *The Politics of Public Housing,* one of the major exemplars of this sort of new scholarly attention, Rhonda Williams traces the tenant activism of black women in Baltimore's public housing. Deftly integrating more than fifty oral history interviews, she shows that this activism began as early as the 1940s and continued throughout subsequent decades as conditions worsened. Even as public housing "increasingly became disreputable in the eyes of much of the American electorate" and sometimes "simply unlivable for tenants," her book demonstrates that "it also provided a measure of subsistence and a political context in which some low-income black women educated themselves about their rights" (Williams 2004: 8).

Other recent scholarship has highlighted similar sorts of tenant activism, often related to efforts to secure significant roles and rights for residents during major redevelopment of distressed projects. At Boston's Columbia Point, for instance, Ellen Pader and Myrna Breitbart stress the actions of impoverished African American women tenants (Breitbart and Pader 1995). Jane Roessner's book about the transformation of Columbia Point into the mixed-income, mixed-race privately managed gated community of Harbor Point also gives ample weight to the contributions of the resident leaders, even though the book was quietly bankrolled by the developer (Roessner 2000). Roberta Feldman and Susan Stall's *The Dignity of Resistance: Women Residents' Activism in Chicago Public Housing* (Feldman and Stall 2004), makes especially notable contributions to accounts of public housing tenant empowerment. The authors narrate the transformation between what they call "*everyday resistance* in the expanded private sphere" and the more politically effective "*transgressive resistance* in the public sphere." Despite the poverty of their circumstances, the poor African-American women at Chicago's Wentworth Gardens have been anything but passive and powerless. "Wentworth residents' actions were not mere adaptations to the conditions of poverty—they were not merely 'coping' or just 'getting by.' Rather, they have been empowering themselves through their ongoing acts of resistance" (Feldman and Stall 2004: 6, 7, 11, 345).

Much of my own work falls clearly into this category of revisionism, especially the three fifty-year neighborhood sagas featured in *Reclaiming Public Housing: A Half-Century of Struggle in Three Public Neighborhoods* (Vale 2002) and in related articles. Hundreds of interviews with residents made it clear that a large urban public housing development is more than a locus of pathology; it is often also a source of empathy and community. Taken together, these projects might be described as empathological places, an uneasy confluence of social center and economic wasteland (Vale 1997, 2002). Increasingly, detailed accounts of resident life in public housing provide similar narratives of ambivalence, making it clear why residents often sue to protect housing projects—their homes and neighborhoods—from demolition.

Where Are Poor People to Live? Transforming Public Housing Communities, edited by Larry Bennett, Janet Smith, and Patricia Wright, asks trenchant questions about the Chicago Housing Authority's "Plan for Transformation"—a massive effort to tear down much of the city's distressed public housing stock and replace some of it with mixed-income communities (Bennett, Smith, and Wright 2006). Like other books in the revisionist genre, this one looks at the problems of public housing communities chiefly from the perspective of residents. The authors view the plethora of lawsuits and the intensive organizing efforts by residents of some Chicago developments as opportunities to re-make public housing more equitably, and not as roadblocks to the Plan. Mary Pattillo's *Black on the Block* (2007) adds an important new chapter to the saga of public housing in Chicago by focusing on the new complexities of the black-led gentrification that has coincided with public housing redevelopment in the North Kenwood-Oakland neighborhood. Similarly, Mark Joseph's exemplary studies of the mixed-income communities that are replacing Chicago public housing show how the class complexities of a post-public housing environment play out on a day-to-day basis (Joseph 2008, 2010).

Perhaps the most controversial examples of this genre of tenant-centered revisionism are Sudhir Venkatesh's gripping accounts of gang life (and death) during the waning years of Chicago's now-demolished Robert Taylor Homes (Venkatesh 2000, 2008). Venkatesh, a sociologist who has engaged in extensive ethnographic investigation since the early 1990s, argues that gang life should not be narrowly seen as a destructive force. Rather than blaming the gangs for instilling a climate of fear and directing young black residents into a drug-centered economy, he calls for a more balanced assessment, one that sees value in the community-building contributions gangs can also provide in terms of safety and welfare. It is a mark of how far the revisionist public housing scholarship has come that the most vilified aspects of the most vilified project could be the subject of provocative re-framing.

Rethinking the Role of Design

A third dimension of revisionist thinking about public housing focuses on the contested role of design. Clare Cooper's study of the Easter Hill Village public housing development in Richmond, California—initially launched as an MCP thesis in 1965—was among the first accounts to take seriously the viewpoints of public housing residents and survey them about the importance of the built environment (Cooper 1975). Cooper's purpose, most explicit in a long chapter entitled "User Needs in Multifamily Housing: Some Recommendations," was to examine the disconnect between the design ideas of architects and landscape architects and their reception by low-income tenants. Armed with such data, environment-behavior researchers have long sought greater influence in decisions about the redesign of public housing. The initial designs of public housing developments, they reason, were made without input from the people who would use the projects; improvement would surely entail a much more engaged form of consultation.

Some parts of this design-centered revisionism have taken a rather explicit environmental determinist stance. Rooted in Serge Chermayeff and Christopher Alexander's little-remembered book *Community and Privacy* (1965) and nurtured by the attack on "project"-centered mentalities launched by the wildly influential work of Jane Jacobs (1961), architect Oscar Newman's classic volume *Defensible Space: Crime Prevention Through Urban Design* (1972) initiated a rethinking of the power of urban design to shape behavior. Newman's work focused on crime reduction and provided early case studies of how public housing projects could be retrofitted and redesigned to make them safer for residents through encouraging territoriality. More controversially, Newman's follow-up volume, *Community of Interest* (1980), carried his arguments forward into the domain of social policy, pairing ideas for redesigning the physical environment with proposals to place caps on the number of welfare-dependent households. At a time when quotas had become a highly racialized phenomenon (epitomized by the U.S. Supreme Court decision in the *Bakke* case in 1979), Newman's strident critique of welfare-dependent tenants antagonized many public housing advocates and, he once recalled to me, got him effectively banned from the university lecture circuit for well over a decade.

That said, it seems clear in retrospect that Newman's arguments actually won out, even if Newman the messenger was personally resisted. First, beginning in Boston and Cambridge during the early 1980s, urban designers and architects started using Newman's ideas about defensible space. Designers rejected the modernist superblock and sought every possible way (within the constraints of HUD-imposed restrictions on total demolition) to re-introduce streets and enhance the street life of casual self-surveillance by residents. Newman's ideas about territoriality and defensible space eventually became part of the mainstream assumptions about public housing redesign and redevelopment in the mid-1990s. HUD secretary Henry Cisneros commissioned Newman to prepare guidelines for use by housing authorities engaged in the massive public housing rebuilding efforts of the federal HOPE VI program (Newman 1996). This program authorized several billion dollars to turn the most "severely distressed" projects into new mixed-income communities, financed by a variety of public and private sources.

Closely allied to this, HUD also embraced the New Urbanist movement, particularly its neotraditional development wing, and sought to re-think the overall image of public housing developments (Congress for the New Urbanism 2000). Rather than the image of public housing as a deliberately different-looking modernist alternative to the decrepit and ill-provisioned rows of wooden or brick townhouses that had come to signify mid-century "blight" and "slum" conditions, the New Urbanist paradigm sought to sanitize and update the reputation of these earlier premodernist urban models and to make future public housing resemble its private sector neighbors, rather than stand implacably apart from them. This is revisionism in its most literal sense, an attempt to instill a different vision of what public housing ought to be, both in terms of how it should look and who should be served (see Franck and Mostoller 1995). The goal, taking defensible space and new urbanism together, is to create a tableau of middle-class Americana that would normalize the appearance of public housing to the point where it could be accepted again into the fabric of existing market-friendly neighborhoods.

As the result of several decades of research and activism, it has also become possible to regard design not simply as a primary locus of blame for public housing failures, but also as a source of progressive re-thinking of project environments. This is true in a double sense: bad design can be retrofitted or entirely rethought and, more complexly, the *process* of design can be both an index and an instigator of community empowerment. By emphasizing issues of design implementation, stressing the place-specific nature of every redevelopment attempt, and examining the intrinsic links between matters of design and matters of management, security, and neighborhood socioeconomic conditions, it becomes possible to bridge the persistent and unfortunate gap between questions of housing design and issues of housing policy.

Public Housing and the Displacement of Poor Neighborhoods

The more one looks closely at American public housing, the more apparent it becomes that social planning is not at all equivalent to humanitarian intervention. We see this as early as the 1930s when there was an unacknowledged disconnect between slum clearance (the priority) and efforts made to actually help people in those slums (a secondary matter and one not directly affected by the provision of public housing). Similarly, there is a cognitive dissonance between the Depression-era concern to put the construction industry back to work and the lack of attention paid to the joblessness of those displaced from slums but not offered a place in the new public housing that replaced their homes. In Baltimore, as Rhonda Williams observes, the Maryland State Advisory Board that surveyed housing needs during the depths of the Great Depression "seemed more concerned with providing jobs, removing blight and disease and, therefore, black nuisances, and preserving white neighborhoods—not attacking black people's poor living conditions" (Williams 2004: 31–32). In Boston, records show that 50–80 percent of the site residents sought entry into the first four public housing projects completed under the Housing Act of 1937, yet my own examination of the lists of tenants in these places revealed that, depending on the project, somewhere between 2 and 12 percent of those households actually gained a place (Vale 2000). Similarly, figures for New York City demonstrate that, as of 1957, only 18.1 percent of the former residents of public housing sites had been rehoused in the new public housing (Bloom 2008: 119). If such patterns were consistent across the country, as I suspect they have been, this provides yet more evidence that the goals of public housing were not centered on serving the people who were displaced to create it.

In this context, it is striking that the principal mechanism for public housing redevelopment, the HOPE VI program deployed by the Department of Housing and Urban Development since 1993, has a similar track record of failing to re-house the vast majority of former public housing residents in the new developments built to replace projects judged to be failures. The New Urbanist design standards popularized in HOPE VI projects across the country are not only rooted in a nostalgic effort to reclaim a vision of picket fence and front porch-centered pseudo-suburbia; they also signal a parallel intent to re-think the intended beneficiaries of the housing. Re-imaged to appeal to and reassure the middle class, the HOPE VI developments were handed over to a clientele from a broad range of incomes, rather than re-tenanted with the very-low-income households who had been desperately drawn to the former projects and still overwhelmingly populate the waiting lists of those seeking public housing nationwide. One widely circulated study, purporting to use HUD's own figures, concluded that only 11.4 percent of the former site tenants of public housing demolished as part of HOPE VI redevelopment efforts had been, or were slated to be, rehoused in the new mixed-income communities as of 2002. Most, the study found, were offered either apartments in other unrenovated public housing or housing subsidy vouchers to be used to find housing with willing landlords in the private sector (National Housing Law Project et al. 2002: iii). More recently, as of September 30, 2008, HUD figures showed that 24 percent of "the total households relocated" had returned to HOPE VI sites, though this figure may overstate the return rate since it does not take account of households lost to the public housing system before they could be temporarily relocated (Cisneros and Engdahl 2009: 302).

Whatever the exact level of re-housing, it is certainly clear that the HOPE VI processes have been used to re-think the intended clientele for public housing (Keating 2000). First, the majority of the new housing created in most HOPE VI projects around the country was either intended for those able to pay market rates or targeted at those who needed only a shallower subsidy, such as the housing created by the Low Income Housing Tax Credit program, which enables units to be occupied by those earning up to 60 percent of the area's median income. Most former public housing residents earned less than 20 percent of the area median, making them a much less attractive prospect for rehousing. To financially strapped housing authorities, it made much more sense to attract some tenants who could pay market rates (or even own their own homes) and find as many other tenants as possible with higher incomes (since subsidized tenants paid 30 percent of their income in rent). Moreover, many former tenants who sought re-entry to the reinvented developments created under HOPE VI proved unable to meet the more stringent requirements imposed by the private management companies that served as the new gatekeepers. Households that had struggled to keep up with rent payments, had family members with criminal records, or simply had a poor credit history could easily be kept out of the new housing.

Under HOPE VI, public housing is being forcibly returned to an earlier era of high selectivity, one that favors households with stable records of employment. This is wholly in keeping with the public housing reform legislation, known formally as the Quality Housing and Work Responsibility Act of 1998. Proponents of public housing, in this new form, treated "work responsibility" as a co-requisite for housing assistance, harking back to the days of the nineteenth-century Homestead Act or even to the attitudes of the early Puritan settlers (Vale 2000). No longer intended as a coping mechanism for dealing with the least advantaged or the so-called "hard to house," public housing is again intended to be a reward for good behavior, a government perk allocated only to those judged worthiest among the poor. Meanwhile, the buzzword to justify this radical reallocation of resources and replacement of communities has been "deconcentration" of poverty. Just as the early housers viewed slum clearance as benefiting former slum dwellers regardless whether they were "re-housed" in the new public housing, so today's advocates of the HOPE VI program view release from the shackles of distressed public housing as its own reward. Increasingly, in response to an extended period when public housing policy actively worked to concentrate the poor, policy-makers now seek ways to purge the poorest from public housing (Vale 2013).

For me, the subject of American public housing has been more than an exercise in policy analysis or an occasion to muse on the power and limitations of design. Instead, it has been an opportunity to think through the basic structures and strictures of inequality in the United States. This underlying inequality pits the role of expert knowledge against the latent expertise of local residents, and invokes the appeals of design determinism against the need for a more subtle accounting of socio-spatial relations. Analysis of public housing offers a window into the priorities of a society and the workings of a polity.

My quest has been to understand not just how programs and policies and building complexes were developed, but to seek out answers about why they have developed the way they have. Ultimately, for me at least, these "why?" sorts of questions are more meaningful and therefore more powerful. Yet, too much focus on that kind of question risks both insularity and self-indulgence. It is not enough to ask *why* Americans have had so much trouble investing in housing for the least economically advantaged. One must also ask what actions, given this, can and should be taken. This is what turns the fields of "history" or "urban studies" into the professional quest we call planning.

Public housing has long been societally filed under the broad heading "failures," but it is much more useful to ask the question in the other direction:

when, where, and why has public housing been successful? What can this tell us about the power of human agency under the most distressed conditions? What can we learn about the sorts of difficult but resilient institutional relationships that can be forged in the midst of dysfunction? In short, what does success look like, and how can it be both measured and replicated?

All too often discussion about the relationship between housing and planning centers on documenting failures: "Let me show you what's wrong with this and who is at fault." It is not a coincidence that there is a famous book called *Great Planning Disasters* (Hall 1982) (even though some of the book documents projects like the Sydney Opera House and the BART system that later gained more appreciation). I want planning to ask the other side of the question. Why did some things succeed in a particular place working through a particular institution via particular processes with a particular design solution? Where do we find good performance in unexpected places? Where are the surprising success stories and how do we measure them and explain them? Who will write the *Great Planning Successes* book?

Conclusion: The Lessons of Public Housing History in the United States

Defining success and advancing efforts to implement successful transformation of traumatized housing environments means coming to terms with seven lessons from the historical struggle of public housing in the United States.

1. It is always necessary and useful to examine the stated and hidden rationales for any complex program. Public housing is a classic example of a series of programs that have been both championed and vilified in accordance with a succession of mixed motives.
2. Housing has always been treated as a moral good and, for low-income people, this perspective has been neither moral nor good.
3. There is a difference between eliminating the problem of public housing and solving the problem of public housing. Demolition techniques can do the former, but only profound policy changes and substantial public investment can bring about the latter.
4. The erstwhile "ownership society" has been an illusory fusion of economics and ideology, indicative of a society that counts only low-income rental housing as "subsidized" and ignores the larger subsidies

in the form of tax expenditures that support homeownership for the majority of Americans. All too often, we structure our housing economics to serve our ideology.

5. Physical renewal of neighborhoods is usually treated as inseparable from population renewal. All too often, the HOPE VI program has seemed a cruel acronym for "House Our Poor Elsewhere."

6. Public housing is as much about the nature of who counts as "public" as it is about measuring what counts as "housing."

7. Ultimately, the changing fate of public housing is a diagnostic window into the socio-spatial place of the least-advantaged Americans.

Public housing forces urban planners to focus on a key question: Who benefits from urban development? The answer is more complicated than the useful injunction to "follow the money." Answers depend fundamentally on sorting through institutional and ideological complexity.

Looking forward, if past is prologue, the saga of public housing redevelopment suggests that neighborhood renewal efforts in the United States will increasingly attempt to minimize the presence of the poor in the new communities. In some cases, the displaced poor are given genuine choice and are able to parlay the use of a portable "Housing Choice Voucher" into new residences in what are often referred to as "opportunity neighborhoods"— places of low poverty and reduced racial segregation. All too often, however, the poor have merely shifted the site of their poverty, while distancing themselves from previous networks of social and emotional support.

How can we do better? In the best situations, instead of attempting to re-house the *political minimum* number of low-income households in mixed-income communities, redevelopment teams can attempt to re-house the *political maximum* number of low-income households, while still taking care to produce a community that is secure and well managed. At base, most studies of the presumed advantages of mixed-income communities have done little to distinguish the best types of mix or to clarify the objectives and mechanisms for achieving the goals that this mixing is expected to achieve. In some cases, such as the successful revitalization of the Commonwealth development in Boston during the 1980s, the Mixed-Income New Communities Strategy (MINCS) briefly implemented by the Chicago Housing Authority in the early 1990s, and some HOPE VI initiatives such as the North Beach Place transformation in San Francisco, American public housing authorities have used sound management, careful tenant screening, enhanced efforts to increase employment, and thoughtful redesign to re-create safe and attractive communities without choosing to turn over any part of the scarce subsidized housing stock to wealthier residents who can afford to pay market rate rents. In other words, it may be possible to end the isolation of the least advantaged poor by increasing their proximity and intermixing with the upwardly mobile working poor, rather than by interspersing them with the rich. What seems needed, then, is a broader application of a narrower mix, and a more concerted effort to identify and learn from the cases where such mixes have been successful (Rosenbaum, Stroh, and Flynn 1998; Carmon 1976, 1999; Vale 2002; Joseph 2008, 2010).

At the same time, planners and scholars need to continue to learn from the results of housing mobility programs, policies that attempt to deliver pathways out of high-poverty neighborhoods. To date, the record of the Moving to Opportunity experiment in the United States has been decidedly mixed—with some important gains in safety (especially for girls and women), but no corresponding gains in incomes (Briggs, Popkin, and Goering 2010). This suggests that portable housing vouchers ought to remain an important part of housing policy, but will not in themselves be a socio-economic panacea.

Housing is one of those great words in English that can be both a noun and a verb. It is the verb part that connects housing to *planning* as opposed to just architecture, a profession that too often seems content to view housing chiefly as a noun. Housing, for me, is about both process and place. Planners hear *housing* as a verb; architects hear it as a noun; residents hear it as "my home." Achieving progress on the relationship among public housing, planning, and people means remembering that housing is always simultaneously a process, a piece of the built environment, and an emotional attachment to a place. To date, the troubled tale of public housing in the United States has followed a cyclical practice of displacement and neighborhood renewal, all too often directed at purging the poorest. Fortunately, however, in recent years planning scholars and activist planners have joined with low-income residents to challenge conventional perceptions and to work toward more equitable solutions.

References

Baranski, John. 2004. Making public housing in San Francisco: Liberalism, social prejudice, and social activism, 1906–1976. Ph.D. dissertation, University of California, Santa Barbara.

Bauer, Catherine. 1934. *Modern housing*. Boston: Houghton Mifflin.

———. 1957. The dreary deadlock of public housing. *Architectural Forum* 106 (May 1957). Reprinted in *Federal housing policy and programs: Past and present*, ed. J. Paul Mitchell, 277–85. New Brunswick, N.J.: Center for Urban Policy Research.

Bauman, John. 1987. *Public housing, race, and renewal: Urban planning in Philadelphia, 1920–1974*. Philadelphia: Temple University Press.

———. 1994. Public housing: The dreadful saga of a durable policy. *Journal of Planning Literature* 8(4): 347–61.

Bauman, John, Roger Biles, and Kristin Szylvian, eds. 2000. *From tenements to the Taylor Homes: In search of an urban housing policy in twentieth-century America*. University Park: Pennsylvania State University Press.

Bennett, Larry, Janet L. Smith, and Patricia A. Wright, eds. 2006. *Where are poor people to live: Transforming public housing communities*. Armonk, N.Y: M.E. Sharpe.

Bloom, Nicholas Dagen. 2008. *Public housing that worked: New York in the twentieth century*. Philadelphia: University of Pennsylvania Press.

Bowly, Devereux, Jr. 1978. *The poorhouse: subsidized housing in Chicago, 1895-1976*. Carbondale: Southern Illinois University Press.

Bratt, Rachel G. 1986. Public housing: The controversy and contribution. In *Critical perspectives on housing*, ed. Rachel G. Bratt, Chester Hartman, and Ann Meyerson Philadelphia: Temple University Press.

Bratt, Rachel G., Michael E. Stone, and Chester Hartman, eds. 2006. *A right to housing: Foundation for a new social agenda*. Philadelphia: Temple University Press.

Breitbart, Myrna Margulies, and Ellen J. Pader. 1995. Establishing ground: Representing gender and race in a mixed housing development. *Gender, Place and Culture* 2(1): 5–20.

Carmon, Naomi. 1976. Social planning of housing. *Journal of Social Policy* 5(1): 49–59.

———. 1981. Housing policy in western countries: Toward broader social responsibility, *Social Praxis* 8(3–4): 53–71.

———. 1999. Three generations of urban renewal policies: Analysis and policy implications. *Geoforum* 30(2): 144–58.

Chermayeff, Serge, and Christopher Alexander. 1965. *Community and privacy: Toward a new architecture of Humanism*. Garden City, N.Y.: Anchor.

Cisneros, Henry, and Lora Engdahl, eds. 2009. *From despair to hope: HOPE VI and the new promise of public housing in America's cities*, app. A-2. Washington, D.C.: Brookings Institution Press.

Connerly, Charles E. 2005. *"The most segregated city in America": City planning and civil rights in Birmingham, 1920–1980*. Charlottesville: University of Virginia Press.

Congress for the New Urbanism, HUD. 2000. *Principles for inner city neighborhood design: HOPE VI and the new urbanism*.

Cooper, Clare. 1975. *Easter Hill Village*. New York: Free Press.

Coyle, Daniel. 1993. *Hardball: A season in the projects*. New York: Putnam.

De Leeuw, Frank. 1970. *Operating costs in public housing: A financial crisis*. Washington, D.C.: Urban Institute.

Fairbanks, Robert. 1988. *Making better citizens: Housing reform and the community development strategy in Cincinnati, 1890–1960*. Urbana: University of Illinois Press.

Feldman, Roberta M., and Susan Stall. 2004. *The dignity of resistance: Women's resident activism and Chicago public housing*. Cambridge: Cambridge University Press.

Franck, Karen, and Michael Mostoller. 1995. From courts to open space to streets: Changes in the site design of U.S. public housing. *Journal of Architectural and Planning Research* 12(3): 186–220.

Friedman, Lawrence. 1968. *Government and slum housing: A century of frustration*. Chicago: Rand McNally.

Fuerst, J. S. (with D. Bradford Hunt). 2003. *When public housing was paradise: Building community in Chicago*. Westport, Conn.: Praeger.

Goetz, Edward. 2003. *Clearing the way: Deconcentrating the poor in urban America*. Washington, D.C.: Urban Institute Press.

Hall, Peter. 1982. *Great planning disasters*. Berkeley: University of California Press.

Heathcott, Joseph. Forthcoming. *The projects and the people: Public housing in the life of an American city*.

Hirsch, Arnold R. 1983. *Making the second ghetto: Race and housing in Chicago, 1940–1960*. New York: Cambridge University Press.

Housing and Home Finance Agency. 1955. *The workable program: What it is*. Washington, D.C.: Government Printing Office, September.

Hunt, D. Bradford. 2009. *Blueprint for disaster: The unraveling of Chicago public housing*. Chicago: University of Chicago Press.

Jacobs, Jane. 1961. *The death and life of great American cities*. New York: Vintage.

Joseph, Mark L. 2008. Early resident experiences at a new mixed-income development in Chicago. *Journal of Urban Affairs* 30(3): 229–57.

———. 2010. Creating mixed-income developments in Chicago: Developer and service provider perspectives, *Housing Policy Debate* 20(1): 91–118.

Keating, Larry. 2000. Redeveloping Public housing: Relearning urban renewal's immutable lessons. *Journal of the American Planning Association* 66(4): 384–97.

Kotlowitz, Alex. 1991. *There are no children here*. New York: Doubleday.

Marcuse, Peter. 1995. Interpreting "public housing" history. *Journal of Architectural and Planning Research* 12(3): 240–58.

Meehan, Eugene. 1975. *Public housing policy: Myth versus reality*. New Brunswick, N.J.: Center for Urban Policy Research.

———. 1979. *The quality of federal policymaking: Programmed failure in public housing*. Columbia: University of Missouri Press.

Moore, William. 1969. *The vertical ghetto: Everyday life in an urban project*. New York: Random House.

National Commission on Severely Distressed Public Housing. 1992a. *The final report of the national commission on severely distressed public housing*. Washington, D.C.: Government Printing Office.

———. 1992b. *Case study and site examination reports.* Washington, D.C.: Government Printing Office.

National Housing Law Project, Poverty & Race Research Action Council, Sherwood Research Associates, and Everywhere and Now Public Housing Residents Organizing Nationally Together (ENPHRONT). 2002. *False HOPE: A critical assessment of the HOPE VI public housing redevelopment program.* http://www.nhlp.org/files/FalseHOPE.pdf, accessed May 2011.

Newman, Oscar. 1972. *Defensible space: Crime prevention through urban design.* New York: Macmillan.

———. 1980. *Community of interest.* Garden City, N.Y.: Anchor /Doubleday.

———. 1996. *Creating defensible space.* Washington, D.C.: U.S. Dept. of Housing and Urban Development, Office of Policy Development and Research.

Pattillo, Mary. 2007. *Black on the block: The politics of race and class in the city.* Chicago: University of Chicago Press.

Peterman, William. 1993. Public housing resident management: A good idea gone wrong? *Shelterforce* 72 (November/December): 6–9.

Popkin, Susan J., Victoria E. Gwiasda, Lynn M. Olsen, Dennis P. Rosenbaum, and Larry Buron. 2000. *The hidden war: Crime and the tragedy of public housing in Chicago.* New Brunswick, N.J.: Rutgers University Press.

Radford, Gail. 2000. The federal government and housing during the Great Depression. In *From tenements to the Taylor homes: In search of an urban housing policy in twentieth-century America,* ed. John F. Bauman, Roger Biles, and Kristin M. Szylvian, 102–20. University Park: Pennsylvania State University Press.

Rainwater, Lee. 1970. *Behind ghetto walls: Black families in a federal slum.* Chicago: Aldine.

Roessner, Jane. 2000. *A decent place to live: From Columbia Point to Harbor Point.* Boston: Northeastern University Press.

Rosenbaum, James E., Linda K. Stroh, and Cathy Flynn. 1998. Lake Parc Place: A study of mixed-income housing. *Housing Policy Debate* 9(4): 703–40.

Sugrue, Thomas. 1998. *The origins of the urban crisis: Race and inequality in postwar Detroit.* Princeton, N.J.: Princeton University Press.

Thomas, June Manning. 1997. *Redevelopment and race: Planning a finer city in postwar Detroit.* Baltimore: Johns Hopkins University Press.

Vale, Lawrence J. 1993. Beyond the Problem projects paradigm: Defining and revitalizing "severely distressed" public housing. *Housing Policy Debate* 4(2): 147–74.

———. 1996. Public housing redevelopment: Seven kinds of success. *Housing Policy Debate* 7(4): 491–534.

———. 1997. Empathological places: Residents' ambivalence towards remaining in public housing. *Journal of Planning Education and Research* 16(3): 159–75.

———. 2000. *From the Puritans to the projects: Public housing and public neighbors.* Cambridge, Mass.: Harvard University Press.

———. 2002. *Reclaiming public housing: A half century of struggle in three public neighborhoods*. Cambridge, Mass.: Harvard University Press.

———. 2007. The ideological origins of affordable home ownership efforts, in *Chasing the American Dream*, ed. William Rohe and Harry Watson, 15–40. Ithaca, N.Y.: Cornell University Press.

———. 2013. *Purging the poorest: Public housing and the design-politics of twice-cleared communities*. Chicago: University of Chicago Press.

Venkatesh, Sudhir Alladi. 2000. *American project*. Cambridge, Mass.: Harvard University Press.

———. 2008. *Gang leader for a day: A rogue sociologist takes to the streets*. New York: Penguin.

Von Hoffman, Alexander. 2000. A Study in contradictions: The origins and legacy of the Housing Act of 1949. *Housing Policy Debate* 11(2): 299–326.

Williams, Rhonda Y. 2004. *The politics of public housing: Black women's struggles against urban inequality*. New York: Oxford University Press.

Chapter 15

Neighborhood Social Mix: Theory, Evidence, and Implications for Policy and Planning

George C. Galster

Progressive thinkers about the residential composition of neighborhoods have long held that population socioeconomic diversity was desirable (Gans 1961; Sarkissian 1976). Similar sentiments still undergird a rich palette of official pronouncements and planning initiatives in Europe, Australia, and the United States. Programmatic examples include: urban regeneration measures that replace concentrations of social housing with more diverse housing stocks; social housing management and tenant allocation reform; tenant-based housing allowances; and land-use planning rules requiring mixed developments (see Berube 2005; Briggs 2005; Musterd and Andersson 2005; Norris 2006).

Despite its longstanding, exalted place in the pantheon of planning nostrums, the goal of "socially mixed neighborhoods" has been challenged on conceptual and empirical grounds by a wide range of scholars, including Atkinson and Kintrea (2000, 2001), Ostendorf, Musterd and de Vos (2001), Kearns (2002), Musterd (2002, 2003), Musterd, Ostendorf and de Vos (2003), Meen et al. (2005), Galster (2005), Delorenzi (2006), Joseph (2006), Joseph, Chaskin, and Webber (2006), Cheshire (2007), Van Kempen and Bolt (2009), and Darcy (2010). It behooves planners to take the challenges seriously, not to pursue social mix as a matter of faith.

This chapter aims to assist planners in this quest. It synthesizes and extends the challenges to social mix and assesses comprehensively the empirical evidence from many disciplines and nations as it interfaces with the topic considering both the goal of social mix and the means to achieve it. It tries to clarify what questions we need to ask and the degree to which answers seem certain regarding concepts, policy rationales, and causal mechanisms, and then draws appropriate, pragmatic implications for planners.

The Slippery Concept of Social Mix

"Social mix" is an intrinsically vague, slippery term; it is typically used to mean different things by different planners and policymakers. Three thorny aspects lie at the heart of this ambiguity (Tunstall and Fenton 2006; Kleinhans 2004):

- *Composition*: On what bas(es) are we mixing people: ethnicity, race, religion, immigrant status, income, housing tenure—all, or some of the above?
- *Concentration*: What is the amount of mixing? Which amounts of which groups comprise the ideal mix, or are minimally required to produce the desired outcomes?
- *Scale*: Over what level(s) of geography should the relevant mix be measured? Does mixing at different spatial scales involve different causal processes and yield different outcomes?

Planners must be precise and explicit in specifying the parameters of these three aspects of social mix before they can evaluate evidence in a precise way or recommend specific planning policies and practices. Below I examine the evidence base related to all three aspects, after establishing an evaluative framework in which evidence can be assessed.

The Equity and Efficiency Rationales
for Social Mix as a Goal

Policy documents and the scholarly literature are replete with a wide range of objectives for a neighborhood social mix strategy. Important insights can be gained by reframing all these rationales in terms of *who, ultimately, is the desired beneficiary* of the policy. I would suggest this tripartite classification of potential beneficiaries:

- *Disadvantaged Families, Adults, and Children* (potentially defined according to tenure, economic, racial-ethnic, national-origin, and/or religious status, depending on context)
- *Advantaged Families, Adults, and Children*
- *Society* (all advantaged and disadvantaged individuals aggregated, though not necessarily benefiting equally or weighted equally by cultural norms)

I assume the typical reader here is not a planner whose goal is to help the advantaged exclusively.[1] Thus, I will only amplify on the first and the third, which hereafter I will refer to as the "equity" and the "efficiency" rationales, which I now define.

Defining Equity and Efficiency Rationales

I specify that *equity* is improved if any social mix policy increases absolutely the well-being of the disadvantaged group in society. If society wished to pursue a policy of mixing advantaged with disadvantaged individuals *in order to benefit the latter group*, either of two necessary conditions would appertain.[2] Disadvantaged individuals must (1) lose well-being by residing with other members of their group (at least past some point of concentration) and/or (2) gain well-being by residing with members of the advantaged group (at least past some point of concentration). Put differently, neighborhood mix policy can be justified on equity grounds favoring the disadvantaged if and only if the disadvantaged are subjected to (1) negative social externalities from disadvantaged neighbors; (2) positive social externalities from advantaged neighbors; and/or (3) stigmatization/resource restrictions because their percentage in the neighborhood is past a threshold.

I specify that *efficiency* is improved if a social mix policy improves the aggregate amount of well-being summed across all members of society, with the well-being of certain individuals perhaps weighted differentially (if implicitly) according to prevailing cultural norms. This standard does not necessarily require Pareto-improvements (wherein some individuals gain and none suffer a loss of well-being), though such would be sufficient. It does, however, require adherence to the Hicks-Kaldor compensation principle. That is, a policy is efficient if the "winners" could potentially compensate the "losers" sufficiently to hold them harmless and yet still be better off themselves.[3]

To clearly distinguish the two standards, a social mix policy that increased the well-being of the advantaged a great deal and decreased the well-being of the disadvantaged a small amount could potentially be efficient (unless the well-being of the disadvantaged was heavily weighted by society), even though it would not be equitable. On the other hand, if a policy increased the well-being of the disadvantaged and did not harm the advantaged, both equity and efficiency would be enhanced. Thus, the two goals are distinct but not mutually contradictory.

I recognize that planners do not think often of efficiency criteria; nevertheless, they are worthy of consideration. In a context where neoliberal ideology is prevalent, efficiency criteria may well take precedence in the minds of key decision-makers with whom planners interface. In other words, the political feasibility of the proposal may be enhanced substantially if its efficiency can be demonstrated.

The efficiency-based justification for social mix requires considerations of the *mechanisms* of social mix neighborhood effects not relevant in the equity-based justification. Specifically, we must distinguish between neighborhood effects that occur because of social interactions *within* the neighborhood and those that occur because of the perceptions and actions of those *outside* the neighborhood. First, because efficiency requires us to consider the well-being of both disadvantaged and advantaged individuals, a more comprehensive analysis of potential intra-neighborhood social externalities is required. We must consider the possibility that negative social externalities imposed by disadvantaged individuals on their advantaged neighbors outweigh the positive social externalities that may flow in the opposite direction. If such were the case, it is easy to imagine a social weighting scheme (such as utilitarianism) that would register the highest values when the two groups were completely segregated residentially. Second, if *only* the extra-neighborhood process of stigmatization/resource restriction were operative, we would not need to concern ourselves with the potential zero-sum or negative-sum aspects associated with intra-neighborhood social interactions between disadvantaged and advantaged groups. On the contrary, changing the social mix by reducing the share of disadvantaged in a neighborhood so that the stigma/restriction was removed would provide a net gain for the well-being of *both* types of individuals living in the formerly stigmatized neighborhood.

Implications of Equity and Efficiency Rationales
for Standards of Evidence

What does the foregoing framing suggest about what sort of empirical evidence would provide *sufficient* proof that social mixing could be justified on equity or efficiency grounds?[4] In the case of the *equity-based conditions*, the evidence must show that outcomes associated with greater well-being now or in the future for disadvantaged individuals are (1) positively correlated with a higher percentage of advantaged neighbors, and/or (2) negatively correlated with a higher percentage of other disadvantaged neighbors, all else equal.[5]

In the case of *efficiency-based conditions*, the sufficient evidentiary base must be considerably more comprehensive and nuanced, with attention paid to the presumed underlying mechanism of neighborhood effect. First, consider if intra-neighborhood social interactions were the presumed mechanism. In this case, not only does the former equity-based criterion continue to apply for disadvantaged individuals, but the converse must also apply for advantaged individuals. That is, studies must be based on observations of advantaged individuals in different neighborhood contexts and find that they are neither (1) significantly harmed by the negative social externalities generated by disadvantaged neighbors, nor (2) significantly benefited by the positive social externalities generated by other advantaged neighbors. Only if such evidence is gained about how both advantaged and disadvantaged individuals are affected by social interactions associated with neighborhood mix can we be confident that a wide range of normative social weighting schemes would yield neighborhood mixing as the most efficient outcome.

Second, consider if extra-neighborhood stigmatization/resource restrictions were the presumed mechanism. In this case, the statistical evidence would not need to be stratified by group insofar as *both* advantaged and disadvantaged individuals were harmed by the stigmatization and other institutional/resource constraints associated with higher percentages of disadvantaged residents in the neighborhood. Here the evidence must show that outcomes associated with greater well-being for a combined sample of both groups are negatively (positively) correlated with percentages of disadvantaged (advantaged) in the neighborhood, at least past some thresholds(s).

The foregoing may strike some as overly pedantic, given that planners most likely try to pursue polices that simultaneously are equitable *and* efficient. Indeed, we should strive to achieve both when we can. Nevertheless, it is useful to distinguish them as alternative goals, and to urge that planners should be explicit about their goals for social mix, because:

- The evidence base may be supportive of one goal being achieved more than another.
- The more desirable programmatic approaches will differ depending on goals specified.
- It will force planners to determine how and why a particular plan for social mix is likely to achieve the desired effects (i.e., to be clear about the presumed causal mechanisms or "theory of change").
- If outcomes are equitable but not efficient, it will help planners to anticipate opposition from advantaged residents who may be adversely affected, and devise mechanisms to, ideally, hold them harmless.

The Effects of Social Mix on the Disadvantaged: The Evidence Base

The previous section showed that sufficient grounds for social mix on the basis of equity arguments would be provided by evidence that disadvantaged individuals are harmed by disadvantaged neighbors (at least past some threshold) and/or benefited by advantaged neighbors (at least past some threshold). In this section I summarize scholarly evidence of various sorts relevant to establishing these sufficient conditions. I organize the discussion around the potential mechanisms through which composition of a neighborhood might affect individual residents.[6]

There have been numerous studies from the U.S. and Europe of the social relationships of youth and adults from low-income neighborhoods. They consistently suggest that negative social externalities from peers and role models are frequently generated among disadvantaged neighbors, especially youths. See, for example, Case and Katz (1991), Diehr et al. (1993), South and Baumer (2000), Ginther, Haveman, and Wolfe (2000), Oberwittler (2004).[7] The lack of social ties with employed and better-educated people is also an often observed characteristic of disadvantaged neighborhood residents, thereby reducing their opportunities; see Tiggs, Brown, and Green (1998), Fernandez and Harris (1992), Bertrand, Luttmer, and Mullainathan (2000), Buck (2001), Farwick (2004), and Pinkster (2008).

Though it thus seems likely that negative influences from peer groups and role models, and resource-poor and locally constrained networks help perpetuate individual disadvantage in disadvantaged neighborhoods, it does not necessarily follow that all social relationships of the disadvantaged will be significantly altered by mere residence near advantaged individuals in mixed communities. Indeed, there is substantial consistent literature indicating that social mix is insufficient to induce substantial social interactions and social capital between groups that may enhance employment and other resource networks for the disadvantaged. American studies include Rosenbaum (1991), Briggs (1997, 1998), Schill (1997), Kleit (2001a, b, 2002), and Rosenbaum, Harris, and Denton (2003). Western European studies include Atkinson and Kintrea (1998), Blokland-Potters (1998), Jupp (1999), Cole and Goodchild (2001), Van Beckhoven and Van Kempen (2003), and Pinkster (2008).[8]

Galster et al. (2008) provide a methodologically sophisticated study of the effects of both disadvantaged and advantaged neighbors on individual earnings of less-advantaged (part-time employed) adults using Swedish urban data. In the case of men who were not employed full time, the neighborhood with the highest possible share of *middle-income neighbors* was most conducive to their earning more. The fact that even a few low-income neighbors eroded these benefits suggested to the authors that negative role modeling or peer effects transpired here. Replacing middle-income with high-income neighbors also had negative impacts on these less-advantaged males, implying that the former provided positive role models but the latter did not, perhaps because the social distance between the groups was too great for social interactions.

It is noteworthy that studies of social interactions among different income groups in mixed U.S. neighborhoods (cited above) do not reveal compelling evidence of relative deprivation or inter-group competition that would harm disadvantaged neighbors. However, there are enough hints of this effect in a few European studies to make it risky to reject this mechanism completely, at least for some selected health and psychological outcomes; see Sampson and Groves (1989), Duncan and Jones (1995), Shouls et al. (1996), McCulloch (2001), Atkinson and Kintrea (2004), and Oberwittler (2007).

Case study evidence suggests that place-based stigmatization is a frequent process in Western Europe; see Wacquant (1993), Power (1997), Taylor (1998), Atkinson and Kintrea (1998), Forrest and Kearns (1999), Dean and Hastings (2000), Hastings and Dean (2003), Martin and Watkinson (2003), Hastings (2004), and Permentier (2009). Permentier, Bolt and van Ham (2007) found that neighborhood reputations were significantly correlated with their socio-economic characteristics, while their physical and functional features were of less importance. Unfortunately, the degree to which the reputation of a long-stigmatized neighborhood can change as a consequence of more advan-taged households being added to the social mix is unclear, but perhaps discouraging; see Cole et al. (1997), Pawson et al. (2000), Beekman et al. (2001), Helleman and Wassenberg (2004), and Van Kempen and Bolt (2009).

Many additional studies have been conducted that, while not focusing on the mechanism(s) of neighborhood effect, provide evidence on the degree to which social mix influences the well-being of disadvantaged residents.[9] Perhaps the most widely cited because of its random-assignment experimental design is the U.S. Moving to Opportunity (MTO) demonstration. Most investigations of MTO data revealed no substantial neighborhood effects on labor market outcomes of poor minority adults; see Ludwig, Duncan, and Pinkston (2000), Katz, Kling, and Liebman (2001), Ludwig, Ladd, and Duncan (2001), Ludwig, Duncan, and Hirschfield (2001), Orr et al. (2003), and Ludwig et al. (2008).[10] Nevertheless, MTO analysts have observed several important neighborhood effects on the health of mothers and daughters, educational outcomes for daughters, rates of risky behaviors by youth, perceptions of safety, and overall life satisfaction; see Goering and Feins (2003), Kling, Liebman, and Katz (2007), and Briggs, Popkin, and Goering (2010).

Finally, a new Australian study offers intriguing evidence, assuming the results can be generalized. Baum, Arthurson and Rickson (2010) find that low-income individuals are much more likely to be satisfied with their neighborhood if they live in places with more income diversity and a smaller ratio of low-to-high-income households.

What does the foregoing evidence suggest about the effects of social mix on disadvantaged residents and the associated neighborhood effect mechanisms, when all is said and done? With the mandatory caveat that firm conclusions are elusive here, my evaluation provisionally suggests the following.

First, in both the U.S. and Western Europe high concentrations of poverty or socially disadvantaged households (typically heavily Hispanic- and especially black-occupied neighborhoods in the U.S. and immigrant-occupied neighborhoods in Western Europe) have been empirically linked to such negative outcomes as youth delinquency, criminality, school leaving, and mental health distress, especially if exposure is sustained. This is consistent with several alternative mechanisms of impact in disadvantaged neighborhoods: (1) intra-neighborhood role model/peer effects; (2) intra-neighborhood circumscribed, resource-poor social networks that provide few links to labor market opportunities; (3) extra-neighborhood processes of stigmatization/resource deprivation based on the area's inferior class or ethnic status.

Second, most U.S. and Western European evidence indicates that the influence on vulnerable individuals of advantaged neighbors is smaller in absolute value than the influence of disadvantaged neighbors. Many studies have consistently found that there is relatively little social interaction and networking between lower-income and considerably higher-income households or children in the same neighborhood, and this lack is compounded if there are also racial-ethnic differences involved. Thus, there is little to support the version of neighborhood effects that advantaged neighbors create valuable networks of "weak ties" for disadvantaged ones. Role modeling and social control seems a more likely mechanism of positive intra-neighborhood social interactions.[11]

Third, in U.S. neighborhood contexts there is virtually no evidence suggesting that the competition or relative deprivation mechanisms are operating in a meaningful way. The same cannot be said of Western European evidence, however, where there are some hints that mixing of extremely low- and high-income groups results in some harms for the disadvantaged.

In sum, my reading of the evidence is that social mix can be beneficial for disadvantaged residents in terms of intra-neighborhood processes, but this appears most likely when the social gulf between groups in the neighborhood is not excessive. This is not a new conclusion, of course (see Carmon 1976, 1999; Joseph 2010; Vale, this volume). The main benefits seem to transpire as the extremely negative consequences of concentrated deprivation (probably transmitted through both intra- and extra-neighborhood processes) are replaced by the comparatively weak but beneficial consequences of social mix.

The Effects of Social Mix on the Advantaged: The Evidence Base

Above I argued that planners also should be concerned about whether social mixing has positive, negative, or neutral impacts on advantaged residents, applying the evaluative criteria of social efficiency. Unfortunately, only a few European statistical studies directly investigate behavioral outcomes for advantaged individuals living in socially mixed neighborhoods.[12] A few suggest that disadvantaged neighbors may increase the likelihood that nondisadvantaged neighbors will remain unemployed (Musterd and Andersson 2006) or commit property offenses (Oberwittler 2007).[13] Two Swedish studies that more convincingly controlled for selection effects found no negative impacts on advantaged individuals' earnings from disadvantaged neighbors; see Edin, Fredricksson, and Aslund (2003) and Galster et al. (2008). A follow-up study by Galster, Andersson, and Musterd (2010) indicated, however, that higher-income individuals benefit economically somewhat more from similar-income neighbors than lower income individuals benefit from higher-income individuals.

Advantaged (as well as disadvantaged) populations may benefit from social mix if the contact results in a reduction of intergroup prejudices (Allport 1954). U.S. studies have often observed that inter-ethnic and inter-economic group tolerance and subsequent social contacts have been enhanced with greater intra-neighborhood contacts, especially earlier in life (e.g., Ihlanfeldt and Scafidi 2002; Emerson, Kimbro, and Yancey 2002; and the review by Pettigrew and Tropp 2006). The picture seems less clear from Western European evidence, however (e.g., Bourdieu 1999: 128; Farwick 2004) and several preconditions are required for these benefits to transpire (Gans 1961: 176).

In sum, there is mixed evidence whether social mixing creates negative outcomes for advantaged households. On the contrary, there is evidence (at least in the U.S.) that such mixing can (though not necessarily) increase the tolerance and reduce the prejudicial stereotypes of advantaged residents.

The Effects of Social Mix on Society as a Whole: The Evidence Base

There are two types of statistical evidence that help us ascertain whether social mixing of neighborhoods might provide a net improvement of the well-being of disadvantaged and advantaged individuals in aggregate. Both test for the existence of nonlinear relationships between the share of a particular income group in the neighborhood and the change in a particular outcome, because only certain types of nonlinear relationships suggest social efficiency gains from social mixing (Galster 2002).

The first type of studies examine potential nonlinear statistical associations between variations in the share of disadvantaged residents in a neighborhood and outcomes for other individuals residing there. My review (Galster 2002) of the U.S. evidence indicates this relationship can be portrayed as a logit-like relationship, with two thresholds (see Krivo and Peterson 1996; Vartanian 1999a, b; Weinberg, Reagan, and Yankow 2004). The independent impacts of neighborhood poverty rates in encouraging negative outcomes for individuals appear to be nil unless the neighborhood exceeds about 15–20 percent poverty, whereupon the externality effects grow rapidly until the neighborhood reaches approximately 40 percent poverty; subsequent increases in the poverty population appear to have no marginal external effect. By contrast, the Western European evidence related to potential nonlinear neighborhood effects of disadvantaged neighbors focuses on labor market outcomes, and the findings are mixed in the extreme. Several studies (Ostendorf, Musterd, and de Vos 2001; Bolster et al. 2004; McCulloch 2001; Musterd, Ostendorf, and de Vos 2003) detected no important nonlinearities. Other studies detected inconsistent nonlinear relationships (cf. Buck 2001; Van der Klaauw and van Ours 2003; Musterd and Andersson 2006; Gordon and Monastiriotis 2006; Oberwittler 2007; Galster et al. 2008). However, a recent, sophisticated Swedish study shows severe impacts on individuals' incomes once the low-income population share exceeds a 40 percent threshold (Galster, Musterd, and Andersson 2010).

The second type of studies examine potential nonlinear relationships between variations in the share of disadvantaged residents in a neighborhood and housing values there. These studies use the well-known proposition that a variety of localized amenities and disamenities that might be associated with social mixing (larger incidence of social problems, reductions in maintenance of housing, loss of neighborhood prestige, etc.) are capitalized into values of homes in the area. Using data from similarly scaled neighborhoods (wards in England and census tracts in the U.S.), Meen (2006) and Galster, Cutsinger, and Malega (2008) statistically estimate a strong negative relationship between neighborhood property value changes and increases in neighborhood disadvantage (poverty rates), but only after such exceeds roughly the same 15–20 percent threshold as noted above. The overall relationship resembled a negative logistic function.

In sum, the fact that neighborhood poverty rates in the U.S. appear consistently related to a range of individual behavioral outcomes in a nonlinear, threshold-like fashion is consistent with only a few sorts of neighborhood effect mechanisms. Unfortunately, with highly inconsistent evidence regarding nonlinearities of neighborhood impacts on individual behaviors in the Western European evidence, less clear inferences can be drawn. However, both U.S. and UK evidence from studies of nonlinear effects of shares of disadvantaged populations on housing values is consistent with the afore-mentioned U.S. evidence on behaviors. Collectively, this evidence provides strong support for the hypotheses of the neighborhood effect mechanisms of: (1) external stigmatization/institutional resource constraints, and (2) intra-neighborhood effects manifesting themselves past a threshold, such as collective controls and social norms.

Even more important, it clearly suggests that a regime of complete segregation (neighborhoods of concentrated advantage or concentrated dis-advantage) is socially less efficient than one in which every neighborhood has an equal share of the disadvantaged. This improved social well-being can be measured either as lower overall incidences of socially problematic be-haviors or as higher aggregate housing values. However, the evidence also suggests that not every degree of social mix is more efficient than complete segregation; only mixes with extremely low concentrations of the disadvan-taged appear more socially efficient.

The Composition of the Social Mix: The Evidence Base

Thus far, I have reviewed the evidence related to "disadvantaged" as defined by income, but what about immigrant status as the basis for disad-vantage? The latter seems to be a category of higher salience in many Western European contexts. The evidence here is reasonably consistent about whether more intra-neighborhood immigrant contact in homogeneous communi-ties (enclaves) provides net (or long-term) positive externalities for ethnic minorities or immigrants. In most cases, prolonged residential contact with other immigrants (whether own- or other-group) is associated with nega-tive outcomes; see Clark and Drinkwater (2002), Aslund and Fredricksson (2005), and Musterd et al. (2008), and U.S.-based work by Galster, Metzger, and Waite (1999) and Cutler, Glaeser, and Vigdor (2008). However, a neigh-borhood with exceptionally highly skilled and employed immigrants can provide positive externalities to other resident immigrants, resulting in clear economic payoffs; see Borjas (1995, 1998) and Edin, Fredricksson, and Aslund (2003). It therefore appears that among immigrants the mix of ad-vantaged and disadvantaged groups defined in income/employment terms is more powerful than the mix defined purely in terms of ethnicity or national origin.

This conclusion is strongly buttressed by two other studies. Andersson et al. (2007) find that the income mix of a neighborhood is a far stronger statistical predictor of individual Swedes' income growth than other potential measures of neighborhood social mix, including immigrant status, education, social benefit receipt, or housing tenure type. Baum, Arthurson, and Rickson (2010) find for both low- and high-income households in Australia that the relationship between neighborhood satisfaction and neighborhood income mix is much more powerful than either ethnic or housing tenure mix.

The Concentration of the Social Mix: The Evidence Base

The U.S. literature is replete with studies that have investigated the impacts on housing values associated with assisted (social) housing being developed nearby. These studies provide indirect evidence on potential concentration effects of the disadvantaged. When viewed in its totality, the subset of this home price impact literature that employs the appropriate statistical methodology provides a distinct theme (Freeman and Botein 2002; Galster et al. 2003). The impacts of assisted housing on prices of nearby single-family homes will depend in an interactive way on the method of social mixing and neighborhood context.

As for method, it appears that if mixing is accomplished in an erstwhile advantaged neighborhood through either modest infill construction or rehabilitation of previously undermaintained housing that is then used for subsidized dwellings, there can be positive (but diminishing on the margin) price impacts for nearby homes over some range (Galster et al. 1999; Santiago, Galster, and Tatian 2001; Ellen et al. 2001; Schill et al. 2002; Schwartz et al. 2002). This range is highly contingent on the subsidized housing type in question (Galster et al. 2003), with the potential "over-concentration" negative effect particularly apparent in the case of tenant-based subsidy programs like rental vouchers (Galster et al. 1999; Galster, Tatian, and Smith 1999). As for context, subsidized housing seems least likely to generate negative price impacts when inserted into high-value, low-poverty, stable neighborhoods (cf. Galster et al. 1999, 2003; Galster, Tatian, and Smith 1999; Johnson and Bednarz 2002).

Thus, these studies comport well with aforementioned work on nonlinear relationships between neighborhood shares of economically disadvantaged populations and various behavioral and property value outcomes.

The evidence is clear that relatively low concentrations of the disadvantaged group (below roughly 15–20 percent in the case of U.S. poverty rates) do not create measurable negative externalities for neighbors.

The Scale of Social Mixing: The Evidence Base

In an earlier survey of the literature, I noted the multiplicity of conceptualizations of "neighborhood," and that there is a great deal of interpersonal variance in the perceived boundaries of neighborhoods, both within and across bureaucratically defined spaces (Galster 2001). Nevertheless, of more importance to social mix planning is over what scale the mechanisms of (putatively positive) neighborhood effects from mix operate.

The international literature related to this question is difficult to assess because neighborhood data were collected at various scales by different institutions in different nations. The most direct way of answering the question "what scale(s) of neighborhood matter most in influencing individual outcomes" is to conduct parallel analyses of a particular outcome where neighborhood indicators are measured at different scales and estimates of effects are compared. Several Western European studies have taken this tack: Buck (2001), Bolster et al. (2004), Knies (2007), Van Ham and Manley (2009), and Andersson and Musterd (2010). All found statistically significant relationships at various scales, but stronger correlations were observed between individual outcomes and neighborhood variables when the latter were measured at comparatively smaller spatial scales (typically measured in several hundred households instead of many thousand).[14]

At smaller scales the impact of mixing is less clear. Several European (Atkinson and Kintrea 1998) and American (Kleit 2001a, b, 2002, 2005; Clampet-Lundquist 2004) studies show that the degree of social interactions among different groups residing in a common neighborhood was enhanced (albeit still not too significant) if the groups were more mixed at the block- or building-level scale. However, such a small-scale mix may subject the disadvantaged to excessive scrutiny and stigmatization (Briggs 1997; Joseph 2006) and heighten potential intergroup conflicts over differences in lifestyles (Goodchild and Cole 2001; Beekman et al. 2001; Chaskin and Joseph 2010). The evidence therefore suggests that the most certain net beneficial effects on disadvantaged (and, perhaps, advantaged) residents will occur if social mix is achieved at a scale of several hundreds of households.

Conclusions Regarding the Planning Goal
of a Neighborhood Social Mix Strategy

When all is said and done, what does the Western European and U.S. evidence suggest about whether the goal of neighborhood social mix can be justified and, if so, on what grounds? There is convincing evidence from both regions that disadvantaged individuals are significantly harmed by the presence of sizable disadvantaged groups in their neighborhood, likely due to negative peer/role modeling, weak social norms/control, limited resource networks, and stigmatization/institutional resources mechanisms. There also is convincing, broad-based evidence that disadvantaged individuals *may be* helped by the presence of more advantaged groups in their neighborhood, likely due to positive role modeling, stronger social norms/control and elimination of geographic stigma. However, mixing with those of much higher income appears to produce inferior outcomes for the disadvantaged relative to mixing with middle-income groups. In concert, the foregoing suggests that there is a sufficient evidentiary base to justify on *equity grounds* (i.e., improving the absolute well-being of the disadvantaged) a social mix policy that works toward avoiding high concentrations of disadvantaged individuals and promoting residential diversity of groups, preferably of only modestly dissimilar socioeconomic status.

By contrast, there is evidence that prejudices of advantaged (and disadvantaged) groups may be eroded by closer residential contacts. Moreover, there is evidence (in both regions but more convincingly so in the U.S.) of increasing marginal negative consequences of disadvantaged neighbors past a threshold neighborhood share. However, there is evidence that advantaged individuals in the U.S. and Western Europe *may be* harmed by the presence of disadvantaged groups (both via social interactions and property market reactions) when there are high concentrations of disadvantaged residents and weaker neighborhood housing markets. In concert, these points suggest a sufficient evidentiary base to justify on efficiency grounds a goal of neighborhood social mix, but *only* if the concentration of disadvantaged residents stays relatively low in all neighborhoods.

Implications for Planning:
The Means to Achieving Social Mix

Thus far I have concentrated on analyzing whether neighborhood social mix was a goal worthy of pursuing on equity and efficiency grounds. Given that the answer is a qualified "yes," here I turn to a general analysis of means to achieving this goal. I do not provide prescriptions, but rather a set of issues that planners must deal with in the context of the particular situation they confront. Worthy goals do not justify all conceivable means of achieving them, so the planner must assess the equity and efficiency dimensions of particular program(s) being considered for enhancing social mix. I will argue below that these considerations must be highly contingent; thus, I can provide no general rules.

However, the foregoing review does provide several desirable parameters of social mix that help guide practical planning practice:

- *Composition*: mixing on the basis of economic status seems more important than on immigrant status; there should not be too great a gap between the economic groups being mixed; little empirical guidance on overall composition (Tunstall and Fenton 2006) or which characteristic(s) producing heterogeneity *within* the disadvantaged are worthy of attention;
- *Concentration*: U.S. research indicates the mix should not exceed roughly 15-20 percent poverty populations; the evidence is less clear for Europe;
- *Scale*: mixing should be accomplished at the spatial scale of multiple hundreds of households.

Other issues related to the means of achieving social mix are specific to the programmatic vehicle chosen. For example, social mix could be encouraged in the U.S. by encouraging and assisting recipients of Housing Choice Vouchers (formerly Section 8) to locate in areas with relatively few assisted households or other low-income families, and by encouraging or requiring landlords to participate in the program. For discussions of these issues, see Galster et al. (2003), Goering and Feins (2003), and Galster (2011b). Another strategic possibility is inclusionary zoning, whereby a minimum percentage of dwelling units in developments exceeding a certain threshold are set aside and offered at below-market-rate rents or prices. The UK and some places in the U.S. have experimented with this strategy. Yet another is to provide economic incentives to private developers (like density bonuses, tax credits, or low-interest mortgages) to provide more affordable units as part of the mix of dwellings in a new development (see Brophy and Smith 1997). Yet another approach is to develop (or preserve) social housing in areas that are gentrifying (see Levy et al. 2006).

Whenever site-based solutions are contemplated, a planner must take four key contingencies into account beyond the aforementioned composition, concentration, and scale parameters: *maintenance, design, community building, location* (cf. Brophy and Smith 1997; Joseph 2006; Tunstall and Fenton 2006).[15] Maintenance of socially mixed estates (especially the units occupied by the disadvantaged) is crucial to the success of the development. Not only does a well-managed and maintained area raise all residents' satisfaction levels, but it also reduces potential for inter-group tensions and intolerance (Jupp 1999; Martin and Watkinson 2003) and minimizes chances that the larger housing market will perceive social mix as associated with negative externalities that can lower proximate property values (Galster et al. 2003).

Design of the dwellings and the larger residential complexes that encompass them is also important (Joseph 2006). Dwellings, common areas, parks, and pathways designed to encourage inter-household interactions and defensible spaces will maximize the opportunities for different groups to interact and collectively create secure, satisfying residential environments. Architecture that minimizes the visible distinctions among dwellings for the different groups will also reduce chances for intra-development stigmatization.

But physical attributes of socially mixed places are likely to be insufficient to generate the types of nonsuperficial interactions that may lead to more significant network and friendship formation that may prove instrumental for the disadvantaged. "Community-building" efforts aimed at developing more informal events and formal institutions in the neighborhood will probably be required to help different groups facilitate interpersonal connections and find common interests (Joseph 2006).

Finally, the location of the mixed development must be assessed. Some sites have poor access to jobs, shopping, recreation, quality schools, and other amenities. Merely altering the physical quality of dwellings and the social mix on the site may do little to enhance the opportunities of low-income households.

The above strategies have a common element: they expand over the longer-term opportunities for lower-income families to live in communities with households of somewhat higher economic means and are voluntary in nature. I advocate for these strategies, because they are more gradualist and impose fewer hardships on the disadvantaged. There is another social mix strategy, however, that deserves mention here because it typically imposes severe costs on low-income families, reduces their residential options in the short term, and is involuntary. I am referring to the redevelopment (often involving substantial demolition) of public housing estates and their transformation into mixed-income developments, as has been widely practiced in Europe, the U.S., and Australia. Planners must recognize that rarely are "areas of concentrated disadvantage" all uniform in their function. Some indeed may operate as "poverty traps," as is often feared. But others may operate as springboards launching residents into improving life trajectories. Such has often been seen as the function of "immigrant enclaves," for example. Though disadvantaged by most conventional indicators, they nevertheless may provide crucial human, financial, and social capital in a linguistically and culturally sensitive way that simply could not be replicated were the area to be "deconcentrated." Thus, demolishing existing developments must always be undertaken gradually and voluntarily to the extent feasible, with the utmost sensitivity to context and potential inequities imposed on disadvantaged residents (Kleinhans and Varady 2011).

Before closing, I would be remiss not to mention several daunting challenges of achieving the sort of productive socially mixed places meeting all the criteria above. Not only are substantial financial and human resources involved, but some of the aforementioned parameters may be mutually contradictory. A "pepper-pot" approach of keeping low concentrations of the disadvantaged in all neighborhoods might be desirable from the standpoint of increasing their exposure to positive role models and social controls, eliminating place stigmatization, and gaining political acceptability from the advantaged. However, it also may thwart the maintenance or development of vital institutions serving the disadvantaged and expose them to more within-development stigmatization and intrusive monitoring. Mixing the disadvantaged with those who are not too dissimilar in socioeconomic status may prove more beneficial to the former group. But it may be difficult to accomplish if deconcentration strategies are taken to scale and policy-makers wish to avoid destabilizing middle- and working-class neighborhoods with additional assisted housing.

Whether all these challenges can be surmounted or not, social mix planning should be approached with a substantial dose of circumspection, sensitivity to contextual nuance, and modest expectations. Despite the volume of research related to social mix, I believe that many of the fundamental questions I have posed have not been answered with sufficient clarity and unanimity to warrant uncritical formulations of policy and plans. The literature is so inconsistent in its statistical methods and how it measures "neighborhood"—its "mix," scale, duration of exposure to residents, many other facets—that a definitive meta-analysis is impossible.[16] In this context I recommend a wide variety of programmatic responses to achieve social mix within the guidelines outlined above that are rigorously evaluated, and avoiding the error-prone "one-size-fits-all" approaches of the past.

Moreover, planners should not be lulled into thinking that social mix—even at its most successful—is a panacea for disadvantage (Joseph, Chaskin, and Webber 2006). Neighborhood environment alone may be insufficient to change drastically the economic prospects of adults who lack basic human capital, social skills, or means of transportation that would unlock doors of opportunity. Similarly, youth may gain few payoffs from a mixed neighborhood if their networks predominantly connect them to their previous environments of concentrated disadvantage or they continue to enroll in inferior, underachieving school systems (Briggs, Popkin, and Goering 2010). It will take a more comprehensive set of social welfare interventions and supports to provide fair opportunities for all citizens, even in a world of socially mixed neighborhoods.

Conclusion

The thrust of the international evidence suggests that social mix policy can be justified on both equity and efficiency criteria if it aims to avoid high concentrations of disadvantaged individuals and instead promote residential diversity of groups according to the following principles:

- The key *compositional* aspect of mix is income, preferably of only modestly dissimilar socioeconomic status.
- Desired mixes should keep *concentrations* of low-income below thresholds (15-20 percent poverty in U.S. terms).
- Mixing below the *spatial scale* of hundreds of households is probably neither required nor beneficial.
- Many programmatic alternatives representing various compositions, concentrations, and scales within the above guidelines should be tried and evaluated.
- Strategies to achieve these goals should emphasize expansion of options for disadvantaged populations to live in socially mixed neighborhoods, which might involve either their voluntary moves

to such places and/or remaining in place as their original neighborhoods diversify.

Notes

This chapter has greatly benefited from commentary from Roland Atkinson, Naomi Carmon, Michael Darcy, Norman Fainstein, Derek Hyra, Mickey Lauria, Peter Marcuse, Phil Thompson, Ivan Tosics, Larry Vale, and anonymous reviewers. Daniel Beard and Claire Nowak-Boyd provided clerical assistance.

1. I recognize that there have been several critical writings claiming that social mix strategies involving redevelopment of social housing estates benefit the advantaged by displacing the disadvantaged from valuable land; see Smith and Stovall (2008) and Imbroscio (2008).

2. An unusually explicit articulation of such a position can be found in Andersson (2004).

3. I recognize that equity and efficiency goals are not mutually contradictory; one might achieve gains in both with a singular policy.

4. There are undoubtedly other frameworks in which to evaluate the relevance and import of the scholarly literature than the one I have offered here. I claim that my approach is innovative and sensible, but hardly definitive.

5. These statements apply to social mix per se, not to improvements in housing and neighborhood quality for lower-income families that might accompany the process of creating social mix.

6. I consider here only mechanisms related to social mix of the neighborhood. I also recognize that intra-neighborhood social processes are vitally contextualized by the local institutional infrastructure available, but variations in this dimension are overlooked here for simplicity. For reviews of neighborhood effect mechanisms, see Jencks and Mayer (1990), Duncan, Connell and Klebanov (1997), Gephart (1997), Friedrichs, (1998), Dietz (2002), Sampson, Morenoff, and Gannon-Rowley (2002), Ioannides and Loury (2004), and Galster (2011c). I also note that the evidence base is weak on the question of duration of exposure, i.e., how long exposure to neighborhood mix is supposed to take before consequences transpire (see Galster 2011c). However, sustained exposure to disadvantaged environments appears to generate more harms for adults (Musterd, Galster, and Andersson, 2012) and youth (Wodtke, Harding, and Elwert, 2011; Crowder and South, 2011).

7. Also see Leventhal and Brooks-Gunn (2000), Friedrichs, Galster, and Musterd (2003).

8. See the reviews in Kleinhans (2004) and Kleit (2008).

9. For a review, see Galster (2005).

10. Based on this, it has become fashionable for some to boldly and publicly assert that "MTO has proven that there are no important neighborhood effects." This is unjustified for many reasons. See Galster (2008, 2011a), Sampson (2008), and Clampet-Lundquist and Massey (2008).

11. Summary claims about specific mechanisms can be made with somewhat less assurance based on Western European statistical evidence on neighborhood effects, given the comparatively limited scope and mixed findings of this literature. See Musterd and Andersson (2005); van der Klaauw and van Ours (2003); McCulloch (2001), Buck (2001); Bolster et al. (2004).

12. Social mix in neighborhoods may lead to social mix in public schools, depending on local student assignment policies. Reviewing this literature is beyond the scope of this chapter, but might well be relevant when tallying benefits and costs to various groups.

13. In addition, Baum, Arthurson and Rickson (2010) find that high-income Australian individuals are much less likely to be satisfied with their neighborhood if they live in places with more income diversity, though the particular reasons for this are not disentangled.

14. Crowder and South (2011) have found substantial spatial spillovers from disadvantaged conditions in nearby census tracts.

15. This assumes a decision has already been reached that social mix is a superior option for residents than their current situation. It assumes, e.g., that social networks, collective efficacy, local institutions, and other potential assets have been thoroughly assessed.

16. For more on the challenges of quantifying neighborhood effects, see Galster (2008, 2010).

References

Allport, Gordon. 1954. *The Nature of Prejudice.* Cambridge, Mass.: Perseus.

Andersson, Eva. 2004. From valley of sadness to the hill of happiness: The significance of surroundings for socioeconomic career. *Urban Studies* 41(3): 641–59.

Andersson, Roger, and Sako Musterd. 2010. What scale matters? Exploring the relationships between individuals' social postion, neighbourhood context, and the scale of neighbourhood. *Geografiska Annaler: Series B, Human Geography* 92(1): 23–43.

Andersson, Roger, Sako Musterd, George Galster, and Timo Kauppinen. 2007. What mix matters for whom? Exploring the relationships between individuals' income and different measures of their neighborhood context. *Housing Studies* 23(5): 637–60.

Aslund, Olaf, and Peter Fredricksson. 2005. Ethnic enclaves and welfare cultures: Quasi-experimental evidence. Manuscript, Department of Economics, Uppsala University.

Atkinson, Roland, and Keith Kintrea. 1998. *Reconnecting Excluded Communities: Neighbourhood impacts of owner occupation.* Edinburgh: Scottish Homes.

———. 2000. Owner-occupation, social mix and neighborhood impacts. *Policy and Politics* 28: 93–108.

———. 2001. Area effects: What do they mean for British housing and regeneration policy? *European Journal of Housing Policy* 2(2): 147–66.

———. 2004. Opportunities and despair, it's all in there: Practitioner experiences and explanations of area effects and life chances. *Sociology* 38(3): 437–55.

Baum, Scott, Kathryn Arthurson, and Kara Rickson. 2010. Happy people in mixed-up places: The association between the degree and type of local socioeconomic mix and expressions of neighborhood satisfaction. *Urban Studies* 47: 467–85.

Beekman, Tony, Frank Lyons, and John Scott. 2001. *Improving the understanding of the influence of owner occupiers in mixed tenure neighborhoods.* Report 89. Edinburgh: ODS Limited for Scottish Homes.

Bertrand, Marianne, Erzo Luttmer, and Sendhil Mullainathan. 2000. Network effects and welfare cultures. *Quarterly Journal of Economics* 115(3): 1019–55.

Berube, Alan. 2005. *Mixed Communities in England: A U.S. perspective on evidence and policy proposals.* York: Joseph Roundtree Foundation

Blokland-Potters, Talja. 1998. *Wat Stadsbewoners Bindt: Sociale relaties in een achterstandswijk.* Kampen, Netherlands: Kok Agora.

Bolster, Anne, Simon Burgess, Ron Johnston, Kelvyn Jones, Carol Propper, and Rebecca Sarker. 2004. *Neighborhoods, households and income dynamics.* CMPO Working Paper Series 04/106. Bristol: University of Bristol.

Bourdieu, Pierre. 1999. *The weight of the world: Social suffering in contemporary society.* Palo Alto, Calif.: Stanford University Press.

Borjas, George. 1995. Ethnicity, neighborhoods, and human-capital externalities. *American Economic Review* 35: 365–90.

———. 1998. To ghetto or not to ghetto: Ethnicity and residential segregation. *Journal of Urban Economics* 44: 228–53.

Briggs, Xavier. 1997. Moving up versus moving out: Researching and interpreting neighborhood effects in housing mobility programs. *Housing Policy Debate* 8: 195–234.

———. 1998. Brown kids in white suburbs: Housing mobility and the many faces of social capital. *Housing Policy Debate* 9: 177–221.

———, ed. 2005. *The Geography of Opportunity.* Washington, D.C.: Brookings Institution Press.

Briggs, Xavier, Susan Popkin, and John Goering. 2010. *Moving to Opportunity.* New York: Oxford University Press.

Brophy, Paul, and Rhonda Smith. 1997. Mixed-income housing: Factors for success. *Cityscape* 3(2): 3–32.

Buck, Nick. 2001. Identifying neighborhood effects on social exclusion. *Urban Studies* 38: 2251–75.

Carmon, Naomi. 1976. Social Planning of Housing. *Journal of Social Policy* 5(1): 49–59.

———. 1999. Three generations of urban renewal policies: Analysis and policy implications. *Geoforum* 30(2): 144–58.

Case, Anne, and Lawrence Katz. 1991. *The company you keep: The effects of family and neighborhood on disadvantaged youth*. NBER Working Paper 3705. Cambridge, Mass.: National Bureau of Economic Research.

Chaskin, Robert, and Mark Joseph. 2010. Building "community" in mixed-income developments. *Urban Affairs Review* 45: 299–335.

Cheshire, Paul. 2007. *Are mixed-income communities the answer to segregation and poverty?* York: Joseph Rowntree Foundation.

Clampet-Lundquist, Susan. 2004. HOPE VI relocation: Moving to new neighborhoods and building new ties. *Housing Policy Debate* 15(3): 415–47.

Clampet-Lundquist, Susan, and Douglas Massey. 2008. Neighborhood effects on economic self-sufficiency: A reconsideration of the Moving to Opportunity experiment. *American Journal of Sociology* 114(1): 107–43.

Clark, Kenneth, and Stephen Drinkwater. 2002. Enclaves, neighborhood effects and employment outcomes: Ethnic minorities in England and Wales. *Journal of Population Economics* 15: 5–29.

Cole, Ian, Glen Gidley, Charles Ritchie, Don Simpson, and Benita Wishart. 1997. Creating communities of welfare housing? A study of housing association developments in Yorkshire/Humberside. Coventry: Chartered Institute of Housing.

Cole, Ian, and Barry Goodchild. 2001. Social mix and the "balanced community" in British housing policy: A tale of two epochs. *Geo Journal* 51: 351-60.

Crowder, Kyle, and Scott South. 2011. Spatial and temporal dimensions of neighborhood effects on high school graduation. *Social Science Research* 40: 87–106.

Cutler, David, Edward Glaeser, and Jacob Vigdor. 2008. When are ghettos bad? Lessons from immigrant segregation in the United States. *Journal of Urban Economics* 63: 759-74.

Darcy, Michael. 2010. Deconcentration of disadvantage and mixed income housing: A critical discourse approach. *Housing, Theory and Society* 27: 1–22.

Dean, Jo, and Annette Hastings. 2000. *Challenging images: Housing estates, stigma and regeneration*. Bristol: Policy Press and Joseph Rowntree Foundation.

Delorenzi, Simone 2006. Introduction. In *Going Places: Neighbourhood, Ethnicity and Social Mobility*, ed. Simone Delorenzi, 1–11. London: Institute for Public Policy Research.

Diehr, Paula, Thomas Koepsel, Allen Cheadle, Bruce Psaty, Edward Wagner, and Susan Curry. 1993. Do communities differ in health behaviors? *Journal of Clinical Epidemiology* 46: 1141–49.

Dietz, Robert. 2002. The estimation of neighborhood effects in the social sciences. *Social Science Research* 31: 539–75.

Duncan, Craig, and Kelvyn Jones. 1995. Individuals and their ecologies: Analyzing the geography of chronic illness within a multi-level modeling framework, *Journal of Health and Place* 1: 27–40.

Duncan, Greg, James Connell, and Patricia Klebanov. 1997. Conceptual and methodological issues in estimating causal effects of neighborhoods and family conditions
on individual development. In *Neighborhood poverty*, vol. 1, *Context and consequences for children*, ed. Jeanne Brooks-Gunn, Greg J. Duncan, and J. Lawrence
Aber, 219–50. New York: Russell Sage.

Edin, Per-Anders, Peter Fredricksson, and Olaf Aslund. 2003. Ethnic enclaves and the
economic success of immigrants: Evidence from a natural experiment. *Quarterly
Journal of Economics* 113: 329–57.

Ellen, Ingrid, Michael Schill, Scott Susin, and Amy Schwartz. 2001. Building homes, reviving neighborhoods: Spillovers from subsidized construction of owner-occupied
housing in New York City. *Journal of Housing Research* 12(2): 185–216.

Emerson, Michael, Rachel Kimbro, and George Yancey. 2002. Contact theory extended.
Social Science Quarterly 83(3): 745–61.

Farwick, Andreas. 2004. Spatial isolation, social networks, and the economic integration of migrants in poverty areas. Paper presented at Inside Poverty Areas conference, University of Koln, November.

Fernandez, Roberto, and David Harris. 1992. Social isolation and the underclass. In
Drugs, crime and social isolation, ed. Adele Harrell and George Peterson, 257–93.
Washington, D.C.: Urban Institute Press.

Forrest, Ray, and Ade Kearns. 1999. *Joined-up places? Social cohesion and neighbourhood
regeneration*. York: Joseph Rowntree Foundation.

Freeman, Lance, and Hilary Botein. 2002. Subsidized housing and neighborhood impacts: A theoretical discussion and review of the evidence. *Journal of Planning
Literature* 16: 359–78.

Friedrichs, Jürgen. 1998. Do poor neighborhoods make their residents poorer? Context
effects of poverty neighborhoods on their residents. In *Empirical poverty research
in a comparative perspective*, ed. Hans-Jurgen Andress, 77–99. Aldershot: Ashgate.

Friedrichs, Jürgen, George Galster, and Sako Musterd. 2003. Neighborhood effects on
social opportunities: The European and American research and policy context.
Housing Studies 18(6): 797–806.

Galster, George. 2001. On the nature of neighbourhood. *Urban Studies* 38: 2111–24.

———. 2002. An economic efficiency analysis of deconcentrating poverty populations.
Journal of Housing Economics 11: 303–29.

———. 2005. *Neighbourhood mix, social opportunities, and the policy challenges of an increasingly diverse Amsterdam*. Amsterdam: University of Amsterdam, Department
of Geography, Planning, and International Development Studies.

———. 2008. Quantifying the effect of neighbourhood on individuals: Challenges, alternative approaches and promising directions. *Journal of Applied Social Science
Studies (Schmollers Jahrbuch/Zeitscrift fur Wirtschafts- und Sozialwissenschaften)*
128: 7–48.

———. 2011a. Changing the geography of opportunity by helping poor households
move out of concentrated poverty: Neighborhood effects and policy design. In

Neighborhood and life chances: How place matters in modern America, ed. Harriett Newburger, Eugenie Birch, and Susan Wachter, 221–34. Philadelphia: University of Pennsylvania Press.

———. 2011b. U.S. Assisted housing programs and poverty deconcentration: A critical geographic review paper. Presented at ESRC conference on neighbourhood-based policies, Glasgow, April.

———. 2011c The mechanism(s) of neighbourhood effects: Theory, evidence, and policy implications. In *Neighbourhood effects research: New perspectives*, ed. Maarten van Ham, David Manley, Nick Bailey, Ludi Simpson, and Duncan Maclennan, 23–56. Dordrecht: Springer.

Galster, George, Roger Andersson, and Sako Musterd. 2010. Who is affected by neighborhood income mix? *Urban Studies* 47(14): 2915–44.

Galster, George, Roger Andersson, Sako Musterd, and Timo Kauppinen. 2008. Does neighborhood income mix affect earnings of adults? New evidence from Sweden. *Journal of Urban Economics* 63: 858–70.

Galster, George, Jackie Cutsinger, and Ron Malega. 2008. The costs of concentrated poverty: Neighborhood property markets and the dynamics of decline. In *Revisiting rental housing: Policies, programs, and priorities*, ed. Nicholas Retsinas and Eric Belsky, 93–113. Washington, D.C.: Brookings Institution Press.

Galster, George, Kurt Metzger, and Ruth Waite. 1999. Neighborhood opportunity structures and immigrants' socioeconomic advancement. *Journal of Housing Research* 10(1): 95–127.

Galster, George, Sako Musterd, and Roger Andersson. 2010. Threshold effects on individuals from changing neighborhood income composition. Paper presented at Association of Public Policy Analysis and Management meetings, Boston, November.

Galster, George, Anna Santiago, Robin Smith, and Peter Tatian. 1999. *Assessing property value impacts of dispersed housing subsidy programs*. Washington, D.C.: U.S. Department of Housing and Urban Development, Policy Development and Research.

Galster, George, Peter Tatian, Anna Santiago, Kathryn Pettit, and Robin Smith. 2003. *Why NOT in my back yard? Neighborhood impacts of assisted housing*. New Brunswick, N.J.: CUPR/Rutgers University Press.

Galster, George, Peter Tatian, and Robin Smith. 1999. The impact of neighbors who use Section 8 certificates on property values. *Housing Policy Debate* 10(4): 879–917.

Gans, Herbert. 1961. The balanced community: homogeneity or heterogeneity in residential areas? *Journal of the American Institute of Planners* 27(3): 176–84.

Gephart, Martha. 1997. Neighborhoods and communities as contexts for development. In *Neighborhood Poverty*. Vol. 1, *Context and Consequences for Children*, ed. Jeanne Brooks-Gunn, Gregory J. Duncan, and J. Lawrence Aber, 1–43. New York: Sage.

Ginther, Donna, Robert Haveman, and Barbara Wolfe. 2000. Neighbourhood attributes as determinants of children's outcomes. *Journal of Human Resources.* 35: 603–42.

Goering, John, and Judith Feins, eds. 2003. *Choosing a better life? Evaluating the Moving to Opportunity experiment*. Washington, D.C.: Urban Institute Press.

Goodchild, Barry, and Ian Cole. 2001. Social balance and mixed neighbourhoods in Britain since 1979. *Environment and Planning D* 19(1): 103–21.

Gordon, Ian, and Vassilas Monastiriotis. 2006. Urban size, spatial segregation and inequality in educational outcomes. *Urban Studies* 43(1): 213–36.

Hastings, Annette. 2004. Stigma and social housing estates. *Journal of Housing and the Built Environment* 19(3): 233–54.

Hastings, Annette, and Jo. Dean. 2003. Challenging images: Tackling stigma through estate regeneration. *Policy and Politics* 31(2): 171–84.

Helleman, Gerben and Frank Wassenberg. 2004. The renewal of what was tomorrow's idealistic city: Amsterdam's Bijlmermeer high-rise. *Cities* 21: 3–17.

Ihlanfeldt, Keith, and Benjamin Scafidi. 2002. The neighborhood contact hypothesis. *Urban Studies* 39: 619–41.

Imbroscio, David. 2008. "United and actuated by some common impulse of passion": Challenging the dispersal consensus in American housing policy research. *Journal of Urban Affairs* 30(2): 111–30.

Ioannides, Yannis, and Laura Loury. 2004. Job information networks, neighborhood effects, and inequality. *Journal of Economic Literature* 42: 1056–93.

Jencks, Christopher, and Sandra Mayer. 1990. The social consequences of growing up in a poor neighborhood. In *Inner-city poverty in the United States*, ed. Laurence E. Lynn and Michael F. H. McGeary, 111–86. Washington, D.C.: National Academy Press.

Johnson, Jennifer, and Beata Bednarz. 2002. *Neighborhood effects of the low income housing tax credit program: Final Report.* Washington D.C.: U.S. Department of Housing and Urban Development.

Joseph, Mark. 2006. Is mixed-income development an antidote to urban poverty? *Housing Policy Debate* 17(2): 209–34.

———. 2010. Creating mixed-income developments in Chicago: Developer and service provider perspectives. *Housing Policy Debate* 20(1): 91–118.

Joseph, Mark, Robert Chaskin, and Henry Webber. 2006. The theoretical basis for addressing poverty through mixed-income development. *Urban Affairs Review* 42(3): 369–409.

Jupp, Ben. 1999. *Living together: Community life on mixed-tenure estates.* London: Demos.

Katz, Laurence, Jeffrey Kling, and Jeffrey Liebman. 2001. Moving to Opportunity in Boston: Early results of a randomized mobility experiment. *Quarterly Journal of Economics* 116(2): 607–54.

Kearns, Ade. 2002. Response: From residential disadvantage to opportunity? Reflections on British and European policy and research. *Housing Studies* 17(1): 145–50.

Kleinhans, Reinout. 2004. Social implications of housing diversification in urban renewal: A review of recent literature. *Journal of Housing and the Built Environment* 19: 367–90.

Kleinhans, Reinout, and David Varady, 2011. Moving out and going down? A review of recent evidence on negative spillover effects of housing restructuring programmes in the United States and the Netherlands. *International Journal of Housing Policy* 11(2): 155–74.

Kleit, Rachel. 2001a. The role of neighborhood social networks in scattered-site public housing residents' search for jobs. *Housing Policy Debate* 12(3): 541–73.

———. 2001b. Neighborhood relations in scattered-site and clustered public housing. *Journal of Urban Affairs* 23: 409–30.

———. 2002. Job search networks and strategies in scattered-site public housing. *Housing Studies* 17(1): 83–100.

———. 2008. Neighborhood segregation, personal networks, and access to social resources. In *Segregation: The rising costs for America*, ed. James Carr and Nandinee Kutty, 237–60. New York: Routledge.

Kling, Jeffrey, Jeffrey Liebman, and Laurence Katz. 2007. Experimental analysis of neighborhood effects. *Econometrica* 75(1): 83–119.

Knies, Gundi. 2007. Keeping up with the Schmidts: Do better-off neighbours make people unhappy? Paper presented at the workshop: Neighborhood Effects Studies on the Basis of European Micro-Data, Humboldt University, Berlin, March.

Krivo, Lauren, and Ruth Peterson. 1996. Extremely disadvantaged neighborhoods and urban crime. *Social Forces* 75: 619–50.

Leventhal, Tama, and Jeanne Brooks-Gunn. 2000. The neighborhoods they live in. *Psychological Bulletin* 126(2): 309–37.

Levy, Diane, Jennifer Comey, and Sandra Padilla. 2006. *In the face of gentrification: Case studies of local efforts to mitigate displacement.* Washington, D.C.: Urban Institute.

Ludwig, Jens, Gregory Duncan, and Paul Hirschfield. 2001. Urban poverty and juvenile crime: Evidence from a randomized housing-mobility experiment. *Quarterly Journal of Economics* 116(2): 655–79.

Ludwig, Jens, Gregory Duncan, and Jeff Pinkston. 2000. Neighbourhood effects on economic self-sufficiency: Evidence from a randomized housing-mobility experiment. JCPR Working Paper 159. http://www.nber.org/mtopublic/baltimore/mto_balt_employment.pdf, accessed 22 February 2012

Ludwig, Jens, Helen Ladd, and Gregory Duncan. 2001. The effects of urban poverty on educational outcomes: Evidence from a randomized experiment. *Brookings-Wharton Papers on Urban Affairs* (July 16): 147–201.

Ludwig, Jens, Jeffrey B. Liebman, Jeffrey R. Kling, Greg J. Duncan, Lawrence F. Katz, Ronald C. Kessler, and Lisa Sanbonmatsu. 2008. What can we learn about neighborhood effects from the Moving to Opportunity experiment? *American Journal of Sociology* 114(1): 144–88.

Martin, Graham, and Judy Watkinson. 2003. *Rebalancing communities by mixing tenures on existing rented housing estates.* York: Joseph Rowntree.

McCulloch, Andrew. 2001. Ward-level deprivation and individual social and economic outcomes in the British household panel survey. *Environment and Planning* A 33: 667–84.

Meen, Geoffrey. 2006. Modelling local deprivation and segregation in England. Unpublished paper, University of Reading.

Meen, Geoffrey, Kenneth Gibb, Jennifer Goody, Thomas McGrath, and Jane Mackinnon. 2005. *Economic segregation in England*. York: Joseph Rowntree Foundation.

Musterd, Sako 2002. Response: Mixed housing policy: A European (Dutch) perspective. *Housing Studies* 17(1): 139–44.

———. 2003. Segregation and integration: A contested relationship. *Journal of Ethnic and Migration Studies* 29(4): 623–41.

Musterd, Sako and Roger Andersson. 2005. Housing mix, social mix and social opportunities. *Urban Affairs Review* 40(6): 761–90.

———. 2006. Employment, social mobility and neighbourhood effects. *International Journal of Urban and Regional Research* 30(1): 120–40.

Musterd, Sako, Roger Andersson, George Galster, and Timo Kauppinen. 2008. Are immigrants' earnings affected by the characteristics of their neighbours? *Environment and Planning* A 40: 785–805.

Musterd, Sako, George Galster, and Roger Andersson. 2012. Temporal dimensions and the measurement of neighbourhood Effects. *Environment and Planning* A 44: 605–27.

Musterd, Sako, Wim Ostendorf, and Sjoerd de Vos. 2003. Neighborhood effects and social mobility: A longitudinal study. *Housing Studies* 18(6): 877–92.

Norris, Michelle. 2006. Developing, designing and managing mixed tenure housing estates, *European Planning Studies* 14(2): 199–218.

Oberwittler, Dietrich. 2004. Neighborhood disadvantage and adolescent adjustment: Responses of adolescents to disorder and violent subcultures. Paper presented at Inside Poverty Areas conference, University of Cologne, November.

———. 2007. The effects of neighbourhood poverty on adolescent problem behaviours: A multi-level analysis differentiated by gender and ethnicity. *Housing Studies* 22(6): 781–804.

Orr, Larry, Judith D. Feins, Robin Jacob, and Erik Beecroft. 2003. *Moving to Opportunity: Interim impacts evaluation, final report*. Washington, D.C.: U.S. Department of Housing and Urban Development, Policy Development and Research.

Ostendorf, Wim, Sako Musterd, and Sjoerd de Vos. 2001. Social mix and the neighborhood effect: Policy ambition and empirical support. *Housing Studies* 16(3): 371–80.

Pawson, Hal, Kirk Karryn, and Sarah McIntosh. 2000. *Assessing the impact of tenure diversification: The case of Niddrie, Edinburgh*. Edinburgh: Scottish Homes.

Permentier, Matthieu. 2009. Reputation, neighbourhoods and behaviour. Ph.D. dissertation, Faculty of Geosciences, Utrecht University, Netherlands Geographical Studies 383.

Permentier, Matthieu, Gideon Bolt, and Maarten van Ham. 2007. Comparing residents' and non-residents' assessments of neighbourhood reputations. Paper presented at American Association of Geographers meetings, San Francisco, April.

Pettigrew, Thomas F., and Linda R. Tropp. 2006. A meta-analytic test of intergroup contact theory. *Journal of Personality and Social Psychology* 90(5): 751–83.

Pinkster, Fenne. 2008. Living in concentrated poverty. Ph.D. dissertation, Department of Geography, Planning, and International Development Studies, University of Amsterdam.

Power, Anne. 1997. *Estates on the edge: The social consequences of mass housing in Northern Europe.* London: Macmillan.

Rosenbaum, Emily, Laura Harris, and Nancy Denton. 2003. New places, new faces: An analysis of neighborhoods and social ties among MTO movers in Chicago. In *Choosing a better life? Evaluating the Moving to Opportunity experiment,* ed. John Goering and Judith Feins, 275–310. Washington, D.C.: Urban Institute Press.

Rosenbaum, James. 1991. Black pioneers: Do moves to the suburbs increase economic opportunity for mothers and children? *Housing Policy Debate* 2: 1179–213.

Sampson, Robert. 2008. Moving to inequality: Neighborhood effects and experiments meet social structure. *American Journal of Sociology* 114(1): 189–231.

Sampson, Robert, and W. Byron Groves. 1989. Community structure and crime: Testing social disorganization theory. *American Journal of Sociology* 94(4): 774–802.

Sampson, Robert, Jeffrey Morenoff, and Thomas Gannon-Rowley. 2002. Assessing "neighborhood effects": Social processes and new directions in research. *Annual Review of Sociology* 28: 443–78.

Santiago, Anna, George Galster, and Peter Tatian. 2001. Assessing the property value impacts of the dispersed housing subsidy program in Denver. *Journal of Policy Analysis and Management* 20(1): 65–88.

Sarkissian, Wendy. 1976. The idea of social mix in town planning: An historical overview. *Urban Studies* 13(3): 231–46.

Schill, Michael. 1997. Chicago's new mixed-income communities strategy: The future face of public housing? In *Affordable housing and urban redevelopment in the United States,* ed. Willem Van Vliet, 135–57. Thousand Oaks, Calif.: Sage.

Schill, Michael, Ingrid Gould Ellen, Amy Ellen Schwartz, and Ioan Voicu. 2002. Revitalizing inner-city neighborhoods: New York City's ten year plan. *Housing Policy Debate* 13(3): 529–66.

Schwartz, Amy, Ingrid Ellen, and Ioan Voicu. 2002. Estimating the external effects of subsidized housing investment on property values. New York: Report Presented to NBER Universities Research Conference.

Shouls, Susanna, Peter Congdon, and Sarah Curtis. 1996. Modeling inequality in reported long term illness in the UK. *Journal of Epidemiology and Community Health* 50: 366–76.

Smith, Janet L. and David Stovall. 2008. "Coming Home" to new homes and new schools: Critical race theory and the new politics of containment. *Journal of Educational Policy* 23(2): 135–52.

South, Scott, and Eric Baumer. 2000. Deciphering community and race effects on adolescent pre-marital childbearing. *Social Forces* 78: 1379–407.

Taylor, Marilyn. 1998. Combating the social exclusion of housing estates. *Housing Studies* 13(6): 819–32.

Tiggs, Leann M., Irene Browne, and Gary P. Green. 1998. Social isolation of the urban poor. *Sociological Quarterly* 39(1): 53–77.

Tunstall, Rebecca, and Alex Fenton. 2006. *In the mix: A review of mixed income, mixed tenure and mixed communities.* York: Joseph Rowntree, English Partnerships, and Housing Corporation.

Van Beckhoven, Ellen, and Ronald Van Kempen. 2003. Social effects of urban restructuring: A case study in Amsterdam and Utrecht, the Netherlands. *Housing Studies* 18(6): 853–75.

Van der Klaauw, Bas, and Jan van Ours. 2003. From welfare to work: Does the neighborhood matter? *Journal of Public Economics* 87: 957–85.

Van Ham, Maarten, and David Manley. 2009. The effect of neighbourhood housing tenure mix on labour market outcomes: A longitudinal investigation of neighbourhood effects, *Journal of Economic Geography* online, May 8: doi:10.1093/jeg/lbp017.

Van Kempen, Ronald, and Gideon Bolt. 2009. Social cohesion, social mix, and urban policies in the Netherlands. *Journal of Housing and the Built Environment* 24(4): 457–75.

Vartanian, Thomas. 1999a. Adolescent neighborhood effects on labor market and economic outcomes. *Social Service Review* 73(2): 142–67.

———. 1999b. Childhood conditions and adult welfare use. *Journal of Marriage and the Family* 61: 225–37.

Wacquant, Loïc. 1993. Urban outcasts: Stigma and division in the black American ghetto and the French periphery. *International Journal of Urban and Regional Research* 17(3): 366–83.

Weinberg, Bruce, Patricia Reagan, and Jeffrey Yankow. 2004. Do neighborhoods affect work behavior? Evidence from the NLSY79. *Journal of Labor Economics* 22(4): 891–924.

Wodtke, Geoffrey, David Harding, and Felix Elwert. 2011. Neighborhood effects in temporal perspective: The impact of long-term exposure to concentrated disadvantage on high school graduation. *American Sociological Review* 76(5): 713–36.

Chapter 16

Suspicion, Surveillance, and Safety: A New Imperative for Public Space?

Tridib Banerjee and Anastasia Loukaitou-Sideris

Openness, access, trust, freedom of speech, and diversity have always been the essential tenets of Western liberal democracies, in contrast to the non-democratic societies where such features are conspicuously absent. For the purposes of this chapter this assumption does not require empirical validation from polling data affirming that a certain percentage of the general population believes in these values. Instead we will simply accept them as a normative proposition which has guided the ideals of liberal democracies. In other words, these are precisely "democracy's values," as Shapiro and Hacker-Cordon (1999) have emphasized.

Accordingly, we argue that these features, which have historically defined the normative essence of Western liberal democracies, are increasingly compromised by a rising obsession with safety, security, and surveillance in the post 9/11 era. If 9/11 symbolized a terrorist act designed to damage the core values of Western liberal democracy, seemingly it has succeeded—not because of the loss of many thousands of lives and two iconic skyscrapers—but because of the chipping away in its after-effect of many of those things that are important to liberal democracies.

Our focus here is on public space, how it functions, how it is conceived, and, indeed, its very nature, which is now being challenged or redefined. Even before 9/11, the increasing privatization of public space in the name of efficiency had curtailed some of the rights and privileges of its use. The market provision of public goods has contributed to a decline in the intensity and diversity of social contacts as certain social groups are excluded through implicit price mechanisms. With public space being treated as a market "good," the public realm has begun to atrophy. This chapter will examine the roots, causes, and human consequences of these phenomena, which some have called "the assault on public space" (Smith and Low 2006).

We argue here that this "assault" is of two varieties: The first is intellectual in tenet, neoliberal to be specific, that promotes the growing trend of the "enclosure of the commons" as an efficient outcome of public service provision, as in the case of Common Interest Developments (or CIDs) (Webster and Lee 2006). This position treats public space as a "public good" that is undersupplied, and therefore over-used, leading to a decline in the quality of resource. It sees an efficient outcome obtained from institutional design that offers exclusive rights to certain groups willing to pay a price to consume public space (Webster 2007). The second kind stems from the ever-increasing "seeing" needs of the modern state, to draw from the critiques of James C. Scott (1998). In the current context, the obsession for visibility and "legibility" is facilitated by the ascendancy of modern technology, and legitimized by the fear of disorder, subversion, and insurgency resulting from geopolitical tensions. Consequently, the ubiquity and proliferation of surveillance of the commons become a form of encumbrance of civil liberties and public trust, and often involve targeting and "profiling" selected social groups.

In this chapter, we examine the rise of a surveillance society in a historic context associated with risk, danger, and the fear of disorder, tracing its roots in the proliferation of state bureaucracies and the development of nation states. We also examine the role of information and communication technologies—advances that have not only obviated face-to-face interactions and place-based social contacts, but have also made the public realm subject to the constant "gaze" of security cameras in a "panopticon" society (Foucault 1977).

Moreover, we explore how modernist urban planning practices have exacerbated the segregation of urban life, the social construction and vilification of the "other," and the scrutiny of the "stranger" by separating the city into "single-minded" spaces (Walzer 1986), socially uniform territories, exclusive locales, and privatized public spaces, what critics refer to as "fortress communities" and "fortress cities" (Coaffee 2009; Blakely and Snyder 1995; Davis 1990). Finally, we conclude the essay by re-imagining the future of public space.

The Concept of Public Space

But what is public space? The common tendency is to define it by what it is not, or in contradistinction to private space, as in a mutually exclusive bipolar relationship. This distinction between the private and the public has become contentious, however. It has undergone deep transformations both existentially and theoretically, influenced by the social, political, and institutional developments of the last century. We now turn to the more nuanced views of this concept and the intellectual traditions that have influenced them.

In Western liberal democracies, the roles and purposes of public space and its functions are intrinsic to the larger concepts of the public sphere and public realm. These two notions in turn are foundationally related to the distinction between the private and the public in liberal political philosophy, a distinction based on imperatives of property and citizenship rights as they are understood in the modern era. In the Habermasian conception of the bourgeois public sphere, private citizens (albeit the bourgeois and elite classes only) participated in public discourse about the affairs of the state. Although Habermas (1991) was not very specific about existential spaces of that discourse, we can assume that he had in mind the Greek agora of pre-modern times, which served such a purpose. Thus, the public sphere and public space were synonymous in the direct democracy of the city state (Sennett 1994). It is this notion of the public in the Greek city state that inspired Hannah Arendt's (1959) distinction between the private realm of the home and the public realm of all that lies outside the threshold to one's home. While this public realm includes streets, alleys, passages, walkways, parks, plazas, and squares, it may no longer map easily onto the current idea of the public sphere, which essentially comprises a space of communication—of dialogue, discourse, and debate. In the modern era, this space of communication is a product of social and political institutions, the media, and the internet. Thus the recent rise of the "blogosphere" and social network sites, with its associated *cybercivitas*, continues to obviate the possibilities of material public space as an arena of public discourse.

The issue is further confounded by the distinction between public and private. How to map them on urban space remains a vexing challenge, as the boundaries between the two often blur or remain implicit, and are dictated by institutional or temporal changes (Steinberger 1999). Referring to this tension between public and private as the "grand dichotomy," Weintraub (1995) names four different intellectual traditions that have historically addressed it: political theory, liberal economic theory, social theory, and feminist theory. These theoretical categories offer us a framework to explore the changing notions of the public space in the context of our explorations here.

Political theorists define the "public" in the context of citizenship, public sphere, democracy, and civil society, as espoused by such authors as Kohn (2004), Bickford (2000), and Barber (1998). Kohn argues quite forcefully that political imperatives of public space are fundamentally linked to First Amendment rights in the United States, and thus must be protected, nurtured, and expanded. Street demonstrations, the Bible preacher, the Hyde Park style soap box oratory, or street corner advocacy for the local unions or ballot initiatives during election times ("honk if you support us"), are all exercises of the First Amendment rights that require a physical setting, which still has no counterpart in the *cybercivitas*. Eminent examples are the demonstrations in Tiananmen Square, Beijing, in 1989, downtown Seattle in 1999, Paris in 2005, Tahrir Square in Cairo in 2011, and many other instances where public spaces served as the setting for the expression of citizens' beliefs, ideology, or dissent.

Liberal economic theory, on the other hand, often conflates the distinction between public and private with that between state and market, or between public and private goods. This distinction is, however, becoming increasingly tenuous. The state is becoming increasingly "hollow"[1] (Milward and Provan 2000) and entrepreneurial (Frieden and Sagalyn 1990), outsourcing conventional public goods to the market place and assuming the corporate role of a firm, often in partnership with the private sector.

This blurring of the distinction between the two sectors, where the public sector emulates and behaves like the private sector, is now well established in academia and the professions. In the 1990s, the profession of public administration tried to reinvent itself as "public management," and the neoliberal notion of servicing the customers supplanted the old norm of serving the citizens. Now we are in the decade of celebrating and promoting the notion of cross-sectoral governance (that includes the nonprofit sector) and the possibility of the voluntary city (Beito, Gordon, and Tabarrok 2000).

The third distinction between the private and public arises out of various tenets of social theory: social life, social contact, sociability, civility, community, and public life. All of these constructs involve our engagement in the public, our public personae, our public encounters, social contacts, conviviality, and so on. In this conception of the public, the conventional representations of public space—parks, squares, plazas, promenades, and so on—are quite relevant and indeed remain one of the few claims for the role of the public space in building the public sphere, civil society, and perhaps social capital. Nevertheless, the modern era has seen a rise of privatism that includes withdrawal from public life. Sennett (1977) bemoans this trend as "the fall of public man," an outcome also opposite to what Hannah Arendt desired in her classic treatise *The Human Condition*—the development of a public persona. Bickford (2000) suggests that two elements were central to the notion of public life that concern public space: (a) diversity and multiplicity of ideas and opinions; and (b) exposure to risk, vulnerability, and individual control. Public life also prepares one to cope with such risks and uncertainties, deal with diverse views, and even develop a sense of community.

Finally, in feminist theories the distinction between the family and the household, or the household and the political community (to invoke Aristotle) is the essence of the private and the public. Indeed, many feminist theorists have argued that in some cultures—Islamic, Korean, and up to the mid-nineteenth-century European—this distinction is tantamount to a gendering of urban space (Fraser 1992). According to these cultural norms, public space is a male domain—where women are intruders and hence have to cover themselves with *hijab* or *burkah*, as if to become invisible (Mernissi 1987). In contrast, the domestic space of the dwelling is a female domain with varying degrees of restrictions on male access.

These perspectives frame our discussion of the changing imperatives of public space and the implications for planning and urban design.

Risk and Danger in Public Space

The intrinsic qualities of public space—openness, accessibility, freedom of speech, and diversity—are a threat to state authorities and private agencies who view those very properties as contributing to anomie, disorder, risk, and danger. Public spaces provide opportunities for unpredictable encounters with diverse social elements, which may involve discomfort, disruption, or even danger (Loukaitou-Sideris and Ehrenfeucht 2009).

Public feelings of vulnerability have become widespread even though the probability of being a victim of random street crime or a terrorist attack remains small. Yet, it is this fear of being victimized—or worse—blown up en masse that leads to a different form of public vulnerability, where civil liberty is conceded to a higher state authority, the result being a "prostrate civil society" (see Scott 1998). The post-9/11 U.S. is a case in point, as Michael Sorkin and others have pointed out (Sorkin 2008).

And it is not only in the United States, but also in other parts of the world, where public spaces have taken on additional and unpredictable risks. Typical targets of car bombs and suicide bombers are buildings, the people inside, and those in the vicinity. Settings like shopping streets, bazaars, bus stops, train stations, market places, stadiums, mosques, temples, and the like, which are part of the quotidian life, become targets because of the predictable assembly of crowds (Coaffee et al. 2009). Similarly, political rallies, as well as religious or civil celebrations, which draw crowds in conspicuous public spaces, are vulnerable targets of terrorist attacks.

But streets and squares also have the potential to serve as theaters of dissent, and this right to "take to the streets" underlies the freedom of expression and democracy (Mitchell 1996). The scripts of dissensus in public space are quite familiar in modern times: marches, sit-ins, rallies, candlelight vigils, and other forms of peaceful civil protests. Occasionally, protests may involve more aggressive and violent disorder like trashing and burning public properties or even hostile confrontation with police and the throwing of rocks or Molotov cocktails, met with the predictable response of water jets, tear gas, and even bullets from state authorities. These are all a part of the historical dynamic of cultural, political, and social change (Irázabal 2008).

Uses of public space for the expression of dissent and for the safeguarding of democracy represent a fundamental "right to the city" (Lefebvre 1968; also see Kohn 2004; Smith and Low 2006), one that is progressively threatened by the "dark side" of public spaces, their perception as settings fraught with risk, danger, and crime. Indeed, the fear of disorder and risk in public space has resulted historically in counter-actions on the part of the authorities, the state, and individual citizens. In the sections that follow, we will examine two phenomena that have had profound impacts on public spaces: (1) the rise of a surveillance society; and (2) the enclosure and encroachment of the commons.

The Rise of a Surveillance Society

The 9/11 terrorist attacks in the U.S. and the subsequent bombings of commuter trains in Madrid and public transportation in London have led to heightened feelings of fear, vulnerability, and suspicion that have been used to justify efforts to enclose, protect, privatize, and control the settings of public life. In reality, current events have simply exacerbated processes that were long under way (Sorkin 2008). At least three distinct phenomena have contributed to the rise and expansion of a surveillance society in Western democracies: (a) the development of state bureaucracies associated with the emergence of modernity in the early nineteenth century; (b) the proliferation and mass marketing of computer and digital technologies in the second half of the twentieth century; and (c) the fear of and reaction to terrorist attacks in the twenty-first century. In the following section, we will discuss these events and trace their spatial implications on the public space and public realm of cities.

Emergence of nation states, public bureaucracies and their "seeing" needs. The roots of the current preoccupation with surveillance and the emphasis on control, regulation, and order go back to the emergence of modernity and the rise of the modern nation-state in Western societies (Sennett 1977; Giddens 1985). As James C. Scott (1998) has effectively argued, the authority of the modern state essentially stems from scientific and technological advances that allow for organization, order, and efficiency in administration. The modern state has always had a need to see everything, and this quest for "legibility" leads to a propensity for collection and storage of information: cadastral mapping, census, tax rolls, aerial photography, soil survey, land use data and the like (Scott 1998). In a modern state, all individuals must have some traceable identity that comes with citizenship rights, an ability to earn income, obtain credit, and many other such requirements of being a modern individual. In the process, self and identity become two different things. Identity de-linked from self becomes a mere possession that can even be stolen these days. The "seeing" need of the modern state has reduced the humanity of society to mere digital identities that can be accessed and stored. This has now matured into ubiquitous electronic surveillance, which includes routine gathering of information about people and objects, and continuous oversight of people's activities in urban spaces (Dandekar 1990).

Modernity has been associated with the materialization of state bureaucracies and municipal organizations whose power grew with their capacity to collect, classify, and store information about people, their property, and their activities (Giddens 1990). The emergence of the modern nation-state brought about the proliferation of specialized bureaucratic institutions with the goal of supervising and managing the external and internal affairs of the state. While pre-modern societies had limited capabilities of surveillance, the development of policing and criminal justice systems enabled the modern state to exercise unprecedented degrees of control and supervision over its subjects (Giddens 1985).

The surveillance capabilities of modern states also had spatial connotations. In earlier times, the need for surveillance and control was primarily geared towards external enemies and forces. Danger and disorder were perceived to be external threats. With the rise of modern capitalist states and evolving class societies, the accumulation of wealth in the hands of a few, and the conceptualization of cities as worlds of strangers, the danger of upheaval, crime, disorder, and rioting was increasingly perceived as coming from the inside. Whereas acropolises and castles were once raised to protect from attacks of external enemies, prisons and asylums were built by modern states to warehouse troublesome citizens. Baron Haussmann's wide and straight new boulevards of Paris had a strategic motive: to facilitate troop movement for the effective policing of neighborhoods and the squelching of possible riots in Napoleon III's capital. Additionally, Haussmann's massive reconstruction was intended to modernize and give "a high level of orderliness" to city streets and public spaces (Lofland 1998: 191-92).

The drafting of city charters in the cities of the early nineteenth-century United States, with the ensuing issuance of municipal ordinances, and later zoning regulations, provided instructions for orderly spatial arrangements, but also gave a legal framework to cities against which the appropriateness of citizen actions and behavior in public space could be measured. The development of a system of municipal taxation for revenue collection and the establishment of legal doctrines such as eminent domain and police powers strengthened the visible hand of public bureaucracies and their capacities for control (Chudacoff and Smith 2005).

Proliferation of information and digital technologies. The next major leap in the surveillance capacities of both state and corporate bureaucracies came roughly a century later when new computer technologies allowed the storage and sorting of immense quantities of information. Our health records, bank records, even consumer preferences are now readily available to interested parties and can be retrieved with the click of a button. Closed circuit television (CCTV) technology[2] allows remote surveillance of public spaces, while cameras on arterial intersections wait to snap pictures documenting our traffic violations. Global positioning satellites (GPS) in space maintain a watchful gaze on our houses, backyards, driveways —even the brown patches on our grass—which can be viewed by anyone with access to the World Wide Web. Dana Cuff (2003: 46) calls this digital intrusion of our everyday life "pervasive computing," arguing that its results are paradoxical as they combine greater connectivity with increased isolation and privacy with publicity. She cautions that "the most recent technological advances and social transformations threaten to dissolve the public-private continuum altogether."

Surveillance capabilities are not limited to state bureaucracies. Corporate actors and even households mirror some of the surveillance practices of the state. For example, digital technologies allow companies to invisibly track the medical records of their employees, retail corporations to draw a very detailed picture of the consumer preferences of their customers based on their purchases, and parents to trace the movement of their children.

The increasing affordability of digital technology has made the use of surveillance devices widespread. It is not clear if the preponderance of CCTV cameras today can be entirely explained by a commensurate rise in crime statistics, or their effectiveness, for that matter, by a decline in crime rates, but clearly their installation is based on a perception that such cameras are a deterrent to public space crime and disorder. To be sure, increasing affordability has made the use of these surveillance devices quite widespread. In the city of London, known to have the largest number of CCTV cameras in public spaces, the bulk are privately owned and installed to watch the immediate public interface of private establishments. What began with banks, ATMs, all-night convenience stores, supermarkets, and department stores has now expanded to public spaces including major intersections, streets, plazas, parking lots, and the like.

Other places have quickly followed London's lead. CCTV cameras are now omnipresent train stations in Japan and Germany, while in Los Angeles, the University of Southern California campus police have installed fifteen surveillance cameras in various locations around the campus neighborhood. Attached to apartment complexes owned by the university, these cameras watch the adjacent sidewalks and street corners where potential criminals may prey on their victims.[3] In many U.S. cities, cameras at traffic lights on street intersections for spotting errant drivers or for broader traffic management purposes have further expanded the space of surveillance. Even though data on the effectiveness of surveillance technology in reducing crime remain less than definitive—critics argue that the crime is simply transferred to another location—their use continues to increase in public settings.

Reactions to the threat of terrorism. The 9/11 attacks and subsequent terrorist incidents in different parts of the globe have generated an unprecedented
reaction of "anti-terrorist" and surveillance policies. In the U.S. the passing
of the Patriot Act, just one month after 9/11 eased restrictions on electronic
surveillance. As argued by Graham (2008: 6), "urban public life is being satu-
rated by intelligent surveillance systems, checkpoints, defensive urban design
and planning strategies and intensifying security." The planning and design
of buildings and streets, transportation planning and traffic management,
migration and refugee policy, even library lending policies are all now con-
ditioned by requirements set by the U.S. Homeland Security. As a number
of authors have noted (Sorkin 2008; Cuff 2003; Solove 2004), the ubiquitous
and often invisible 24/7 surveillance brings to mind the dystopian images of
the Panopticon, aptly discussed by Michael Foucault (1977) as a metaphor for
the contemporary surveillance society.[4]

Privatism, Territoriality, and the Enclosure
of the Common

The feelings of fear and vulnerability by the public have given justification to
a privatization and fortification of public spaces and a tightening and close
scrutiny of public space uses, in the name of public safety. As we will explain below, this encroachment of the common is not new; its roots go back a
couple of centuries. At the same time that emerging nation-states used their
burgeoning bureaucracies to increase control over their populace, a capitalist
market system started fostering individualism and concentration of wealth in
the hands of a few. The transformation of Western economies from mercan-
tile to capitalist in the late eighteenth century and the Industrial Revolution
in the early nineteenth century brought dramatic changes in the social organization of cities by creating both a "class society" and an impersonal "world
of strangers" (Lofland 1973; Dandekar 1990).

Upper-class citizens aspired for privatism and retreated into more exclusive territories as a way of emphasizing their status but also separating themselves from the perceived disorder and unpredictability of the public city. The
first planned U.S. suburb, Llwellyn Park in New Jersey, was built in 1855 as a
gated community separating its affluent residents from the public city outside its gates. This drastic distinction between public and private realms was
fueled by an increasing segregation and spatial separation of classes. They fed

feelings of suspicion and mistrust between the "haves" and the "have nots," which were only exacerbated by the flow into cities of new immigrants and blacks from the southern plantations. This new "other" population, perceived as "unholy" and "unwashed" by the "natives," had to be disciplined and controlled, kept under scrutiny for possible disorder, and at a distance from well-to-do neighborhoods. Some of the first municipal police forces in the U.S. were the natural extensions of private security officers hired by wealthy citizens to safeguard their property.

The trend toward privatism accentuated in Western societies after World War II, when middle-class families would become increasingly able to isolate themselves in the "single-minded" spaces of postwar suburbs, and erect homeowner associations, covenants and restrictions to protect their privacy and exclude from their communities those who "did not belong." In the suburbs, community-private or "parochial" spaces (cf. Lofland 1989) flourished as traditional public spaces declined, became inhospitable, or were perceived as dangerous. Suburban zoning ordinances helped bring about the segregation of people and uses, banning mixed land uses, separating residential space from work, social, and public activities. They stripped public space of its most vital component: the coexistence of diverse people and the overlay of social activities in a single territory. The encroachment of public space was also the result of its perceived urban pathology. Many urbanites became eventually more concerned with their personal and property safety than with public life. It has been argued that "'being inside' becomes a powerful symbol of being protected, buttressed, coddled, while 'being outside' evokes exposure, isolation, vulnerability" (Boddy 1992: 140).

While by the middle of the twentieth century some traditional public spaces in Western societies (streets, sidewalks, public markets, urban parks) started losing their users, new spaces under private auspices and control became increasingly popular. Enclosed shopping malls, shopping plazas, and commercial arcades proliferated in cities, zealously guarding and protecting their customers from the disruption and unpredictability of traditional public spaces. The idea of a public space where anything can happen has been replaced by the provision of safe and controlled places for strolling, entertainment, and consumption.

The fear of rising urban crime and social unrest in U.S. cities during the 1960s provided the impetus to use urban design and planning strategies to fight incivility, disorder, and crime, and "defend" public spaces. Jane Jacobs (1961) was among the first to assert that crime and the physical environment are related in systematic and controllable ways. In a similar manner, Jeffrey (1971) advocated the use of urban design as a means to reducing crime. His crime prevention through environmental design (CPTED) strategies were coupled with Oscar Newman's (1972) ideas about the importance of territoriality, sense of ownership, and surveillance opportunities by neighbors so as to create "defensible space." Such strategies, which advocated "designing out crime" through the use of physical features, enhancing surveillance capabilities and restricting public access, became widely popular on both sides of the Atlantic in the 1970s and 1980s.

In practice, many of these ideas led to gated communities, privatized public spaces and streets, and more generally, the "enclosure of the urban commons" (Lee and Webster 2006). Privatized spaces were designed as inward-oriented territories, turning their back to the public city outside. The negation of and dramatic contrast to the outside environment was achieved by enclosing walls, the positioning of entrances through parking structures, the choice of architectural materials. Such design "inventions" constituted "soft control" practices, as we have argued elsewhere, aiming at discouraging the wrong type of users from entering the space (Loukaitou-Sideris and Banerjee 1998).

In the 1990s, new generations of CPTED strategies evolved, which included surveillance technologies such as CCTV, access control, and "target hardening" measures (Coaffee 2009). The events of 9/11 made these design interventions less subtle by adding jersey barriers and blast-proof planters in public spaces as visual reminders of a reformulated fear that urbanites now have because of terrorism.

Looking Toward the Future:
Implications for Public Space

"She said the man in the gabardine suit was a spy / I said 'Be careful, his bowtie is really a camera" (Paul Simon, "America," 1968). Paul Simon's lyric, written some forty years ago in the context of FBI surveillance of antiwar movements of the 1960s, may have suggested the dawn of an Orwellian surveillance society. The ubiquitous digital and electronic surveillance today confirms that the era may have finally arrived. This surveillance regime comprises suspicion and snooping. Suspicion displaces trust or at least suggests a loss of trust. This in turn makes more attractive defensive strategies that involve withdrawal, disengagement, "bystander apathy," and gradual decline in the sense of community—a result of what social psychologist Stanley Milgram (1970) has called "stimulus overload." Suspicion of strangers grows when they are perceived as the "other" according to common stereotypes or racial/ethnic profiles. The "othering" of strangers makes surveillance and enclosure of the commons even more compelling.

The trend is likely to continue, as we surrender our privacy, identity, and associated rights to the panoptic gaze of the all-seeing state and the privately owned cameras that monitor the public edges of private property. We willingly surrender such rights in the cause of collective safety and security. In the post-9/11 era, the new fear of terrorism and random catastrophic violence has further exacerbated the already growing fear of crime and violence in the public sphere.

Today, not the "bowtie" but the cell phone is a camera and available to all, which sends images instantly to web sites for wide dissemination, if not evidence for police investigation. We are now not only the object of, but also collaborators in our own surveillance. Indeed, we succumb to the fun and intrigue of these technological possibilities and promises and are willing participants and consumers of the new marketplace of technological surveillance. Parents are known to give cell phones to their children at a very early age to easily track their whereabouts.

Analyzing the effect of the surveillance regime on the future of public life and space, we cannot help but note that the contemporary trends suggest a gradual atrophying of the commons and the spirit of what Seymour Mandelbaum (2000) refers to as "open moral [and trusting, we might add] communities." But while the cause of a surveillance regime has benefited from our fears of crime, violence, and terrorism on the one hand, and technological advances on the other, the vitality of the public realm has further eroded with the enclosure of the commons, or what can be seen as the privatization of the public good, life, and space.

If this trend continues it is not too difficult to imagine a scenario of a dystopic future where much of the commons will be enclosed by common interest developments, if not outright corporate ownership on the one hand, and surveillance of the commons on the other. Every pixel of the residual public realm—the streets, squares, and plazas—will be framed by a mosaic of privatized "patches" (Pickett et al. 2004) with interstitial spaces of flow. The public life will be contained within privatized spaces of enclosed commons, while the residual spaces will be defined by ethnic enclaves, or ghettoes. These residual spaces are likely to become urban panoptica, exposed to the gaze of surveillance cameras with algorithms to categorize, sort, and profile users of the space, especially those whom we consider the "other," "the unholy and the unwashed" (Lofland 1973), or in Julia Kristeva's (1991) term, "the abject."

One of the pernicious outcomes of this new regime of public space is the construction of "abjection" in two mutually reinforcing manners driven by the imperatives of exclusive consumption of urban space on the one hand, and suspicion, surveillance, and safety on the other. In both instances the result is social exclusion, as Blakely and Snyder (1995) and Madanipour (2011) have argued in the case of enclosed commons, and as Graham and Wood (2003) have pointed out in the case of surveillance. Such dystopic scenarios and trends raise indeed issues of social justice in public space that planners must address.

So, the question for us to consider is whether there are any possible planning options to resist the trend or redress the dystopic outcome. First, it is not clear whether anything can be done about the advances in technology, since these advances also bring efficiency and empowerment, other than enforcing constitutional rights to privacy. Yet, the literature critical of surveillance in the public realm is growing, especially in the UK, where such surveillance is widespread not just in London, but in many other cities. In the U.S., major cities like New York, Baltimore, Chicago, Washington, and Los Angeles all have extensive surveillance programs and plans for further expansion (see Blitz 2004). Legal scholars in the U.S. are revisiting the Fourth Amendment protection for "The right of the people to be secure in their persons, houses, papers, and effects, against unreasonable searches and seizures" (U.S. Constitution, Amendment IV). According to a 1967 Supreme Court decision (*Katz v. United States*), this protection, however, did not extend to the public space because "what a person knowingly exposes to the public . . . is not a subject of Fourth Amendment protection." Thus CCTV surveillance and archiving of surveillance videos are not being constrained by the Fourth Amendment. But questioning this outcome, Blitz (2004: 1348–49) argues that government agencies equipped with visual records of citizens' public activities are highly problematic as "even a video archive that includes only a person's movements through public settings would inevitably reveal much that he would rather not share with an audience, let alone have incorporated into official records," such as a visit to a psychiatrist's office, marriage counseling center, or abortion clinic. Blitz argues further that the best way to extend the constitutional limits to public spaces like parks, plazas, sidewalks, and the like is to emphasize that while the Fourth Amendment "does not protect the privacy of places," it should extend to "the privacy of the *people* in these places, and its protections can move *with* people as they leave their homes and move from place to place, taking private information with them" (1363). It is difficult to predict whether these legal challenges will bring about change in the surveillance regime. In the absence of such change, we might see people "covering" (see Yoshino 2006) themselves, literally—women wearing wigs or hiding under parasols, men wearing hats and sunglasses or even false moustaches—while crossing the town square or walking on streets.

Meanwhile we could be vigilant about the enclosure of the commons, or encroachments on the public realm. One of the arguments against the enclosure of the commons is that the process leads to social exclusion, while helping what Robert Reich calls "secession of the successful." Even if we were to accept the neo-liberal argument that enclosing the commons—thus encouraging "club domains" for provision of public goods instead of the conventional "public domain" (Webster and Lai 2003)—leads to fiscal efficiency, it should address demands for distributive justice as well. Thus, the condition of enclosure must stipulate a mix of income class, so that the voluntary city does not become an exclusionary city.

In the closing of our chapter we want to recall Jane Jacobs's (1961) ideal city environment, where pedestrians on public sidewalks, store-owners, and their employees and customers provided the "eyes on the street." This was a scenario of "manned surveillance," driven not by fear but by concern for the safety of other human beings. It was also a narrative of conviviality.

We are afraid that planners and urban designers alone cannot reverse the tide that has privileged fear of the other human being over the concern for collective well-being. They can, however, help amplify some of the more dire consequences of fear, suspicion, and surveillance, by producing plans and designs that promote rather than preclude human interaction. Design elements should emphasize and reinforce the bonds of public space to the rest of the urban structure (Loukaitou-Sideris 1996). At the neighborhood level, the ways that buildings relate to the public realm, the articulation of ground floor uses, the relationship between open and enclosed space, and the land use mix could all encourage the kind of convivial sidewalk spaces that Jane Jacobs tried to inspire among planners. Such outcomes may even obviate, at least partially, the need for surveillance. Thus diversity, disorder, unspecialized and open-ended spaces that engender spontaneous social contact should be the guiding principles of urban design and planning. We can hope that vigorous pursuit of the goals of propinquity, conviviality and social contact in urban design and planning will bring some redemption to the otherwise inexorably dystopic future of public space.

Notes

1. According to Milward and Provan (2000: 359), "The hollow state is a metaphor for the increasing use of third parties, often nonprofits, to deliver social services and generally act in the name of the state."

2. Great Britain has been at the forefront of installing CCTV cameras on streets and in public spaces (Coaffee et al. 2009)—according to Solove (2004), since 1994, about 2.5 million.

3. According to the chief of the U.S.C. campus police, this has been a major deterrent to crime.

4. Designed by English philosopher Jeremy Bentham in 1785, the Panopticon was a prison layout that allowed an invisible guard to survey his prisoners, creating a constant fear among them that ensured their obedience and discipline.

References

Arendt, Hannah. 1959. *The human condition.* Garden City, N.Y.: Doubleday.

Barber, Benjamin. 1998. *A place for us: How to make society civil and democracy strong.* New York: Hill and Wang.

Beito, David, Peter Gordon, and Alexander Tabarrok, eds. 2000. *The voluntary city: Choice, community, and civil society.* Ann Arbor: University of Michigan Press.

Boddy, Trevor. 1992. Underground and overhead: Building the analogous city. In *Variations on a theme park: Scenes from the new American city and the end of public space,* ed. Michael Sorkin. New York: Hill and Wang.

Bickford, Susan. 2000. Constructing inequality: City spaces and the architecture of citizenship. *Political Theory* 28(3): 355–76.

Blakely, Edward J., and Mary Gail Snyder. 1995. Fortress America: Gated and walled communities in the United States. Working Paper, Lincoln Institute of Land Policy, Cambridge, Mass.

Blitz, Marc J. 2004. Video surveillance and the constitution of public space: Fitting the fourth amendment to a world that tracks image and identity. *Texas Law Review* 82(6): 1349–1481.

Chudacoff, Howard P. and Judith E. Smith. 2005. *The evolution of American urban society.* 6th ed. Upper Saddle River, N.J.: Pearson Prentice Hall.

Coaffee, Jon. 2009. *Terrorism, risk, and the global city: Towards urban resilience.* Farnham: Ashgate.

Coaffee, Jon, David Murakami Wood, and Peter Rogers. 2009. *The everyday resilience of the city: How cities respond to terrorism and disaster.* London: Palgrave Macmillan.

Cuff, Dana. 2003. Immanent domain: Pervasive computing and the public realm. *Journal of Architectural Education* 57(1): 43–50.

Dandaker, Christopher. 1990. *Surveillance, power, and modernity: Bureaucracy and discipline from 1700 to the present day.* Cambridge: Polity Press.

Davis, Mike. 1990. *City of quartz: Excavating the future in Los Angeles.* London: Verso.

Foucault, Michel. 1977. *Discipline and punish: The birth of the prison.* Paris: Gallimard.

Fraser, Nancy. 1992. Rethinking the public sphere: a contribution to the critique of actually existing democracy. In *Habermas and the public sphere,* ed. Craig Calhoun, 109–42. Cambridge, Mass.: MIT Press.

Frieden, Bernard J., and Lynne Sagalyn. 1990. *Downtown Inc.: How America Builds Cities.* Cambridge, Mass.: MIT Press.

Giddens, Anthony. 1985. *The nation-state and violence.* Cambridge: Polity Press.

———. 1990. *The consequences of modernity.* Stanford, Calif.: Stanford University Press.

Graham, Stephen. 2008. Cities and the war on terror. In *Indefensible space: The architecture of the national insecurity state,* ed. Michael Sorkin. New York: Routledge.

Graham, Stephen, and David Wood. 2003. Digitizing surveillance: Categorization, space, inequality. *Critical Social Policy* 23(2): 227–48.

Habermas, Jürgen. 1991. *The structural transformation of public sphere: An inquiry into a category of bourgeois society.* Cambridge, Mass.: MIT Press.

Holston, James. 1991. Spaces of insurgent citizenship. *Planning Theory* 13: 35–51.

Irázabal, Clara. ed. 2008. *Ordinary places, extraordinary events: Citizenship, democracy and public space in Latin America.* London: Routledge.

Jacobs, Jane. 1961. *The death and life of great American cities.* New York: Random House.

Jeffery, C. Ray. 1971. *Crime prevention through environmental design.* Beverly Hills, Calif.: Sage.

Kohn, Margaret. 2004. *Brave new neighborhoods: The privatization of public space.* New York: Routledge.

Kristeva, Julia. 1991. *Strangers to ourselves.* New York: Columbia University Press.

Lee, Shin, and Chris Webster. 2006. Enclosure of the urban commons. *Geo Journal* 66(1–2): 27–42.

Lefebvre, Henri. 1968. *Le droit à la ville.* Paris: Anthopos.

Lofland, Lyn H. 1973. *World of strangers: Order and action in urban public space.* New York: Basic Books.

———. 1989. The morality of urban public life: The emergence and continuation of a debate. *Places* 6(1): 18–23.

———. 1998. *The public realm: Exploring the city's quintessential social territory.* Hawthorne, N.Y.: de Gruyter.

Loukaitou-Sideris, Anastasia. 1996. Cracks in the city: Addressing the constraints and potentials of urban design. *Journal of Urban Design*, 1(1): 91–103.

Loukaitou-Sideris, Anastasia, and Tridib Banerjee. 1998. *Urban design downtown: Poetics and politics of form.* Berkeley: University of California Press.

Loukaitou-Sideris, Anastasia, and Renia Ehrenfeucht. 2009. *Sidewalks: Conflict and negotiation over public space.* Cambridge, Mass.: MIT Press.

Madanipour, Ali. 2011. Living together or apart: Exclusion, gentrification, and displacement. In *Companion to Urban Design,* ed. Tridib Banerjee and Anastasia Loukaitou-Sideris, 484–94. London: Routledge.

Mandelbaum, Seymour J. 2000. *Open moral communities.* Cambridge, Mass.: MIT Press.

Mernissi, Fatima. 1987. *Beyond the veil: Male-female dynamics in modern Muslim society.* Bloomington: Indiana University Press.

Milgram, Stanley. 1970. The experience of living in cities. *Science* 167(3924): 1461–68.

Milward, H. Brinton, and Keith G. Provan. 2000. Governing the hollow state. *Journal of Public Administration Research and Theory* 10(2): 359–80.

Mitchell, Don. 1996. Political violence, order, and the legal construction of public space: Power and the public forum doctrine. *Urban Geography* 7(2): 152–78.

Newman, Oscar. 1972. *Defensible space: Crime prevention through environmental design.* New York: Macmillan.

Pickett, Steward T. A., Mary L. Cadenasso and J. Morgan Grove. 2004. Resilient cities: Meanings, models, and metaphor for integrating the ecological, socio-economic, and planning realms. *Landscape and Urban Planning* 69: 369–84.

Scott, James C. 1998. *Seeing like a state: How certain schemes to improve the human condition have failed.* New Haven, Conn.: Yale University Press.

Sennett, Richard. 1977. *The fall of public man: A history of public culture and public space.* New York: Norton.

———. 1994. *Flesh and stone: The body and the city in western civilization.* New York: Norton.

Shapiro, Ian, and Caciano Hacker-Cordon, eds. 1999. *Democracy's value.* Cambridge: Cambridge University Press.

Smith, Neil, and Setha Low. 2006. Introduction: The Imperative of Public Space. In *The politics of public space.* ed. Setha Low and Neil Smith, 1–16. New York: Routledge.

Solove, Daniel J. 2004. *The digital person: Technology and privacy in the information age.* New York: New York University Press.

Sorkin, Michael. 2008. Introduction: The fear factor. In *indefensible space: The architecture of the national insecurity state,* ed. Michael Sorkin, vii–xvii. New York: Routledge.

Steinberger, Peter J. 1999. Public and private. *Political Studies* 47: 292–313.

Walzer, Michael. 1986. Public space: Pleasures and costs of urbanity, *Dissent* 33(4): 470–75.

Webster, Christopher J. 2007. Property rights, public space, and urban design. *Town Planning Review* 78(1): 81–101.

Webster, Christopher J. and Lawrence Wai-Chung Lai. 2003. *Property rights, planning, and markets: Managing spontaneous cities.* Cheltenham: Edward Elgar.

Weintraub, Jeff. 1995. Varieties and vicissitudes of public space. In *Metropolis: Center and symbol of our times,* ed. Philip Kasinitz, 280–319. New York: New York University Press.

Yoshino, Kenji. 2006. *Covering: The hidden assault on our civil rights.* New York: Random House.

Chapter 17

Beyond the Ladder: New Ideas About Resident Roles in Contemporary Community Development in the United States

Rachel G. Bratt and Kenneth M. Reardon

During the second half of the twentieth century, the role of residents in community development programs across the United States gained considerable attention as civil rights leaders and community activists pushed municipal governments and their federal partners to develop more participatory planning processes. This greater resident voice in community development programs was stimulated by the negative effects of many Urban Renewal programs as well as the launch of the War on Poverty in the early 1960s, with its requirement of "maximum feasible participation" by the poor. Sherry Arnstein's seminal 1969 paper "A Ladder of Citizen Participation," written during this period of growing interest in resident participation, has framed much of the subsequent discourse on this topic in the United States.

Since that time individuals and community groups have become involved in public debates in ways that were not envisioned four decades ago. In addition, recent years have witnessed growing dissatisfaction and upheaval resulting from the deregulation of housing and financial markets. This has been accompanied by a precipitous decline in public confidence in the ability of elites to manage either the economy or the delivery of basic government services. It is timely, therefore, to reconsider the role residents should play in the planning of a diverse set of public initiatives. By revisiting the Arnstein

Ladder, we hope the next generation of planning students will be better able to appreciate the range of strategies through which residents can meaningfully participate in shaping their own future.

This chapter focuses on community development rather than the broader spectrum of planning activities for a number of reasons. First, because we are using the Arnstein Ladder, it is logical to stick to community development programs, since this was her focus. Second, the bulk of the planning literature on participation is concentrated in community development. Finally, an examination of resident participation in a single planning subfield is far more manageable for a paper, as opposed to a full treatment of the history/lessons of participation in planning, which would require a book.

By tracing forty years of community development practice, and the dramatic changes in context in which this practice has taken place, we hope to offer a new theoretical understanding of the role of residents in community development. The over-arching goal is to ensure that the next generation of planners looks to the needs of residents, especially those of the poor, as the focus of future urban policy debates and community development practice; appreciate the breadth and complexity of the strategies that foster resident participation; and reflect on how their roles can interact with and support resident initiatives.

Definitions

A number of phrases have been used to refer to the role residents play in community development. Most of the participation literature uses the word "citizen." Since many residents in countries throughout the world are not citizens, and many of these are poor and of color, we do not want to exclude these groups from a role in planning initiatives, even at a rhetorical level. Therefore, we feel that "resident" is a more inclusive term than "citizen" when discussing participation in planning. We prefer this term to the more inclusive "public participation," since our focus is on the individuals living in a particular community, as opposed to a broader array of stakeholders. In most of this chapter, therefore, we use the term "resident participation." However, in discussing Arnstein's Ladder and other relevant literature, we use the language of the author, which is typically "citizen participation."

Arnstein defines citizen participation as a "categorical term for citizen power":

It is the redistribution of power that enables the have-not citizens, presently excluded from the political and economic processes, to be deliberately included in the future. It is the strategy by which the have-nots join in determining how information is shared, goals and policies are set, tax resources are allocated, programs are operated, and benefits like contracts and patronage are parceled out. (216)

Clearly, this definition includes the desired end-result of participation, more equitable policy outcomes, not simply the act itself. As to the meaning of community development, a "textbook" definition states that it is

Asset building that improves the quality of life among residents of low-to moderate-income communities, where *communities* are defined as neighborhoods or multigenerational areas. [In this context, assets include] *physical capital* in the form of buildings, tools, and so forth; *intellectual and human capital*, in the form of skills, knowledge, and confidence; *social capital*—norms, shared understandings, trust, and other factors that make relationships feasible and productive; *financial capital* (in standard forms); and *political capital*, which provides the capacity to exert political influence. (Ferguson and Dickens 1999: 5, 4; emphasis original)

Going beyond a focus on improving quality of life, Marie Kennedy argues that

Genuine community development combines material development with the development of people, increasing a community's capacity for taking control of its own development.... A good planning project should leave a community not just with more immediate "products"—for example, more housing—but also with an increased capacity to meet future needs. (Kennedy 2007: 25)

Kennedy's definition of community development significantly overlaps with Arnstein's definition of citizen participation by emphasizing resident power. Thus, at least to some practitioners, community development and resident participation are synonymous or, at least, you can't have one without the other.

As planners embraced resident participation in the 1960s, a number of distinct planning paradigms emerged. "Advocacy planning" attempted to provide residents with opportunities to enter into negotiations with public officials and private developers. Paul Davidoff (1965) offered that planners neither can, nor should, be value-neutral technocrats whose role is to carry out the plans of those in power. Instead, the role of the planner is to assist multiple interests, with a particular focus on poor and minority concerns, to argue their alternative proposals.

The concept has remained important to planners, as Tom Angotti (2007) has noted: "advocacy planning is still the foundation for all progressive planning today . . . It is relevant because it allows us to distinguish between progressive community planning and the generic community planning." The former entails "opposition to the conditions that produce and reproduce the inequalities of race and class. Without that, advocacy would be just a conservative appeal for pluralism—everybody do their own thing and don't challenge existing relations of economic and political power" (Angotti 2007: 21, 23).

"Empowerment planning," which also falls within the broad conceptualization of progressive community planning, seeks to enhance the capacity of community organizations to influence the investment decisions that, to a large degree, determine the quality of life local residents enjoy. This is accomplished through an approach that integrates the core concepts of participatory action research, direct action organizing, and popular education into a powerful social change process (Reardon 2000).

"Equity planning" is essentially synonymous with the practice of progressive community planning, except that it refers to planners working inside government who "use their skills to influence opinion, mobilize underrepresented constituencies, and advance and perhaps implement policies and programs that redistribute public and private resources to the poor and working class" (Metzger 1996). Urban planning educator Norman Krumholz is closely linked with this form of practice, based upon work he did in the government of the City of Cleveland (Krumholz and Forester 1990).

The American Planning Association has been critical of "the traditional practice of planning" because it does not sufficiently consider resident voices. It states that traditional planning practice, "in which a municipal planning department plans for the physical future of the entire jurisdiction from city hall, often fails to provide effective planning for the full range of community components that affect families at the neighborhood level" (2008). The Association has encouraged a new definition of "neighborhood collaborative

planning" that seeks "to enhance the quality of life in a specific area by join-
ing attention to the economic, social, and physical infrastructure of the
neighborhood to realize the goals defined by a resident-driven/managed/led
vision" (1996).

This view of planning is nearly identical to the textbook definition of
community development. But both stop short of Arnstein's definition of citizen participation and Davidoff, Angotti, and Kennedy's views of advocacy
planning and community development. We have intentionally limited the
previous discussion to planning theories that explicitly focus on outcomes, as
opposed to those that are more process oriented, such as consensus building
and communicative/collaborative planning. In a communicative framework,
for example, the planner's role is to "listen to people's stories and assist in the
forging of consensus among different viewpoints" (Fainstein 2000: 454). In
addition, in our analysis we take as a "given" the inequality of power between
residents and other stakeholders as a critical element in the context of community development practice.

Thus, in this chapter we embrace Arnstein's definition of participation
with its focus on the outcome of enhancing power among the participants, as
well as the act of participation. We further believe that the appropriate aim
of community development is to improve and protect the quality of life in
an area, while also providing residents with greater power and control over
their environments. Community development and resident participation are,
then, inextricably linked.

Impact of the Ladder on Community Planning and Development

The Ladder challenged activists, planners, and officials to reexamine the role
residents were playing within federal revitalization initiatives, especially the
Community Action and Model Cities Programs. Influenced by the social
movements of the 1960s, Arnstein was committed to building a society in
which the voices of the poor could be heard within all urban policy and plan-
making programs.

Seeking to maximize the influence poor and working-class individuals
exerted within the planning process, Arnstein used the ascending rungs of
a ladder to illustrate the degree to which formal resident participation processes resulted in real power (see Figure 17.1). At the bottom of the Ladder

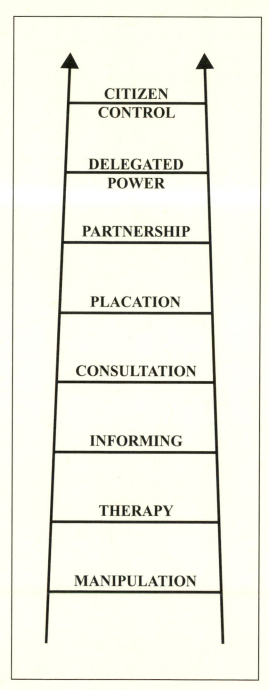

Figure 17.1. Arnstein's ladder of citizen
participation.

of Citizen Participation are two forms of citizen engagement, manipulation and therapy, in which citizens are offered ceremonial opportunities to participate during public planning processes, giving them the illusion of power while decision-making remains in the hands of local elites. The middle of the Ladder, the informing, consultation, and placation rungs, offers limited participation in which residents provide input on policies while officials representing elite interests maintain their privileged positions. At the top of the Ladder are the partnership, delegated power, and citizen control rungs that offer residents significant influence and control.

Since its first publication in the *Journal of the American Institute of Planners*,[1] the Ladder has been used by innumerable professionals and academics to evaluate the degree to which public planning processes offer residents, especially the poor, opportunities to influence decisions affecting their communities. Published in 1969, this article continues to be featured in most introductory planning texts, including Stein's *Classic Readings in Urban Planning* (2004) and LeGates and Stout's *The City Reader* (2003). In addition, the article remains required reading in many graduate planning programs, including Berkeley, Cornell, Illinois, Michigan, and Tufts. Despite the decades that have passed since its initial publication, the article remains one of the most frequently cited planning articles. According to Google Scholar, it was referenced in 1,988 articles and books in 2007. Planetizen reported that more than 1,100 visitors downloaded Arnstein's article in the first 90 days of its posting on www.planetizen.org. In recent years, it has also become one of the most frequently read articles by Chinese planners seeking to increase resident participation in what have essentially been closed planning processes.

The importance of power and power sharing in public planning processes, as described by Arnstein, continues to occupy a vital place within contemporary planning practice and discourse. For example, 10 percent of the questions on the 2008 American Institute of Certified Planners (AICP) Exam focused on resident participation, and the most popular AICP Exam preparatory text continues to quiz candidates regarding their knowledge of Arnstein's Ladder.

Within community development, questions raised by Arnstein related to resident power remain important themes in the scholarly literature. Mel King's *Chains of Change* (1984), Chester Hartman's *Between Eminence and Notoriety* (2002), and Peter Medoff and Holly Sklar's *Holding Ground: The Fall and Rise of an Urban Neighborhood* (1994), describe how low-income residents confronting large-scale redevelopment and displacement have organized to oppose such efforts. Many of the stories in these volumes describe how residents rejected various forms of officially sponsored participation to organize grassroots movements to restructure local revitalization efforts.

Issues raised by the Arnstein Ladder are further explored in many influential-planning texts. In *The Deliberative Practitioner*, John Forester (1999) explains how equity planners are frequently asked to transcend their technical analyst role to organize communities to make their voices heard within elite controlled planning processes. Martin and Carolyn Needleman's *Guerrillas in the Bureaucracy* (1974), Pierre Clavel's *The Progressive City: Planning and Participation, 1969–1984* (1984) and Norm Krumholz and Pierre Clavel's *Equity Planners Tell Their Stories* (1994) review the formidable opposition local planners encounter while seeking to implement redistributive development policies and participatory planning processes.

Ron Shiffman and Susan B. Motley's "A Comprehensive and Integrative Approach to Community Development" (1989), William Peterman's *Neighborhood Planning and Community Development: The Potential and Limits of Grassroots Action* (1999), Herbert J. Rubin's *Renewing Hope Within Neighborhoods of Despair* (2000), and Randy Stoecker's "Challenging Community Development Practice" (1997) highlight the conflict community development professionals experience when attempting to balance their commitment to community organizing and empowerment with the need to successfully complete their next development project upon which their organizations often depend for economic survival.

Robert Putnam's *Bowling Alone* (2000) emphasizes the challenges local leaders face in promoting participation when out-migration from our cities has reduced the number of residents participating in civil society. Leonie Sandercock's *Cosmopolis* (1998) and *Mongrel Cities* (2004) emphasize the importance and difficulty of promoting resident participation in urban areas that have become increasingly diverse.

The Ladder has also influenced scholars from other fields who are committed to understanding how individuals from economically marginalized groups can influence government policy and plan-making. Among these are scholars from environmental psychology, public health, and international development who have incorporated the Ladder into their work (see, for example, Hart 1992; www.freechild.org/ladder.html; Checkoway and Gutierrez 2006; Choguill 1996; Pretty 1995).

Strengths and Limitations of the Ladder

Arnstein's Ladder has withstood the test of time. Still widely taught in planning courses, the model's simplicity makes it accessible and understandable to students and practitioners. Arnstein highlights the centrality of resident involvement and underscores the importance of their voices not only being heard, but resulting in greater power sharing and improved policy outcomes.

The Ladder also offers practitioners, funders, and evaluators a usable framework for measuring the power sharing that exists among stakeholders within specific community development projects. In addition, the Ladder emphasizes the possibility of moving toward greater resident involvement. While not offering detailed guidance as to *how* to advance along a specific empowerment pathway, it does provide a general roadmap for those interested in adopting more collaborative approaches to practice. Finally, the lower rungs of the Ladder provide a strong cautionary message that not all forms of resident participation are positive! Indeed, the most modest forms of participation may create illusions of participation, lulling residents into believing their opinions are being considered, providing legitimacy to projects that may actually cause harm.

Despite the Ladder's many strengths, there are also some weaknesses. These include

1. Arnstein offers only anecdotal evidence to support her conceptions of how various types of participation play out in the world. The logic of the Ladder notwithstanding, Arnstein offers no empirical data to support her argument that greater participation results in improved planning outcomes, including a redistribution of power or opportunity for lower income residents and members of racial minorities.

2. The Ladder assumes a single form of participation—residents becoming involved with programs that originate outside their neighborhood through "top-down" planning.[2] The article fails to acknowledge the other ways residents may influence the community development process.

3. Although Arnstein defines participation as including both strategies and outcomes, the Ladder confuses the two. While the highest three rungs of the Ladder—partnership, delegated power, and control—may be viewed as both strategies and outcomes, the lower rungs focus exclusively on the outcomes of inadequate or misguided resident

participation. The Ladder also does not acknowledge that the "best" form of resident participation may vary based upon the planning context. While it is almost certain that the three highest rungs on the Ladder represent the most desired outcomes, it may not always be the case that control is preferable to a partnership arrangement.

4. Arnstein does not offer reasons why participation, even on a theoretical basis, is important. For example, she might have elaborated on how resident involvement may lead to a better process if local stakeholders are involved. In addition, fewer delays and greater cost effectiveness may result from a decreased likelihood of local opposition. In view of the importance of lay knowledge, there is also a greater chance that the project will be consistent with resident needs. Resident involvement may also result in benefits going to those most in need, thereby promoting a more equitable distribution of resources.

5. Arnstein does not acknowledge some potentially important drawbacks of participation. For example, residents who participate can voice anti-social attitudes, including subtle messages of white privilege/racism, income segregation, sexism, ageism, and homophobia. In other words, there are times when resident involvement can result in the exclusion of those not considered part of the community.

6. The Ladder does not acknowledge the extent to which mandated resident participation can undermine grassroots movements. "Official" resident committees appointed by local officials often stifle legitimate community voices that may be expressed through religious and/or civic organizations. Certainly, at the time the Ladder was constructed, there were historic and contemporary examples of how grassroots movements and activism stimulated significant changes.

7. While the Ladder acknowledges that "neither the have-nots nor the power holders are homogeneous blocs" in planning practice, these variations need to be more fully considered. Decades of planning experience have underscored that diverse stakeholders are likely to view a particular project from their individual perspectives. Yet, the Ladder does not take into account how different voices can be heard, how different racial or ethnic identities might influence participation, or how to balance competing community demands.

8. Although Arnstein notes that the Ladder "does not include an analysis of the most significant roadblocks to achieving genuine levels of participation," a more robust model would provide guidance to those

stuck on lower rungs regarding how to progress to higher levels of collaboration.

Moreover, it is worth noting that there is a lack of clarity regarding the unit of analysis that is being used. Is Arnstein talking about individual, organizational, or community empowerment?

Changing Context of Community Development Since the 1960s

Arnstein developed her Ladder during the 1960s, a period with a very different set of social concerns from the present era. These differences are important to understanding our proposals for a new framework. The Department of Housing and Urban Development (HUD), the federal agency in charge of housing and community development initiatives, had just been created with a broad new mission of consolidating federal urban programs and expanding its mission to neighborhood revitalization. Accompanying these developments were the deep, direct federal subsidies provided through such programs as Urban Renewal and programs that offered mortgages at below-market interest rates to developers and lower income homeowners. With the current troubled state of the economy and two wars being fought, the problems facing economically challenged urban neighborhoods have not been a priority in the United States. In addition, since the 1980s, responsibility for urban policy has shifted to state and local governments, as devolution has become the standard federal approach and public-private partnerships have become commonplace.

Along with federal involvement in a wide array of domestic issues in the 1960s, federal officials and policy-makers began to articulate concerns about evaluation. Questions were being asked about how the costs and benefits of urban initiatives would be assessed. However, when Arnstein created the Ladder she was still writing from a "pre-evaluation" perspective. Her arguments were persuasive and her anecdotal observations were accepted as facts. At present, if one were to argue for enhanced resident involvement in public decision-making, policy-makers would demand convincing evidence and a compelling rationale about why such participation is necessary and what the benefits will be. With evaluation "the name of the game," outcome data on participation have become essential. Indeed, a new construct could better serve as a tool for assessing levels of participation in any given initiative.

While there was tremendous growth in the African American and Latino populations in central cities, there were few elected officials from these groups in the 1960s. There are now more than 9,000 non-white elected officials in U.S. state and local governments. All this suggests that, at present, resident participation can and does take the form of voting candidates into office and running for office.

In addition, the current U.S. population is significantly more diverse than in the 1960s, with about a third classified as non-white. While African Americans were the dominant minority group in the 1960s, today they constitute a smaller group than Hispanics and others with Latino roots. Each ethnic and racial group has its own history and cultural connections to resident participation (or not).[3] Therefore, it is unlikely that we can prescribe a "one size fits all" approach to resident participation.

In recent decades, too, there has been a proliferation of small-scale community development corporations and other social service agencies assuming responsibility for public service delivery in distressed areas, eclipsing in many localities the role formerly played by federally funded public agencies. Neighborhood residents, as well as professionals living outside these areas, typically staff these organizations. Opportunities for residents to participate in these organizations simply did not exist in the 1960s. The nonprofits, then, may be serving as effective vehicles for residents to become involved in a wide variety of community development issues. Whereas in Arnstein's era public officials were concerned about how to encourage resident participation and what types of new participation committees should be created, in today's context an important challenge is to involve already-existing groups in local decision-making. The same is true for those for-profit private sector entities that have become important players in urban revitalization partnerships in recent years. While these partnerships often involve private developers and local governments, there may also be explicit roles for non-profit neighborhood associations and local residents to play influential roles.

It is worth noting that the old style of community development was easier to understand than present-day practice. No longer dependent on a single (i.e., federal) source of funding, contemporary programs typically require leveraging public dollars, layering subsidies from multiple sources, and navigating the difficult-to-understand world of tax credits. Even residents who want to get involved may get discouraged by the complexity of the programs. Although it is true that there is a great deal of information on the web, we do not know the extent to which residents actually use it for their own analyses and advocacy. Are we disempowering residents by overwhelming them with information while, at the same time, offering them relatively few web-based, analytic tools to make sense of these data?

Finally, we are now experimenting with various indirect methods of participation that are faster and, perhaps, less costly, such as "electronic town halls." However, to the extent that such approaches are used, residents lose the opportunity to participate in the "give and take" that direct participation offers.

In view of the many differences between the 1960s and the first years of the twenty-first century, there is a need for a more contemporary conceptual framework that can enhance our understanding of the range of resident roles in community development and other planning initiatives.

Illustrative Examples of Innovative Practice

Arnstein's scholarship has prompted community development planners to approach their work in a more participatory fashion. These planners have come to appreciate how an inclusionary approach to practice can expand the base for progressive community development while enhancing the capacity of community organizations to implement increasingly ambitious local development projects.

This section presents two resident-driven planning processes from the United States that reflect the highest level of resident control described by the Ladder.[4] From these examples we will be able to outline a number of more contemporary forms of innovative practice that will inform the model we develop.

Emerson Park Development Corporation
(East St. Louis, Illinois)

In the mid-1980s, a group of women from the Emerson Park neighborhood of East St. Louis, Illinois, became alarmed by the collapse of their neighborhood's manufacturing, transportation, and retail sectors. As unemployment and poverty mounted, they watched increasing numbers of families move away in search of living wage jobs. When one third of the building lots became vacant and a quarter of the remaining buildings became seriously deteriorated, they formed the Emerson Park Development Corporation (EPDC).

Mobilizing dozens of unemployed men, these women dismantled three abandoned buildings, recycled useful materials, raised additional funds, and mobilized volunteers transforming these properties into a beautiful children's playground. Following this success, the group recruited University of Illinois planning students to prepare a comprehensive revitalization plan. Using participatory methods that included mapping community assets, oral histories, children's planning murals, resident interviews, and stakeholder focus groups, EPDC and their student planners prepared the Emerson Park Neighborhood Improvement Plan, which was awarded the 1991 AICP Best Student Plan Award.

When funders refused to invest in the plan, residents completed a series of self-help projects to address some of the identified problems. Working together, they removed trash from vacant lots, painted low-income seniors' homes, replaced the roof of the community center, and created a community garden. These small successes attracted an influx of new volunteers and renewed interest from local funders. During the next ten years, EPDC, in partnership with University of Illinois, completed more than one hundred increasingly challenging neighborhood improvement projects.

With this track record, and based on research from the University of Illinois, EPDC convinced regional transportation officials to extend a light rail line connecting Lambert International Airport and the City of East St. Louis. Having purchased a significant number of parcels close to the Emerson Park light rail station, EPDC recruited an experienced developer to build a new mixed-use/income planned community serving Emerson Park. By 2005, EPDC had completed the $29 million Parsons Place Project, which features a public park, a Montessori school, a charter high school, and more than one hundred forty units of market- and below-market-rate housing.

Sacred Heart Parish (New Brunswick, New Jersey)

The City of New Brunswick, New Jersey, a former manufacturing, transportation, retailing, and government center, has experienced a significant influx of Asian and Latino immigrants in recent years, many of them undocumented. Attracted by the hospitality, transportation, warehousing, and landscaping jobs available to those with limited language and technical skills, these workers earn modest wages, enjoy few work-related benefits, and are frequently denied state unemployment benefits and worker compensation. Although most of them work for well-known multinational corporations in New Brunswick, they are actually employed by "temporary employment contractors" who assume responsibility for verifying their eligibility to work.

The workers employed by these contractors receive only a small portion of the hourly compensation the corporations pay for their labor. Contractors typically require workers to travel to and from their places of employment in their vans, for which they charge a hefty fee. The contractors also hold a monopoly over the mobile food wagons that provide meals to the laborers enabling them to charge a premium for such services. Finally, the contractors provide costly check-cashing services to workers who are often unable to establish local bank accounts because of their lack of appropriate ID.

In 2002, Sacred Heart Roman Catholic Church in downtown New Brunswick experienced a significant increase in parishioners from among the city's new immigrants. In addition to offering a number of services, the church initiated a comprehensive planning effort in collaboration with the Affordable Housing and Community Development Network of New Jersey. With the Network's assistance, Sacred Heart secured a $50,000 foundation grant to undertake a resident-driven revitalization plan. In 2006, a participatory planning process identified the neighborhood's most important assets, challenges, and development opportunities. More than 250 residents participated in the discussions, meetings, and charrettes that formed the core of this process.

The plan that emerged from this process proposed improved police and fire protection, expanded job training, enhanced neighborhood retail services, improved health care services; additional affordable housing; and greater food security. Following completion of their plan, Sacred Heart secured $1 million in Neighborhood Revitalization Tax Credits through the New Jersey Department of Community Affairs. Novartis, a Swiss pharmaceutical corporation, purchased the tax credits enabling Sacred Heart to begin implementation of the plan. Achievements include new wellness services, rehabilitation of twelve units of affordable housing, a Building and Fire Code Enforcement Campaign, and a large-scale community garden. Based on these early successes, Novartis renewed its financial commitment enabling the parish to leverage other community development grants.

Broadening the Resident Participation Framework

From this exploration come a number of recommendations aimed at broadening the resident participation framework. We are suggesting several new categories that explicitly focus on direct and indirect bottom-up resident strategies; and new supporting roles for professional planners. In the

Column #1 Direct bottom-up resident strategies	Column #2 Indirect bottom-up resident strategies	Column #3 Professional roles in support of resident participation	Arnstein's Ladder top-down resident participation strategies
Citizen Control	Citizen Control	Citizen Control	Citizen Control
Delegated Power	Delegated Power	Delegated Power	Delegated Power
⇧	⇧	⇧	⇧
Partnership Status			
⇧	⇧	⇧	⇧
Negotiation and Mediation	Running/Serving in Public Office	Advocacy Planning	Placation
Participatory community Planning	Voting/Working on an Electoral Campaigm	Working for a Local/State CD Agency	Consultation
Organizing	Writing/Engagement in Public Interest Campaign	Working for a Privete Sector Firm (CRA Officer in a Bank)	Informing
Activism and Protest	Volunteering with a Non-Profit	Working for a Local CD Corporation	Therepy
			Manipulation

Figure 17.2. Professional and resident roles that lead to participation and control of community development initiatives.

following discussion we explore how each of these new strategies may be appropriate depending on three contextual variables.

New Categories of Resident Participation

Over the past four decades, poor and working-class communities have pursued planning approaches not represented on the Ladder to achieve more equitable forms of community development. These new approaches are not based on an ever-progressing increase in resident power, so they are not presented as Ladders. Rather, they encompass a type of intervention aimed at expanding opportunities for residents to have their concerns acknowledged within particular planning contexts.

As shown in Figure 17.2, in each of the participation strategies, residents seek to enter into negotiations with local development officials, which hopefully will result in a partnership arrangement, placing them on the sixth rung on the Ladder. There would then be the possibility of moving up the Ladder to outcomes that involve delegating power to residents or residents being in control of a given program. In fact, rather than the sequential progression that the Ladder metaphor suggests, we believe the image of a pole vault may more accurately convey how specific strategies falling under the new categories may result in a situation where powerful stakeholders are willing to negotiate with residents.

It is important to recall that the Ladder is primarily concerned with outcomes achieved through various federally funded "top-down" participation initiatives. In contrast, the categories being proposed delineate three broad types of strategies that residents, or professionals, can pursue to enable residents to get to "yes," which we consider forming a partnership arrangement with the local government or other entities in control of community resources. Moving above the Partnership level, there may be opportunities for residents to be delegated power and/or to assume control of the community development initiative.

Direct Bottom-Up Resident Strategies (Column 1)

This category includes four types of resident-driven initiatives. Residents may be able to enter into negotiation with key city officials or other powerful decision-makers directly, or they may need to pursue one of the other three strategies that result in some form of negotiation. Through this process, residents may be able to form a productive partnership or, beyond that, achieve control over key community development initiatives.

- **Negotiation and mediation**—a resident group may enter into a negotiation process with key power-holding stakeholders as a prelude to forming a mutually beneficial partnership
- **Participatory community planning**—residents can collaborate with a university or with an advocacy organization to develop a plan, independent of city hall, that meets their needs.
- **Organizing**—residents can also work through citizen organizations and public interest coalitions to create more nurturing environments in which local economic and community development can be pursued.

- **Activism and protest**—oppositional campaigns that cause disruption of "business/politics as usual" have helped many communities influence local development policies.

Indirect Bottom-Up Resident Strategies (column 2)

The following initiatives are grouped together because they seek to enhance the general level of resident involvement in civic affairs, indirectly enabling residents to influence local community development. As with the direct, bottom-up resident strategies (column 1), these aim at helping residents achieve a position from which they can enter into productive negotiations with key stakeholders that may then result in a partnership or higher form of resident involvement.

- **Volunteering with a nonprofit**—participation in these groups may range from membership and occasional meeting attendance, to volunteering in sponsored programs, to serving on the board.
- **Writing/engagement in public interest campaign**—Residents have opportunities to participate in political dialogue in ways that would have been unimaginable in the 1960s. The Internet has revolutionized communication methods. While some Model Cities programs had newsletters, today's resident groups can have their own web sites presenting their views electronically and reporting their activities in their own community.
- **Voting/working on electoral campaign**—participation through established channels of engagement, including voter registration and "get-out-the-vote" campaigns.[5]
- **Running for/serving in public office**—participation through leadership in the political process. If you can't get "them" to fix or change the situation, consider changing it yourself.

Professional Roles in Support of Resident Participation (column 3)

The final category includes professional roles residents or nonresidents may assume. The immediate goal of these approaches is to assist residents in entering into partnership arrangements with powerful stakeholders to promote resident voice and resource control within community development.

- **Working for a local community development corporation.**
- **Working for a private sector firm.**
- **Working for a local/state CD agency**—Whether the employee is a professional from outside the community or a resident working on the inside of a key firm or agency, they can influence policies, processes and resource allocations.
- **Advocacy planning**—Planners who serve as advocates for specific communities still play a critical role for practitioners of progressive planning.

Thus, some residents (as well as outside professionals) may assume different roles in support of resident participation in community development (column 3). Other residents may engage in direct (column 1) or indirect bottom-up strategies (column 2). The combined impact of these strategies is to empower residents to enter into negotiation whenever possible, so they can form partnerships with city officials, while continuing to move up the Ladder.

Resident Strategies in Context

One of our earlier criticisms of the Arnstein Ladder is that it does not sufficiently acknowledge how local contexts may impact the effectiveness of alternative participation strategies (See also work by Churchman, 1987, in which the importance of context is underscored.) As shown in Figure 17.3, we suggest that there are three contextual variables that community development participants need to monitor and adjust their activities accordingly: level of economic resources, level of support for community development/participatory planning, and concentration of power within the local community. Each of these variables is shown as a continuum. The more hostile the context, in terms of limited resources, weak support for community development, and high concentrations of power in the local community, the more residents will need to start their efforts through activism and protest, organizing and community planning with the goal of "pole-vaulting" to the negotiation/mediation stage.

Hostile Environment

Where powerful institutions no longer believe in the possibilities for revitalization of a community and have reduced services that threaten the

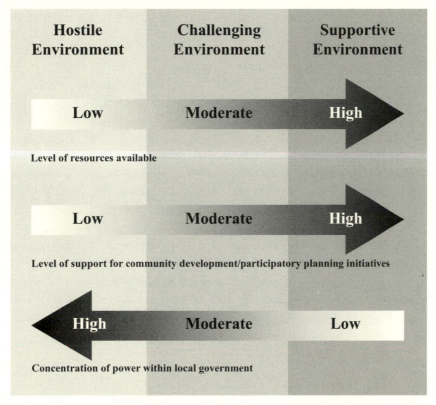

Figure 17.3. Attributes of local environments that affect resident participation strategies.

community's future, resident organizing may take the form of adopting a self-help approach to basic service provision while also pursuing a protest strategy involving legal action to prevent powerful outside actors from destroying the community.

When New Orleans officials appeared to be embracing a "planned shrinkage" approach to post-Katrina planning, in which heavily damaged eastside neighborhoods were being reprogrammed as urban wetlands to serve as buffer areas in the event of future storms, the Association of Community Organizations for Reform Now (ACORN) responded by helping local families and businesses "gut" their buildings in preparation for future renovation, while suing the city to prevent it from demolishing the community's building stock. ACORN then entered into a partnership with a group of universities to formulate a comprehensive revitalization plan for the Ninth Ward. The combination of ACORN's self-help, legal defense and neighborhood planning activities enabled them to capture $140 million in Federal infrastructure funds for the severely damaged Ninth Ward.

Similarly, when powerful institutions are interested in redeveloping a neighborhood in a manner that significantly benefits outside economic interests, while displacing long-time residents and businesses, the latter groups may be forced to mobilize a broad-based coalition to ensure basic equity within publicly-supported community development programs.

In the Greenpoint-Williamsburg neighborhood of Brooklyn, residents and religious leaders came together to ensure that a proposed up-zoning of the waterfront designed to accommodate new residential development featured a significant "set-aside" for affordable housing. By organizing a broad-based coalition of faith-based organizations, local stakeholders secured the support of elected officials; forty percent of new housing units built within their community were required to be permanently affordable. Through these efforts, the community was also able to construct a waterfront promenade, restore two parks, build a public library, implement subway station improvements, install public art, and preserve and/or create 7,800 units of affordable housing.

Challenging Environment

When powerful development interests focused their attention on the revitalization of other parts of the city, such as the downtown, the riverfront, and/or university/medical districts, all the while ignoring the needs of residential neighborhoods where the poor live, residents of these areas may need to undertake organizing campaigns to encourage a more balanced approach to economic and community development.

In Memphis, Tennessee, one of the city's largest developers proposed redevelopment of the Mid-South Fairgrounds—a 156 acre city- and county-owned site that serves as the home for the Liberty Bowl Stadium, a basketball arena, and an agricultural exhibition area. The developer sought to transform the facilities into a world-class athletic and cultural center by securing more than $100 million in state tourist development bonds. While asserting his desire to see the project positively affect the neighborhoods surrounding the site, the developer has, to date, taken few steps to guarantee this outcome. Jacob's Ladder Community Development Corporation, representing a poor residential area adjacent to the site, proposed the negotiation of a community benefits agreement between the developer and the affected neighborhoods. With the support of local institutions and elected officials, an effort was made to mitigate the negative impacts of the project through local hiring preferences, minority business set-asides, park improvements, affordable housing provision, energy conservation assistance, and a new charter middle school.

Supportive Environment

Where powerful institutions readily acknowledge the influence that local residents and institutions exert over critical resources (e.g., land, buildings, capital, media coverage, and local government institutions such as planning commissions), residents may be able to pursue a more collaborative approach to planning. In these cases, residents, along with representatives of these outside interests, can cooperate with local economic and community development organizations as co-investigators, co-designers, and co-developers.

Since establishing its Neighbors Building Neighborhoods (NBN) Program in the early 1990s, Rochester, New York, has delegated increasing levels of responsibility and power over critical economic and community development decisions to local residents and institutional representatives participating in community planning councils. Initially seeking input over the use of Community Development Block Grant funds for brick and mortar projects in their neighborhoods, the NBN Councils are now routinely involved in setting priorities for the city's ongoing service delivery programs and capital budgets.

Future Initiatives

In order to move the field of resident participation forward, research is needed in the following areas.

- **how various resident participation strategies, pursued in a range of contextual environments, result in particular outcomes**—To what extent are resident efforts resulting in productive partnership arrangements that provide additional opportunities to enhance resident empowerment?
- **how the range of cultural backgrounds represented in a given community relates to participation strategies**—To what extent do

views of resident participation vary depending on race, ethnicity, or other attributes and how can diverse populations become involved?
- **how to engage youth in community development**—What can we learn about how community planners have promoted youth involvement in economic and community development policy-making and planning?

At a more applied level, another initiative could build on existing knowledge and research to develop guides to assist planners working in the public, nonprofit, and private sectors to support more productive resident participation strategies. These might also prove to be useful texts in graduate planning programs. The guides could also assist residents by providing information on the range of participation strategies and highlight the role context plays in determining which approach would be most appropriate in a given environment.

Concluding Note

When the Ladder was created, the practice of incorporating residents in community development, as well as a broad range of other planning activities, was brand new. Practitioners at that time often viewed federal directives to engage residents in planning efforts as a nuisance required to secure federal funding. Increasingly, planners have come to understand that better plans will be created and better outcomes achieved if those most likely to be affected are involved throughout the process.

This exploration into the Ladder, viewed from a contemporary perspective, is intended to underscore both the importance of a broad range of resident participation strategies and the complexity of these efforts. The Ladder has been an enormously helpful tool, but ultimately its set of rungs does not adequately support the subtlety or complexity of resident participation in the twenty-first century. Revisiting the Ladder provides an opportunity to better understand its many strengths and to articulate the need for a broader framework of resident participation.

We end with two questions. Can this new conceptualization of resident participation provide us with insights and tools for tapping the extraordinary grassroots organization so critical to the successful election of President Obama, to undertake the often daunting task of community revitalization? And, can this framework help educate policy-makers, government officials, and private stakeholders concerning the ways residents can play productive roles in community efforts?

Notes

We are most grateful to Naomi Carmon and Susan Fainstein for conceptualizing the gathering that stimulated this paper and for providing constructive feedback. Also, Avigail Ferdman was enormously helpful before, during, and after the conference. Sincere thanks to Norman Krumholz, Clement Lai, and Janet Smith, who joined us for a roundtable session in Chicago, July 2008, at the Fourth Joint Congress of the Association of Collegiate Schools of Planning/Association of European Schools of Planning, "Beyond the Ladder: What Have We Learned About Community Roles in U.S. Community Development Initiatives?" Their comments were invaluable. We also thank the forty people attending this session, many of whom offered insights that helped us frame this chapter. Finally, we are grateful to Antonio Raciti for significantly improving our graphics.

1. Now *Journal of the American Planning Association*.

2. We make special note of a particularly ambitious effort to engage residents in Israel. Project Renewal, implemented from the late 1970s through the mid-1990s, embraced citizen participation as its central principle and underscored the need for residents to participate "bottom-up," as opposed to the "top-down" framework presented by Arnstein. Nevertheless, the forms of participation advocated by Project Renewal may have been more "top-down" in practice: Local Steering Committees, encouraging residents and public officials to confront one another directly, or by encouraging the formation of "leading groups" (Weinstein 2008).

3. Observation by Cornell University Professor Clement Lai at the July 2008 ACSP-AESOP meeting in Chicago.

4. Both cases presented, as well as the vignettes on context noted later in the paper, are based on the professional experiences of one of the authors (Reardon).

5. This point was emphasized by Cleveland State University Professor Norman Krumholz at the July 2008 AESOP-ACSP meeting. He asked: "Does the best citizen participation involve simply participating in the electoral process and getting people elected to office, where the numbers of voters would allow that?"

References

American Planning Association. 1996. Summary of the Neighborhood Collaborative Planning Symposium. Chicago, November 14–16.

———. 2008. Neighborhood collaborative planning. http://planning.org/casey/summary .html, accessed September 6, 2008.

Angotti, Tom. 2007. Advocacy and community planning: Past, present and future: The legacy. *Progressive Planning* 171 (Spring): 21–24.

Arnstein, Sherry R. 1969. A ladder of citizen participation. *Journal of the American Institute of Planners* 35: 216–24.

Checkoway, Barry, and Lorraine Margot Gutierrez. 2006. *Youth participation and community change.* Binghamton, N.Y.: Haworth Press

Choguill, Marisa B. Guaraldo. 1996. A ladder of community participation for underdeveloped countries. *Habitat International* 20: 431–44.

Churchman, Arza. 1987. Can resident participation in neighborhood rehabilitation succeed? In *Neighborhood and community environment,* ed. Irwin Altman and Abraham Wandersman, 113–62. New York: Plenum.

Clavel, Pierre, 1984. *The progressive city: Planning and participation 1969–1984.* New Brunswick, N.J.: Rutgers University Press.

Davidoff, Paul. 1965. Advocacy and pluralism in planning. *Journal of the American Institute of Planners* 31: 331–38.

Fainstein, Susan S. 2000. New directions in planning theory. *Urban Affairs Review* 35: 451–78.

Ferguson, Ronald F., and William T. Dickens. 1999. *Urban problems and community development.* Washington, D.C.: Brookings Institution Press.

Forester, John. 1989. *Planning in the face of power.* Berkeley: University of California Press.

———. 1999. *The deliberative practitioner: Encouraging participatory planning processes.* Cambridge, Mass.: MIT Press.

Hart, Roger. 1992. *Children's participation: From tokenism to citizenship.* Florence: UNESCO.

Hartman, Chester W. 2002. *Between eminence & notoriety: Four decades of radical urban planning.* New Brunswick, N.J.: Center for Urban Policy Research.

Kennedy, Marie. 2007. From advocacy planning to transformative community planning. *Progressive Planning* 171 (Spring): 24–27.

Krumholz, Norman, and Pierre Clavel. 1994. *Reinventing cities: Equity planners tell their stories.* Philadelphia: Temple University Press.

Krumholz, Norman, and John Forester. 1990. *Making equity planning work: Leadership in the public sector.* Philadelphia: Temple University Press.

LeGates, Richard T., and Frederic Stout, 2007. *The city reader.* Cambridge: Routledge.

Medoff, Peter, and Holly Sklar. 1994. *Streets of hope: The fall and rise of an urban neighborhood.* Boston: South End Press.

Metzger, John T. 1996. The theory and practice of equity planning: An annotated bibliography. *Journal of Planning Literature* 11: 112–26.

Needleman, Martin, and Carolyn Needleman, 1974. *Guerrillas in the bureaucracy: The community planning experiment in the United States.* New York: Wiley.

Peterman, William. 1999. *Neighborhood planning and community-based development: The potential and limits of grassroots action.* Thousand Oaks, Calif.: Sage.

Pretty, Jules. 1995. Ladder of participation. *Community Development Journal* 43: 269–83.

Putnam, Robert D. 2000. *Bowling alone: The collapse and rise of American community.* New York: Simon and Schuster.

Reardon, Kenneth M. 2000. An experiential approach to creating a community/ university partnership that works: The East St. Louis Action Research Project. *Cityscape: A Journal of Policy Development and Research* 5: 59–74.

Rubin, Herbert J. 2000. *Renewing hope within neighborhoods of despair: The community-based development model.* Albany: State University of New York Press.

Sandercock, Leonie. 1998. *Towards cosmopolis: Planning for multicultural cities.* Hoboken, N.J.: Wiley.

———. 2004. *Cosmopolis II: Mongrel cities in the 21st century.* Vancouver: Continuum International.

Shiffman, Ronald, and Susan B. Motley. 1989. *A comprehensive and integrative approach to community development.* New York: Community Development Research Center.

Stein, Jay M. 2004. *Classic readings in urban planning.* Washington, D.C.: American Planning Association Press.

Stoecker, Randy. 1997. The CDC model of urban development: A critique and an alternative. *Journal of Urban Affairs* 19: 1–22.

Thompson, J. Phillip III. 2006. *Double trouble: Black mayors, black communities, and the call for a deep democracy.* New York: Oxford University Press.

Weinstein, Zvi. 2008. Citizen participation in Israel: The case of Israel Project Renewal. *Journal of Urbanism* 1: 129–55.

Contributors

Alberta Andreotti is a Researcher at the Department of Sociology and Social Research at the University of Milano-Bicocca. Her main research interests are social capital and social networks, local welfare systems, poverty and social exclusion, and the middle class in comparative perspective. She has participated in several European projects, including comparative UrbEx-The Spatial Dimensions of Urban Social Exclusion and Integration.

Tridib Banerjee is Professor of Planning and James Irvine Chair in Urban and Regional Planning in the School of Policy, Planning and Development, University of Southern California. His research focuses on design and planning of the built environment from a comparative perspective. He is interested in the political economy of urban design and development, and the effects of globalization on transitional urban forms and urbanism.

Rachel G. Bratt is Professor and former Head of the Department of Urban and Environmental Policy and Planning, Tufts University and a Fellow at the Joint Center for Housing Studies, Harvard University. She also worked as a professional planner in the city of Worcester, Massachusetts, and has served on a number of boards and advisory committees. Her research is focused primarily on the role of nonprofit organizations in supplying decent, affordable housing to low-income households.

Naomi Carmon is Professor of Urban Planning and Sociology and Joseph Meyerhoff Chair in Urban and Regional Planning at the Faculty of Architecture and Town Planning, Technion-Israel Institute of Technology. She is former President of Israel Sociological Society (ISS) and was a visiting professor at MIT and UCLA, University of British Columbia, and University of Auckland. She has served on Israeli government committees on land and planning issues and consulted with public and civic organizations. Her areas of teaching and research have focused on social aspects of planning and evaluation of urban and regional plans, with an emphasis on urban regeneration and housing, social capital, and quality of life of minorities and immigrants.

Karen Chapple is Associate Professor of City and Regional Planning at the University of California, Berkeley and Theodore Bo Lee and Doris Shoong Lee Chair in Environmental Design. She specializes in community and economic development, metropolitan planning, and poverty, with a focus on the relationship between job growth and housing price appreciation, regional fair share housing programs, workforce development in information technology, housing dispersal programs, and regional collaboration.

Norman Fainstein is Chair and Professor of Sociology at Connecticut College. He was President of Connecticut College, chief academic officer at Vassar College, and Dean of Faculty at the City University of New York (CUNY). His research and writings focus on urban history and politics, city and regional planning, economic development, race, social movements and public policy.

Susan Fainstein is Senior Research Fellow at the Graduate School of Design, Harvard University, where she was previously Professor of Urban Planning. She has also taught at Columbia and Rutgers Universities and been a visiting professor at the University of Amsterdam, and the University of Witwatersrand. Her teaching and research have focused on comparative urban public policy, planning theory, and urban redevelopment. Among her books are *The Just City*, *The City Builders: Property, Politics, and Planning in London and New York*, *Restructuring the City*, and *Urban Political Movements*. She is a recipient of the Distinguished Planning Educator Award and the Davidoff Book Award of the Association of Collegiate Schools of Planning.

Eran Feitelson is Professor at the Department of Geography and Head of the Federmann School of Public Policy and Government at the Hebrew University of Jerusalem. Since 1999 he has also served as chair of the Israeli Nature Reserves and National Parks Board. He has published widely on planning, water policy (including transboundary water) and transport policy issues.

Amnon Frenkel is Associate Professor at the Faculty of Architecture and Town Planning and Head of the Graduate Program for Urban and Regional Planning at the Technion-Israel Institute of Technology. His research interests are land use projection models, regional and metropolitan planning, urban spatial dynamics and regional aspects of technology diffusion.

George Galster is Clarence Hilberry Professor of Urban Affairs at the Department of Geography and Urban Planning, Wayne State University. His research interests are metropolitan housing markets, racial discrimination and segregation, neighborhood dynamics, residential reinvestment, community lending and insurance patterns, and urban poverty.

Penny Gurstein is Professor and Director of the School of Community and Regional Planning at the University of British Columbia. Her research interests focus on planning for equitable and healthy communities; and technology, work and society. She specializes in the socio-cultural aspects of community planning with particular emphasis on those who are the most marginalized in planning processes.

Deborah Howe is Professor and Chair of the Department of Community and Regional Planning at Temple University, and Principal Investigator on Robert Wood Johnson Foundation Active Living grant. She served as co-editor of *JAPA*, the *Journal of the American Planning Association*. Her current research and professional interests include housing alternatives, land use innovations, and community planning for aging.

Norman Krumholz is Professor in the Levin College of Urban Affairs at Cleveland State University. He is past president of the American Planning Association and American Institute of Certified Planners. He served as Director of Planning for the city of Cleveland for ten years. His writings focus on equity planning and neighborhood planning.

Jonathan Levine is Professor and Chair of Urban and Regional Planning at the University of Michigan, and Visiting Professor at Princeton University, the University of Pennsylvania, and the Technion-Israel Institute of Technology. His research and writings focus on transportation and land-use planning, measuring and comparing transportation accessibility.

Anastasia Loukaitou-Sideris is Professor and former Chair at the UCLA Department of Urban Planning. Her research focuses on the public environment of the city, its physical representation, aesthetics, meaning and impact on residents, and includes documentation of the socio-physical changes in the public realm as a result of privatization, revitalization of inner city areas, cultural determinants of design, and environmental attributes of crime and their implications for design and policy.

Enzo Mingione is Professor of Sociology, Dean of the Faculty of Sociology, and Coordinator of the European Doctorate Urbeur "Urban and Local European Studies," University of Milano-Bicocca. He is one of the founding editors of the International *Journal of Urban and Regional Research* and member of the Editorial Executive Board of the journal *Inchiesta*. His main fields of interest are poverty, social exclusion, informal sector, unemployment, and economic and urban sociology.

Kenneth Reardon is Professor and Director of the Graduate Program in City and Regional Planning at the University of Memphis. Former Associate Professor and Chairperson of the Department of City and Regional Planning at Cornell University, he also taught at the University of Illinois at Urbana-Champaign. His fields of interests are neighborhood planning, community development and municipal reform.

Izhak Schnell is Professor of Social and Cultural Geography and former Head of the Department of Geography and Human Environment at the University of Tel Aviv. He specializes in social spaces in a globalizing reality, in particular, sociospatial segregation of ethnic groups in Tel Aviv, and Israeli Arabs' embeddedness in sociospatial networks.

Daniel Shefer is Professor Emeritus of Urban and Regional Economics at the Technion-Israel Institute of Technology, holds the Kunin-Lunenfeld Chair in Urban and Regional Planning, and is the former Dean of the Faculty of Architecture and Town Planning at the Technion. He served as Senior Economist in the urban and regional economics division of the World Bank in Washington, D.C., and as a Visiting Professor at the Tinbergen Institute in Amsterdam and the Kennedy School of Government, Harvard University. His areas of expertise include urban and regional economics, joint transportation and land use modeling, and various aspects of transportation and environmental economics.

Michael Teitz is Professor Emeritus and former Chair of the Department of City and Regional Planning at UC Berkeley and President of the Association of Collegiate Schools of Planning. He received the Berkeley Citation, the Distinguished Educator Award from the Association of Collegiate Schools of Planning, and the ACSP Jay Chatterjee Award for Distinguished Service for career-long service to the planning academy. He has been advisor to numerous government and private organizations, including U.S. Department of Housing and Urban Development, U.S. Army Corps of Engineers, State of California, and City of Los Angeles. His fields of expertise are urban development and planning, housing planning and policy and regional and local economic development.

Iván Tosics is one of the principals of Metropolitan Research Institute (MRI), Budapest. He is Vice Chair of the European Network of Housing Research (ENHR) and executive committee member of the European Urban Research Association (EURA). He is Policy Editor of the journal *Urban Research and Practice* and member of the Editorial Advisory Boards for the *Journal of Housing and the Built Environment* and *Housing Studies*. He was the leader of a consortium working on the medium- and long-term Urban Development Strategy of Budapest. He is an urban sociologist, interested in strategic development, housing policy, and EU regional policy issues.

Lawrence Vale is Ford Professor of Urban Design and Planning, faculty member, and former head of the Department of Urban Studies and Planning, MIT. He is the recipient of many awards of best books and best papers of the year from ACSP and Urban Affairs Association, among others. His current research includes disaster recovery, comparative housing redevelopment, and urban security. Other research examines the architectural and urbanistic expression of institutional power, and the growth of design and marketing efforts aimed at "imaging" places.

Martin Wachs, Director of the Transportation, Space and Technology Program and of the Supply Chain Policy Center at the RAND Corporation, is former Professor of Civil & Environmental Engineering and Professor of City

& Regional Planning at the University of California, Berkeley, and Director of the Institute of Transportation Studies, and Chair of the Department of Urban Planning at UCLA. He is a Lifetime Associate of the National Academy of Sciences and was named Distinguished Planning Educator by ACSP. His research and writings focus on relationships between transportation, land use, and air quality, transportation needs of the elderly, techniques for evaluation of transportation systems, and use of performance measurement in transportation planning.

Index

Acknowledgments

The chapters in this book are the work of individual authors, but the book as a whole is the product of extensive collaboration. The project was conceived at the Center for Urban and Regional Planning at the Technion-Israel Institute of Technology, where issues of Planning with/for People have been high on the agenda for the last three decades. A series of meetings with colleagues at ACSP (American Collegiate Schools of Planning) conferences led to a continuous collaboration among a group of senior planning educators who shared the wish to deliver their social legacy to students, scholars, and practitioners interested in urban development.

We are grateful to the anonymous foundation whose very generous financial support enabled us to carry out the various stages towards the publication of this book. In particular, we want to convey our gratitude to the Director of the Foundation's environmental division for his professionalism and responsiveness.

For supporting us in various ways we thank the Faculty of Architecture and Town Planning and Orit Yimalkovski at the Center for Urban and Regional Studies, both at the Technion-Israel Institute of Technology. Thanks are due to the planning schools that supported the time and travel expenses of participants. Our English editor Peter Wissoker cooperated willingly and effectively throughout the process. Ofer Lerner deserves our thanks for his high administrative capabilities. Finally, special appreciation and gratitude are due to Avigail Ferdman, a doctoral student at the Hebrew University in Jerusalem, who accompanied us throughout the process, providing intelligent, effective, and efficient assistance on academic and administrative matters.